Geography of Gender in the Third World

*Edited by Janet Henshall Momsen
and Janet G. Townsend*

State University of New York Press

Hutchinson

London   Melbourne   Sydney   Auckland   Johannesburg

Hutchinson Education

An imprint of Century Hutchinson Ltd

62–65 Chandos Place, London WC2N 4NW

Century Hutchinson Australia Pty Ltd
PO Box 496, 16–22 Church Street, Hawthorn,
Victoria 3122, Australia

Century Hutchinson New Zealand Limited
PO Box 40–086, Glenfield, Auckland 10, New Zealand

Century Hutchinson South Africa (Pty) Ltd
PO Box 337, Bergvlei, 2012 South Africa

US edition published by
State University of New York Press, Albany

For information in US, address State University of New York
Press, State University Plaza, Albany, N.Y., 12246

Set in 10 on 12pt in VIP Melior by
D P Media Limited, Hitchin Hertfordshire

Printed in Great Britain by
Butler & Tanner Ltd, Frome and London

British Library Cataloguing in Publication Data

Geography of gender in the Third World.
   1. Women—Developing countries—
   Social conditions I. Momsen, Janet Henshall   II. Townsend,
   Janet   III. Geography Study Group of the IBG

   305.4′2′091724   HQ1870.9

Library of Congress Cataloging-in-Publication Data

Geography of gender in the Third World.

   Includes papers from meeting of the Women and Geography
Study Group of the Institute of British Geographers.
   1. Women in development. 2. Sexual division of labor –
Developing countries. 3. Sex role – Developing countries.
I. Momsen, Janet Henshall. II. Townsend, Janet, 1944–
III. Women and Geography Study Group of the IBG.
HG1240.G46   1987   305.4′2′091724   86-14564

ISBN (UK) 0 09 170821 4 (pbk)
ISBN (US) 0-88706-441-8 (cased)
ISBN (US) 0-88706-440-X (pbk)

Contents

We've come a long way baby!
But, the best is yet to come.
We are still the poorest of the poor,
The most powerless of the powerless,
The least understood of those without a voice,
The most excluded from the benefits of our toil.
But we have strengths, sisters,
And a unique knowledge of what is real:
The pain and beauty of reproduction,
Of nurturing the next generation –
An essential share in the work of creation!
And we can use these strengths,
And insights,
And unique experience of the life force,
To end the wars,
To change the world,
To build our societies into places
Where people can find purpose and peace.
But first, we must believe –
That we are rich in our experience of life,
Powerful in our personhood,
And hold the keys
To the relationships and systems
Which keep the best at bay.

Peggy Antrobus 1982

Acknowledgements

Our thanks are due to David Hume, who drew the maps, to Abrayyik Abdelaziz Bukachiem and to Sinclair Sutherland, who did the computing, to Barbara Patterson, who typed the text, and to Alan Townsend, who read it.

Notes on contributors

Bina Agarwal Ph.D.   Economist working at the Institute of Economic Growth in New Delhi, India. Has published widely on regional contrasts in gender roles.

Peggy Antrobus B.A. Bristol and diploma in Social Work.   Tutor in Extra-Mural Studies and Head, Women and Development Unit, University of the West Indies, Barbados.

Deipica Bagchi Ph.D. Oregon State University.   Presently geography professor at S. Illinois University, USA and working on women and technical change in rural India.

Jane Benton Ph.D. in geography based on field study in highland Bolivia.   Lecturer in geography at Hertfordshire College of Higher Education, UK.

Aida Beshara Ph.D. Newcastle upon Tyne.   Professor and Head of Department of Geography, Faculty of Women, Ain Shams University, Heliopolis, Cairo, Egypt.

Rex A. Casinader M.A.   Formerly Senior Research Officer, People's Bank, Sri Lanka. Currently doctoral student in geography at University of British Columbia, Canada.

Sylvia Chant Ph.D. London.   Lecturer in geography at the University of Liverpool, UK. Researching on urban problems in Mexico, especially the housing of the poor.

Susan Cunningham Ph.D. London.   Lectures in geography in the UK and writes extensively on the changing geography of Brazilian industrialization.

Sepalika Fernando B.A.   Researcher in the Research Department of the People's Bank, Sri Lanka.

Karuna Gamage B.A.   Researcher in the Research Department of the People's Bank, Sri Lanka.

Barbara Harriss Ph.D. is a geographer now working on nutrition at the London School of Hygiene and Tropical Medicine, UK, and continuing her research on India.

Janet Henshall Momsen Ph.D.   Lecturer in geography at Newcastle University, UK. She has taught in Brazil and Canada and is researching gender issues in rural areas.

Michael McCall Ph.D.   Geographer in the Technology and Development Group at the University of Twente, the Netherlands, working on Tanzania.

Terry McGee Ph.D.   Professor of Geography and Director of the Asian Studies Centre, University of British Columbia, Vancouver, Canada.

Maggie Pearson Ph.D. is a geographer and qualified nurse who now lectures in Medical Sociology at Liverpool University, UK, after research in Nepal.

Jane Pryer M.Sc. is a research student in nutrition at the London School of Hygiene and Tropical Medicine, and is still engaged in fieldwork in Bangladesh.

Kamal Salih Ph.D.   Economist formerly at Universiti Sains Malaysia. He is now Director of the Malaysian Institute of Economic Research, Kuala Lumpur.

Anchalee Singhanetra-Renard Ph.D. lectures in geography at Chieng Mai University, Thailand, and researches in the field of population geography.

Heather Spiro Ph.D. is a geographer who works on women's time allocation: she has measured this in detail in Nigeria.

Janet Townsend D. Phil. lectures in geography at Durham University, UK: she specializes in the colonization of the rainforest in the tropical Americas.

Esther Trenchard M.Sc. is working on nutrition in Zimbabwe after training at the London School of Hygiene and Tropical Medicine, UK.

Elizabeth Watson M.Sc. in nutrition from the London School of Hygiene and Tropical Medicine. She now works for the UK Association of Community Health Councils.

Clive Wilkinson Ph.D. lectures in geography at Sunderland Polytechnic, UK. He has taught in Zimbabwe and carried out research in Lesotho.

Sally Wilson de Acosta M.Sc. is a nutritionist in Colombia. After a geography degree she studied nutrition at the London School of Hygiene and Tropical Medicine.

Mei Ling Young Ph.D. Demographer. Taught development studies at Universiti Sains Malaysia and now runs a consultancy group in Penang.

Preface

This is the second book to appear under the auspices of the Women and Geography Study Group of the Institute of British Geographers. The Group's collectively written *Geography and Gender* (1984) was the first introductory text on feminist geography; its success was such that it was felt that companion volumes of more specialized readings on particular branches of feminist geography should follow.

The Women and Geography Study Group of the Institute of British Geographers was formally constituted in 1982. At the Institute's 1983 annual meeting, it was decided that the theme for the group's main session at the next annual meeting should be 'Women's role in changing the face of the developing world'. This session, held in Durham, was organized by the editors of this volume. We were struck that most of the papers were derived from recently completed doctoral theses. This brought home to us that the field of geography and gender in the developing world was both very new and of great interest to today's students. The reception of the papers proved it to be also of great interest to our colleagues. Here was a new research frontier on which very little published work was available.

As background to the Durham session, we had produced preliminary versions of the papers (Momsen and Townsend 1984)* and a bibliography for geographers on women in developing areas (Townsend *et al*. 1984). Contributions to the session from Bagchi, Benton, Pearson and Spiro appear in a much revised form here; the papers by Chant (1984) and Simon (1984) were published elsewhere, but Chant has provided us with a different paper here. McCall, of Twente University, the Netherlands, was present at the Durham meeting, and has written a paper for this book. A meeting of the study Group at Newcastle upon Tyne in April 1984 focused on women and the urban environment. It attracted two papers on

* Full references quoted in the text are contained in the bibliography beginning on p. 373.

the developing world: Cunningham, on women in Brazilian industries, and Wilkinson, on the effect of migration on women in Lesotho: both have been developed into chapters for this collection.

It was with the encouragement of our editor, Mark Cohen, that we decided to try to put together a representative collection of current geographical research on gender and development. With help from many people, especially David Drakakis-Smith of the Developing Areas Research Group of the Institute of British Geographers, we were able to broaden the geographical range of both topics and contributors and to include work on Asia, Africa and Latin America by researchers from the Third World, North America and Europe.

The world-wide distribution of geographers working on research topics related to gender issues in the world's developing capitalist economies, the mobility of these geographers – our contributors – and woman's double day itself have all complicated the production of this volume. During the gestation of this book, both editors carried out fieldwork on geography and gender in Latin America, and both presented papers on this theme at a colloquium in Mexico City in September 1984. The enthusiasm of the Mexican geographers rekindled the excitement aroused at the Durham meeting. Domestic crises required the caring roles of women. 'But we have strength, sisters, and a unique knowledge of what is real.' We thank our contributors, our editor, our patient and supportive families and, in particular, Hope Page for her meticulous emendations.

Part One

Context

Map 1 Location in the Third World of the studies in this book, by chapter number

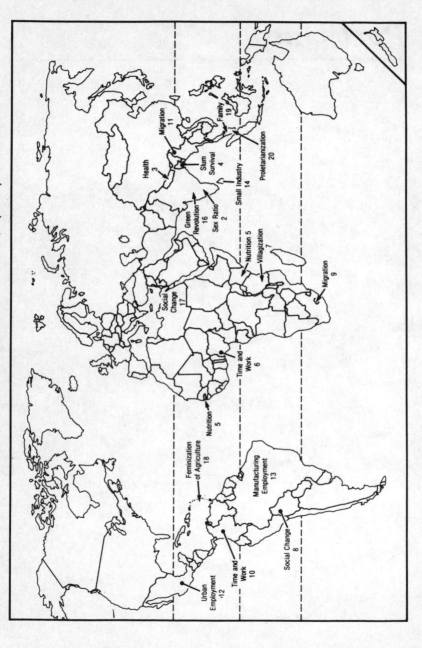

Introduction

Janet Henshall Momsen

We are now in the middle of the Third United Nations Development Decade and at the end of the Decade for Women. It is a time for reassessment of our approaches to development and to the role of women in the Third World. At the end of the first two Development Decades it was found that levels of disease, poverty, unemployment and illiteracy had increased. Now in the Third Development Decade we have achieved the worst crisis since the 1930s in the world monetary system and famine has reached tragic proportions in Africa, while malnutrition remains a permanent condition for many people in the developing world. The Decade for Women, 1975–85, has seen little real change in patriarchal attitudes and only very limited and locationally specific improvements in the overwhelming subordination of women. Perhaps the most striking feature in the world today is the advent of an ever more complex pattern of gender relations at all scales of analysis. The geography of gender has a vital role to play in improving our understanding of the rapidly changing spatial mosaic of gender relations in developing capitalist economies.

In this exploratory survey, we present case studies from a range of developing capitalist economies, nations commonly considered to constitute the Third World. It is in the Third World that the greatest variety of constructions of gender is encountered but frequently fertility is high (Map 4), incomes are low and the female share of the paid labour force is small (Maps 5, 6, 7). By comparison, in the advanced industrial economies, or First World, and the centrally planned economies, or Second World, there is a fairly consistent pattern of low fertility (Map 4) and a substantial female contribution to the paid labour force. Fertility and wage labour are not the only dimensions around which gender is constructed, but they form significant parameters for the geography of gender. Feminism is an important force in industrial economies, while in centrally planned economies the state is committed to the transformation of gender roles. Once again the developing capitalist economies present a kaleidoscopic variety but, in general, the process of development appears to increase the burdens of Third World women. Our case studies illustrate this variety with examples taken from Latin America, Africa, the Middle East and South and South-East Asia.

Concepts of development remain predominantly economic, despite the preamble to the international Development Strategy for the Third Development Decade which defined development as 'the constant improvement of the well-being of the entire population on the basis of their full participation in the process of development and a fair share of the benefits therefrom' (Antrobus 1984). This attempt to link social and economic activities and to encourage equality of participation has failed; partly, at least, because the spatial separation of the home and the work world and the division of responsibilities between men and women prevent women being fully integrated into the development process as long as this process is male-defined.

Overwhelmingly, the debate on development has focused on two paradigms emerging from two different ideological positions. One blames underdevelopment on shortages of skilled labour, entrepreneurship, capital and technology and sees the solution in terms of the transfer of resources from rich to poor; the other approach argues that underdevelopment is the result of the exploitative nature of capitalism with its concentration on profits rather than people. Each paradigm involves different strategies, priorities and methodologies. Yet each strategy is based on economic considerations and both are still characterized by the centralization of power and decision-making in the hands of small elites, bankers and industrialists in one case, the state in the other. Neither paradigm has yet offered an alternative to development based on industrialization: both are still patriarchal and fail to take into account the needs, perceptions and strengths of women.

Many writers are now supporting the importance of a more holistic approach to development if we are to overcome problems of poverty and inequality and avoid the mistakes of previous development efforts. This new development discourse has been invoked by a growing attitude of responsibility to the environment, by a search for alternatives to 'alienated labour and commodity fetishism' (Redclift 1984) and by the spotlight feminists have trained on the social construction of divisions of labour by gender.

It is not just a question of adding women to development theory, but demands a fundamental reassessment of the very foundations of development theory and practice (Cebotarev 1982). The traditional argument for industrialization as a necessary step towards the elimination of poverty in developing countries is hard to refute (Kitching 1982), but, as Sutcliffe (1984) points out, industrialization, in practice, has not led to the satisfaction of human needs, particularly within rural areas and for women. Boserup (1970) in her seminal work on women and development, was first to identify women as victims of development, but development theory has only recently begun to take cognizance of this situation. In 1977, Elliot criticized developmentalism for its assumption that modernization would automatically lead to a 'trickle down' of benefits to women. She felt that a new theory of development was needed that incorporated an evaluation of women's work outside the formal paid labour force and took into account changes in household structure, particularly the growing importance of female-headed households. Finally she stressed that the impact of development on change or lack of change in women's roles, in light of the double burden of work imposed on women in the First and Second Worlds following their increased incorporation into the labour force, must be considered. These factors identified by Elliot have provided foci for work on geography and gender, as the case studies in this volume show. Today, a rapidly expanding group of Third World women is committed to a search for a more equitable development paradigm based on a feminist ethic with associated decentralization of power and with an emphasis on the sustainable use of resources and a people-centred approach to the satisfaction of human needs (Antrobus 1985).

Various trends in development research have encouraged the recent growth of interest in topics relating to women. The World Bank's redirection of certain funds to the poorest countries and to rural areas where women's work is of major importance; the establishment in 1975 of the United Nations Decade for Women; and the recognition of the process by which many activities of women are relocated from the household to the market place so that control over the local environment is removed from the hands of the poor, especially women, and relocated as a link in the international division of labour (Redclift 1984), have all stimulated an upsurge in research into the role of women in changing the face of the developing world.

Boserup (1970) made a major contribution to the geography of gender when she drew our attention to regional patterns in the division of labour by gender. She argued that social stratification, as reflected in land tenure systems and the composition of the labour force, was of great importance in determining the division of labour in agriculture. She also pinpointed international differences in the gender division of rural to urban migration flows and their impact on labour markets and household structures. These patterns are examined in detail in some of the contributions included here, especially in Chapters 5 and 6, on divisions of labour in agriculture, and Chapter 9 on migration. As our contributors show, changes in the scale of study from national to regional, community and household level add enormously to the intricacies of gender relations in labour processes (Long 1984). Boserup perceived very clearly that her analysis was severely limited by lack of data. The outpourings of research on women over the last decade now make it possible to provide a more detailed synthesis of spatial variations in women's roles, as outlined in our Chapter 1, and to offer this volume as an introduction to the geography of gender in the Third World.

This explosion of information on the socially created differences in the lives of men and women, or gender differences, in the countries of the capitalist periphery of the world-economy has enabled the United Nations to document many of the changes in gender relations throughout the world over the Decade for Women, 1975–85. Looking at these country by country statistics demarcating change over the Decade, the overwhelming picture is one of similar trends in both core and periphery, although distinctive regional identities are preserved.

Statistics relating to reproduction over the Decade show that early marriage is generally less common, most markedly in Ethiopia, contraceptive use has increased, except in Pakistan, and maternal mortality has declined in all the developing countries for which data are available, although over three-quarters of pregnant women still suffer from nutritional anaemia in Egypt, Gambia, Guinea Bissau, Malaysia and Mauritius. Everywhere, people are living longer but gender differences remain: life expectancy in all 150 countries enumerated increased over the Decade, with women continuing to live longer than men (mainly because of hormonal differences) except in the countries of South Asia, that is Bangladesh, Bhutan, India, Nepal and Pakistan. The fertility rate also shows regional patterns: the world-wide trend of declining fertility is not apparent in most countries of Africa, where indeed fertility has markedly increased during the Decade, as it has in the two southern countries of the Americas, Argentina and Uruguay, which in 1970 had the lowest fertility rates in South America. Statistics on education reveal some of the greatest changes over the Decade, with gender differences being reduced and even reversed in some cases. The proportion of illiterates in the population of each country has decreased, but generally the percentage of women unable to read or write has remained higher than that of men. However, among the population aged 15 to 24, in most of the countries of Latin America and the Caribbean, more women than men are now literate. Enrolment in education has increased throughout the periphery, and in post-secondary education the Decade has seen a reversal of gender differences in Latin America and the Caribbean with more women than men now in higher education, except in those countries of the region with large Indian populations such as Peru, Bolivia, Paraguay and Mexico, and in poverty-stricken Haiti. In the labour-reserve areas of Botswana and Lesotho (Chapter 9) women are more likely to be well-educated than men and this educational superiority has increased over the Decade. A reversal of male educational dominance has also occurred in the oil-rich states of Kuwait and Qatar and in the Philippines.

It is clear that even at the scale of national comparisons there are marked regional patterns in an ever-changing matrix of gender-based differentiation. The causal processes involved are more complicated than their surface manifestations, and we need to recognize the contextual nature of all such information. Not only must we have statistics for gender differences between states but we also need to identify intra-state variations. Contrasts between the peripheral states of the world-economy are no more striking than the differences between core and periphery within a state.

Data for national comparisons are still limited in their coverage. How much more difficult is it to find time-series data for regions within a country. Fortunately the Peruvian Women's Centre (Franke 1985) has supplied us with detailed information on the changes in women's lives in their country over the period of the Decade for Women. Peru is a nation of extreme physical environments ranging from coastal desert to high mountains and tropical forest. The society is multi-racial and multi-lingual, with the Indian languages of Quechua and Aymara being spoken as well as the dominant Spanish. Peru offers a microcosm of urban/rural, core/periphery, modern/traditional contrasts in a multi-stranded social matrix and thus enables us to explore in depth some of the changes in gender relationships revealed in the national comparisons of the United Nations' data.

Inter-regional differences in the Peruvian sex ratio have widened between 1972 and 1981 as sex-specific migration has increased. Young men move to the employment opportunities offered by industry and fishing on the coast or to the expanding frontier zone of the tropical forest, leaving women and children behind in the mountains. In the cities the proportion of 'economically active' women has increased only slightly from 25 per cent in 1972 to 28 per cent in 1981, but in the rural areas the reported increase over this period has been much greater, rising from 14 to 21 per cent. The dramatic change in rural areas is more apparent than real and the Women's Centre authors suggest that the agrarian reform, which took place during this period, has made peasant women more aware of the economic importance of their traditional role in farming, so that they are now proud to declare themselves economically active for the purpose of official statistics. The fertility rate also shows a marked urban/rural differential. In Lima metropolitan area the fertility rate is 3.5, rising to 5.5 in other urban areas and reaching 8.1 in rural areas despite the desired number of children for rural women being only 3.3.

Clearly, as we change the scale, the interrelationships of gender with race and class, core and periphery, rural and urban make for a very complex picture. Women and men are facing real dilemmas as they grapple with systematic constraints, unexpected consequences and ever-changing conditions in the countries of the developing periphery. It must be accepted that 'the implications of gender in the study of geography are at least as important as the implications of any other social or economic factor which transforms society and space' (WGSG 1984).

Geography has lagged far behind the other social sciences in its appreciation of the importance of gender. Zelinsky, Monk and Hanson (1982) suggest two reasons for this, both related to the nature of the subject: much of the research on women is done by women scholars, and the proportion of women in geography is very low and more akin to the situation in the physical sciences than in the social sciences and humanities (Henshall Momsen 1980); and, second, many geographers work in cartography and physical geography where they are unlikely to come face to face with women's issues in their research. Women have remained invisible to geography until very recently but 'once our perspective shifts away from a preoccupation with spatial structures to a focus on processes in society, the political economy and the ecosystem then, rather magically, great new vistas of unexplored territory open up' (Zelinsky, Monk and Hanson 1982).

Not surprisingly the first territory to be explored is that closest to home and most of the work done by European and North American feminist geographers focuses on labour markets, housing and urban planning in developed capitalist economies, while the problems of the periphery remain a minority interest. The first session on geography and gender in developing countries held at a major geographical conference was that organized by Oscar Horst for the 1978 Annual Meeting of the Association of American Geographers in New Orleans. This meeting was held in honour of Lucia C. Harrison, 'an early American geographer, whose academic experiences, it was felt, encapsulated the many frustrations encountered by women in their attempts to forge a niche within the higher echelons of our discipline' (Horst 1981). As Harrison's primary area of interest had been Latin America, the five papers presented all dealt with this region and later formed the first published collection by geographers on aspects of gender relations in developing capitalist economies (Horst 1981). Other sessions have since been held with a systematic focus on changes in the position of women in rural areas of the developing world. The first of these was at the meeting of the International Geographical Union Commission on Rural Development in Fresno, California in 1981. This was followed by a session at the commission meeting at the IGU Regional Congress in Brazil in 1982. In 1983 the Rural Geography Speciality Group of the Association of American Geographers organized a meeting on rural women in both developing and developed countries. Not until January 1984 did the Institute of British Geographers discuss gender in a session entitled 'Women's role in changing the face of the developing world'. Four months later, at the Women and Geography Study Group of the IBG meeting on 'Women and the urban environment' two papers on Third World urbanization were presented. The editors of this volume have been involved as organizers and/or contributors at all these meetings, and the papers given at the two British meetings form the core of this volume.

Most, but by no means all, of the work on the geography of gender in the developing world has been carried out by women geographers. Some of us became interested in the topic when we returned to field areas we had first visited many years earlier and were either struck by obvious societal changes or, because of a new awareness of the importance of gender, were able to reinterpret relationships and to look at a familiar area with a new perspective. In 1981, when Jane Benton revisited a community in Bolivia after a ten-year interval, she was surprised to find a great change in gender roles brought about by the expansion in the marketing of local produce in La Paz, a role in which women excelled (Chapter 8). For one of the editors, it was Oscar Horst's request in 1977 for a paper on women which stimulated a re-examination of field data leading to an appreciation of many important gender-based effects which had hitherto been ignored (Henshall 1981). Many others in this book, after long experience in particular developing countries, have felt the need to focus on gender issues in their field areas, as for example Townsend on Colombia (Chapter 10), Harriss on India (Chapter 2), McCall on Tanzania (Chapter 7), and Cunningham on Brazil (Chapter 13). Growing interest in feminism has led to increasing numbers of postgraduate students choosing to look at geographical aspects of gender when undertaking research in developing countries. This work is revealing some surprising relationships and some unexpected effects of development, as for example in Chant's study of family structure and labour force participation in Mexico (Chapter 12), Spiro on rural women's productive work in Nigeria (Chapter 6), Pearson on women's roles in health care in Nepal (Chapter 13), and Wilkinson on the impact of sex-specific migration on women in Lesotho (Chapter 9).

Among women in the Third World, feminism, as expressed by scholars of the industrialized North, has often seemed largely irrelevant. This attitude was well expressed by Nora Astorga, Vice-Minister of Foreign Affairs in Nicaragua, when she said 'In Nicaragua we cannot conduct a struggle of a Western feminist kind. This is alien to our reality. It doesn't make sense to separate the women's struggle from that of overcoming poverty, exploitation and reaction. We want to promote women's interests within the context of that wider struggle' (Molyneux 15/10/82). Peggy Antrobus of the Women and Development Unit of the University of the West Indies, Barbados, admits that she has now moved from this position to an acceptance of feminism as 'a *consciousness* of women's oppression and a commitment to work against it . . . [to seeing] feminism as a process of the "decolonization" of women by the "conscious demolition of images" which fail to reflect women's reality and the deliberate explosion of patriarchal myths about power, status and the production process' (Antrobus 1984).

Third World geographers have sometimes tended to move to an espousal of feminism in their work after a period spent in North America or Europe, and in this way they have been stimulated to look at the geography of gender in their own countries. Professor Beshara was encouraged to consider the role of women in rural development in her native Egypt (Chapter 17), after a year's sabbatical spent in North America and England. Anchalee Singhanetra-Renard (Chapter 11) and Nora Huang (1982) both gained their doctorates at the University of Hawaii. Others are provoked by the commitment of international agencies to research programmes aimed at the greater involvement of women in the labour market. 'Without cognizance of issues relating to women and industrial work, the research outpourings of industrial geographers may become divorced from one of the central issues of concern for key development agencies' (Martin and Rogerson 1984). Expansion of women into the formal and informal labour market of the capitalist periphery has stimulated local Non-Governmental Organizations, particularly women's groups, to look into the issues raised and has led to the involvement of geographers as for instance in Sri Lanka (Chapter 14; Casinader 1983). In the industrialized core area of Brazil feminist groups proliferate and thus several geographers from the University of São Paulo were encouraged to publish papers on women in the labour force of Latin America in a special issue of *Revista Geográfica* (**97**, 1983).

Women have been invisible to geography for a long time and we are only beginning to take into account 'half the human in human geography' (Monk and Hanson 1982). The main focus of geographical work on gender has been on the growing conflict between women's roles in production and reproduction in the face of the new international division of labour and rapid urbanization. Women's specific function in capitalist accumulation is viewed as particularly critical, in that their role in subsistence agriculture and the urban informal economy facilitates the sale of men's labour power to large-scale capitalist enterprise at less than the subsistence family wage. Milton Santos (1979) and Terry McGee (Chapter 20) have led the way in the geographical study of the urban informal sector and many studies have followed focusing particularly on women (Beavon and Rogerson 1984; Simon 1984). The feminization of some export-processing industries has also attracted attention from geographers (Christopherson 1983) as has the broader function of women in modern manufacturing industries on the periphery (Cunningham, Chapter 13). Carl Sauer (1961, 1967) first aroused interest in women's contributions to food production and agricultural innovation. More recently, it has been shown that women's role on farms can lead to gender-related differences in cropping patterns (Henshall 1981). Trenchard (Chapter 5) shows how the competition between male-dominated cash-crop production and female subsistence production for land, labour and capital underlies the food crisis in many African countries.

A common thread running through many of these studies of women's productive activities in urban and rural areas and their reproductive role is the increasing pressure of time. Chant (1984c) examined the effect of building materials and architecture and of household structure on the time use of women. Spiro (Chapter 6) reveals the importance of seasonality for rural women's time use pattern. Time geography (Chapter 1) allows us to examine the constraints that time and space place on women, sometimes preventing the acceptance of innovations and general changes in life-style.

The changing spatial division of labour in the capitalist periphery has led to increasing flows of workers both within and between countries. The gender differentiation of these flows was one of the first topics to be considered by geographers (Rengert 1981; Monk 1981). In Part Four of this volume we focus on two aspects: the specific impact of long-term circular, international migration by men and of short-term commuting from rural to urban areas by men and women; and the household strategies devised by women left behind in labour reserve areas. Pearson shows that although Nepali women may have gained power in running farm and home during their husband's absence they have made little headway in health care (Chapter 3). Wilkinson (Chapter 9) examines the solutions found by the highly educated women of Lesotho, prevented by a sex-specific frontier from following their menfolk to work in South Africa.

To those who see geography as an environmental science, the link between ecology and feminism offers opportunities for a new direction to research. For many feminists the link between feminism and ecology is inevitably based on the significance of the concept of home to both philosophies. Ecologists view the earth as the habitat or home of all living organisms, but home, the place where life is sustained, is traditionally the sphere of women (Monk 1984). Others reject this connection seeing it merely as reinforcing sex role stereotyping (Redclift 1984). In their examination of gender in relation to environment and landscape preferences, Zelinsky, Monk and Hanson (1982) note the pervasive influence of women's link with private space while men tend to dominate public spaces. This private/public distinction carries through into environmental attitudes. McStay and Dunlap (1983) reported that women appeared to be generally more environmentally concerned than men but that they expressed their involvement in different ways. Women were more likely than men to relate to the environment through personal actions such as avoiding environmentally damaging products or conserving energy, whereas men were more often found to engage in public behaviour such as attending public meetings or contacting officialdom. These differences appear to hold true in the developing world. Harry (1981), in her study of women farmers in Trinidad, identified their resistance to the use of chemical inputs on the grounds of risk to both the environment and their own health while Bagchi (Chapter 15) stresses the important role played by women in rural energy programmes in India. The structure of housing has also reinforced the gender-based private/public dichotomy not only in terms of separate houses as with the Mundurucu (Chapter 1) but also in relation to the architecture of individual houses (Monk 1984).

It is clear that the field of geography and gender is in a state of flux with new and exciting research initiatives emerging. We see the cornerstone of much of our work being provided by the spatial divisions of labour and so we have taken this as the organizing theme of our book. In Chapter 1 we provide an overview of the topics and problems involved in a study of the spatial patterning of gender in the developing capitalist periphery. In Chapter 2, an examination by Harriss and Watson of the sex ratio in South Asia illustrates the need to focus on the effects of scale, time and space if we are to move towards a general understanding of the geography of gender. This study of discrimination at the sub-continental scale is followed by analyses of the problems of survival at the household level for women in Nepal by Pearson and in Bangladesh by Pryer. The next three sections provide case studies illustrating regional differences in specific aspects of the division of labour. Part Three looks at changing roles of women in agriculture: Trenchard (Chapter 5) using data from five African ethnic groups, identifies the generally depressant effect of the introduction of cash cropping on women's subsistence production and consequently on family nutrition; Spiro (Chapter 6) challenges our image of West African women traders by demonstrating through careful use of time data that women spend more time farming, usually on their husband's plot, than in commerce; McCall (Chapter 7) and Benton (Chapter 8) illustrate both negative and positive effects of capitalist penetration with villagization increasing the workload of women in Tanzania while commerce has opened up new opportunities for women in Bolivia. In Part Four we concentrate on a particular type of region – the labour reserve – with Wilkinson on Lesotho and Townsend and Acosta on Colombia providing an inter-continental comparison of the changes in gender roles brought about by the long-term, usually international, migration of men. In the final chapter in this part, Singhanetra-Renard describes how daily commuting in northern Thailand, of rural men and women to urban jobs in the construction industry, has created incompatibility between motherhood and employment and awakened women to the new opportunities for education and consumption offered by the city. The theme of Part Five is the impact of the incorporation of women's labour into industry. We have two contributions looking at the role of women in the urban industrial environment of Latin America at different scales: Chant (Chapter 12) examines the role of household structure in influencing the access of women from the shanty towns of Querétaro in Mexico to income earning opportunities in both the formal and informal economy; while Cunningham (Chapter 13) considers the specific functions of women in different types of manufacturing industry in Brazil. The third chapter in this part is set in Sri Lanka and describes the impact on the community and on household divisions of labour of the recent establishment of women entrepreneurs in agricultural processing. These first five parts provide us with thirteen studies covering Asia, Africa and Latin America.

In Part Six we recognize the dynamic nature of our subject and bring this collection to a conclusion by looking to the future. We can perceive no easy answer, no facile explanations in our exploration of the geography of gender, but our voyage of discovery continues. We present six brief reports on research in progress in Egypt, India, Malaysia and the Caribbean and note a research frontier characterized by studies of household survival strategies, nutrition and the impact of new technology.

Underlying much of the work included in this volume is the generally negative effect on women of capitalist penetration in the periphery (Henshall 1984). Yet the picture is not universally depressing. Our contributors offer a sampling of the enormous variation, both within and between developing nations, in the process and impact of changes in the division of labour, and in the relationships between women, men and the environment. This variation is explored at all scales from the sub-continental to the national, regional, community and household level and our case studies have been chosen so as to provide a broad and balanced geographical coverage (Map 1). In this introduction to the geography of gender in the Third World we explode some myths, offer some hypotheses, and indicate the infinite possibilities for both negative and positive change in gender relations which characterize developing capitalist economies.

1 Towards a geography of gender in developing market economies

Janet Townsend and Janet Henshall Momsen

Contents

Introduction

Geographers have come sadly late to a recognition of gender. It is a phenomenon of remarkable *variation from place to place*, as well as from time to time and class to class; the joke that woman's place is at the typewriter may have meaning in New York, but hardly in Delhi or Tehran, where typists are male. As we seek for pattern and cause, or for insight and empathy, we encounter the complexity of explanations. As we begin to recognize the variety, we realize the consistency of the theme on which the variations take place: the *theme of women's subordination*.

This book is about spatial variations in gender (and its significance, at all scales from the human individual to the world economy) and the causal relationships involved. But we must begin with the theme, which will recur through all the variations discussed in our case studies. Despite geographical variations, class variations, and individual variations, the world-wide theme of the geography of gender is female subordination. Gender is a social phenomenon, socially created. As we shall see, some consider gender a purely social construction, independent of biology, while others define it as derived, directly or indirectly, from the interactions of material culture with the biological differences between the sexes; in either case, gender is socially constituted while sex is biologically determined (Oakley 1972; Rogers 1980). As it is socially determined, this meaning will vary with society; yet, in the history and geography of humanity, women's subordination is omnipresent; no society has so constituted gender as to produce male subordination. The forms of subordination differ greatly, but, all over the world, women's work tends to be defined as of less value than men's and women tend to have far less access to all forms of social, economic and political power.

The geography of gender has both this world-wide continuity and regional and local diversity. The diversity is not only in readily comparable aspects such as gender roles but in the historically and spatially specific nature of relationships and their significance. To take a crude example, in one society a woman's control over the family budget may be a measure of realizable power and autonomy; in another, custom may prescribe that she deprive herself and her children in favour of the menfolk: she may control the family food and clothing, she may technically be the 'gatekeeper', but she will not allocate them to herself. These are complex relationships, given meaning by their context, not carrying a stable, consistent meaning across space and time.

Many contributors to this book do not live in the Third World; some of us are not women. To date, the Third World has been presented to us in male terms. How can we attempt to explain the geography of gender in the Third World? Unfortunately, we cannot just appeal in the last resort to the views of the Third World women. By definition, cultures provide a design for living; practices will have their own rationale. To the outsider, purdah may seem a coercive control over women's liberty and sexuality, yet high caste Hindu and Muslim women may regard themselves as 'privileged by being able to enjoy the relative cool of their compound while their menfolk have to face the heat of the day' (Epstein 1982), and Hausa women have argued in favour of seclusion as reducing their work load (Tinker 1976).

The work of Murphy and Murphy (1974) on the Mundurucu in Brazil illustrates how difficult this area is for researchers. They studied one small group in the process of change. The sexes had traditionally lived apart, in the men's house and the women's house, and the forest had been the domain of the men; any woman caught there had been punished by group rape. The group was changing to a nuclear family life-style, modelled on that of incoming Brazilians, and redefining women's spatial freedom. In the view of the anthropologists, the Mundurucu women were losing autonomy and control over their own lives by this transition, but the women themselves promoted the change specifically because they perceived themselves as gaining independence. As in this example, we shall accept that there are many difficulties not only in the demanding task of explaining the geography of gender but even in describing it.

Describing the geography of gender

Our case studies illustrate some of the diversity of possible approaches to the geography of gender as well as the diversity of women's worlds. This chapter seeks to set our case studies, which are national, regional and local, in a world background. No one yardstick could measure for us what it means to be a labouring woman in India, in Nigeria and in Brazil. Two kinds of international comparisons can nevertheless be made: comparisons between women in different countries (a geography of women) and comparisons between the differentials between women and men in different countries (a part of the geography of gender): who earns more, and how much, who lives longer, and how much? Appropriate indicators would cover not only the well-being, or the physical quality of life of females and males but the roles of the two genders in production, in reproduction, in society and in the household. We shall first consider specific indicators for these themes and then come to a discussion of associations and explanations.

Indicators of women's physical well-being

Survival

Life expectancy is the most useful single measure of well-being in the Third World. Despite the data problems, the disparities between the very poorest countries do relate to very real differences in well-being. A woman's life expectancy at birth is estimated at 72 in China, 70 in Sri Lanka, 47 in Somalia and 44 in Afghanistan – yet all have per capita incomes of approximately US$300 p.a. Such findings have been used to argue that even poor countries can materially improve the well-being of their people by adopting 'basic needs strategies'. Discussion of 'basic needs' immediately involves women, both as a frequently disadvantaged group and as the main caretakers of basic needs (Stewart 1985).

As is shown by Map 2, in all advanced industrial countries (First World) life expectancy for a female born in the early 1980s was over 75 years. This was also true in most centrally planned economies (Second World); the exceptions included China and Albania, at 72 years. It is within the Third World that a wide range is to be found, from a reported 44 years in Chad to 74 in Guyana. In the present state of medical knowledge, relatively few people live beyond 80, but in most countries, many of the prosperous will reach the 70s. National life expectancy is increased much less by the rich living longer than by the poor living longer; poverty takes a heavy toll of life, particularly among children. Long-term gains in well-being for the poor therefore contribute heavily to a raised national life expectancy.

Within the Third World, there are general regional differences, but marked contrasts within regions. Latin America is relatively wealthy and its women are relatively long-lived, but Haiti and Bolivia, the poorest countries, have average expectancies of only 56 and 55 (Chapter 8). Income differentials are high and welfare provision low in the Third World countries of Latin America, so

Map 2 Female life expectancy at birth in the early 1980s

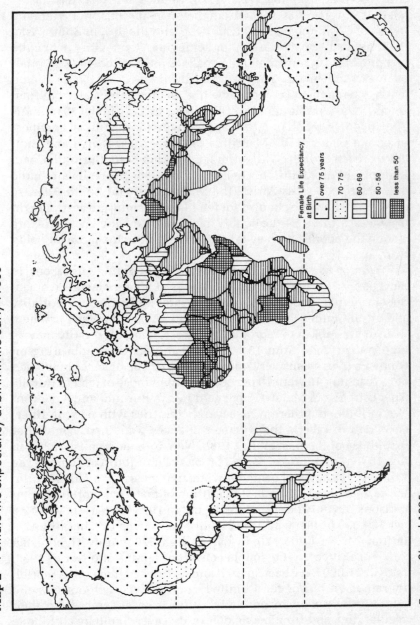

Female Life Expectancy at Birth

- over 75 years
- 70 - 75
- 60 - 69
- 50 - 59
- less than 50

Source: Sivard 1985.

that the highest expectancy is 74 – while Cuba (Second World), although much poorer, reaches 75. South-East Asia, despite its relative poverty, has several countries in the 60s, but Vietnam, Indonesia, Kampuchea and Laos drop into the 50s. In South Asia, Sri Lanka is highly regarded for achieving 70 on a low per capita income, but Afghanistan and Nepal are only in the 40s and other countries are in the 50s. The Middle East–North Africa region tends to be in the 60s, with some high scores in oil states but Iran, Oman, Saudi Arabia and the PDR Yemen are only in the 50s and AR Yemen, 48. Sub-Saharan Africa is both the shortest-lived and most disparate region: only Mauritius, South Africa, Kenya and Zimbabwe reach the 60s, while Angola, Burkina Faso, Burundi, Chad, Ethiopia, Mali, Mauritania, Niger, Senegal and Somalia are in the 40s. Scattered across Africa, the Middle East and South Asia are countries where the chances for female well-being are very poor. In many cases, these are the doubly disadvantaged: their countries are among the poorest in the world, and they suffer the more for being women.

Women usually live longer than men, for hormonal reasons; in most countries, age-specific death rates at all ages favour women. Specific explanations are required for the higher female mortality among the under 5s in northern South Asia (Chapter 2). Where women are subject to reproductive stress, female mortality may be higher than male from 15 to 45, but the tax of childbearing on women's lives seems very uneven. In 1970, the chances of women of 15 reaching 45 were 10 per cent less than those of men in Burma, 6 per cent less in Malawi, 5 per cent less in Burundi and 4 per cent less in India, but there were several countries with no real difference, and in Liberia the women's chances were 9 per cent better than those of the men (WHO 1980; New Internationalist 1985). In this 15 to 45 age-range, complications of childbirth are among the five leading causes of death for women in most of the Third World. In the absence of a standard definition of maternal mortality comparisons can only be approximate, but in 1975 the US rate was 12.8 per 100,000 births, while the rate in Mexico was 123, in Chile 126, in Iran 249, in India 370, in Bangladesh 570 and in Afghanistan 700. For Eritrea, in the double context of famine and war in 1985, rates of 25,000 have been quoted and a 27 per cent maternal mortality rate is on record for a limited sample. Even without war and famine, these women normally suffer from anaemia from their regular diet, and from pelvic deformity caused both by childhood rickets and by the practice of binding girls' legs together until forty days after infibulation, to let the wounds heal; infibulation is performed before the age of 2 (Firebrace 1985). Culture as well as childbearing can bear heavily on female life expectancy.

Sex ratio

It might appear that the sex ratio, or the number of males per hundred females in a population, would both define the relative quality of life and denote the value placed by society on the sexes (Map 3). Numbers are not equal at birth: it seems that more males than females are conceived, but that males are more vulnerable both before and after birth; the better the conditions of gestation and birth, the more likely boys will be to survive. The sex ratio of new-born babies is usually masculine. As we have seen, given basic nutrition and health care, age-specific death rates favour females. In the Soviet Union, the sex ratio is highly feminine; in Europe (save for Greenland and Iceland), the Americas, Australasia, East and South-East Asia and several African countries, it is also feminine. Yet so masculine are ratios in South Asia, China, the Middle East, North Africa and some other African countries that there are more males than females in the world − 20 million more. Explanations, global, national, regional or local, are not simple.

Nutrition

Information on the nutrition of women in the Third World tends to relate only to pregnant and lactating women, and to the consequences for the infant's viability and health (Hamilton *et al.* 1984) rather than to the incidence of, for example, anaemia among all women. Yet nearly two-thirds of pregnant women and half of other women in low income countries are thought to be anaemic, with all the physical and psychological problems which follow (WHO 1979; New Internationalist 1985; anaemia is less prevalent in Latin America, more prevalent in Africa and Asia). Most poor women in the Third World work long and hard; caloric and protein intake are often deficient. In rural Bangladesh, Chen *et al.* (1981) found the caloric consumption of males to exceed females' by 29 per cent in the childbearing age group. Evidence of women eating less than men per kilogramme of body weight is limited.

Other data

For an adequate geography of the physical well-being of the sexes,

Map 3 Sex ratios in the early 1980s

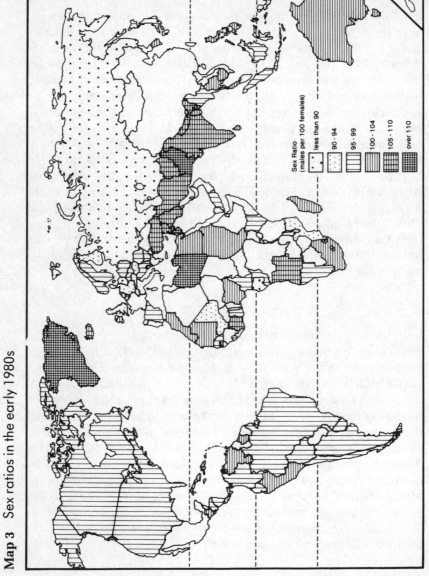

Sex Ratio
(males per 100 females)

less than 90

90 - 94

95 - 99

100 - 104

105 - 110

over 110

Source: *UN Demographic Yearbook* 1983.

we would need exact data for morbidity, mortality and nutritional status by age, sex, income and locality. In poor countries the information is sparse and tends not to be comparable. So we are forced to return over and over again to the surrogate measure of life expectancy and to the importance of current fertility, discussed below.

For most of the components of physical well-being that are specific to women, it seems that international data simply do not exist. There are no comprehensive cross-national tables on age at menarche or puberty (important in itself and related to nutrition) or on such important phenomena as rape, wife-beating and wife-murder. Violence against women is a central feminist theme and appears to vary geographically in form and incidence, being clearly a fundamental aspect of culture, but statistics are simply not collected.

Compound indices?

Attempts have been made to develop compound measures of physical well-being. Morris (1979) produced a 'physical quality of life index' based on infant mortality, adult literacy and life expectancy at age 1. When these measures are taken for the population as a whole, the Third World scores badly, but on his calculations, the countries with a marked difference between the male and the female 'physical quality of life' belong to no specific region; they are scattered across the Third World. But the weighting of Morris's index is doubtful (Lipton 1983b) and the data for many countries are weak.

Andrews (1982) sought to produce a 'female quality of life' index for comparing women's lives in different countries. She used the same weighting methods as Morris, and compounded her index from Morris's data for female literacy and female life expectancy, plus a measure of fertility (the number of births per woman): literacy and life expectancy are seen as positive measures of well-being, fertility as negative. When world maps are drawn for the whole population from Morris's index and for women from Andrews's (Andrews 1982), there is a poorer showing on Andrews's index by some of sub-Saharan Africa and particularly by a belt from South Asia through the Middle East to North Africa. This is selected by Andrews's emphasis on fertility and on female literacy.

Life expectancy and literacy are not simply functions of material wealth; although per capita GNP accounts for some 70 per cent of the variation between Third World countries in literacy or life expectancy (Stewart 1985). At least Morris's and Andrews's indices do examine outcomes. But why these variables? Why include literacy as a measure of well-being? For Morris, literacy is a measure of benefits going to the very poorest groups; it may indeed be the best available indicator of this. Fertility is more of a problem. To class high fertility as a negative feature is to identify Kenya as having poor female well-being; it also brings the Soviet Union and Eastern Europe down relative to Western Europe and North America. If the total fertility rate in the USSR is 2.4 and in the UK 1.7, is the well-being of women therefore higher in the UK? Compound indices seem to have more drawbacks than advantages: doubtful data and doubtful interpretations are not improved by being added together.

Childbearing

In biological reproduction the roles of the sexes are physically determined. Both sexes are required for conception, but childbearing and lactation are female functions; fertility becomes an important statement about women's lives. (The total fertility rate, or TFR, is the number of children who would be born per woman through her childbearing years if she were to have children at the age-specific fertility rates of her society.) Fertility (Map 4) more than any other aspect of life distinguishes Third World women from those of the First and Second Worlds. 30 per cent of Third World women of childbearing age are either pregnant or lactating at any one time. In advanced industrial economies, the total fertility rate is usually under two and always under three; in the centrally planned, it is often over two, but is over three only in Albania. In the Third World, the range is from 2.0 in Barbados to 7.9 in Kenya.

Aspects of fertility are the best documented features of women's lives in the Third World. We disagree with Andrews (1982) and other geographers who define number of children per se as a direct negative measure of female well-being, yet it remains true that repeated, closely spaced pregnancies can have direct harmful results on the health and nutrition of mother and child. Such mothers may show progressive weight loss, premature ageing and anaemia; they are also more liable to complications in pregnancy and to chronic ill health. The severity of stress from recurring pregnancy and lactation is amply illustrated in studies of nutrition and energy use in highly seasonal environments and of the effects on infant birth-weight and survival and on maternal

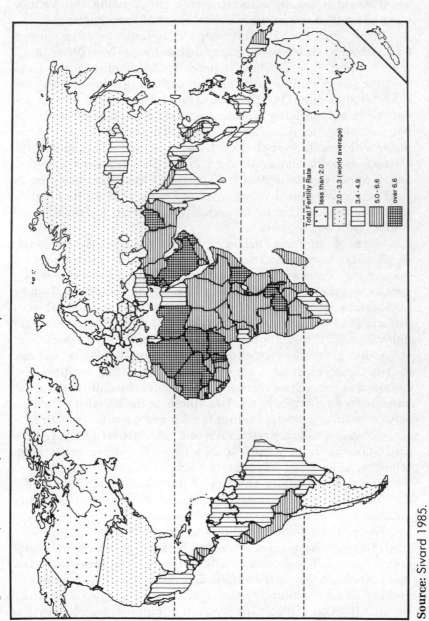

Map 4 Fertility in the early 1980s: the total fertility rate

Total Fertility Rate

- less than 2.0
- 2.0 - 3.3 (world average)
- 3.4 - 4.9
- 5.0 - 6.6
- over 6.6

Source: Sivard 1985.

mortality (Chambers et al. (eds.) 1981). Women's well-being in the Third World is closely associated with childbearing, but fertility must be understood in the whole context of reproduction.

In the Third World, women depend primarily on other women for any help in childbearing; many deliver themselves. Better nutrition (Chapter 5) and better hygiene would greatly improve the survival rate of mother and child: grassroots primary health care (Chapter 3) and food together could make vast inroads into maternal and infant mortality without formal medical treatment. But as Pearson shows us (Chapter 3), painful contradictions and paradoxes will remain. In societies where menstruation and childbirth are seen as polluting, as among Hindus, it is this very pollution which renders midwifery strictly women's business, reserving to women some degree of autonomy. Yet Pearson did not find female solidarity in Nepal, but rather a socially generated and maintained conflict between women.

Not even the most strictly biological functions can be considered apart from their social reality. A myriad restrictions on women may serve simply to secure knowledge of paternity. As a simple and direct example, there is really no other satisfactory explanation of clitoridectomy (excision of the clitoris) and infibulation (removal and suturing of the labia). These are found today primarily from the Sahel to East Africa and affect more than 100 million women, even though they decrease fertility and can cause grave medical complications, including septicaemia, haemorrhage, shock and serious urinary infections, throughout the woman's reproductive years. They increase the certainty of paternity by reducing or eliminating the woman's sexual pleasure.

Compared to this drastic intervention in women's lives, mere restrictions such as purdah and other forms of seclusion seem relatively mild. We shall see that for Engels, the express purpose of the family is to produce children of undisputed paternity (1884) and that many anthropologists derive the whole of women's subordination from their unique role in procreation.

For an understanding of biological reproduction, certain statistical indicators have value – the total fertility rate, infant mortality and, if possible, maternal mortality and morbidity, rates of abortion and availability of contraception. But again the picture these can yield is notably incomplete: the significance of women's sexuality for their lives may derive largely from interpretations of this sexuality and from hidden structural features. On Goody's logic (1983), the current western identification of marriage as a central point in the life-cycle, and the whole popular culture attached to this derive simply from the European tradition of the dowry system.

Sustaining society

The caretakers

Goods and services must be produced for human use; human life and society must be reproduced to continue in existence. For our purposes, the categorization is a convenient one for locating variations in gender roles. The reproduction of human life and the reproduction of society are closely interrelated (Evers *et al.* 1984; Harris and Young 1981), but both neo-classical and Marxist economists have tended to ignore them; both have focused rather on production for exchange or on production and circulation.

Children must be cared for and taught: this is usually a female task, but often not that of the mother. But there is more to *social reproduction* than this: food, water, warmth, clothing, shelter, hygiene and care for the sick must be provided as well as personal support and comfort. In the First and Second Worlds, much is provided by the cash economy and the state, but in the Third World, with an absence of investment in public utilities and welfare facilities, more is provided within the domestic sphere, usually by women. For the majority of Third World people, all water for drinking, cooking and washing must be carried, usually by women (5 to 45 litres per person per day); in extreme cases the distance is so great that the return journey cannot be accomplished in a day, and the woman has to sleep at the watering place. More than 1000 million rural people depend on firewood for cooking and warmth, and almost as many again on dung and crop wastes: all must be collected and carried, usually by women (Chapter 15). Only a minority of Third World people have any form of sanitation, but considerable effort is usually devoted to keeping the house, people and their clothes clean. It is perhaps easier to think of rural women's struggle for fuelwood as a relationship between people and their environment than that of urban women to develop hygienic habits in children who must excrete on an exposed rubbish tip (Chant 1984a). All these 'caring' roles are primarily female. Although they have long been out of focus, as if they had either no importance or no variability in space and time, society would break down without them, as, in disasters, it does.

Basic care of health is women's work (Chapter 3), though official practitioners may be male. Providing a house is often a male

activity, but 'after a house has been built it is necessary to reproduce a habitat' (Evers *et al.* 1984), usually a female role. Reproductive activities will vary with place, time and wealth, both in their
content and in the division between the sexes, but there remains a
recognizable element of 'household subsistence reproduction' for
which labour and much management are provided by women,
from the remotest rural areas to the most affluent city suburbs. As
Deere *et al.* (1982) and Beneria (1982) point out, the domestic
labour of advanced industrial society merely 'stretches' the wage,
while domestic and self-provisioning activities in the Third World
replace much of the wage, making labour cheaper in the Third
World.

'The most fundamental and stable fact of women's lives
throughout the world is their responsibility for the home, the
family, and domestic labour. To whatever extent women are integrated into production . . . they still bear the responsibility for this
basic element of human existence' (UNESCO 1984). For much
research, women's action-space is divided into that within the
household versus the outside: women's worlds are seen as a
dichotomy of private and public spheres, of the world of home and
family against the world of work (Sanday 1974).

Are households units?

In the industrialized world it is the nuclear family, co-resident as a
household, which dominates the reproduction of human life and
labour: the relation central to reproduction is the family, and the
locale is the household. This structure belongs to definite times
and places and we cannot usefully generalize from it: Harris (1981),
Oppong (1982), Safilios-Rothschild (1982) and Youssef (1982)
therefore argue against the use of the household in the study of
Third World women. Kindred groups may not be co-resident; co-
resident groups may not be kin. Effective pooling of income is rare,
whether within a 'family', a 'household' or a 'co-resident group':
conflict, tension and inequality are normal. There has now crept
into the data and the literature the identification of a 'household
head', conventionally male, who is assumed to centralize and
allocate resources. This is often an inapplicable model (Chapter 5).

Yet we are not willing to discard the household level of
analysis, because this is the arena of subordination. The household
should not be viewed as a cohesive unit; mutual dependence does
not guarantee lack of conflicts or of basic differences of interests.
Nevertheless, it is within the household, by agreement, custom or

conflict, that income is distributed: often a mixture of wages, payment in kind, household products that can be directly consumed (perhaps crops, textiles or clothing), profits from petty trading and other informal sector activities, rents and gifts (see Chapter 4). Household activities may add as much as 40 per cent to GNP in some countries (Stewart 1985). Excessive attention to the wage labour force not only excludes a majority of the world's population (only a minority engage in regular wage labour for most of their adult lives) but, as we have seen, takes for granted the reproductive activities without which there would be no labour force and no society. There is no 'natural' universal unit common to all societies which organizes these activities in the same way, but the household is one level at which the activities meet and interact: we must not oversimplify the interactions, but we must examine them.

We shall follow some of Pahl's (1984) usages. For Pahl, *'households are simply units for getting various kinds of work done', 'work' including production and reproduction* (our emphasis). The composition and sources of work used by the household vary in space and time. It is this which Pahl defines as a household work strategy, without inferring conscious decision.

The New Household Economics (Binswanger *et al.* (eds.) 1980) has attempted to examine the economic behaviour of the household and specifically to explain in economic terms the household demand for children. As with many neo-classical approaches, this cannot incorporate social attitudes and expectations, intra-household disagreement or, indeed, differential access to resources (Mueller 1982). It does not admit the external influences on the household that form the environment within which the household supposedly maximizes utility. It does at least, however, serve to emphasize the value of children and of the labour time of household members, since economic utility is formally assigned to each.

W(h)ither the household?

First World and particularly British readers will be aware that Pahl (1984) and others have been paying increasing attention to subjects which are very familiar in Third World research, such as informal (or unwaged) activities, the household and time allocation. Both neo-classical and Marxist economists had tended to assume that informal and self-provisioning activities would wither away as cash and wage relations penetrated more areas of life – that they were in some way marginal, residual features. The last two decades have seen a pronounced revival of self-provisioning activities in, for example, the UK (Pahl 1984) and the USSR (Gordon and Klopov 1975). This revival of domestic production is perceived not as a transient feature of recession, but as a trend to be expected for the foreseeable future. In the Third World, domestic production may prove similarly durable.

Income-earning: indicators of women's roles

Direct production seems at first a less problematic category of work, as it includes all the orthodox 'economic' activities. The main problem here in studying the geography of gender is that there are serious discrepancies in the calculation of work done by each gender. 'Direct production' by women should include not only factory employment (Chapter 12) and wage work in offices and services, but agriculture, domestic service and income-generating activities in the informal sector: the last three are quite commonly missed. Women's 'economic' activities are still grossly underestimated, particularly where there is relatively little commoditization or where unpaid family labour bulks large. Comparison between countries is particularly difficult, since different definitions are still adopted for 'economic' activity. Two points generate confusion: the conceptual problem of the definition of 'work', which is not agreed by all countries, and the empirical problem of measurement, in which there were, in 1985, serious discrepancies. At the UN conference in Nairobi which marked the end of the Decade for Women, delegates agreed to urge their countries to put an economic value on women's productive and reproductive work in their statistics.

The System of National Accounts (SNA), which is fairly widely employed, requires household surveys to include an estimated value for some goods and services produced and consumed within the household, including farm products – but it specifically excludes food preparation, child care, cleaning, etc., as well as the collection and transport of wood and water. Reproductive activities performed within the household are simply not counted, and much women's work is therefore concealed. National censuses do not even achieve the SNA information. Far more countries report demographic and educational data by sex than have any information on female participation in the labour force. Where information exists, the 'economically active population' (EAP) is that which furnishes labour for the production of economic goods and services for market or exchange, in contrast to those for individual or family use, subsistence or consumption.

Geography of gender roles in 'economic' activity

In all parts of the world, nearly all men aged between about 25 and 55 are 'in the labour force' or 'economically active': the pattern is for men to spend their adult years in labour market activities. Women on the other hand may spend all or part of their adult lives as 'economically inactive homemakers' or may be 'economically active' but invisible. According to official figures, the tendency in advanced industrial economies (First World) and centrally planned economies (Second World) is for more than a third of the wage labour force to be female. In developing market economies (Third World) the proportion is usually much less, being lowest in certain Islamic states of North Africa, the Middle East and South Asia and highest in South-East Asia. The most sharply varying patterns are found in Africa, where Angola reports that 9 per cent of women aged 15 to 64 are in the labour force, and that 9 per cent of the total labour force is female; the corresponding figures for nearby Botswana are 73 per cent and 52 per cent. As we have seen, there are serious doubts about how 'real' these aggregate statistics are, particularly where the figures are low. On official figures, few Third

Table 1 Female activity rates

Region	Rural	Urban
Arab countries	very low	low
Latin America	very low	high
Africa and India	high	low
South-East Asia	high	high

Source: After Standing (1978).

World states reach the levels of female wage labour which are commonplace in the First and Second Worlds; the exceptions are mainland South-East Asia and a scatter of African states. Internal patterns vary not only by class, income and ethnic group but systematically by urban–rural residence, as is shown in Table 1. To achieve as much comparability as possible, we shall discuss not overall 'participation rates', but specific sectors where the sources of bias and omissions are more apparent and the data more readily evaluated.

Maps 5, 6 and 7 show estimates for the percentage of the labour force in 1970 which was thought to be female. For the industrial

Map 5   Women's estimated share in agricultural work in the Third World, 1970

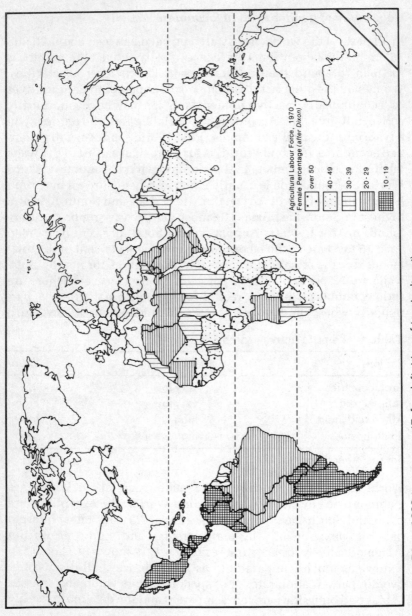

Agricultural Labour Force, 1970
Female Percentage (after Dixon)

- over 50
- 40 - 49
- 30 - 39
- 20 - 29
- 10 - 19

Source: Dixon 1983 (see text, p. 47, for definition of 'agriculture').

Map 6   Women's estimated share in industrial work in the Third World

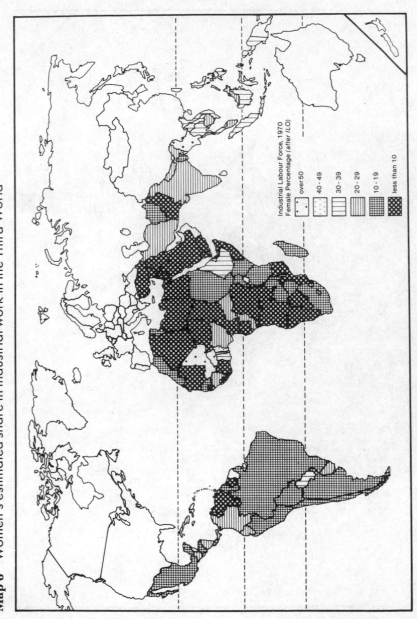

Industrial Labour Force, 1970
Female Percentage (after ILO)

over 50
40 · 49
30 · 39
20 · 29
10 · 19
less than 10

Source: ILO 1977 (see text, p. 47, for definition of 'industrial').

Map 7   Women's estimated share in work in the service sector in the Third World, 1970

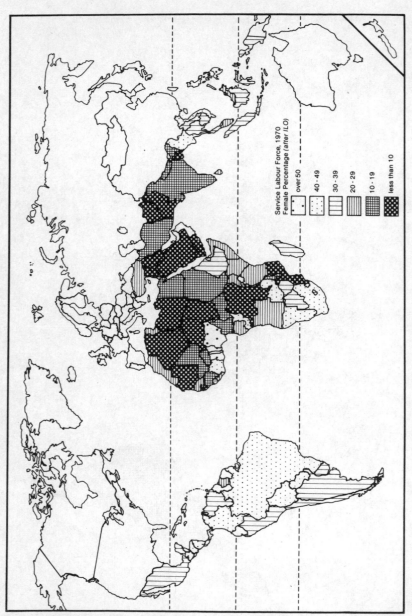

Service Labour Force, 1970
Female Percentage (after ILO)

over 50
40 - 49
30 - 39
20 - 29
10 - 19
less than 10

Source: ILO 1977 (see text, p. 47, for definition of 'service').

and service sectors we have mapped the ILO (1977) estimates; for agriculture, we have preferred Dixon's (1983) corrections of these same estimates from FAO surveys. We would ascribe some of the variation, despite the best efforts of Dixon and the ILO, to inconsistent recording and inaccurate data; some of the regional patterns may also derive less from reality than from ILO's use of neighbouring countries to interpolate missing data. Notwithstanding these caveats, these maps still demonstrate remarkable variation in female 'economic' activity both between sectors of activity and across the Third World.

In general, the estimated female share in *agricultural* work is high: Dixon's figures suggest that, in 1970, three-quarters of the people of the Third World lived in countries where women made up more than a third of the agricultural labour force. (Agriculture here includes also hunting, forestry and fishing.) In the *industrial* sector (mining and quarrying, manufacturing, electricity, gas, water and construction), the female share is usually considerably less. In *services* (wholesale and retail trade, restaurants, hotels, transport, storage, communication, financing, insurance, real estate, business services, community, social and personal services), the female share is higher again. But the variations are very considerable. Few countries are consistent across the three sectors. Among these, South-East Asia is notable for consistently high female shares, while the Islamic states from Mauritania to Bangladesh (but not Indonesia or Malaysia) consistently have low to very low female shares in all sectors. India, however, has a high female participation in agriculture, low in industry and very low in services; sub-Saharan Africa has a great range of female shares in all sectors, with little repetition of pattern; Latin America has a remarkably low female share in industry (as defined above) and a high female share in services – the opposite to India.

Patterns of the female share in economic activities within these broad sectors are even more idiosyncratic in the few countries for which we have 1980s data. In *manufacturing industry*, for example, the tendency in the First and Second Worlds is for some 20 to 40 per cent of the labour force to be female (ILO 1983). In the Third World, a map of the female share of the labour force in manufacturing industry would show high levels in South-East Asia, fairly high levels in Latin America and low levels elsewhere. The Islamic states are unexpectedly varied: Tunisia, Egypt and Pakistan all have significant manufacturing (and employment data), but the reported female share varies from 49 per cent in Tunisia to 6 per cent in Egypt and Pakistan. Similarly, in India the female share is only 15 per cent, but in Sri Lanka it is 33 per cent. It is in the very small states where export processing dominates manufacturing that the female share is very high: in Singapore, 56 per cent of the labour force in manufacturing is female. Where there is a larger, traditional manufacturing sector, this new phenomenon of female-dominated export-processing industry may be substantial in size, but cannot dominate labour force statistics against the older foundries, brickworks and breweries.

There is no simple explanation for the relative level of the female share in manufacturing employment, and above all there is no correlation with the female share in agriculture. (We should note that much of this development postdates the 1970 data of Map 6.) Gender roles can be entirely reconstructed between the sectors.

Data for the gender structure of *clerical* occupations (ILO 1983) have interest, since there is such a stereotype in the advanced industrialized countries of all clerical workers being female. In the Third World, the female share in clerical occupations is less than half in almost every country for which data exist. In Latin America it may be as small as a third; elsewhere it is usually much less, save in South-East Asia, where the share may be over 40 per cent. In India, it is 6 per cent. What is overwhelmingly a 'female' occupation in Europe and North America is even more overwhelmingly masculine in India.

Geography of gender roles in society

In the Third World, we rarely have national data on the discrepancies between men's and women's wages for the same type of work: data are similarly lacking for many other important aspects of gender roles. We can map the legality of and conditions for abortion (Kidron and Segal 1984) or divorce, or the state position on contraception. These maps are not without meaning – but for the mass of poor women, the meaning can be limited. Abortion may be legal, but is it available? (or rather, are qualified abortionists available?). How immediately relevant is divorce legislation in a country where the majority of poor women do not marry, and those who do could not afford divorce proceedings?

Education

In most Third World societies, literacy is an important measure of life options. In 1980, 48.5 per cent of females aged 15 and over in developing countries were illiterate, against 32.3 per cent of males

(UNESCO 1983). Most countries had successfully committed resources to improve female literacy: for 1960, Sivard (1985) records forty-seven Third World countries where the female adult literacy rate was only half the male; for 1980, only sixteen. In most countries, female literacy gained substantially on male levels. Large discrepancies between the sexes are still found in the Middle East and North Africa, but in South-East Asia and especially Latin America literacy tends to be much more equal (Map 8). Of the initial enrolment in primary schools in the Third World in 1980, 44 per cent were girls (UNESCO 1983), but this proportion still fell to 39 per cent in secondary education and 34 per cent in tertiary. These global figures conceal some very poor performances, as in Afghanistan (17, 15 and 18 per cent respectively) or Nepal (27, 20, 18 per cent). Drop-out rates are also often much higher for girls. For those Third World countries for which data are available, women form a progressively smaller group through higher education, except in Kuwait. At higher levels the significance of education is ambivalent: a high female presence may merely represent women from wealthy families for whom the gender construction of society does not leave other options open. That some women are highly qualified may be of importance to the nation but irrelevant to poor women.

High female adult literacy (over 70 per cent) and high equality in literacy between the sexes (over 80 per cent) are found in many Latin American and some South-East Asian countries and in Sri Lanka and Tanzania. Countries of very low female literacy tend also to have much lower female than male literacy, although this is less true of the African countries in the group (see Table 2). Countries where less than 11 per cent of women can read and write have one thing in common: their poverty. If we consider income, we find that the following countries have low literacy and high gender inequality for their per capita income: Saudi Arabia (male literacy 44 per cent, female 19), Iraq (75, 41), Iran (62, 39), Algeria (69, 32): all Muslim oil-exporters. (Gabon is not Muslim, but its oil wealth has clearly also gone towards male rather than female literacy (70 and 50 per cent).) There are also poor countries of high literacy such as Sri Lanka (88, 78).

Although education is so important to life options, there is no clear evidence for a universal association between education and female participation in the 'labour force', though the spread of education does tend to create a social climate favouring female 'economic activity'. Empirical research has tended to show that the relationship between female education and 'economic activity' is

Map 8 Female literacy as a percentage of male in the early 1980s

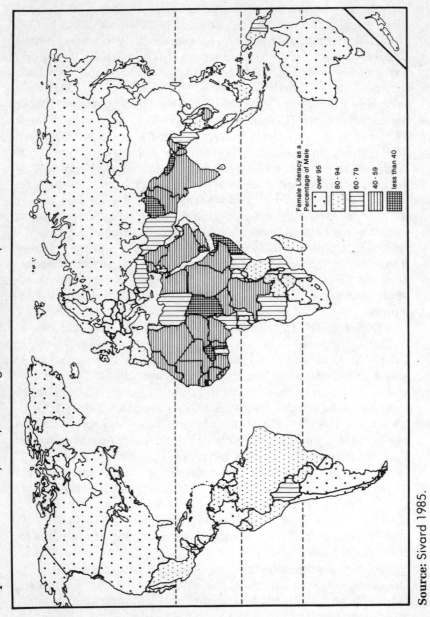

Female Literacy as a
Percentage of Male

- over 95
- 80 - 94
- 60 - 79
- 40 - 59
- less than 40

Source: Sivard 1985.

Table 2   Countries of low female literacy

Country	Percentage of women of 15 and over able to read and write	Adult female literacy as a percentage of adult male literacy
Yemen Arab Republic	3	11
Nepal	9	21
Afghanistan	8	24
Chad	11	28
Burkina Faso	6	29
Somalia	6	33
Ethiopia	5	46
Niger	9	47
Mali	11	48

Source: UNESCO 1983.

highly dependent on factors such as place, income and class (Standing and Sheehan (eds.) 1978).

Social indicators

Other information we would wish to have to compare women's lives in countries of the Third World would include indicators such as those of Safilios-Rothschild (1970, 1982). They must measure two features: first, women's ability to control important events in their lives, and second, the extent to which women have the same life options as men in the same age group and social class with respect to food, education and training, occupations, remuneration, occupational advancement, migration, use of time and leisure, land and property ownership and life expectancy.

For intra-household variables, only survey research will elucidate international contrasts in women's power – their ability to decide about their own activities and those of others, their control over subsistence decisions and resources, the amount of help received in reproductive activities, their membership of groups outside the household, their role in the formation and dispersal of the household or other productive group. Only at the micro level is it possible to assess women's informal power, which may be very significant in many societies (Whyte 1978).

Widowhood and marital breakdown

Many phenomena must be studied in their regional context. The poignancy of very low remarriage rates for widows is realized only when we think of the realities of South Asia. There, an Indian ideal has been that the bride should be one-third the age of her husband, ensuring early widowhood for many, which for widows of the higher Hindu castes has meant social death. Low caste South Asian women can remarry, although they may then lose property rights and access to their children. 'Self-immolation was expected only of high-caste women, but widowhood has been a particularly unhappy state for most' (Whyte and Whyte 1982). The worst outcome is possibly for the childless widow, so the incentives to child-bearing are high. Widows are a widespread phenomenon, since many societies have a large age difference between spouses; where tradition has meant widows, tradition has commonly enforced some sort of provision for them, but this is often disrupted by urbanization and economic change (Youssef and Hetler 1983).

Marital breakdown is also an intractable phenomenon. In societies with many informal or consensual unions (mainly Latin America and the Caribbean), the breakdown, like the union, may go unrecorded. In Islamic societies, divorce rates have been relatively high but male kin have owed full support to a divorced woman. It appears that this obligation is becoming less effective; in the Middle East, North Africa, Malaysia and Muslim Indonesia, divorced women are increasingly entering the labour market. At the other extreme, in Latin America, divorced women have been few, ostracized and rejected; they are increasing in numbers, and they too appear in the labour market. Buvinic and Youssef (1978) consider that in all countries it must be divorced and separated women who most lack economic support, as against the married, single and even the widowed, since the divorced and separated are the most heavily involved in the labour force.

Female-headed households

The proportion of all households in the world headed de facto by women has been estimated as being as high as a quarter to a third (Tinker 1976), but Buvinic and Youssef's calculations (1978) would suggest a figure nearer a sixth for the Third World. Some female-headed households have arisen from male-headed households through death, marital breakdown or migration; some are 'naturally' female-headed, either because the woman has no permanent partner (Caribbean) or because there are other wives in other dwellings and settlements (West Africa). Patterns are regional: in Asia, widowhood is still the main cause, but international migration is an increasingly important factor; in North Africa and southern Africa, international migration dominates (Chapter 9); in the rest of Africa, male migration to the cities leaves rural households female-headed; in Latin America, unstable unions are the main cause, but very high migration often yields such households in both urban and rural areas.

'The female-headed family is a type of domestic unit produced by modern conditions; it has no counterpart in any pre-industrial tradition' (Mair 1984). This is inexact: such households were a majority in colonial Sao Paulo. Nevertheless, the ubiquitous occurrence of such households is new; wider family responsibilities are often breaking down, leaving widows and single mothers and (in very large numbers) the wives of migrant workers in a new situation of isolation and insecurity. In a squatter settlement near Nairobi, Kenya, Nelson (1979) estimated that 60 to 80 per cent of women in the settlement were independent heads of households. In the Caribbean, female urban migrants often leave their children behind with their mothers, so that the rural areas of many territories become dominated by households headed by grandmothers (Henshall 1981). A large, new problem is being widely ignored; fragments of the mosaic have become visible to planners and academics, but inadequate account is still taken of the whole.

Scattered across the Third World (Part Four) are labour reserve areas from which adults, usually male, migrate in search of temporary or permanent employment. Farming continues, in the hands of the young, the old and the female; remittances may be sent to the family. Often, families are effectively female-headed: we are beginning to be aware of the problems faced in gaining access to extension and credit, but we have little idea of the geography of remittances. Research has been focused on the role of remittances in productive investment; an important question. But what is the role of remittances in reproduction? What fraction of such female-headed households receive no remittances?

A convention has arisen that female-headed households tend to be poor. Lipton (1983a) has challenged this, claiming that such households are not, other variables being held constant, more at risk of great poverty. Where they are poor, he ascribes this to the social disadvantage of widowhood rather than the sex of the household head. Youssef and Hetler (1983) conclude that the shortcomings of the data are of serious magnitude in all regions: the controversy may simply reflect regional variation.

Are women really poorer?

Again, it is possible for Boulding to assert (1983) that 'The majority of those estimated to be seriously poor and destitute in the Third World are women and children', while Lipton (1983a), in a World Bank report, maintains that there are only slightly more females than males among the poor. The problem is partly one of definition, but again largely of inadequate data. What minimum agreement is there? At the least, it is more difficult for poor women to escape from poverty than poor men, and specific problems attach to being female and poor: women suffer more severe and less remediable effects of poverty (Lipton 1983a).

For Visaria (1977), writing on Maharashtra and Gujarat, the real problem is that women's chances of escape – either from rural poverty via townward migration, or from urban poverty via upward mobility – are far less than men's. Women in the Third World are indeed often more immobile than men, particularly in the Old World. In India, ladders of success are more open to males, yielding a 'new demography of urban poverty' where males predominate in richer urban groups and elite, decision-making groups may become powerfully male (Lipton 1983a). It is not agreed that women are often paid less for the same work, but all concur that women have less access to (and training for) work with better earnings prospects. Women are more trapped in poverty.

We would argue that the life of women in poorer groups is harder than that of men. Almost everywhere, the poorer women are, the more likely they are to engage in paid labour (until the very poorest group of all). Poorer groups of households have a very much higher ratio of children to adult women (Lipton 1983a). It is women who are under social pressure to work a double day, at home and at work. In India at least, poorer women are actually less likely to have access to complex household structures to help with children; cycles of poverty follow, via inevitably inadequate child stimulation and care (Lipton 1983a; compare Chapter 4 for Bangladesh). The whole meaning of the double day in productive and reproductive activities is most acute for poorer women: they are more likely to be in the labour force, and to be providing and caring for more children on (by definition) a lower income.

Migration

Migration is at once a cause and a measure. It is an essential component of the geography of gender: an important factor in women's lives in the Third World, and an indicator for observers of life options at different places (see Chapters 3, 9, 10, 11, 18). At the regional scale, Latin America and 'areas of European settlement' are characterized by a predominance of female migration at both young and older ages (Chapter 10); this is also a European pattern; in Africa (Chapter 9), the Middle East and South Asia (Chapter 3), youth migration is more commonly male-selective, and the level of old-age migration among women is low (United Nations 1980). In South-East and East Asia (Chapter 11) there is no consistent dominance of one sex over another in the migration process (Smith *et al*. 1984), and migration has been characterized as 'family migration' (Standing 1978). At the national and more local scales there is remarkable variety.

In the Third World, it is migration to cities that involves most people (Chapter 11), although international labour migration (Chapters 3, 9, 18) may have a more dramatic economic impact, and migration to frontiers of settlement (Chapter 9) may alter more of the landscape. The construction of gender has some very consistent and other very local effects on male/female differences in migration. Broadly, either sex may migrate to improve livelihood or status through education and/or employment of themselves or their children, but it is usually (though not invariably) women who migrate to marry. Marriage migration is an important component of migration in both Africa and South Asia, and women's subsequent isolation may be a major factor in their lives. Nevertheless, the notion that patterns of female migration are simply a compound of marriage, family and household migration is a gross distortion; autonomous female migration is a real and widespread feature. The differing regional patterns of migration identified by the United Nations (1980) relate roughly to regional contrasts in urban and rural activity rates (Table 1), suggesting a strong link to employment possibilities. Low-wage service employment, particularly in domestic service, is an urban attraction open (outside South Asia) primarily to females. The feminine sex ratios and substantial presence of female-headed households in Latin American cities are commonly ascribed to this attraction. Conversely, male migration may determine women's lives (Chapter 18).

How women vanish: a hidden geography

How can half of humanity be so consistently overlooked by scholars and planners, particularly in the world of work? Many working women are obscured because they are 'economically inactive homemakers' who only produce food for home consumption, or they are too young or too old to be recorded – this is a familiar concept. But Boulding (1983) has shown that remarkable numbers are not accounted for at all. She identified thirty-two countries which record both the percentage of women participating in the labour force and 'economically inactive homemakers'. These two categories, plus students, retired women, women living on their own means and employing a housekeeper, the totally dependent and the institutionalized should by definition total 100 per cent of women over 15. Yet in four African and Middle Eastern countries, 49 per cent of the women do not appear either in the 'labour force' or as 'economically inactive homemakers'. It is clearly impossible that they should all fall into the residual categories just listed. All experience of Third World women suggests rather that the poor majority work all the time. Many countries omit 'unpaid family workers' with a very substantial effect on the 'number of women in the labour force', especially in agricultural societies with significant numbers of family farms. Statistics of *female labour force participation* (the percentage of women participating in the labour force) are thus of *very poor international comparability*.

Further inconsistencies in the recording of women's roles in direct production appear in part-time work and in informal sector activities. Obscurities over part-time work are not confined to the Third World: in the EEC, the female share of the UK labour force appears high, but 41.5 per cent of these UK women work less than thirty hours per week. If part-time jobs are converted to full-time equivalents, the female share of the labour force in the UK drops to the EEC average (Townsend 1986). Similar inconsistencies beset the data worldwide. There is some overlap between part-time work and that in the informal sector, where activities are insecure, do not provide full-time employment and often generate low incomes. The informal sector concept has proved of little explanatory value but is descriptively telling: the relative lack of legal incorporation and restrictions has a powerful effect on workers (Lipton 1984). Family enterprises, casual work, outworking, home production for the market – all may have in common a very low level of protection for workers and a very high propensity to be overlooked in statistics. None of these activities is ascribed to the same gender worldwide: casual labour on construction sites in Thailand may be female (Chapter 11); domestic service is commonly female, but in India and parts of East Africa it is male. 'These combinations can only be discovered by examining each particular economy. They cannot be deduced from abstract constructs, which are useful only as guidelines' (Heyzer 1981).

Meanwhile, the 'unpaid family workers' remain such an awkward category that there is some excuse for countries which refuse to enumerate them. (They form an important fraction of the informal sector.) By definition, unpaid family workers work in non-domestic activities for at least one-third of the normal hours (usually during a stated period, such as the two weeks prior to the census). A typical figure would be fifteen hours a week – but Leon (1984) examined Latin American censuses and found six countries stipulating no minimum time, nine requiring thirty-five hours and eight requiring between one and eighteen hours. (These abstract quantities of time probably render the question useless in most semi-literate communities.) Leon believed that in Colombia's 1973 census only 1 per cent of unpaid family workers were registered as such. Wherever household surveys have been taken, they have seriously challenged the official national data. In Algeria in 1956, 96,000 women were reported as unpaid family workers. This figure was subsequently revised upwards to 1.2 million after undercounting had been recognized. Technical points such as the form of questions also promote inconsistency (Leon 1984). Questions about 'main occupation' and 'subsidiary occupation' lead to extensive under-reporting of economically active women (Beneria 1982). Social, cultural and ideological problems also intervene, as respondents (and even census takers) deliberately conceal women's economic activity.

Confused definitions, inconsistencies between countries and genuinely difficult concepts probably all derive from, as well as worsen, social confusions over 'women's role'. Some men are under-enumerated because of the same difficulties, but the numbers of women affected are much larger. Women are also obscured more than men by the invisibility of productive work carried out in the household: handicraft activities, petty trading, the selling of cooked food (Chapters 6, 12), processing, as of cashew nuts (Chapter 14), and the brewing of ale and beer (Chapter 7).

Does it matter?

Definitional detail and the form of census questions seem very remote from women's real worlds. Clearly, the inconsistencies of information about women's activities, particularly in the Third World, make life very difficult for geographers. Does it matter to Third World women?

An array of high quality studies has shown that it does. Rogers

(1980) demonstrated most elegantly how development planning is often dominated not only by western male ideology but by a lamentable lack of knowledge about what women do. She cites Galbraith's highly applicable dictum that 'what is not counted is usually not noticed'. Under development 'schemes', agricultural training is usually given to men even where women do the farming; credit is commonly restricted to men; so is title to land, even where this is not the local tradition. Projects directed at women tend to be segregated: 'a woman's place is home economics' (Rogers 1980). Rarely, if ever, do projects seek to render more productive the work women are actually doing. All too often they assume, quite wrongly, that women have free time which they could devote, say, to handicrafts or even good works. Far too much feminist talk about Third World women still also presupposes women enclosed in the home, engaged exclusively in childcare, cooking and cleaning, and ignores the 'economically active' who are being squeezed out of their roles in direct production.

Academic answer: survey research

Two approaches are advocated to improve our information on the world of work: household surveys, and time-budget studies. The UN has advocated household surveys since 1950 as a basis for data collection in poorer countries; the results on the labour force are regarded as much more reliable than census data, particularly for women. At present, most countries have a small number of such local surveys of high quality: these may often be a more reliable guide for national trends than the apparently more substantial findings of the census. Most contributors to this book either draw heavily on such surveys or present the significance of a survey they have themselves conducted.

Gender and time

Time is an increasingly scarce resource for many women in the developing world. Many Third World women carry a very heavy burden of a double or even a triple workload involving a very long working day (Chapter 10). Until recently the full extent of gender differences in time use was not widely appreciated. However, with the advent of increasing numbers of women field-researchers to whom women's domestic responsibilities are both accessible and of interest, much more detailed information has become available.

Boserup (1970) was first to detect regional patterns of gender differences in time utilization within the household. She noted that in Africa women put in a much longer day than men gathering fuelwood, fetching water, and carrying out housework, childcare, food preparation and much of the agricultural labour (Table 3). In

Table 3 Percentage of hours of work associated with specific tasks attributed to women in Africa

Task	Women's Percentage of total hours
Food production/crop cultivation	70
Domestic food storage	50
Food processing	100
Animal husbandry	50
Marketing	60
Brewing	90
Supplying water	90
Providing fuel	80

Source: Dixon 1985.

addition to the very high proportion of work associated with food production undertaken by African rural women (see Chapter 15, and Table 55) they also spend about 25 per cent of their working day on domestic labour (Chapter 6). In the Gambia, women spend 159 days per year, compared to 103 days for the men, in work on the farm (Mair 1984). African women then spend an additional four hours a day on collecting fuel and water and on housework and childcare. The type of agriculture itself will often determine the gender division of labour time: Harry (1981) in her work on Trinidad found that women worked longer hours than men on rice and dairy farms but fewer hours than men on sugar plantations.

Change associated with capitalist penetration also affects women's workload (Part Three). New technology may reduce the time women spend in processing crops (Bagchi 1982), but an expansion of the cultivated area may force women to spend longer collecting firewood as the most accessible forests are cleared (Chapters 11, 16). Consolidation of settlements may also increase the length of the woman's work day by forcing her to walk further to her traditional fields as McCall found in Tanzania (Chapter 7). Easier access to education deprives women of the assistance of their older children who traditionally have helped their mothers by guarding stock and taking care of younger siblings.

Temporal environmental changes such as seasonality are of particular interest to geographers but we have yet to explore fully the role of seasonality in gender, particularly in tropical areas (Townsend 1984). It is not just the direct impact of wet and dry seasons, but also the variability in the time of onset, intensity and extent of these seasons which affect the workload of household members. Chambers (1979) sees wet/dry seasonality as providing an explanation of tropical poverty. Seasonal stresses often coincide in the wet season; in some localities, births also tend to be most frequent at this time of year (Chambers et al. (eds.) 1981) as are deaths of newborn children (Mair 1984). Lactating mothers suffer a decline in both quantity and quality of their milk and are forced to wean their babies earlier, thus increasing the infant's vulnerability to infection. Yet much of the extra labour demand at these busy times of the agricultural year falls on women at the expense of time normally spent on childcare and leisure. Spiro shows (Chapter 6) that Yoruba women reduce the hours they spend on domestic work when farmwork demands more of their time (Table 33). They are able to halve the time they spend each day collecting water because in the wet season they can use wells near the village while in the dry season they have to walk long distances to the river. Even in urban areas seasonal differences affect domestic labour. Chant in her study of shanty towns in Mexico showed that dirt-floored huts need constant sweeping because of dust in the dry season but in the wet season they often become seas of mud which are a very time-consuming problem for housewives (Chant 1984a). Chant has shown how both the design of the house and the structure of the family can affect the workload of women. She was able to demonstrate that the women in shanty towns around Querétaro in Mexico found that housework in tiny, flimsy, dirt-floored shacks was harder and took more time than in the concrete-floored and brick-walled houses occupied by half her sample. The feeling of interminable work involved in keeping clean a shack with a floor of beaten earth was aggravated by the fact that the results were barely perceptible. The shortage of space in these shacks also meant that a woman's day was spent constantly rearranging furniture, bedding and domestic items. Lack of piped water, sewage, garbage disposal and paved roads, especially in crowded city slums, makes hygiene, health care and the training of small children extremely difficult and very time-consuming. Chant showed that housework took an extra two hours in the most poorly serviced shanty towns, so it is perhaps not surprising that women have led community demands for infrastructure improvements in many parts of Latin America.

In Malaysia and the Philippines, surveys have found that where there is an infant in the house its presence increases domestic work by between three and five hours per day while toddlers require about half this amount of extra time (Mueller 1982). Most of this time is found at the expense of the women's leisure time but in these surveys the mother's participation in the labour market is also reduced by the presence of small children.

In nuclear families these domestic burdens fall very heavily on the mother who receives very little help from the other members of the family in most cases. Chant (1984a) showed that in nuclear families women had a working day 45 per cent longer than that of the husband, while in extended families women work only 31 per cent more hours than men.

These various constraints on women's use of time may be examined by means of the concepts of time geography, developed by Torsten Hagerstrand (1970). Time geography, with its emphasis on the individual, allows us to examine the links between individual life paths, macro-level social phenomena and social change (Pred 1984). A study of individual paths over time and space in a time-geographic framework may also be used to identify gender differences in innovation adoption, and activity space. One of the editors has used this approach in her own work in the Caribbean and found that the use of individual life paths and their linkages with those of other individuals over time and space was of considerable help in explaining land use and other differences between farms operated by men and women (Monk and Momsen 1984). Christopherson (1983) has also used time-geographic concepts in her study of the relationship between young women's employment and family structure in Ciudad Juárez, Mexico. For women, time geography can illustrate how innovation may merely serve to increase the workload when it does not take into account the distribution of tasks within the household or the time–space environment of the family.

Time-budget surveys

Time surveys do not present a simple solution, since all the problems of survey research arise, with others specific to the study of time (Anker *et al.* (eds.) 1982). 'Work' can be carried out with different degrees of intensity; housework is known for expanding to overfill the time available; conversely, in domestic work, several tasks may be on hand at the same time. To be accurate, this must be a very expensive and time-consuming method. The examples in this collection take very different approaches: Spiro (Chapter 6) seeks accuracy in hours spent on tasks; Townsend and de Acosta ask only whether an individual participates in a task 'always', 'sometimes' or never (Chapter 10).

Time use surveys have brought many assumptions into question. For the first time, we can perceive leisure as an activity: an activity which a woman may forgo in favour of childcare or income-earning activity, so that children and 'economic activity' are not in direct competition (Mueller 1982). Conversely, we are learning more about poverty and 'underemployment': so often the poor are not 'idle', and the slack agricultural season is not one of leisure. Rather, in both cases, people are working very long hours for low returns. 'Work' can be called into question and redefined: King and Evenson (1983) in Laguna, the Philippines, found the home time of the wife to be the largest single component of total household production. At present, time use surveys seem the most powerful tool for improving our information on the geography of gender in the Third World: it is in time that it is possible to bring together well-being, production, reproduction and gender.

Explaining the geography of gender?

We have reviewed the problems of describing the geography of gender, with special attention to a range of concepts and indicators. These have in general been discussed in isolation. The problems of integration, explanation and understanding have yet to be faced. We shall sketch out here some current views on the nature of gender and some explanations of the geography of gender itself. We shall then outline the success (or otherwise) of some explanations in accounting for gender under specific forms of production: the pre-industrial, the colonial and the Third World today. We shall conclude with a proposed integrating framework: spatial divisions of labour.

How 'natural' is gender?

Is gender derived wholly, directly or indirectly, from the interactions of material culture with the biological differences between the sexes? Or is it a purely social construction, independent of biology? Feminism has been much concerned to discredit the former position, and may even be said to have medical support. 'Intersexuality' is a case in point. Physically, the biological demarcation of males from females is not sharp: in a tiny minority of cases, the apparent sex of an individual (and therefore their sex of upbringing) fails to match their biological sex, for organic reasons. Physicians are advised normally to treat such individuals as belonging to their sex of upbringing, not their chromosomal sex. In cytogenetics textbooks, gender, social sex and psychological sex are all described as matters of upbringing (Stanley 1984).

Sociobiologists are now emphasizing both the biological and the social. Early biological explanations of gender (e.g. Jay 1963) now stand discredited, and more recent ones (Tiger 1977) face widespread criticism. Hrdy's view (1981) is one of the more provocative and compelling. A 'committed Darwinian', she argues that sexual asymmetries are nearly universal among primates (compare Rosaldo and Lamphere (eds.) 1974, for humans). Among non-human primates, for instance, it is typically the male which can approach, threaten and displace the female; among humans, it is typically the male who can coerce the behaviour of females (for some, this is a definition of patriarchy). The features unique to humanity among primates are our elaborate division of labour by sex, our reliance on sharing, the existence of authority among us and our remarkable ingenuity. As a result, 'our species possesses the capacity to carry sexual inequality to its greatest known extremes, but we also possess the potential to realize an unusual social equality between the sexes should we choose to exercise that potential' (Hrdy 1981). Our biological capacity is for a great range of social constructions of gender.

In answer to myths about biologically determined, passive, submissive and compliant females (Jay 1963; Tiger 1970), Hrdy demonstrates that other female primates are highly competitive, socially involved and sexually assertive; they have a universal commitment to reproduction, but they have an equally powerful and universal commitment to compete, and in particular to quest for high status which gives access to resources. (There is still variety: among baboons, female status is derived from males, but among some macaques, male power is transient beside the matrilineal clans.) If a human mother is passive, withdrawn, and apolitical, this is not a biological function of primate motherhood, but requires considerable *social explanation*.

Explanations of the geography of gender

Current explanations of regional patterns in the constitution of gender range from a focus on reproduction to a focus on production. All seek to explain both the subordination of women and the varying construction of gender in time and place. There is a continuum of explanation between the biological determinists and the feminists; a continuum also exists from those who see gender roles as created by and functional to the economic base (Deere *et al.* 1982) to those who see them as interacting with economic affairs, but as derived independently – as some sort of historical accident. Each explanation would have different outcomes in different circumstances, producing a regional geography. We shall not discuss non-materialist explanations, because their relation to other phenomena is still obscure, whether they call on the symbolization of femaleness (Ortner 1974) or on the psychoanalytic (Chodorow 1974). It will be seen that many explanations overlap, and none are mutually exclusive.

Force

For John Stuart Mill (1806–73), the subordination of women rested solely on the law of the strongest. This subordination had originally been achieved by force and remained a kind of slavery, distorting female personality so that no one could know what the capacities of women might be in a free and equal society. The maintenance and variety of the subordination were social, although the origin was physical; technical change could free women (Rossi (ed.) 1970).

Force and sex

Collins (1971, 1975) presents a sophisticated sociological explanation incorporating male strength, used to control women by violence in the interest of male sexual gratification. In his scenario, changing political and economic conditions (over time and space) greatly alter female bargaining power, since there are changes not only in female access to resources, but also in the role of force in society. Examples are 'low technology tribal societies', 'fortified households in stratified society' (identified by Collins as the worst general situation for women, as in medieval Europe), 'private households in a market economy' where the state takes over the control of legitimate violence, and 'affluent market economies' where women improve their economic bargaining power. Collins is heavily criticized by anthropologists on empirical grounds, and his emphasis on violence and sexual gratification is not widely accepted, but his other insights are well regarded.

Female biology

For Firestone (1970), before the advent of modern contraception women were helpless, baby-making machines, dependent on males for their physical survival. With contraception, women can escape their weakness and gender can be reconstituted; the geography of gender becomes a geography of contraceptive technology. This hardly coheres with the reality of women's work or with current views on fertility, but it remains true that strenuous physical labour in late pregnancy and early lactation is damaging to maternal health.

Children as labour power

For many anthropologists, whole societies are shaped by the institutions which expropriate the fecundity of women and allocate their progeny. Meillassoux (1981) describes the 'hidden, subordinate role of women' as 'always linked to the exploitation of women's reproductive functions'. A woman's value is in her reproductive capacity; control over this is control over the rights in children. From these institutions other aspects of gender and indeed of society are shaped. On this model, women's procreative capacity is more important and more stringently controlled in agrarian societies of low technology and, therefore, heavy demand for labour. The spatial transfer of females to the family of the male is the rule for most human societies, and is an important cause of female powerlessness (Chapter 3). This is another human idiosyncrasy: among most primates, females define a territory and occupy it from generation to generation (Hrdy 1971).

Children as genetic survival

For Engels (1884), 'the family is based on the supremacy of the man, the express purpose being to produce children of undisputed paternity'. For sociobiologists, the prime aim of all parties is genetic survival (survival through descendants). Strategies for genetic survival will characterize a society. To give one example, Dickemann (as cited by Hrdy 1981) links the concern with paternity to sociobiology. She examines stratified societies in which women seek to marry 'up' into families of higher standing. On the assumption that the chances of reproductive success are better for the better off, since the progeny will be guaranteed better access to resources, a woman's family has a direct, biological stake in her marrying up. Since access to a wealthy family is competitive, they have a stake in her reputation and eligibility, which will normally require her chastity. Since competition can, in this case, not only require chastity but exaggerate behaviour over it, biological interest may intensify seclusion, purdah and other restrictions on women. Different genetic survival strategies may create whole cultures.

Marriage transfers

Cultures may also be derived from institutions, such as the forms of transfer of wealth on marriage. Goody (1976) has argued that the social effects of these systems are extremely pervasive, and that there are strong regional patterns; we shall consider them in more detail below.

Sexual divisions of labour

Relations of production are much more commonly invoked, often in conjunction with the explanations just listed.

The sexual division of labour emerges as an expression of women's roles in both production and reproduction; these roles in turn derive from those social relations which regulate the formation of families and the bearing and rearing of children, and those social relations which govern the production of goods and services (Deere et al. 1982).

Sexual divisions of labour do not themselves determine other aspects of the geography of gender, nor are they directly determined by them: there is a complex interplay with the forces and relations of production at a given place. For instance, the existence of a sexual division of labour does not logically require the subordination of either sex: the relation could be complementary, not one of dominance. Feminist literature is much concerned with this problem: crudely, if there is 'women's work' which is essential to society, as it often is, why is a low value set on it?

Many writers place sexual divisions of labour at the centre of the social construction of gender. Once again, early writers placed much more emphasis than is now used on male strength in explaining divisions of labour. A more usual focus now is to examine the compatibility of tasks with simultaneous responsibilities for childcare, particularly breastfeeding. Lactating women will tend to avoid tasks that are distant and/or dangerous, leaving to men the early stages of production (extraction of raw

materials, clearing the land) while women work in secondary processing and harvesting. The more mobile males are assumed to
derive dominance from this situation. Yet even in pre-industrial
societies, non-biological factors can modify or override women's
'nursing compatibility constraint' since women who are important
subsistence producers often introduce supplementary foods for
their babies at an earlier age. In many societies, lactating women do
work in 'incompatible' activities; in industrial societies, for
instance, most women's paid work is in activities incompatible
with breastfeeding. Neither male strength nor the requirements of
lactation can adequately explain sexual divisions of labour as they
actually exist.

The Engels scenario

One explanation has itself caused geographical outcomes. Engels,
in *The Origin of the Family, Private Property and the State* (1884),
was perhaps the first to describe women's position as varying
according to the prevailing economic and cultural relationships
(Sacks 1975). His work has strongly influenced thinking, not only
among Marxist and feminist academics but among legislators in
socialist countries. Engels presents a historical development from
communal, egalitarian societies through the rise of private property and the family to exploitative class societies. Women in this
scenario were initially dominant, but became subordinate with the
appearance of means of production which could be privately
owned, specifically domesticated animals. When men held private
property in productive assets and an exchangeable surplus,
women came to work for their husbands and families instead of for
society: the division of labour between the sexes became exploitative. With the rise of capitalism, production and reproduction are
spatially separated. Home and workplace are no longer the same;
home becomes the locale of reproduction. Subsequent research has
not supported Engels's initial matriarchy, and there have been
serious challenges over the significance of private property (Whyte
1978), but the general argument that *women are subordinated by
their alienation from direct production* has become fundamental
to legislation (if not practice!) in socialist states. Molyneux (1981)
demonstrates the socialist commitment to make entry into the
labour force a normal expectation for every active woman as a
necessary precondition not only for the emancipation of women
but for the creation of socialism. A belief that 'productive' labour or

waged work is liberating is widespread among feminists and not uncommon among Third World governments. In practice, the woman who does a 'double day', of income-generating and reproductive activities, is all too familiar in the Third World as in the First and Second Worlds.

Explaining gender: is there a 'status of women'?

Most of our explanations have strong connotations of value. There is a whole literature on the 'status of women' which seems to offer us both a cross-cultural measure and a sense of determinate relationships. Sometimes a single variable is presented as describing or predicting this 'status', as when it is assumed that high fertility connotes low 'status'; more often a package of variables is presented as measuring 'status' (Mazey and Lee 1983). There are sharp differences of opinion on whether or not the 'status of women' is a useful or valid concept. It clearly has considerable political value in the struggle for women's rights, locally, nationally and internationally; the term is then used very loosely, with different meanings and interpretations in different times and places; it is a deliberately value-loaded expression, effective and emotive, not intended to refer to a measurable quantity.

We can measure and map sex ratios, fertility, women in the enfranchised population or women at work in factories, knowing that these phenomena may have very different meanings for women in different places. A predominance of males in the population may relate to a low valuation of women (Chapters 2, 3), or it may be a function of a military presence (as in the Falklands/ Malvinas), or of 'male' occupations (Alaska today; California in the gold rush): the results for the women may be very different. Similarly, the significance of a constitutional right to vote varies widely between countries. We would argue that no single or compound indicator of the 'status' of women can produce a useful geographical comparison. The abstraction is mystifying rather than useful (Rogers 1980), and there is no consistent causation.

From a study of ninety-three pre-industrial societies, Whyte (1978) concludes that 'there is no coherent concept of the status of women that can be identified cross-culturally . . . *aspects or indicators of the status of women are essentially unrelated things'* (our emphasis). Modern feminism may construct a package of 'women's rights' and campaign for them, but they have had no particular tendency to occur together in recorded cultures. In comparisons of modern nation-states, the result is the same. Stewart and Winter

(1977) took UN data (mainly for the 1960s) for 'variables presumed to measure the status of women': these included political, educational and economic indicators, as well as illegitimacy, age of marriage and measures of well-being. Their factor analysis produced one factor involving the 'social and educational equality' of the sexes, another for 'economic equality'. Most variables have relatively pure loadings on one of these factors. Labour force participation, franchise and education have not loaded with each other, nor with measures of female well-being, such as male–female differentials in suicide, homicide, infant mortality, life expectancy and divorce rates. As for pre-industrial cultures, the indicators appear essentially unrelated.

Women's worlds: pre-industrial

Few serious attempts have been made to identify or explain regional construction of gender in the Third World. The most influential has been that of the economist, Boserup (1970), who made two outstanding points. First is her scenario of technical change in agriculture, under which *change profits men rather than women*: 'in the course of agricultural development, men's labour productivity tends to increase, while women's remains more or less static' – she ascribes this largely to European colonial intervention. She is perhaps the leading exponent of the argument that 'modernization' is at the expense of rural women. Second is her identification of *male and female farming systems*. These are defined by the gender roles, as to which gender contributes most agricultural labour. Boserup contends that in extensive, shifting, non-plough agriculture, as in most traditional societies of Africa and tribal societies of South and South-East Asia, most field work is done by women: farming systems are female. Where plough cultivation is the rule, low female participation in farm work is usual, as in Latin America and the Arab countries, and farming systems are male. In regions of intensive, irrigated cultivation, both men and women must put hard work into agriculture, as in much of South and South-East Asia (Map 5).

How direct is the relationship between forms of production and patterns of gender roles? In the foraging and horticultural societies of which we have record, a range of divisions of labour and constructions of gender are found. Although these constitute only a fraction of humanity today, such forms of production account for 'all but the last fraction of 1 percent of our three-to-four-million-year human history'; and women were the primary producers in most such societies (Blumberg 1984; see also Sauer 1961, 1967). Patterns are heterogeneous: the highly egalitarian Tasaday of the Philippines have almost no division of labour; the Chipewyan women of Canada produce almost no food, but they process it, and control food and food sharing in this hunting society (Sharp 1981). Contrary to popular belief, peoples whose subsistence is based on hunting large animals tend to be more egalitarian than others (Whyte 1978).

Gender roles are equally heterogeneous among horticultural-ists and among herders, although horticulturalists include most if not all of Boserup's female farming systems. There are no simple relationships between the division of labour and other facets of culture. The Iroquois and the Hopi have highly separated male and female domains in work and other aspects of life, but are regarded as egalitarian; among the Azande, women are the main source of labour, but are treated like slaves. There is no necessary relation between women's contribution to subsistence and their rights over property, decision-making or their own sex lives (Whyte 1978), although such a contribution may be necessary but not sufficient condition for household and social power.

Moving from foraging and horticultural societies to agrarian, plough-based societies (without irrigation), we find major changes. Women tend to play only a minor productive role, to have less domestic authority, less control over their own sex lives and less rights in property than in non-plough societies (Whyte 1978). This is the recent past of most of the rich world: hence the rich world's view of women having 'historically' been subjugated non-producers (Blumberg 1984). (It is in irrigated paddy rice that female labour tends again to be significant.) All these points are relationships with exceptions. Without exception, however, 'once societies develop complex economies and stratification systems extending beyond the community level, these are dominated by men' (Blumberg 1984, editors' emphasis). As the forces and rela-tions of production develop, the human experience has been that both plough agriculture and complex societies have been adverse for women. In complex pre-industrial societies Whyte (1978) found women, on balance, to suffer disadvantages relative to men that women in simpler societies do not; the relationship is clear, the causes less certain.

Goody (1969, 1976, 1983) links the increased subordination of women indirectly to pressure on land and directly to marriage transfers. The transfer of women on marriage may be accompanied by many forms of transfer of wealth. 'Dowry' is given by the bride's parents to the new couple. 'Bridewealth' is given by the groom's parents to the bride's; it is a payment within the same generation, between males, for the transfer of the woman. There are strong regional patterns. In Africa, bridewealth predominates, while Europe and North Africa have, since the Roman Empire, seen a change to dowry; as has much of India in this century. Remnants of the dowry system characterize western society. In complex, highly differentiated societies, land is the scarce resource. Parents pass land on to their sons, and dower their daughters in search of a 'good match' to a man with land: the dowry system, therefore, tends to occur in agrarian societies with plough agriculture, intensive farming, high population density and land shortage. Daughters cannot be left to mate where they will; their behaviour is strictly controlled, and their virginity at marriage essential. Tight control over females follows. In bridewealth societies, the difference between a 'good match' and a 'bad match' is trivial by comparison because there is no land shortage.

Goody (1976) linked his work to that of Boserup (1970) by a quantitative analysis of pre-industrial societies: female farming was strongly associated with hoe agriculture and simple polity, while male farming was associated with more advanced agriculture (plough plus irrigated), with more complex polities and with inheritance systems of diverging devolution (under which property is transmitted to women, either as dowry or inheritance). Goody follows Boserup (1970) in ascribing male dominance in advanced agriculture to the plough as an instrument employed almost entirely by men, and to the almost exclusive concentration of large livestock, whether horses, cattle or camels, in male hands (compare Hecht, forthcoming; Chapter 10). Dyson and Moore (1983) have sought to apply such arguments in some detail to India, but Harriss and Watson in Chapter 2 question the empirical basis for this. This epitomizes the state of our knowledge on pre-industrial gender: promising explanations and inadequate information.

Women's worlds: gender and the rise of the west

Over the last 500 years, the expansion of the world market to impinge on the life of virtually every human being has been accompanied by unprecedented changes in the way work is structured around the world.

The experience of women under the European empires was diverse indeed, but commonly they lost relative to men, and often this was through the imposition of a new, 'western' gender ideology. Colonial rule, direct or indirect, was carried out through male hierarchies; the new sources of cash, in cash crops or in wage labour or plantations, in mines or in the towns 'were overwhelmingly imposed on or offered to men' (Rogers 1980). Later, the 'western' gender ideology became more coherent and more consistent in all continents: promotion of the 'ideal' domestic life was coupled with pseudo-theories that the children of mothers engaged in direct production will be deprived. Education in the periphery was offered primarily to males; girls were taught domestic science, if anything. On the land, women lost access to the means of production (Chapter 5) when new legal codes and land tenure systems vested ownership in the (male) head of household; in industry, they were commonly excluded by 'protective' legislation and (male) trade union action; in the new urban areas, they lacked the education for the more attractive work.

'Since the rise of the world system, most women have lived within the confines of a feudal or precapitalist mode of production in the home vis-à-vis the larger capitalist society' (Ward 1984). For many feminists, capitalism cannot exist without *patriarchal relations*: that is, the institutionalized patterns and ideologies of male dominance and control over resources that have empowered men to define the productive and reproductive roles and behaviour of women. Whether or not they are essential, patriarchal relations have become highly characteristic of the whole modern, urban, industrial world – and of the Third World.

Women's worlds: the Third World Today

The two great disjunctures between women's worlds in 'traditional' societies and in the Third World today are in the present dominance of capitalism and the decline in infant mortality. The former has reworked both gender roles and spatial divisions of labour; the latter has been followed by a new scale of use of 'artificial' methods of birth control (contraception, abortion and sterilization). None of these methods is new, and most societies also had social control of population, but until the last few decades, mortality, particularly of infants, was a major control on population growth. Fertility has now become by far and away the most studied aspect of women's lives in the Third World.

As this chapter has shown, we lack the information for a rounded, comprehensive view of women's worlds in the Third World today. Three integrated statistical comparisons will, however, provide a cross-national context for the regional, national and local studies of our chapters. Dixon (1983) has related the female share in the agricultural workforce to structural characteristics across the Third World. Ward (1984) has attempted to relate women's worlds to dependency. Sivard (1985) has provided us with a data set for a cross-national summary of women's worlds. Ward's (1984) analysis and our own from Sivard's (1985) data will bring us again to fertility.

Are indicators of women's worlds more related to each other under capitalism than in pre-industrial societies? Specific areas show strong relationships, as we shall see, but the common experience is that of Stewart and Winter (1977). On their factor analysis, Third World regions tended to score high on one set of indicators of 'equality' between the genders and low on the other (Table 4). This was also the case for most Third World countries; on these measures, these forms of equality are negatively related. Certain Islamic countries scored low on both factors: Algeria, Egypt, Iran, Iraq, Libya, Morocco, Pakistan and Tunisia; stereotypes drawn from these are applied widely and inaccurately to Third World women at large.

Table 4 Third World Regions by Stewart and Winter's factors

Region	Social-educational equality	Economic equality
Latin America	high	low
Sub-Saharan Africa	low	high
South Asia	low	high
South-East Asia	low	high
Middle East and North Africa	low	low

Source: Stewart and Winter (1977); 1960s data.

Geography, agriculture and gender

Dixon (1983) is looking for statistical relationships with a single gender variable: the sex composition of the agricultural labour force in the Third World (Map 5) is examined against structural characteristics of the rural economy. Geographical region seems to be a major explanatory variable in women's share in agriculture in the Third World, but structural characteristics prove more important. The percentage of farms which were 'small holdings' of 1 to 5 ha correlates quite strongly (0.67) with the female share of farm labour; land distribution explains 44 per cent of the total variation in the female share and no less than 80 per cent of the variation attributable to regional differences. The highest proportions of smallholdings are found in sub-Saharan Africa, Asia and the Caribbean, the lowest in Latin America. This mirrors differences in Stewart and Winter's 'economic equality' factor in Table 4 and, more importantly, fits Boserup's scenario of plough and wage labour displacing women. In short, the female share of the agricultural labour force in the Third World 'appears highest where the rural economy is characterized by smallholder agriculture oriented towards production for subsistence or for local markets, and by low levels of urbanization combined with male-dominated outmigration to towns and cities' (Dixon 1983). Male dominance in the agricultural labour force is related to highly skewed land distribution, to export agriculture, to wage labour and to female urban migration. Dixon emphasizes that these characteristics may act independently or in concert: this is a description, not a functional model. She appears to have established that in the Third World today women *perform a much larger share of agricultural field tasks where there are large numbers of small farms*. Gender roles are directly linked to economic phenomena in rural areas.

Gender, dependency and the world system?

There has been no comparable success in linking gender roles to other specific structural phenomena across the Third World. Ward (1984) attempts to analyse gender at the national level from a world systems viewpoint, but, in measuring gender roles, her labour force variables show very weak correlations not only with her political and social variables but with her other economic variables. Causal relationships are difficult to establish. Poor countries do tend to have relatively high proportions of foreign investment, low per capita energy consumption, high concentrations of exports on a single commodity, highly unequal income distributions and a heavy dependence on raw material exports; overall, poorer countries also have a smaller reported female share in the labour force. Does this demonstrate causation? Ward argues that 'classical dependency and dependent development have negative effects on women's share of economic resources'. We also consider dependency and dependent development to characterize the Third World and to be implicated in constructions of gender, but we expect a general cause to have different local effects, contingent upon its nature and local conditions.

Correlations between indicators at the national level

We examined correlations between our indicators using Sivard's (1985) data for 140 countries in the early 1980s. We encountered the expected set of correlations, with some instructive insights when countries were grouped by income or region. Over the 140 countries, female life expectancy correlates at almost 0.9 with the percentage of women able to read and write. (A high relationship between life expectancy and literacy is a very common finding. Stewart (1985) suggests a causal relationship, running from education/literacy to life expectancy, but it is possible that both are merely surrogate measures for social expenditure on the poor.) We found the correlation less strong in sub-Saharan Africa, and found other literacy variables showing weaker relationships there, supporting our hypothesis of regional variations. Predictably, the literacy–life expectancy relationship is much stronger among the world's poorer countries than among the richer; similarly, the proportion of girls in schools is strongly related to life expectancy in poor countries (0.7) but not in the richer (0.3).

Female life expectancy is not highly correlated with national per capita income, but if the log of the per capita income is taken, so that differences among poor countries are emphasized and differences among rich ones reduced, the correlation with female life expectancy is 0.8; another expected finding. Sex ratios are remarkably uncorrelated with other phenomena. The percentage of women aged 15 to 64 whom the ILO consider to be in the labour force and the percentage of that labour force which the ILO record as female are notably uncorrelated with anything except each other – but this may be because the cross-national comparability of the data is poor. The exception is Latin America, where women's participation and women's share of the labour force correlate highly with women's literacy, the percentage of girls who are in school, GNP (as a log) and national energy use per capita (as a log); Latin American countries are, of course, much more literate and very much more urban, with a much bigger urban service sector.

Apart from the correlation of female life expectancy with female literacy and with per capita GNP (as a log), the really striking feature of recent national data is the strength of the negative correlations between the total fertility rate and female life expectancy, literacy and income (log). The negative correlations between TFR and female life expectancy and literacy are both over 0.8. Factor analysis of the Third World countries yields a similar outcome: the literacy and education variables, with per capita GNP

(log) and per capita energy use (log) load strongly with life expectancy and against fertility and quite separately from the labour
force variables and sex ratio. Ward's (1984) more impressive
findings are also in connection with fertility.

Fertility – key indicator?

At present, high fertility almost defines the Third World (Map 4)
but the direction of causality has proved difficult to determine.
Ward (1983) argues that economic dependency at the national level
increases fertility. Over 126 countries, she found strong correlations with the total fertility rate for 1975:

per capita energy use (1965)	−0.8
social insurance programme experience (1970)	−0.8
diversified foreign trade structure	−0.6
women's share of tertiary education (1970)	−0.6
dependence on a single export (1965)	0.5
income inequality (1967), using the Gini coefficient	0.6
infant mortality (1968)	0.8

On data for the early 1980s for 140 countries (Sivard 1985), we
found the following high negative correlations with the total
fertility rate:

female life expectancy	−0.9
female literacy	−0.8
the log of GNP per capita	−0.6

When the countries are examined in groups, the relationships
between fertility and literacy, between fertility and the proportion
of girls in school and between fertility and life expectancy are all
much greater in the poor world than the rich. Literacy, education
and life expectancy all tend to be low in poor countries, and to be
inversely related, at a national level, to fertility. There are also
strong regional effects: in Africa, the inverse correlation between
fertility and literacy is weak; in Asia, the inverse correlation between fertility and the proportion of girls who are in school is much
stronger than elsewhere.

   Those Third World countries where female well-being
appears relatively good on such indicators as life expectancy, education and literacy tend to be those where fertility is less high. For
many years, this encouraged scholars to regard *high fertility as a*

cause of poor female well-being (Andrews 1982). The World Population Conference at Bucharest, however, accepted that 'Development is the best contraceptive' or, broadly, that 'Poor people are not poor because they have large families; they have large families because they are poor' (Mamdani 1972). On this explanation, *poverty causes both high fertility and poor well-being.* At the macro-level, either explanation fits the correlations just listed, since all the indicators which have such strong negative relationships with fertility are in some sense measures of wealth or social provision.

Fertility is now seen as a complex and multicausal phenomenon, and high fertility is no longer always assumed to be unintentional and unwanted. The World Fertility Survey (1984) found that the average number of children that young African women say that they want is 6.5: twice as many as Latin American and Asian women say, but in keeping with actual fertility patterns. The survey also found that about half the world's women now have access to modern birth control.

We may not dismiss high fertility as a negative cause or outcome of poverty. Children may be essential – in quantity or quality – to the self-esteem of either or both parents. In many cultures, and perhaps for the majority of the human race, children are the leading life-satisfaction. In specific circumstances, poverty may be an important incentive to high fertility; hence the popularity of the New Household Economics, discussed above. Cain (1980) has shown that male children in rural Bangladesh may have become net producers by age 12, compensate for their own cumulative consumption by age 15 and for that of one sister by age 22. In selected villages in Nepal and Java, Nag *et al.* (1980) concluded that parents' interests were best served by maximizing the numbers of surviving children, and they found that child-spacing was a traditional part of this. Such findings have been widespread in the Third World. Such strategies, of course, may be rational for the parents but not for society at large or even for the long-term welfare of the children, but it is important to recognize children's work input to household productivity as a factor influencing the fertility behaviour of parents in peasant societies. Parents also need children as protection, as insurance for old age and times of sickness and crisis.

Both economic and sociological models of fertility (Anker 1982) raise the question of conflict between women's roles in direct production and in reproduction. In practice, the compatibility of work and childcare depends on the activity involved (Chapter 6), the family structure (Chant 1984c), the cost of domestics and the presence in the family of surrogate mothers, such as other siblings and other adults (Chapter 11); it is the exception rather than the rule for Third World women to do most of the childcare unaided. There is therefore no simple relationship between fertility and female involvement in direct production. If no substitute mother is available, women may forgo leisure to earn income; they may neglect their children (Chapter 4); they may seek out tasks compatible with childcare (Chapter 13). In the Third World, it seems that the negative relationship between employment and fertility is found almost entirely in urban, industrialized settings, and even there it is mainly in the formal sector. Fertility does tend to be lower among those urban women who leave their home for full-time work (Youssef 1982).

Fertility is a social as well as a biological phenomenon. Like marriage or widowhood, its meaning and significance vary greatly from one social group to another, being strongly defined by mode of production, social class, perhaps ethnicity. As an aspect of gender, it can only be appreciated in the context of national, regional and even local incorporation into the world economy.

Spatial divisions of labour

Gender roles in production and reproduction must answer to changing spatial divisions of labour, local, regional, national and international. Localities, regions and nations may specialize in their productive or reproductive activities: the scale of this specialization is always limited by available organization and technology, and is expressed in a spatial structure. Gender roles may on occasion derive from new spatial divisions of labour: in a labour reserve area of high male out-migration women may take on new productive and organizational tasks; the development of an export processing zone may depend on incorporating them into new forms of production. By definition, gender roles are a part of the spatial structure of the labour force, whether as cause or effect.

We have already seen something of the way spatial divisions of labour have changed as the rise of the West altered gender roles around the world. Massey (1984) has described the structure of a local economy and society as the product of a combination of layers, each layer representing the successive imposition over the years of new forms of activity. The metaphor of a 'combination of layers' is not a happy one, since 'layers' in common parlance do not combine and rarely interact, yet here the interaction is of the essence. The structure of a local economy and society offers certain possibilities: if one develops, the old structure will strongly influence the shape of the new.

Countries, regions or localities in the Third World may serve as suppliers of raw materials or of labour power, they may be markets for the advanced industrial countries, they may be receivers of capital exports. At a specific time, any one may be playing one or more of these roles; over time, their incorporation into the wider economy will change. We expect the geography of gender roles to respond very strongly to the history of the insertion of each country into the changing international divisions of labour.

The New International Division of Labour

This has included a sharp reconstitution of gender for certain ages and social classes in specific countries (Fröbel, Heinrichs and Kreye 1980; Chapters 13, 14 and 20). In the new 'world market factories . . . production processes are standardized, repetitious, call for very little modern knowledge, and are highly labour intensive' (Elson and Pearson 1981). Wages may be a tenth of those in comparable factories in the advanced industrial countries, working hours may be 50 per cent longer, and workers' rights are strictly limited. The majority of the labour force are young women. Elson and Pearson (1981) argue convincingly that girls are already trained by their experience of domestic labour in the 'manual dexterity' which so many of these jobs require, and that their subordination as a gender renders them docile, subservient and cheap. These continuities are encountered through a wide range of relations of production, from home-based piecework through subcontracting to factories with attached hostels.

Other features are more specific to particular activities, as with health in electronics. Here, the short product-cycle imposes a highly competitive structure which has encouraged the 'global assembly line': hourly wages of US$6.96 in the United States and $5.97 in Japan compare with $0.45 in Indonesia or $0.42 in Malaysia (Lin 1985). In Asia, in particular, labour-intensive, export-oriented industries have brought large numbers of women into the formal sector labour force for the first time ever in these societies: Lin sees this as a very positive historic precedent, but Elson and Pearson (1981) are less optimistic about the potential for positive change.

In electronics, there are widespread reports of stress, fatigue, eyesight deterioration and overall health problems. In almost 1000 interviews with female workers in Malaysia and Singapore, Lin

(1985) found that more production than clerical workers suffer complaints of the eye, ear, nose and throat and musculoskeletal system and sleep disorders. In the case of eye trouble, the incidence is double among those using microscopes and VDUs. Those using chemicals regularly are more prone to menstrual complaints, pregnancy problems and infertility. Other health problems are related not to the technical conditions of production but to the shiftwork, which appears to produce sleeping problems, gastro-intestinal problems, central nervous system complaints and psychological complaints.

This sudden incorporation of young, female labour previously excluded from 'economic' activity has been particularly pro-nounced in electronics and other labour-intensive manufacturing over the past two decades; it is a major feature of the New International Division of Labour. But the phenomenon is not exclusive to manufacturing: it is encountered, for example, in the Colombian flower export industry (Cuales 1982). Gender roles in Colombia have shifted with forms of production. It seems that in pre-Columbian times and in the colonial period, women participated in production. Usually tasks were gender specific, although this applied less under slavery. When capitalist relations of production started to emerge, the participation of women in production ceased to be a matter of course; they were incorporated in some sectors and not others. They have been described as the major labour power in coffee production towards the end of the nineteenth century; at that time they were also important in textiles, but they were later pro-gressively displaced. Since 1967, Colombia has been committed to (and highly successful in) export promotion, and one dramatic new export is cut flowers. Exports began in 1965 with 17 tonnes; by 1978, they totalled 26,759 tonnes and constituted the country's fourth export. The flowers are mainly grown under plastic near the capital and airfreighted to their destination. Most of the production workers are women, of peasant origin but now living around the capital, without previous employment experience in the formal sector, single, and semi-literate. Employment turnover is high, health is injured by the heavy use of chemicals. The division of labour is sharp: management, supervision and maintenance are overwhelmingly male, while tasks 'directly related to the flower' are female, since 'women are delicate by nature'. This gender ideology compares directly with the preference of manufacturers for women in tasks requiring 'dexterity'; the flower workers are again seen as docile, as second earners in their household who need not be paid a family wage.

These two case studies, of electronics workers in Malaysia and Singapore and of flower workers in Colombia, illustrate the sudden shifts in constructions of gender which can be a part of changes in the spatial division of labour. In Holland, male (migrant) workers handle flowers; in Colombia, this is a female task. Commonly, the shifts are less apparent and the economic content less obvious, but the shifts are and have been a continuing feature of human existence, and the economic content of gender change has been common and, under capitalist relations of production, ubiquitous. It is remarkable that electronics factories could perform essentially the same manoeuvre in so many different social formations around the world.

Towards a regional geography of gender?

We would argue that a better understanding of the variety of constructions of gender in time and space will be necessary to an understanding of the construction of gender itself. In particular, we need a regional geography of gender. At one level, we need to know how certain aspects of people's lives vary around the world (often we have reasonable information for males but poor information for females); this chapter has been concerned to report some of the little we know, and to call attention to the immense amount we do not know. At another, we need to know how different countries are incorporated into the world economy, and what are the links between the form of their incorporation and their socio-economic structure, including the construction of gender. This is a grossly underresearched aspect of social formations. We need to know the regional variations within countries, both in causes and outcomes (Chapter 2). We need locality studies (Chapters 8, 10). Descriptions at the level of the household and the individual (Chapter 4) must cohere with macro-studies (Chapter 2).

We regard the spatial division of labour as a major organizing principle in the geography of gender, and have therefore arranged our contributions in such a framework. We must make a beginning in moving towards a regional geography of gender.

Part Two

Survival

Map 9 Indian states, 1981

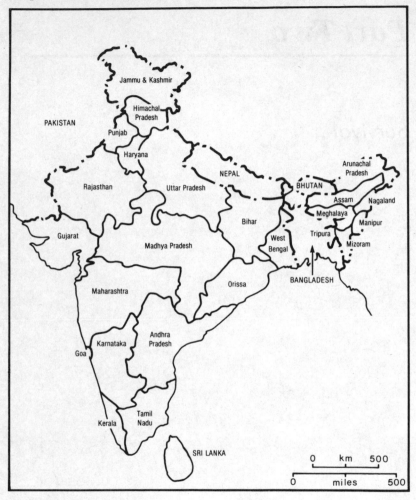

2   The sex ratio in South Asia

Barbara Harriss and Elizabeth Watson

Editors' introduction

The geography of gender does not merely present alluring and intractable intellectual problems; more importantly, it is a dimension of the human condition. Gender is not only a social artefact but a part of that very social fabric which produces gross deprivation for both sexes. It is linked directly to hunger, disease and suffering. Gender-linked explanations are proposed for many patterns, but while many of the explanations are elegant, few have yet resisted rigorous testing. It is the contention of all contributors to this book that such testing is the prerequisite of a better understanding.

In this chapter, we illustrate this problem with Harriss and Watson's review of attempts to account for the sex ratio in South Asia. Why is there an exceptional predominance of males (see Map 3)? Why the marked patterns within the region? Why the change in patterns over time? What processes are operating? By focusing on the sex ratio, Harriss and Watson demonstrate both how gender permeates society and economy and how specific the outcomes may be, by locality, caste or class. Differential sex ratios are linked to variations in well-being and are shown to be vitally related to biological and social reproduction; some say also to economic production. The leading explanations in general use are in terms of marriage transfers and of spatial divisions of labour, but the main finding here is that explanations based on macro-level analysis may simply not withstand thorough empirical checks. This chapter exemplifies the need to conduct research into the geography of gender in the Third World with the most exact attention to scale, time and space, until we can satisfactorily relate the general to the specific. Harriss and Watson expose to us the multidimensional significance of an apparently 'simple' statistic. They present insights not only into gender in South Asia, but into the difficulty of establishing significant relationships in the geography of gender. This, then, is a critique of both data and theory.

The birth of a girl, grant it elsewhere, Here grant a son. (Artharveda)
Woman creates, woman destroys.
Daughters and cows go wherever they are led.
Mother teaches food. Father teaches wisdom.
A woman's mind is in the sole of her foot.
(Proverbs collected by Reaching Out, Mahim, Bombay 1983)

Introduction

Women are physiologically more efficient than men. On average
they are smaller and have a lower proportion of metabolically
active tissue than men, therefore women who are not pregnant or
lactating need less protein and energy. The energy cost of work is
thought also to be lower, and resistance to cold to be higher, for
women than for men (Rivers 1982). In most countries there are
more females than males in the population. The sex ratio is then
said to be feminine. The Middle East, China, and South Asia are
exceptions (Table 5). In South Asia, masculine sex ratios are
associated with high levels of mortality among very young girls
and among women of childbearing age. These levels have been
related to the economic undervaluation and low relative social
status of women (Visaria 1967; Bardhan 1974; Mitra 1978a; Miller
1981; Sen and Sengupta 1983; Sen 1984).

This chapter reviews what earlier writers have said on space–
time variations in the sex ratio and explanations they have given.

Table 5   The sex ratio, 1981–2 (males per thousand females)

Europe and North America[1]	952
Africa[1]	980
SE Asia[1]	990
China, E, SW Asia[1]	1010
S Asia[1]	1075
Sri Lanka[2]	1040
Afghanistan[2]	1048
Nepal[2]	1049
Bhutan[2]	1067
Bangladesh[2]	1067
India[2]	1073
Pakistan[2]	1078

Sources: [1]UN 1983, quoted in Sen 1984, p. 526. [2]Sri Lanka 1982, India
1981, WHO 1983.

Table 6   All India sex ratio, 1901–81 (males per thousand females)

Census year	Sex ratio
1901	1029
1911	1037
1921	1047
1931	1053
1941	1058
1951	1057
1961	1063
1971	1075
1981	1073

Source: India 1981.

We use the synthesizing approach characteristic of geography in the hope of stimulating professional and political action to reduce malnutrition.

The evidence: the masculine sex ratio in South Asia

Not only is the All India sex ratio unusually masculine, but it has become increasingly so (Table 6), while general mortality has fallen from 42.6 per thousand in 1901–11 to 14.5 by 1978 (Padmanabha 1982). Of total deaths, 47 per cent are now of children under the age of 4, and 18 per cent are of newborn infants. In India as elsewhere deaths among newborn boys exceed those among girls; but after the first month, and even more after the first year, female mortality rates increasingly exceed male rates (Table 7). This is especially true in rural areas. Chen's (1982) seminal research in Matlab Thana in Bangladesh shows that by the fourth year female deaths exceed male deaths by 53 per cent; they then

Table 7   Age specific death rates of children aged 0–4 years, 1977, per thousand: India

Age	Males	Females
0–24 days	19.5	16.8
1–12 months	9.9	11.9
0–1 year	29.4	28.7
1–4 years	15.8	20.6

Source: Padmanabha 1982, table 8, p. 1287.

Map 10   Sex ratios in Indian states, 1981

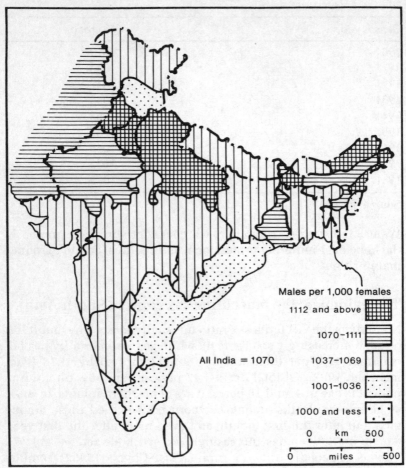

Males per 1,000 females

1112 and above

1070–1111

All India = 1070   1037–1069

1001–1036

1000 and less

0   km   500

0   miles   500

Source: P. Padmanabha. Census of India Series 1, Paper 1 of 1981
Provisional Population Totals, Table 7 UN Demographic
Yearbook 1983.

fall, but are always higher than male deaths. In both India and
Bangladesh, female mortality peaks again during the reproductive
years. So females appear particularly vulnerable in early childhood
and in parenthood – both times of life especially sensitive for
health and nutrition.

There are striking spatial variations in the sex ratio (Map 10).
Save for the small populations of the hill states, states in north and
west of India have the most masculine ratios; those in the south and
east have more balanced or feminine ratios. Comparison of Maps 10

Map 11   Sex ratios in India, 1901

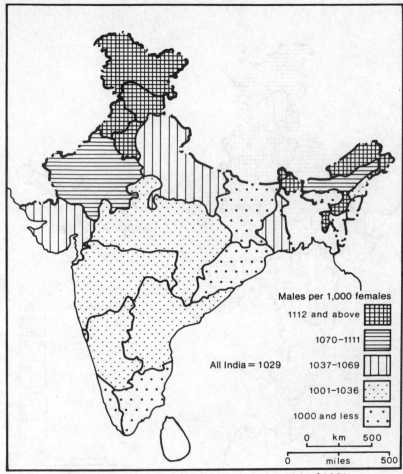

Males per 1,000 females

1112 and above

1070–1111

All India = 1029   1037–1069

1001–1036

1000 and less

0   km   500

0   miles   500

Source: Padmanabha. Census of India Series 1, Paper 1 of 1981
Provisional Population Totals, Table 7. Note: Padmanabha has
reconciled the census data with modern Indian states.

and 11 shows that the regional contrasts were similar in 1901 but
the masculinity has intensified almost everywhere. In rural areas
among children under the age of 4, female mortality was 50 per
cent higher than male mortality in Punjab and Uttar Pradesh in the
north, and 20 per cent higher in Rajasthan and Gujarat. It was
balanced in the central–southern states of Andhra Pradesh and
Maharashtra and in Tamil Nadu in the far south, and mortality of
boys exceeded that of girls in the southern states of Kerala and
Karnataka (Bardhan 1974, 1984). The geographical pattern is

Map 12   Sex ratios for scheduled castes in India, 1981

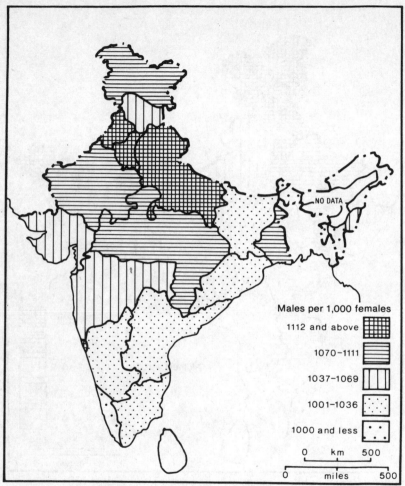

Males per 1,000 females

1112 and above	
1070–1111	
1037–1069	
1001–1036	
1000 and less	

NO DATA

0   km   500

0   miles   500

Source: Census of India, 1981, Series 1 Primary Census Abstracts Part II
BC (ii). Scheduled Castes, Statement 8.

modified if we analyse by social class. The sex ratio among the
poorest decile of rural people (small cultivators and landless
labourers) is masculine in a broad swathe from Bihar and Gujurat in
the north to Tamil Nadu in the south. The masculine ratio among
the poorest decile in Tamil Nadu and the feminine ratio in Haryana
are anomalous when compared with their general ratios (Visaria
and Visaria 1973). Analysis by individual caste is not possible
because caste is no longer called for in the census. Map 12, plotting
1981 census data for all 'scheduled' (low) castes, shows the reg-

ional trend. Sex ratios for scheduled castes are equal to or slightly higher than for total population in the south, but generally worse in northern states.

Evidence for the relative neglect of female children

The sex ratio addresses mortality. For spatial patterns in nutritional status and in morbidity, data are scandalously patchy. We cannot map malnutrition; we can only sample it. We study nutritional status by anthropometry. Anthropometric indicators are conventionally used for children rather than adults: comparisons with a reference western population enable us to evaluate growth by measuring weight for age, weight for height and height for age. Shortfalls in height for age are thought to indicate chronic malnutrition, while shortfalls in weight indicate acute malnutrition.

Nepal, despite a sex ratio of 1045 males per 1000 females, shows no difference between the sexes in the degree of retardation of growth (Nepal 1975; Martorell et al. 1984). In Sri Lanka, with a sex ratio of 1040, there is anthropometric evidence for 'chronic discrimination against girls' in all but two districts (Perera 1983), but no difference in acute malnutrition between the sexes. Evidence from Bangladesh (sex ratio 1067) is strangely contradictory between authors (Chen 1982; Abdullah 1983): Chen found significant sexual but insignificant social differences while Abdullah (with a small sample) found the reverse. In India (sex ratio 1073) there are only three recent anthropometric data sets which are disaggregated by sex and by social categories, two from the north for children and one from the south for adults. In east Punjab, the nutritional status of girls among Ramdasias (a poor and low caste) was much lower than that of boys. Among the wealthier, landed Jat castes, despite discrimination in feeding practices against girls, the difference was less and nutritional status generally higher (Levinson 1972). In West Bengal, a similar relationship was found for children of different castes and sexes (Sen and Sengupta 1983; Sen 1984) but variations between villages were also important. In northern Tamil Nadu, which is less exaggeratedly masculine, research identified women as significantly more undernourished in the poorest socio-economic group, though there was little anthropometric difference between the sexes in the overall adult population (McNeill 1984). A study of preschool children (not socially disaggregated) in the same area found no significant differences in nutritional status between the sexes (Hilder and Steinhoff 1983). Over the subcontinent, the limited data show regional variations and suggest that girls, in all social groups, are more likely to be retarded in growth.

One reason for the differences in growth may be discrimination in *food intake*. The relative neglect of the female in intra-household food distribution is considered to be 'possibly an important influence on the sex ratio' (Kynch and Sen, *Cambridge Journal of Economics*). Ratios of calorie intake to requirements can be measured, adjusted for body weight, and for estimates of the energy needs of activity, pregnancy and lactation. In Bangladesh, these are generally a few percentage points higher for men and male children than for women and girls, except in the age group 5–14, where the ratios are, in aggregate, equal (Chen *et al.* 1981). Abdullah (1983; Abdullah and Wheeler 1985), found that girls younger than 4 had lower intakes than boys in Bangladesh. Similar discrimination in food intake is observed in Morinda, in north-west India (Levinson 1972). By contrast, in Tamil Nadu a nutrition survey shows that women have higher ratios than men of calorie intakes to requirements (Chaudhuri 1982). As with anthropometric data, food intake surveys 'fit' the pattern of sex ratios but are extremely fragmentary. There is a crying need for other, comparable studies.

There is a little evidence of discrimination against females in access to health facilities. Gopalan and Nadamini Naidu (1972, no location given) reported an incidence of the kwashiorkor syndrome 33 per cent higher among girls than among boys, in an area where 13 per cent more boys than girls were admitted to hospital for treatment for it. Nutritional status, however, is not only related to food intake. It interacts with *morbidity* (sickness and propensity to sickness) and with *health care* practices. The immune response is weakened (in a way not fully understood by immunologists) both by inadequate energy intake and by infections. These feedbacks and interactions are hard to measure, let alone explain. Regional differences in mortality have been linked (on data now twenty years old (to variables indicative of the standard of health care (Bardhan 1974). The north–south trend of the sex ratio is broadly mirrored. Uttar Pradesh in the north had the lowest government expenditure per caput on public health, the highest infant and aggregate mortality rates, the lowest number of births attended by trained people and the lowest density of hospital beds and dispensaries. UP has a consistently masculine sex ratio — it was 1129 in 1981. By contrast, Kerala, in the south, has the most feminine sex ratio in India. At 967 in 1981 it is comparable with ratios for Africa and the 'developed world'. Kerala is pre-eminent in India in health facilities although it is a state with widespread poverty, which the welfare facilities alone cannot alleviate. In Bangladesh, even though there were no sexual differences in general morbidity, 66 per cent more boys than girls under 5 were brought for treatment (Chen *et al.* 1981). From official statistics it has been deduced that high female death rates from gastroenteritis, colitis, (broncho) pneumonia, tuberculosis, avitaminosis and other diseases associated with malnutrition are indicative of the late stage at which treatment is sought. But this evidence may *also* reflect influences of nutritional status.

When Sen conjectures that there is a peculiarly Asian problem of intra-household biases in the distribution of food (1984, p. 527), he is making a controversial statement. The nutritional problem may be specific to certain regions and classes and it is part of a larger and highly complex syndrome.

With data so defective, to suggest that the north–south spatial pattern of bias against females in nutrition and in the incidence of and response to ill health can be associated with the same spatial differences in the sex ratio can hardly be more than a working hypothesis. Nevertheless, this 'map' of sexual discrimination has attracted two important approaches to the further task of explanation. One approach stresses the economic undervaluation of women as the cause of discrimination. The second argues that the economic undervaluation of women is a symptom rather than a cause, and that the causes are historically specific cultural and ideological perceptions of women which affect the behaviour not only of men but also of women towards women. In examining each view in turn we therefore touch on the sensitive subject of the material base of culture.

The economic value of women

The discrimination described above has been attributed to the low economic value of women. A low value is assigned to the female part of the sexual division of labour. Neo-Darwinists have suggested that the sexual division of labour is natural, allowing specific traits to develop in each sex in order to enable the species to survive. But empirical evidence of massive spatio-temporal variation in the content of the division discredits notions of naturalness and of sexual complementarity. The sexual division of labour is rather seen to be specific historically, culturally and by class, and the point is often emphasized by referring to it as a 'gender' division of labour.

Women's value in agricultural production: an agricultural determinism

The link between technology, female participation in agricultural production and the social status of women was first proposed in a global analysis by Boserup (1970). It has been argued that operation of the plough requires more physical strength than can be exerted by women; this leads to a lowering of the demand for female labour in other operations such as weeding; and ploughing is incompatible with childcare and domestic work. So female status will be lower in plough systems of cultivation than in hoe systems. South Asian agriculture is predominantly a plough system.

Developing a line of reasoning first put forward by Bardhan (1974), Miller (1981) hypothesizes that the type of agricultural

Figure 1 Production, property and population in India: a north–south model

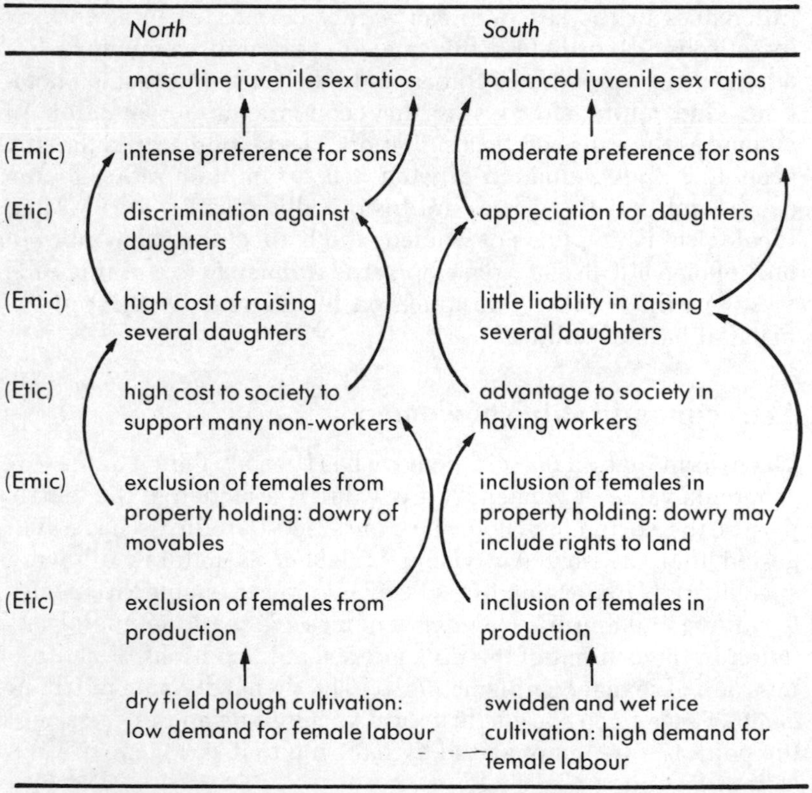

	North	South
	masculine juvenile sex ratios	balanced juvenile sex ratios
(Emic)	intense preference for sons	moderate preference for sons
(Etic)	discrimination against daughters	appreciation for daughters
(Emic)	high cost of raising several daughters	little liability in raising several daughters
(Etic)	high cost to society to support many non-workers	advantage to society in having workers
(Emic)	exclusion of females from property holding: dowry of movables	inclusion of females in property holding: dowry may include rights to land
(Etic)	exclusion of females from production	inclusion of females in production
	dry field plough cultivation: low demand for female labour	swidden and wet rice cultivation: high demand for female labour

Source: Miller 1981.

system determines not only female participation but also the sex ratio and the system of control over, and inheritance of, property. In these respects north and south India offer many contrasts. The northern region is associated with Brahmanical Hinduism, the south with pre-Hindu Dravidian culture. Figure 1 summarizes scenarios for propertied classes and distinguishes etic perspectives (behavioural traits observable from outside the system) from emic perspectives (understandable from within the system). From the etic perspective, worth or value is derived from work. In summary, Miller argues that northern women, who are excluded from wheat cultivation, are less valuable (and are more frequently denied access to property) than southern women, who participate in rice cultivation. From the emic perspective, the costs of marriage condition attitudes towards daughters as liabilities in the north, whereas lower dowries (sometimes brideprice) lead to a greater appreciation of daughters as assets in the south (Miller 1981; see also Bardhan 1984). The prime cause in this explanation is the demand for female labour, which is in turn derived from the nature of agricultural production. We must point out at once that Miller's analysis of labour is confined to landed cultivators and is not analytically extended to the landless, nor to the productive work (post-harvest processing, for instance) or reproductive work (childcare) of women within the home. In this Miller follows the common tendency in research on women: to focus on certain aspects in isolation from others. However, because of its relevance to the geography of the sex ratio, we pursue the analysis of female wage labour.

Status: the social geography of female participation

The participation of women in the Indian workforce is mapped from the latest census data (Map 13) to reveal the familiar north–south trend; the one unusual feature is the low female participation rate of Kerala, the state with the most feminine sex ratio. The important anomaly of Kerala has been hypothesized as resulting from conditions of poverty in which women work at times and in places when men are underemployed, so that female participation levels may vary inversely with those of males (Gulati 1975a; Mencher and Saradamoni 1982).

Our map is of total population. The regional trend is clearer for the rural than for the urban population (Kynch and Sen, forthcoming). Comparison of the geography of female participation with complex agricultural regions (Map 14) shows a certain congruence

Map 13   Female 'main' workers as a percentage of female
population, 1981

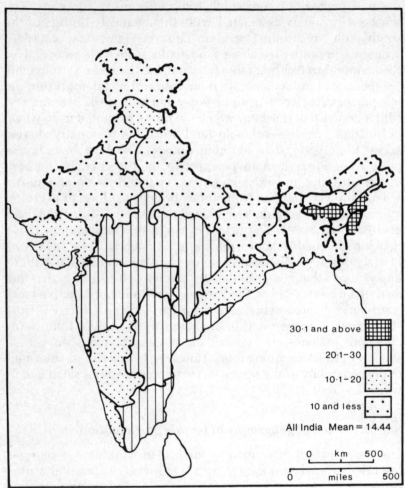

30·1 and above

20·1 – 30

10·1 – 20

10 and less

All India Mean = 14.44

0   km   500

0   miles   500

Source: Census of India, Series 1, India Paper 3 of 1981 Provisional
Population Totals. Workers and Non Workers, P. Padmanabha
pp. 5—7, Statement 3.

between wheat regions (in Punjab and Haryana) and low female
participation rates on the one hand, and the rice regions (of Tamil
Nadu and Andhra Pradesh) and high female participation rates on
the other. But it is quite hard to make sense of the rest of India. High
female participation rates are found in semi-arid tropical areas of
rainfed farming throughout India (Harriss 1984). Low female participation rates go with stockrearing, in Rajasthan, or with

Map 14   Agrarian regions of India

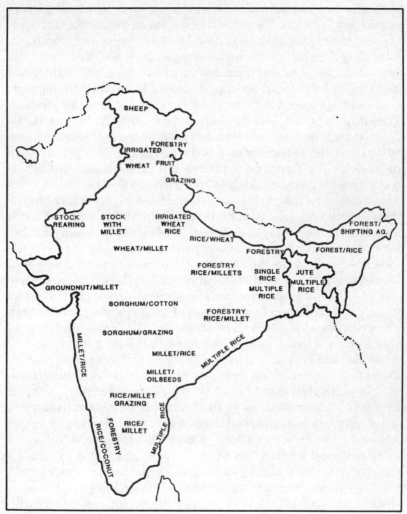

diversified agriculture, in Uttar Pradesh. Miller herself qualifies her argument and pertinently draws attention to a further anomaly caused by the conflation of north with wheat and south with rice: that in West Bengal there are low female participation rates in rice cultivation, since men perform tasks such as transplanting which are done by women in the south.

The participation of women is not only a function of the gender division of labour, but also of types and intensities of poverty. Taking this complication into account, Miller has argued that, since a greater proportion of the population is landless in the southern rice areas than in the northern wheat belt, female participation (and therefore status) will be higher in the south. But landlessness is not the only poverty-related compulsion to work. In Haryana (par excellence a wheat area) women are drawn into the agricultural wage labour force not only from the ranks of the landless but also from small farming households, in order to augment household income. And the same is certainly true for dryland agriculture in central and southern India (Sen 1982; Harriss 1984).

Poverty is not the only social factor influencing female participation. Caste in particular affects the frequency and type of work undertaken. The upper caste poor in West Bengal are confined to food processing and cooking (Mukherjee 1983). The lowest caste poor in Kerala cannot do that and are confined to physically dirty or ritually polluting jobs (Gulati 1978). Demand for such jobs will interact with the regional distribution of castes to muddy further the simple regional contrasts in participation. The stage in the household's life cycle, the number of dependants and the degree of dependence (Cain *et al.* 1979) and education (D'Souza 1975) have also been shown convincingly and unsurprisingly to affect women's participation in agriculture. Female participation is high at low and at very high levels of education. The female agricultural work force has low levels of education (Bardhan 1984).

Wage work, it is alleged, can be regarded by the peasant household as a return on the costs of unproductive years (childhood in particular) (see Vlassof 1979 for Bangladesh). The gender division of labour starts early in childhood: there is considerable social variation, but boys tend to be 'apprenticed' at an early age on field and marketing operations while girls work in the house on housework and preparation of food. Even in regions of Andhra Pradesh where masculinity and female participation rates are both relatively high, there are three times as many boys as girls aged between 10 and 14 working in agricultural production (Parthasarathy and Rama Rao 1973). It is, however, apparently the children of richer households who acquire these sharply different skills, and it can be argued that this is a training for 'management' rather than for future wage work. Lack of land may deny boys this on-farm practical schooling, while intensifying the need for girls to acquire domestic skills in order to liberate adult women for wage work. Our own recent data confirm such reasoning for northern Tamil Nadu, where it is rural weaving, not agriculture, which provides niches for boy wage-workers, while female drop-outs from, or non-entrants to, school do unpaid work on domestic tasks

(Harriss 1985). For rural boys we can thus observe a paradox: that their economically productive role, whether paid or unpaid, will vary positively with the household's class position up to a certain point (above which formal schooling generally removes them from productive work). The importance of this paradox will vary according to local circumstances of land use and distribution of assets. The much more consistent need for girls in domestic tasks is a powerful counterargument to the idea that opportunities for boys in productive agricultural work explain poorer rates of female survival.

The 'agricultural determinist' case does not stand up to the evidence. Regional links between agricultural systems, female participation and (by implication) the economic value and relative social status of girls and women are problematical, and do not square easily with the sex ratio which summarizes the discrimination against them.

Status: the history of female participation

It may now come as a relief to look at time trends in female participation, which seem clear and simple. The masculinization of the sex ratio since 1901 has occurred fairly uniformly throughout India. An association is suggested (see Mies 1978) between this trend and declining female participation, and therefore relative social status. We must now explore this proposition. Our relief is short lived. We are again at the mercy of census data. The definition of active labour has been altered for each of the last four censuses, and is particularly relevant as it affects the measurement and interpretation of women's work. For what it is worth, the census evidence implies that rates of female participation are slightly higher in 1981 than in 1971, but lower than in 1961. Independent official data from large surveys in 1955, 1972–3 and 1977–8 which were consistent in their categories show that the rate of female participation has not changed much (Randeria and Visaria 1984). But Omvedt's (1978) recomputations of census data, using official but small resurveys with standardized definitions (Table 8), show that between 1901 and 1971 the female participation rate, the proportion of females in the total work force and the proportion of females in the agricultural work force, have all substantially declined.

These aggregates conceal contradictory trends. Despite increasing urbanization, employment opportunities for women in manufacturing industry, trade and commerce are contracting and

Table 8   Trends in women's work participation

Year	Female workers as % of total female population	Female workers as % of total workforce	Females as % of total agricultural labourers
1901	n.a.	35.1	50.8
1911	33.7	34.4	49.2
1921	33.7	34.0	48.3
1931	27.6	31.2	45.7
1951	23.3	29.0	36.9
1961	27.9	31.5	45.0
1971	20.4	22.6	38.0

Source: G. Omvedt 1978, p. 375 (table 1), p. 378 (table 3), appendix pp. 398–9.

this is forcing women to seek employment in agriculture. Meanwhile, in agriculture some women may be being displaced, while others withdraw voluntarily for reasons of family prestige. Omvedt has identified a process of marginalization affecting both sexes, but particularly women.

The displacement of female labour in urban areas is poorly documented; it is perhaps best documented for urban agro-industry. In Bangladesh, West Bengal, Tamil Nadu and Sri Lanka, for instance, modern rice mills and technological changes in pre-milling processing and storage have caused a numerically large displacement of unskilled female wage labour in exchange for deterioration, or at the very best small gains, in technical efficiency, and with substantial state subsidies (see Harriss 1979 for Bangladesh, 1983 for West Bengal, 1976, 1977 for S India and Sri Lanka). Similar trends in displacement of wage labour (not in the reduction of drudgery) have been documented for the processing of wheat and maize in Punjab and oilseeds in north and south India (Sharma 1980; Harriss and Kelly 1982). For wage labour displaced by technological change in agro-industry, empirical and historical research in the Bengal region suggests that cottage-based work offers very little scope; sources of income important in the budgets of poor households have been lost, and work is sought in agricultural production (Cain 1979; Mukherjee 1983).

Meanwhile, the diffusion of modern agricultural technology changes the demand for labour. Mechanization reduces the demand unless it brings an increase in cropping intensity. From case studies in West Godavari, the rice bowl of Andhra Pradesh,

Table 9   Sex ratio in West Godavari, 1901–71

Year	1901	1911	1921	1931	1941	1951	1961	1971
Sex ratio	969	966	969	973	994	1000	1008	1006

Source: Mitra 1978.

Mies (1978) deduces (simplistically in our view) a direct causal relation between the new technology, capitalist relations of production, declining female participation in agriculture and masculinization of the population (Table 9). Agarwal's (1984) painstaking review of other rice-cultivating regions of India leads her to the conclusion that the impact of the new technology depends on the class position of women workers, the existing gender division of labour (in and out of the home), the precise gender division of tasks in agriculture, and the pattern of distribution and control over household earnings. The diffusion of 'high yielding varieties' often increases demand for transplanting, intensive weeding, threshing and harvesting. If short-duration crops lead to a rise in cropping intensity, demand for labour is further increased. Casual female labour is often used for transplanting, weeding and harvesting, so demand for female labour may rise. On the other hand, female labour is particularly liable to be displaced by weedicides. Case study research from three eastern rice-producing states does not support easy associations between female marginalization in agriculture and the sex ratio. In the north-eastern state of Orissa (with a masculine sex ratio) male casual labour increasingly dominates the wage labour force. By contrast, in Andhra Pradesh and Tamil Nadu in the south about half the labour time in rice production is provided by casual female labour. In Andhra Pradesh demand for male and female labour is increasing at roughly the same rate, but in Tamil Nadu where the sex ratio is more feminine, demand increases for male labour but not for female casual labour.

To sum up: the gender division of tasks in production is regionally specific and precise. In some regions women may be displaced from agro-processing or industrial work to agricultural labouring; in others, women may be displaced from agricultural production. Women may withdraw their labour voluntarily. In some regions demand for female labour may be becoming more compressed in time and more highly seasonal, but evidence is too poor for generalizations (see Parthasarathy and Rama Rao 1973, for rice in Andhra Pradesh; Sen 1982 for wheat in Haryana; Mencher and Saradamoni 1982 for southern rice areas). We must conclude that female participation in production is not easily linked either regionally or historically to the sex ratio.

Differentials in earnings

Obviously the role of women in agricultural production is inadequately indicated by participation rates unless compared with rates of remuneration. Among the poor, discrimination against women and children in food intake has often been explained as necessary to secure an adequate energy intake for the male household head to find and perform work. This is a variation on the theme of a nutritionally based efficiency wage (a concept referring to a critical base for wages below which the energy requirements of the worker cannot be met), critically reviewed by Binswanger and Rosensweig (1984). The relevant literature takes the gender differences in wages as given.

With respect to the role of earnings in nutrition, analysis of data on village labour throughout the semi-arid tropics of India has revealed a close positive relation between nutritional status and daily earnings among men but not among women (Ryan 1982). Not only is this said to provide an economic rationale for men generally receiving priority at meals but also it is said to explain leakages of food targeted at children in supplementary feeding schemes away from the targets and towards adult males (ICRISAT 1983). As Lipton comments, 'such analysis transfers the quest for lethal discrimination from food allocation' (Sen's crucial variable) 'to labour markets' (1983). Lipton argues that men may need to be relatively overfed to counter the effects of uncertainty in labour markets wasting energy in the search for work. This is to be understood as a desperately poor household's last resort. Unfortunately for Lipton's argument, in the semi-arid tropics of India it is the woman who should need to be 'overfed'. Female labour is important: it varies from 64 per cent of all hired labour inputs on the smallest holdings to 84 per cent of hired labour inputs on the holdings of capitalist farmers, and is an important component in the income of labouring households. Uncertainty in the market for casual female labour apparently exceeds that for male labour by 50 per cent (Ryan and Ghodake 1984).

Female labour is indeed generally paid less than male labour. For six villages in the semi-arid tropics (a zone stretching from Rajasthan in the north down to southern Tamil Nadu), female wage rates are significantly (56 per cent) lower than male wage rates

(Ryan and Ghodake 1984). Parthasarathy and Rao (1975) concluded that women were paid 70 to 80 per cent of the male wage.
There is evidence of a similar differential for north-east and
north-west India (Sen 1982). The evidence on regional variations
tends to be presented in the form of a teaser. A regression analysis
on national data on 1334 households in 1971 shows that the survival chances of girls increased with the female participation rate
and with the narrowing of gender differentials in daily earnings
(Rosenweig and Schulz 1982). Similarly, Bardhan has found that
differential survival chances for females can be related to their
anticipated earnings as adults. But whether female participation
rates and female wage rates are positively associated is the 64,000
dollar question.

A growing body of econometric analysis is directed to explaining wage differentials, and looks to three reasons for lower wages
for women: productivity, skill, and supply–demand relationships.
First, gender–specific productivity in agriculture is very hard to
measure since the gender division of tasks compartmentalizes the
labour market so that female and male labour do not supply comparable commodities and are not interchangeable. Where they are
comparable, differences in productivity cannot explain the differential payment of women. Second, there is no simple allocation of
more highly skilled jobs to male labour. Some low-paid women's
work, such as transplanting (in most wet rice regions), requires
great skill and stamina. The final explanation, that low female
wage rates reflect 'sex differences in demand and supply' in competitive markets, is claimed to be confirmed in a substantial set of
econometric exercises (Rosensweig 1984; Binswanger and Rosensweig 1984; Ryan and Ghodake 1984). Two comments on this are in
order. One is that though the econometric evidence may be statistically significant, the unexplained residuals are so large that
caution is necessary in causal inferences and interpretation. The
second is that, even if markets do operate competitively, there is no
explanation for the very compartmentalization, by gender and task,
within which supply and demand may interact. In West Bengal,
the gender and seasonal division of rural tasks (within which
supply and demand operate) have been concluded to serve the
purposes both of insuring against the out-migration of rural male
labour and of maintaining a reserve of cheap female labour: that is,
the division itself controls supply and demand (Bardhan 1984).

These gender differences in wages have long been entered on
the political agenda. But minimum wages legislation perpetuates
the inequalities. The 1981 law in Tamil Nadu for example gives

wages 25 per cent higher for 'male' tasks than for 'female' tasks. In Kerala the general legal rate for agricultural labour is 45 per cent higher for men. Only in West Bengal (where communist-organized labour movements are very active lobbies) is there no gender contrast in the law.

Would that there were evidence to test the hypothesis that higher participation rates and earnings in wage work increased the control by women over household budgets or decisions about food allocation; or that they were associated with reductions in oppressive practices. Our recent fieldwork suggests the reverse (Harriss 1985). The whole endeavour to link female work and the sex ratio can be criticized, for its economic reductionism. The gender division of labour, it can be argued, is not caused in some deterministic way by the needs of agricultural production. It is a symptom not a result, and serves to reinforce male domination, which leads to results such as the South Asian sex ratio. Status, it can be argued, is not adequately defined by participation in the wage labour force.

Invisible, unvalorized work by women

The sex ratio is the outcome of much more than the paid work of women in agriculture. Both liberal and Marxist economists have conflated work with wage work and ignored domestic work: liberals understand economic activity as the production of goods for exchange, and Marxists recognize domestic work as strictly necessary but unproductive under capitalist regimes. It is Marxist feminists who have argued that, if necessary, domestic labour produces goods which would otherwise have to be purchased as commodities, then wage workers can be paid lower wages than would otherwise be necessary. The value of commodities actually purchased with the wage is increased, and so is the rate of surplus appropriation. We find this analysis convincing, even if this exploitation of women is 'invisible' because of the informal way in which female labour is subordinated within the family, and even if it is impossible to quantify the relationship. It is, moreover, inevitable that the role of domestic labour is changing as a result of the expansion of capitalist production.

Nobody has yet analysed the relationships of female work to health and nutritional status, except to make one theoretical distinction between biological reproduction and the class-specific social control of women's reproductive capacities. Biological reproduction has been hypothesized as lowering women's social status by disabling them from participation in public life, but there is no biological necessity for this (Stolcke 1981). Social reproduction comprises, first, the role played by women in the reproduction of the labour force, and second, the role played by women, or by male control of women, in changes in class relations within society (Edholm *et al.* 1977). Empirical analyses of these categories imply a very different approach from the statistical correlation of macro-level variables and we should not be startled if existing empirical literature does not fit these analytical categories.

Table 10 Allocation of domestic labour, north Indian villages

	Tasks done by females	Tasks done by either sex	Tasks done by males
Children	1 Occasional help with cooking and washing utensils 2 Tending smaller children	1 Fetching water 2 Minor purchases from shops 3 Taking cattle to pasture or to water	1 Helping to handle draught animals
Adults	1 Cooking, post-harvest processing 2 Washing clothes 3 Tending small children and babies 4 Raising vegetables near the house 5 Milking and feeding cattle 6 Sewing and knitting 7 Cleaning house	1 Fetching water 2 Weeding 3 Sowing 4 Threshing by hand 5 Harvesting 6 Operating persian well for irrigation 7 Shopping	1 Ploughing 2 Feeding the threshing machine 3 Operating tube well 4 Digging irrigation channels 5 Operating farm machinery
Elderly people	1 Minding small children 2 Occasional cooking	1 Light agricultural work	

Source: Sharma 1980, p. 90.

Like wage work, domestic labour tends to be precisely allocated, and may be very onerous because of the primitive technologies available. A division of domestic labour in villages in the
north (Punjab and Himachal Pradesh) is given in Table 10. Ethnographic descriptions for the south (Thanjavur and southern Karnataka) are closely similar (Gough 1981; Hill 1982). The domestic
reproductive work of women is central to the survival of the household. Thus women are almost entirely responsible for the first type
of social reproduction identified by Edholm and her colleagues
(1977), and this responsibility appears to be little, if at all, affected
by the agricultural ecology. Our inescapable conclusion is that
women *throughout India* are important not only as unvalorized
domestic producers and biological reproducers, but also as socially
responsible for the reproduction of productive labour.

The ideology of patriarchy

Gender identity is mediated not only through material conditions
but also through ideology and politics. Status can also be derived
from and expressed in social power, which reflects a collective
awareness of control over economic resources and of the ability to
maintain or transform the social structure. So the sex ratio has also
been examined as the outcome of ideologies, particularly the
ideology of patriarchy. Patriarchy takes different forms according
to historical and cultural circumstances. Hence we now need to
find out how the ideology of patriarchy and the exercise of power
over women have affected female morbidity and mortality and the
regional pattern of the sex ratio. We look first at regional variations
in women's ability to control property and then at the socio-
psychological control of women.

Female autonomy and property

Miller's (1981) and Bardhan's (1984) cultural materialist explanation of regional variation in the sex ratio rests on the premise that
practices in the transfer of property on marriage and at death show
north–south regional contrasts. In the north, where the sex ratio is
most masculine, not only are women excluded from holding property, but also they require dowries on marriage, and so are
liabilities. Sons, by contrast, not only contribute to agricultural
production, but also carry the family name and property, support
parents in old age and attract dowries into the household. North–
south contrasts are summarized in Table 11, but the south is chang-

Table 11   Female labour, marriage costs and juvenile sex ratios
in two classes in north and south India

Class	Female labour participation	Marriage costs	Juvenile sex ratio
Northern propertied	low	high	highly masculine
Southern propertied	low to high	low to high	less masculine
Northern unpropertied	high	low	medium
Southern unpropertied	high	low	low to medium

Source: Miller 1981, p. 158.

ing away from brideprice and towards dowry. The diffusion
southwards of dowries may be related to the somewhat controversial evidence for a fall in demand for female labour. Dyson and
Moore (1983) have developed a satisfying argument linking marriage patterns, fertility and regional variations in the sex ratio; this
is summarized in Table 12. They turn attention away from the
notions of worth and status and find that for demographic, cultural
and psychological reasons there is greater female autonomy (the
capacity to manipulate one's personal environment) in the southern socio-cultural region. Their account tends to be descriptive
rather than analytical, does not cover temporal trends and it
explicitly ducks the problems of the material determination of
culture ('Whatever the ultimate material and historical factors
shaping culture, it seems safer and more realistic to take culture as
the primary determining factor for . . . the present'). Nevertheless
we shall examine their thesis in the light of ethnographic evidence.
For Dyson and Moore, transfers of property at marriage are indicators both of the wealth of the households concerned and of the
status and freedom of women within them. In the north, where
females do not as a rule inherit property, they are accompanied at
marriage by a dowry; its purpose is to compensate the groom's
family for the receipt of a new non-earning liability, or at best to act
as an insurance for the bride or perhaps to provide starting capital
for a business for the groom. The bride normally moves outside her
childhood locality. One study of a village near Delhi showed that
266 married women hailed from 200 different villages. The result is
the extreme isolation of the adolescent bride from her female kin
(Lewis 1958, p. 161). In the south, women may and sometimes do
inherit property. Local cross-cousin marriage within the caste is
the norm, and transactions essentially within the family are less
financially debilitating. Land tends to be retained within a close

Table 12 Characteristics of northern and southern socio-cultural regions

Characteristic	North	South
Female social status	Low	Higher
Demography		
Sex ratio	Masculine	More balanced
Fertility	High total fertility	Lower total fertility
Marriage	Low female age at marriage (except in Punjab and Gujurat)	Higher female age of marriage; slightly more non-marriage and dissolution
Mortality	High child mortality rate. High female death rate (0–4 age group)	Fewer female deaths (0–4)
Culture		
Marriage	Exogamous, dominated by search for alliances between males. Spouses less closely related by kin and by location	Endogamous. Emphasis on (fictive) cross-cousin marriage. Marriage more likely to be to known households near natal homes
Inheritance	Females do not inherit property	Females may sometimes inherit and transfer property rights
Status	Wife givers socially and culturally inferior to wife takers. Female chastity important to reinforce honour and power	Tendency to social and ritual equality of affines. Female chastity less important. Communication networks less sex-specific. Greater freedom for women to work. Less restriction on occupation
Psychology		
Male relatives	Blood relatives co-operate. Tension between patrilineally related males	Men enter social, political, and economic relations with affines and blood relatives

Psychology *cont.*

Females	Incoming brides viewed as threat to family solidarity because from another kin group	Affective ties between husband and wife are no threat to descent group. This enables freer discussion of fertility control
Old age	Parents of daughters expect little help from them after marriage. Sons remain in parental home.	Daughters more likely to be near for help and support.

Source: Dyson and Moore 1983.

group of kindred, and on occasions brideprice may be transferred. Its purpose is to recompense the bride givers for the loss of a potential earner ('selling' the bride) or is to be used to gain wives for her brothers.

There is, however, ethnographic evidence on marriage transactions among propertied classes in north and south India (respectively Sharma 1980; Gough 1981) which does not reveal these regional differences. Moreover, there are disagreements on whether the southern system of cross-cousin marriage (and brideprice or two-way payments) is giving way to arranged marriages with strangers within the caste (and two-way payments or dowries) (compare Gough 1981 with Harriss 1981), and on whether there is a trend for dowry payments to daughters to rise towards a level equal to the amount inherited by sons, or whether the dowry merely contributes to the expenses of the immediate ceremony. Practices probably differ between castes. And whether the rise in dowry payments can be linked to the decline in the female participation in the labour market depends upon a definition of active labour which is restricted to wage work. This may or may not be appropriate; and it assumes, against the evidence, that women control their earnings and derive status from that control (Randeria and Visaria 1984). Ethnographic evidence thus suggests that Dyson and Moore's north–south stereotypes are dwarfed by the similarities of the patrilineal descent system, with patrilocal residence requirements on marriage. When a woman (a pubescent or adolescent girl) changes her home on marriage she is controlled by her husband's parents, and is generally unable to claim her statutory rights to inheritance to property in either her natal or her conjugal family.

Socio-psychological control of women

The practice of patriarchy, the male control of property and of women, is sanctioned by both sexes and can be reinforced by repressive means, as well as by the neglect of women's health and nutrition discussed earlier. Documentation of violence against women is improving, but still scanty. There is a long list of restrictive or oppressive practices and cultural ideas associated with them, ranging from the now illegal *sati* (self-sacrifice of a widow on her dead husband's pyre) and female infanticide, through murder for dowry to constraints on freedom, such as strictures against divorce and against the remarriage of widows (who are relatively numerous when girls are married before puberty to much older men), *purdah* and seclusion, to the shunning of women as agents of pollution during menstruation, in late pregnancy and after childbirth (Lannoy 1971; Panigrahi 1973). Many restrictions concern food. Widows obtain virtue by confining themselves to one meal a day. Virtue is generally attached to female fasting (e.g. for one day per week). The (female) cook is held to be subordinate to the (male) eater, who takes priority in eating order. Women are held to be providers of services, including food and sexual intercourse. While a new wife is in an apprentice phase in the kitchen, she may be underfed, may be the last to feed and may eat alone. Later, she may eat with her mother-in-law after the men are fed.

Male control excludes women from power and authority. Purdah restricts the spatial movements of both Muslim and Hindu women, especially in northern India and among the higher castes and classes. The bazaar, where household provisioning decisions are implemented, is not accessible to women observing purdah. The making of cash transactions in public places violates purdah. Even in the south, where purdah is observed only by Muslims, women from higher castes are secluded in their houses between menarche and marriage. Notions of purity and morality are extended not only to space but also to tasks. The management of a male labour force violates purdah. Agricultural work is to be avoided for reasons of 'honour' by the women of upwardly mobile intermediate castes such as Jats. In Himachal Pradesh, where extensive male migration forces poor women to work on the family farm, their work is regarded as an extension of domestic work, which earns moral and social value (Sharma 1980). The same value system obtains in south India, where women may have more spatial freedom and may manage property (Gough 1981). But the control of land by women is diminishing and that trend is not expected to be checked by recent legislation to abolish gender differences in inheritance. The number of registered women cultivator–landowners has fallen from 18 million in 1911 to 16 million in 1971 despite an increase in the female population from 123 to 264 million.

Restrictions on women's spatial mobility and control of property are reinforced by their lack of authority. In the north, the *gunghat* (veiled seclusion) prevents rural women from interacting with senior men who dominate political life in public places. In the south women are explicitly excluded from judgements on disputes in the street and village assemblies. They are regarded, and regard themselves, as legal minors under the guardianship of male relatives. Women are repressed not only by men but also by women. Among women seniority brings enormous rewards not just in status but also in authority over younger women and over younger and lower-caste men. Young women's expectation of power later in their lives may justify their acceptance of suffering earlier. Women also internalize their own repression. Debilitating fertility behaviour by north Indian women during their reproductive years may be explained by the need to create their own affective social group comprising their children, to compensate for submission and subordination during their own childhood (Dyson and Moore 1983). Maltreatment of girls by men may be explained as an aggressive, resentful, adult reaction both to fantasies of Kali (the form of the goddess who represents the overwhelming rather than the nurturing aspects of femininity) and to prolonged dependence of a son upon his mother, often associated unintentionally (through hunger and disease) with a punitive conditioning (Lannoy 1971). Subordination may lead to the reaction of heightened aggression towards males. But there is little evidence for this in India (apart from the sublimations of ballads and jokes about male infantility (Kakar 1981)). Kakar concludes that this aggression tends to be internalized in a conversion of outrage into self-deprecation (see also Cormack 1961).

This oppressive behaviour occurs throughout India, but it is said to be less pronounced in the south because of the influence of pre-Aryan conceptions of a nurturing mother goddess (Kali images in the south being less culturally pervasive). It is also important that moves on marriage are much shorter and thus the psychological separation at marriage is thought to be less traumatic.

If we may revert to the threefold distinction in female reproductive roles, women are not only subjugated but are also responsible for biological reproduction and the reproduction of the productive labour force of the household. However, the position of women affects and will be affected by other social changes. We now look at these.

Patriarchy and social change

While paternity needs social mechanisms such as marriage to make it visible, maternity is incontestable. Control over the special caste attributes of a man's descendants requires male control over female sexuality. The ideology of subordination and the reality of man's control over women's reproductive capacity can be interpreted as underpinning the family. The family brings about the social reproduction of class relations. So changes in class relations may require or bring about changes in the control of fertility. We have found examples for Gujurat and for Punjab.

In central Gujurat, the development of a small elite group in the nineteenth century has been charted by Clark (1983). Members of this elite increased their economic power by enlarging and consolidating their hold over minimally fragmented land. They increased their political power by cornering the market in offices under the British; they achieved social power by virtue of their already high ascribed caste and their kinship and fertility practices. Brides were accepted from lower subcastes upon payment of remarkably large dowries. Land could be tightly controlled by achieving stability or low growth in the size of the elite population. The sex ratio was highly masculine (Table 13). This was brought about by a high rate of bachelorhood among the top families and by female infanticide, which is carefully documented by Clark. By contrast, low status *kolis* 'protected' their women less, and both sexes worked productively in agriculture; their population grew rapidly.

Similar processes are found among elite Rajputs in the Kangra hills (Parry 1979). The options open to the uppermost households were, first, to leave daughters unmarried (incurring shame and spiritual dishonour), second, to marry into lower subcastes (renouncing claims to superiority, in exchange for massive dowries and a long-term flow of gifts from the bride givers), and third, female infanticide. Infanticide is scripturally the worst form of murder, but children under the age of 22 months are in an ambiguous category, being believed not to have sins. This may explain why the death of a baby girl is unpolluting: 'the allegation that the practice is not altogether extinct . . . [is viewed] . . . with a certain amount of complacency' (Parry 1979). The honour of the patriline

Table 13   Average sex ratios, central Gujurat

Year	Total population	Elite Karbis	Low Kolis
1826	1250	1351	1163
1849	n.d.	1428	n.d.
1867	1282	1471	1205
1872	n.d.	1370	n.d.
1891	1162	1282	1111
1901	1123	1250	1111

Source: Clark 1983, p. 9.

is still apparently thought under certain circumstances to be capable of necessitating the death of a daughter.

These case studies of infanticide and female neglect derive from the uppermost castes, not from the lowest, poorest and most destitute.

Patriarchy and catastrophe

The placing of the patriline above the survival of women and children has been noted in the literature on famine; and it is the poor and destitute who do this. The social effects of famine can be viewed in three ways. First, famine can be analysed as an extreme exaggeration of existing social trends. Second, it can be seen as the opposite: the breakdown of routine structures. Third, it works like a ratchet, after the turning of which there is no return to a previous social state or process. The victims of South Asian famines are said to have a clear social profile. Abandoned by the land-controlling classes, rural dependent classes lose their entitlement to food, and the moral order also collapses. In the great Bengal famine the least affected were Hindu, male, adults of the trading or cultivating caste. The most severely affected were Muslim and Hindu women and children, widows, and female-headed households of the lower castes (Greenough 1982). Those in charge of subsistence and nutrition may consciously disenfranchise those dependent on their decisions (Appadurai 1984). Of course, an official declaration of famine is not necessary to set in motion these discriminating processes. An anthropometric survey, lagging by a year serious floods in West Bengal in 1978, showed uniformly larger incidence and severity of undernutrition among female children under 72 months of age than among male children (Sen 1984).

Conclusion

The sex ratio in South Asia shows that female mortality is higher than male. The ratio has a strong geographical pattern, being most masculine in the north and least in the south. It is generally getting more extreme over time. Data on nutritional status, food intake, morbidity and access to health facilities imperfectly reflect the geographical pattern of the sex ratio, and there are many exceptions to the general trend.

Explanations for general variations are of two types. One, exemplified by Miller (1981) and by Bardhan (1984), relates the sex ratio to low social status and the economic undervaluation of women, and emphasizes the role of women in agricultural production. The second, exemplified by Dyson and Moore (1983), relates discrimination to lack of autonomy and lays stress on systems of property control and transfer. Neither approach, we find, is generally supported by empirical material.

Notions of status have led to research on female participation in work. But from the polar extremes of gross generalization or acute detail at which data are available, there is little congruity between specific agricultural regions and distinctive levels of female participation. And the data ignore non-wage work. Female social status cannot be measured by participation in work, whether paid or unpaid, which does not enhance women's authority or power within household or society.

The exploration of constraints on female autonomy has revealed both regional and caste variations in spatial and social freedom and in oppressive practices, but there is little evidence to suggest that women have access to more power or authority in the south than in the north. There is one exception to this. A woman who marries faces a longer migration in the north than in the south; and she is viewed much more as a threat to the cohesion of the patrilineal, gerontocratic household in the north. But these cultural differences cannot alone be the causes of differences in the sex ratio. The sex ratio is clearly the summary outcome of a complex mass of interacting and contradictory variables.

Explanations for the intensification of the masculinity of the sex ratio over time are being sought in discussions about status, the progressive lowering of which is associated with displacement of women's work by technological change in both rural and urban areas (Agarwal 1984). There is also evidence of contradictory social reasons for changes in the work done by women: higher class women withdraw labour or are secluded for reasons of family prestige, while poor women work more or less according to the supply of gender-specific tasks (Sharma 1980). But emphasis on these highly complex changes diverts attention from the discrimination, oppressive practices and exclusion practised throughout the subcontinent. These social forces take their heaviest toll at times in women's lives when they are most physiologically vulnerable.

Finally, the masculine sex ratio could be partly due to the high social value placed on caste endogamy, mediated through the supply of women.

The disturbing geography of the sex ratio and of health and nutritional status is not going to be explained satisfactorily until research is directed to the role of women in property, production and the three types of reproduction (Edholm et al. 1977) in many regions of South Asia.

Postscript

Because experience comes from life rather than from books, we want to pay tribute to Rani, a childless village woman in south India, 18 years old, a wife of twenty months' standing, spice grinder, carrier of slops. She married with an incomplete dowry. Her father quarrelled with her father-in-law over money and over irrigation water. Rani hanged herself with her own sari, bending and holding up her legs to gain height to swing from a low beam in the kitchen hut, till she had put an end to her own misery.

Though at some time in her childhood she may have been netted in a census, she had neither birth nor death certificate. She was a demographic near-invisibility, a brief source of shame to her kin, but she is part of the story of the sex ratio.

Acknowledgement

This review was funded by the Overseas Development Administration through its funding of the Nutrition Policy Unit in the London School of Hygiene and Tropical Medicine. Interpretations here are in no way the official views of ODA.

3   Old wives or young midwives? Women as caretakers of health: the case of Nepal

Maggie Pearson

Editors' introduction

The leading role played by some countries and regions in the spatial division of labour is simply the supply of cheap labour – the reproduction of the labour force for other regions. Nepal is one of the world's poorest, least developed countries and depends almost exclusively on India for trade, transit and outside employment. Internally, Nepal has used its independence to limit capitalist penetration: most Nepalis are peasants who own their own means of production and produce primarily for their own consumption, but the majority of households can barely feed themselves from their own land, and ecological collapse seems imminent. Stagnant technology and the lack of any significant reorganization of production render population growth a serious threat. There is little escape into wage labour, whether in agriculture or industry; the state is the main employer in Nepal, whether in the bureaucracy or the army.

The main opportunity open to households with inadequate resources is for someone to leave for India, to work in civil, or, if possible, army employment. A fifth of males between 20 and 70 may be either in the army or in receipt of pensions. The Indian army appears as supporting the peasant system in Nepal; strategic considerations are involved, since the collapse of Nepal's economy would create instability on India's northern borders. The exchanges of Nepali labour and primary products for wages and manufactured goods have been profitable to India in the past, but the distortions of the Nepalese economy have now become so extreme as to bring its viability into question.

Nepali women, running farm and household in the men's absence, may have gained in household power. No such gain is apparent in women's role in caring for family health, where Pearson finds women belittled by both traditional and modern medicine. This highly specific case study of women and health among poor, remote people suffering a decline in livelihood on the periphery of India has strong general relevance not only to the Third World but to all humanity. Some features are peculiar to Hindu culture or Nepali practice, but the study holds a distant mirror to health systems around the world.

Introduction

In all societies, women are 'caretakers of health and life'; this is an important element of their wider domestic role. The recognition of symptoms; assessment of the need to consult more 'expert' advice; the application of home remedies; self-care during pregnancy and childbirth; all are major components of health care. Yet they are invisible to the professional sector, which, with its increasing control over health care and mystification of medical knowledge, allows no value to the lay sector. In the developing world, 40 per cent of the population is aged under 15 years; a woman may bear as many as twelve children, and 25 per cent may die before the age of 5 years; and institutionalized health care is not widely accessible. Women's invisible role is therefore of crucial importance, but is rarely acknowledged or incorporated into plans to promote health and improve health services. This paper discusses the role of women as wives, mothers and midwives, providing 'informal' health care in Nepal. It is based on field work during 1980–1, which focused on basic health services and control of leprosy in west central Nepal.

Nepal

The small Hindu Kingdom of Nepal clings perilously to the southern slopes of the Himalayas; in its rugged terrain there is much poverty and a rich diversity of peoples and cultures. Within 160 km the country rises from the southern jungle and plains (*terai*), at a few hundred metres above sea level, to the highest mountain peaks in the world, including Everest at 6848 m. Many parts of the country are accessible only on foot, and are often cut off by floods and landslides during the summer monsoon.

Rural economy: declining subsistence agriculture

Over 90 per cent of the economically active population is engaged in agriculture, which accounts for 60 per cent of the officially recorded GDP, estimated at US$170 per capita for 1982. It is essentially a peasant, subsistence economy; an estimated 40 per cent of production is consumed within the household unit, never entering the market. Over 60 per cent of households are those of independent peasants who live mainly in the hills, where the average landholding is 0.4 hectares and is expected to support 5.6 people. Cash crops account for less than 10 per cent of the cropped area, and are produced in the *terai*, largely for export to India. The subsistence economy on which the Nepali population of 15 million is so heavily dependent is rapidly becoming unable to keep pace with an annual population growth of 2.6 per cent. Already in the hills and mountains the low yields of the small cultivated area cannot support the inhabitants. Income has been supplemented for many years by migration south to the *terai* or abroad, for employment, particularly in foreign military forces. Indeed, in some mountainous districts the total population fell by as much as 2 per cent per annum in 1971–81, despite the increase of 2.6 per cent in the national population.

In several districts in the hills the ratio of males to females is 0.9:1, compared with 1.1:1 in some parts of the *terai* which have been recently drained, cleared and settled. It is estimated that in 1977–8 there was a net outmigration of 66,000 people from the hill population of approximately 8 million. Of those 40,000 went to the *terai*, 11,000 to urban areas and 15,000 abroad. The proportion of the population living in the hills and mountains has fallen from 62 per cent in 1971 to 56 per cent in 1981.

History and culture: the dominance of Hinduism

A wide variety between regions is the product of successive migrations and invasions from central Asia and from the Indian subcontinent. The modern kingdom of Nepal was established in 1789, after a series of conquests and annexations of petty hill states. The monarch is believed to be a reincarnation of the god Vishnu; and the first National Code (*Mulki Ain*) of 1854 formalized Hindu ideology into state law. The supremacy of Hindu values was established during a period of fanatical Hinduization in the nineteenth century, though other religions were tolerated if they did not directly contradict basic Hindu values. Contemporary Nepal is the product of this rich history. Approximately 80 per cent of the population are Hindus or 'Hindu-oriented', incorporating significant aspects and principles of this cultural–religious complex into a variety of social configurations. Census data record only 52.5 per cent of the population speaking Nepali, the language of Sanskrit origin, as mother tongue (HMG 1977). Others have retained their own language while adopting some aspects of Hinduism.

Women in rural Nepal

Women and the patrilineal ideology of Hinduism

Gender status varies between ethnic groups; there is more independence for women among non-Hindu hill tribes than among high-caste Hindus living on the lower slopes and in the valleys of the middle hills. This may also be a result of differential male migration.

Hinduism has had varied impact in Nepal, but it is the dominant ideology structuring the lives of the majority of women. Their social and ritual status within Hindu patriarchy is fraught with contradictions and ambiguities. On the one hand, there is profound respect for motherhood; a woman's social identity depends on her success in producing sons. Motherhood of a large and thriving family is a woman's chief source of recognition and status. High fertility also fulfils an important economic function in providing labour for the domestic subsistence economy. Yet childbirth itself, and other manifestations of female sexuality such as menstruation, are seen within the ideology of ritual purity as highly polluting, since they involve the shedding of blood. Ritual cleansing is required before the woman can return to full activity in the household, particularly in the preparation of food.

Women's status is ultimately defined by their direct blood relationship with men. This is most oppressive in widowhood, which in orthodox households brings shame: widows are expected to shave their hair and are unable to remarry. Daughters and sisters have high status as symbols of innocence passing through the family and destined for marriage. Wives and daughters-in-law, on the other hand, are subordinate and potentially dangerous outsiders of low status, who must prove their worth by motherhood. They are always open to suspicion of intending to destroy the extended family for their own selfish purposes. Inexplicable misfortune afflicting a family is often attributed to the witchcraft (bokshi) of a malicious daughter-in-law (Stone 1976).

Patrilineal ideology excludes women from all spiritual functions and requires death rites to be performed by a male relative, preferably a son. Women's role as unpaid productive and reproductive labour carries negligible power or control over economic resources, and therefore no independence. Their rights to property and economic security are dependent upon the social fact of marriage. Women with no surviving children may be destitute.

The dual role of women in rural Nepal: production and reproduction

It is common to see a Nepali woman working in the fields, cutting wood or weaving cloth, with a young baby on her back. This epitomizes her grossly undervalued dual role in production and reproduction. It is a lot which few rural women can escape; they have no independent property rights and few marketable job skills. The average age at marriage is 16.8 years. There is a staggeringly low literacy rate of 3.66 per cent among women aged over 10 years. With such constraints, there is little room for manoeuvre. Most production within the rural domestic subsistence economy is undertaken by women, but is invisible to official statistics. The 1971 census recorded 35.1 per cent of women as economically active. This is a high proportion for the Third World, but a severe underestimate of their actual productive activity, since 'domestic work' and unpaid labour were not included. A further 57.1 per cent were classed as housewives and by implication were economically inactive; but several local studies have shown that women are as productive as men within the domestic economy, in addition to their reproductive role as wives and mothers (Macfarlane 1976; Schroeder and Schroeder 1979). Pregnancy and childcare continue in the midst of other productive activity. While men are away, selling or buying goods in the local bazaar, or in paid employment elsewhere, women are responsible for planting, tending and harvesting crops and tending livestock, as well as collecting firewood and looking after the family.

Statistics summarizing the life-cycle of the 'average' woman cannot quantify her actual reproductive labour. After an early marriage at an age of 16.8 years she will bear 6.1 children (NFS 1976). More than 80 per cent of women then breastfeed for twenty-four months or more (Reejal 1979). In short, a woman is engaged in reproduction for about fifteen years – four and a half years pregnant, and between ten and twelve years breastfeeding. Visible stresses on the mother in her reproductive role include carrying a child, nursing infant sickness, and mourning infant death. All continue along with other, productive activity. The toll taken on women in their dual role is reflected in a higher death rate of 22.8 per thousand population compared with 21.5 for men, and a lower life expectancy of 41.4 years compared with 43.4. Rural women have the highest death rate, at 23.2 per thousand, while urban men have a crude death rate of 8.23 per thousand. Such figures are alarming enough for the lives of rural Nepali women, but they also highlight the vicious circle of ill health when a mother's health is crucial to her unborn or breastfed child.

The need for health care: birth, death and disease in Nepal

Health care is essential for safe childbirth and the prevention and treatment of illness and disease. With an estimated birth rate of 42.6 per thousand (one of the highest in South Asia), there is a great need for expertise in midwifery. The high average fertility rate of 6.1 per married woman takes its toll on the mother's increasingly depleted resources, which need preventive and restorative care and consistently sound nutrition. Only 10 per cent of pregnant women seek any medical care during pregnancy and childbirth, and less than 8 per cent use His Majesty's Government (HMG) midwives (see Table 16). In a population with 15 per cent under the age of 5 years, and 40 per cent under 15 years, childcare is a priority in promoting health and preventing illness and death. Over 50 per cent of the estimated crude death rate of 21–23 per thousand is accounted for by children under the age of 5 years, and infant mortality is estimated at 152 per thousand live births (WHO 1981).

Nepal has also a high general level of illness and a consequent need for general health care. Life expectancy at birth is 43 years. Community health surveys in four districts showed that between 22 and 45 per cent of people in households interviewed had been ill during the previous fourteen days, and between 2 and 10 per cent had been acutely disabled from carrying out their normal duties (Table 14). Respiratory disease was the main health problem in all these districts, accounting for as much as a third of reported illness. Diarrhoea, dysentery and other gastro-intestinal disorders accounted for 15–20 per cent of health problems, but the proportion was far higher (40 per cent) among children under the age of 5 years. Despite this prevalence of ill health 70 per cent of ill people received no treatment at all, and only 20 per cent consulted any service or practitioner (Table 15). Less than 15 per cent of people interviewed in the mid term review of HMG health services in 1979 had acquired their knowledge of health matters from health workers; 50 per cent had learnt from friends or relatives (HMG 1979). The lay health sector, whether friends, relatives or one's

Table 14 Repeated morbidity, acute disability and illness rate in four districts of Nepal

Cause of morbidity (%all reported illness)	Surkhet	Nuwakot	Tanahu	Dhankuta
Respiratory disease	29	26	33	36
Diarrhoea/dysentery/G-I	15	19	18	21
Fever	9	4	6	5
Skin	8	9	4	7
Musculo-skeletal	7	9	7	5
Acute disability (% of population)	10	3	10	2
'Illness rate' per fourteen days (% of population)	32	34	45	22

Source: Institute of Medicine, Kathmandu 1977, 1979 a, b, c.

Table 15 Use of available health services in four districts of Nepal

	Surket	Nuwakot	Tanahu	Dhankuta
% of ill people untreated	78	73	70	68
% of ill people consulting any service	20	10	23	18
% of consulters treated in HMG health facilities	57	56	50	65
% of consulters using TMP	30	18	9	17

Source: Institute of Medicine, Kathmandu 1977, 1979 a, b, c.

own common sense, is clearly the main source of health care and knowledge in rural Nepal. Women play an important part in their reproductive role as wives, mothers and housekeepers. They are the gatekeepers of health care, and caretakers of health.

Patriarchy and professionalism in western and traditional medicine

Western medicine: alienating and technocratic

Until the mid 1970s, health policies promoted by international agencies and adopted by national governments in the Third World exported the technological model of medical care from western industrialized countries. Finance and personnel to establish hospitals with the latest equipment and drugs were an important component of overseas trade and aid to the Third World. The wholesale transplanting of western medicine was generally accepted without criticism; its appropriateness was taken for granted. This medical tradition has a mechanistic view of the body, perceiving it as a set of component parts with discrete functions. That has two important implications. First, it depersonalizes the experience of illness; medical practitioners are detached from the sick person, hidden behind an array of jargon, tests, procedures and equipment. Second, biological explanations of disease restrict treatment to the realms of 'objective science'. This is the jealously guarded domain of an elite of highly trained professionals and drug companies; admission to those ranks is highly controlled, and was until recently confined to men.

Since the early 1970s, there has been increasing concern that technological medicine is inadequate, particularly in the Third World. The increasing failure of established health services to meet the basic needs of the majority of the world's population was in stark and glaring contrast to the radical improvements in health achieved by countries such as China, Cuba and Tanzania, which laid emphasis on primary health care and paramedical workers. This realization led the World Health Organisation (WHO) to make a fundamental change in policy to a basis of Primary Health Care, with the aim of making essential health care universally accessible at a cost that each community and country can afford. This was the basis of the WHO strategy for attaining its goal of Health for All by the Year 2000. It explicitly acknowledged that resources and power must be diverted from the expensive technological medical centres serving the urban elite to provide accessible and flexible primary health care for the rural (and urban) poor.

Government health services in Nepal

Nepal's health policy concentrated on the improvement of hospital care until the mid 1970s. It spent 95 per cent of the health budget on curative care, which reached 5 per cent of the total population (Reejal 1979). In 1975 there was a radical shift to the provision of primary health care, in line with WHO policy. The Government's Basic Health Services aim to make a minimal health care available to the maximum number of people. A hierarchy of regional and district hospitals, providing specialist and technological services, are supported by a network of Basic Health Posts providing preventive and curative primary health care. It is estimated that approximately 66 per cent of Nepal's population now live within half a day's walk of a Basic Health Post (HMG 1979). The staff quota of each health post includes at least one trained health assistant and one auxiliary nurse/midwife. There may also be a Malaria Eradication Officer, a Family Planning and Maternal/Child Health Clinic, and a Village Health Worker who promotes health education and preventive community medicine. Despite the spirit of community participation in primary health care, the HMG Basic Health Services are still the domain of male professionalism. In 1979, between 90 and 100 per cent of the field staff were male, and the majority saw their prime role as curing illness. Few felt any responsibility to promote preventive health measures.

'Traditional' treatments and practitioners

Within the hegemony of western medicine, other systems are invariably assumed to be invalid, ineffective and resistant to change. But people the world over amend their knowledge, beliefs and behaviour in the light of experience. The rural Nepalis are no exception. Far from being impenetrably conservative or ignorant, they have incorporated several aspects of western medicine in their ideas and practices. They consult healers of various traditions and skills for different conditions, and often consult more than one for a single complaint.

Traditional medicine, despite its very different theoretical base, also proves to be professional and patriarchal. Ideas about disease and systems of healing are broadly similar throughout Nepal, despite cultural and religious variations. Illness is generally perceived as but one part of a general system of affliction, in which (wo)man is hopelessly beset by larger forces. Diagnosis of the source of illness is usually undertaken by an astrologer, a *shama* (medium), or a *vaidya*; all are invariably men. If simpler methods of treatment, such as herbal remedies or food prescriptions, are sufficient, more elaborate rituals are not used. For the rituals, first, the pulses of three arteries in both wrists will be read, to divine the source of affliction. Second, rice reading is performed. The source of the trouble is revealed in the way in which rice falls on to a plate, when thrown during a consultation with a ritual healer. The third method of diagnosis, which not all healers can perform, is spirit invocation. There are complex concepts of illness, originating in (wo)man's many links with the impersonal metaphysical forces and highly personal supernatural beings. Misalignment with the planets is associated with general misfortune, which may include rather vague, non-specific illness. Other supernatural sources of illness are, by contrast, often highly personalized in the identity of particular malicious spirits. This spiritual world is conceived along lines similar to the caste structure which pervades Nepali society, and to which women are not admitted in their own right. Higher spiritual beings are angered if neglected or offended. They do not attack their human victim directly, but may work through lower forces. The 'lower' spiritual forces (*lagu*) are malicious evil spirits, who may also attack an innocent victim out of hunger.

Witches (*bokshi*) transcend these rigid categories. Although *bokshi* could theoretically be male or female, in practice they are invariably women. The most usual method of attack is to cast a spell over the victim's food, by blowing a verse of spell-bound words (*mantra*), or to invoke a willing *lagu* as helping agent. Because food is often an instrument of witchcraft, many Nepalis, it is said, prefer to eat at home. The field of potential attack is thus narrowed to the kitchen hearth. The motive for witchcraft is usually jealousy or anger. Rights over property are the most common source of disputes, especially between brothers. Much witchcraft is, inevitably, attributed to the dangerous daughters-in-law who play a major role in the kitchen. The women in a family must bear all the blame for witchcraft and conflict-mongering; this is essential to the survival of the strongly patriarchal society. Conflict between women in a household is acute.

Food pervades concepts of disease and curing, both as the actual cause of certain complaints and more generally as a symbol and metaphor in illness diagnosis and healing. This reflects the ritual importance of food in a society based on caste, even though blended with other traditions in Nepal. Where illness is attributed to an imbalance of temperature between food (or air) and the body, the remedy is, simply, to redress the balance by altering body temperature with food, or by a change in external temperature. 'Hot' (*gharam*) foods include meat, eggs, milk and tea; 'cold' (*sardhi*) foods include yoghurt, cucumber and bananas. Excessive eating of food in either category can result in illness, and many stomach upsets are attributed to the properties of food which has been eaten. The diet is adjusted accordingly to restore the balance. Treatment, prescribed by the male 'experts' who maintain control of diagnosis and receive payment for it, is often carried out by the women of an afflicted person's family. There are several methods of treatment which the lay person can perform, the most important being spell (*mantra*) blowing, the wearing of amulets, food offerings and herbal remedies. The more serious 'treatments' of spirit invocation and exorcism are the domain of the expert *shaman*.

There is an interesting, but unsurprising, sexual division of labour in this sphere of illness and health care, misfortune and its resolution. The flip side of the patriarchal coin, which in practice attributes witchcraft solely to women, endows few women with supernatural healing powers or the ability to learn them. Their role is confined to unspiritual treatments produced easily as part of their domestic role in preparing food, or in the polluting sphere of childbirth, in which men cannot, and do not wish to, be involved. There are few, if any, reports of general or spiritual healers being women. Powers of healing and spirit divination would give women an independence and prestige that is never accorded to them within South Asian caste society, and would necessitate their social and physical mobility to enable them to answer calls for their skills and advice.

Women as caretakers of health and life: the invisible role

The role of women in the promotion of health and maintenance of life is clearly far wider than purely physical reproduction in pregnancy and childbirth. The wider role embraces primary health care within the household, where women are responsible for 40 per cent of the population aged less than 15 years. Women detect and treat symptoms, assess the need to consult more specialized experts, decide when and whom to consult, and carry out treatments prescribed by 'experts' and professionals, whether in technological or in 'traditional' medicine. Their invisible expertise and role as caretakers of health and gatekeepers to health care are crucial, since the HMG Basic Health Services cannot and do not meet the expressed need.

Women as gatekeepers of health in pregnancy and childbirth

Within this strong patriarchal ideology, women are of passing, peripheral and ambiguous importance. They prepare the food (unless menstruating or recently delivered), but eat last and therefore, within poor households, eat little. Nutritious foods such as milk, eggs and vegetables may be scarce, and are invariably offered first to men and honoured visitors. Women's health and nutritional state during pregnancy is often unsatisfactory, and this will affect

Table 16 Source of care received by women giving birth in four districts of Nepal

Source of care	Surkhet	Nuwakot	Tanahu	Dhankuta
Self/none	82.7	57.5	65.0	72.5
Friend/relative	8.7	20.5	30.0	4.8
Traditional midwife	5.1	5.7	2.5	15.0
Hospital/HP	2.6	5.4	1.2	7.6
Other	1.0	10.0	1.2	0

Source: Institute of Medicine, Kathmandu 1977, 1979 a, b, c.

the baby's health and resistance to infection. With high fertility and extensive breastfeeding, there is danger to the woman's own nutritional state and the health of her next child. Dysentery and infectious diseases such as measles and tuberculosis kill 25 per cent of children before the age of 5; their resistance would be higher if they were well nourished within the womb or when breastfed. The critical importance of the pregnant mother's own health is acknowledged. The government plans to promote education in nutrition by village health workers, but there are few of these, and one wonders how effective they will be in promoting the nutrition of daughters-in-law, who do not enjoy a high status in their husbands' extended families.

Childbirth itself is solely the business of women, since it is ritually polluting and therefore dangerous to men. Men, children and women who have had no children (and may be inauspicious) are excluded from the delivery area. Experienced female relatives keep the pregnant woman warm during labour and massage her. The great majority of women deliver themselves in labour; others receive help from friends or relatives (Table 16). Traditional midwives (surehni or dhai-ama) are not widely used, and have apparently declined in rural areas (Bennett 1976; Stone 1976). Most health 'knowledge' is gained from talking to friends, relatives and neighbours – and, in the sphere of midwifery, is based on 'common knowledge' often dismissed as old wives' tales by professionals (HMG 1979). There is increasing recognition by the Department of Health of the importance of this invisible, lay sector in maternal and infant health. The department is now planning a programme of 'increasing support to the local birth attendant' (HMG 1979). There are moves to ensure that old wives' tales relating to care of women during the experience of childbirth do not become displaced by alienation caused by the professional control of young midwives attending patients during labour.

Women in Primary Health Care

Perhaps one of the greatest contradictions in the new vogue of Primary Health Care is that it essentially remains the domain of male professionals and 'experts'. Some of these may have less technological training than their colleagues in hospitals; but nevertheless, there has been a trend to make 'Health for All' para-professional. The majority of ill people in Nepal still turn to lay sources of health care, treating themselves on the basis of 'common knowledge' or 'old wives' tales', or turning to friends and relatives. Many effective and simple treatments fall within the domain of women as housekeepers, child-carers and food-preparers. It is they who give the yoghurt (*dahi*) to the child with a gastro-internal upset; it is the women who adjust the level of spices (*piro*) in the curry when a stomach complaint is diagnosed. Such 'old wives' tales' are not all myth, and many are based on a wealth of know-ledge developed over many years of experience and observation.

Within the realm of infant and childcare, particularly in pre-venting and treating dysentery (the commonest cause of infant mortality), there have been welcome developments in promoting common knowledge of simple, life-saving measures such as the preparation of oral rehydration fluid (*aussadhi pani*, lit. medicine water). Women village health workers would have an important role to play in visiting households, sharing knowledge which would otherwise be inaccessible to women who do not have the time or social mobility to go to the local health post. Health for all depends on power and control over one's own health, and access to information is an important element.

There is a second aspect to women's invisible role in primary health care: the decision to refer to a 'specialist' or 'expert'. The decision to refer is based on awareness of the limitations of a woman's own skills, and a knowledge of other skills available. Given the major role of women in referring to other practitioners for health care, it is vital that they should be aware of the possibilities and limitations of options available. It is also important for the experts to whom she may refer – particularly in health posts, which may entail a day's journey – to be aware of the woman's own potential and limitations. An awareness of the effective remedies which are available within her domain – such as sugar solutions and herbal treatments for infected ulcers – would enable the health post assistant to give information, advice and treatment which relate to the patient's experience. As alarm grows at the meteoric increase in the resistance of common infections to antibiotics which can be bought in single doses in most bazaars, the role of women in deciding when to purchase medicine is crucial to attempts to reverse the tide. Unless women are given information which enables them to make informed choices about their own and their families' health, effective primary health care in Nepal will never be realized.

Women as caretakers of health: invisible to patriarchy and professionalism

Although there may be important differences between the concepts of ill health as mechanistic failure or as holistic dis-ease, there are important similarities which are relevant to this discussion. Established bodies of medical knowledge have largely become the institutionalized domain of the male 'professional', whose expert services are sought and usually paid for in cash or in kind. There is often an element of specialization within the general paradigm: surgeons, physicians and health post workers in technological medicine; astrologers and herbalists in the holistic approach. When a practitioner feels that a health problem is beyond the scope of his expertise, he will refer the patient on to another 'expert'. The masculine gender is used advisedly here, for all institutionalized medical systems are the preserve of male 'professionals'; this is a reflection of the patriarchial structures of society.

A second similarity between the western and Nepali approaches to healing is that childbirth and the 'normal' condition of pregnancy are not easily incorporated into the general schema of dis-ease. The contradictions inherent in a pregnant woman being a 'patient' in a western hospital have been described elsewhere (Doyal 1981). Complications come within the sphere of obstetricians, but straightforward childbirth remains the domain of the midwife. In the developing world, childbirth is very definitely the business of women, and is more explicitly divorced from the general system of dis-ease. In many other parts of the Third World, a new mother and her baby are perceived as polluting and in need of ritual cleansing before they can return to mixed society. The reproduction of life remains the preserve of women, despite attempts to professionalize it within the technical model.

Women in Nepal clearly fulfil an important but invisible role in promoting and protecting health and life. They are the first point of referral for many ill people, and have retained control over their own role in reproduction. They have a wealth of knowledge and experience which is easily accessible to friends and relatives. At the same time they are risking their own and their children's health because of the toll taken by their dual roles in production and reproduction within the ailing, domestic economy. Any effective health programme must incorporate this invaluable role of women, building on it and working through it. Women must also themselves become better informed of the need to take more care of their own health, which is jeopardized by their attempts to fulfil their dual role to the satisfaction of patriarchal society.

Information and training must be given to women to enhance their control over their own health and bodies, and to improve access to health for the whole population. The inclusion of these hitherto invisible caretakers of health and life is a necessary element of any primary health care programme which is meant to be used by the majority of the population.

4 Production and reproduction of malnutrition in an urban slum in Khulna, Bangladesh

Jane Pryer

Editors' introduction

Gender is deeply implicated in human survival. In industrial societies, the social construction of gender is often examined only in economic and psychological terms, as if gender only mattered in labour power and in interpersonal relations. Gender does enter into relations of dominance, relations of production and relations of reproduction, but it does not stop there; it extends to human life and death. Chapters 2, 3 and 4 show the many ways in which gender permeates questions of survival, at widely different scales of analysis; from South Asian examples, they show also how strongly dominance, production, reproduction and survival are linked. At the macro-level, the map of the sex ratio has elusive links with economic requirements and with structures of patriarchy (Chapter 2); all current explanations for the map call on either relations of production or relations of dominance. Harriss and Watson in their search for an explanation have illustrated the remarkable number of aspects of life in which gender is so important that the resulting discrimination against girl children may endanger their lives. In Chapter 3, Pearson has shown how women's role as caretakers of health is shaped by Hindu ideology in Nepal; where childbirth is ritually polluting and disease is attributed mainly to (female) witches, the stigma attached to being female bears heavily on women and affects everybody's chances of survival.

Now we can see at the micro-level how, in a Bangladeshi slum, gender roles in income-earning become crucial to the survival of the individual and the household. In this chapter Pryer describes income as more essential to nutrition and survival than any other factor. For a satisfactory understanding, we must reconcile the macro with the micro. Harriss and Watson have shown that facile explanations of macro-features may not resist empirical testing at that or other levels. Careful reading of this chapter shows us why: the web of life histories and the tragic and complex details show what we must face if we attempt to explain the geography of gender in South Asia. The general lessons hold true for the whole of the Third World: the limitations of our theory, the prime importance of gender, the complexities and the wholly unacceptable conditions.

Introduction

This chapter describes the characteristics and processes at the household level which result in severe undernourishment in one urban slum. It is based on research carried out between January 1984 and January 1985 in Medja Para slum (pseudonym) in Khulna, Bangladesh. The ways in which women, in particular, cope with severe economic deprivation will be illustrated by two household profiles. Most case study research on malnourished children has concentrated on the role of women as caretakers of the children's psychological and nutritional well-being, stressing the nature and quality of the mother–child relationship, and the constraints operating on it. This approach is seriously inadequate because the mother–child relationship is dominated by external social and economic forces. In this chapter the household (defined here as people who live together and eat from a common pot), rather than mother and child, is taken as the unit of analysis; this reflects broader social and economic hypotheses on the nature and origin of nutritional risk.

Khulna is the second seaport and third city of Bangladesh, with a population of some 600,000 in 1981. The city has a modest industrial base and is an important regional trading centre. It has grown rapidly in recent decades, and growth is expected to continue; the estimated population in AD 2000, with a moderate growth rate, is 2 million. The impetus behind this growth has been industrialization and large influxes of dispossessed migrants after political disturbances: the partition of India and Pakistan in 1947, communal riots in Calcutta in 1965, and the Liberation War in Bangladesh in 1971. In addition, immigrants come from the surrounding rural areas in significant and increasing numbers. The result has been a mushroom growth of both legal and illegal slums; these are officially estimated to contain approximately 35 per cent of the present population, though about 50 to 60 per cent is likely to be more accurate. Though not homogeneous, these slums are characteristically insanitary and overcrowded and have much poverty; environmental and nutrition-related diseases are prevalent. A Save the Children Fund nutritional survey of Medja Para slum in 1984 found 67 per cent of children under 5 to be second or third degree malnourished (that is, under 75 per cent of expected weight for age using NCHS growth standards: WHO 1983; Gomez *et al*. 1956).

The seven case studies discussed here were the 'most malnourished' in a cross-sectional sample of 220 households, of which 11 per cent had third degree malnutrition (under 60 per cent of expected weight for age). Wasting and stunting of children under 5 were severe (wasting is leanness indicating current undernutrition, and stunting is height retardation indicating chronic undernutrition (Waterlow 1972)). Each case study was examined by informal but structured interviews over a period of fifteen to thirty hours. Household adults were interviewed independently and statements of events were corroborated from as many sources as possible. Interviews included the following subjects:

1   Household history, with particular concentration on crises, crisis management and loss or accumulation of productive assets.
2   Household economy, including details on how households cope or fail to cope daily and/or seasonally when food is inadequate.
3   General observations on allocation of domestic work.
4   Nutrition and morbidity history of the children under 5 and pregnancy history of the mother.
5   Weight and height of all household members.

The case study households

The seven households (Tables 17 to 20) are not recent immigrants to Khulna; their length of residence ranges from twelve to forty years. All had come in from the surrounding rural areas having been impoverished by loss or decline of productive assets, serious illnesses and/or death of adults. Severe poverty and assetlessness have been associated with the disintegration of the family unit (Blaikie *et al*. 1979; Cutler and Shoham 1985), but that had not happened here. Of the seven households, one is an extended family, five are nuclear families and one is a household headed by a widow. The range of household sizes is four to seven, which is normal for South Asia.

The distribution and severity of undernutrition within the households, and the prevalence and types of illnesses of parents, are shown in Tables 17 and 18. Most household members are acutely and/or chronically undernourished, but women and young female children are particularly so: the average BMI of adult females is 14.35, in comparison with 17.38 for adult men. (BMI or Body Mass Index is weight, in kilograms divided by height

Table 17   Nutritional status of parents and severely undernourished children and health status of adults

	(Mina) 1	(Hasna) 2	3	4	5	6	7
				Case study numbers			
Youngest malnourished child [1]							
sex	F	F	F	F	F	F	M
age (months)	27	21	21	39	44	34	26
weight/height%	75	71	78	71	78	76	75
height/age%	80	83	83	76	73	84	84
weight/age%	52	54	56	45	49	57	55
Mother							
age (years)	40	32	30	26	23	25	27
weight (kg)	25	38	27	33	30	34.5	34
height (m)	1.42	1.55	1.53	1.48	1.45	1.42	1.54
BMI	12.4	15.8	11.5	15.1	14.3	17.1	14.3
Father							
age (years)		50	47	36	28	32	40
weight (kg)	dead	42	50.5	42.5	39.5	49	45
height (m)		1.59	1.66	1.59	1.52	1.67	1.60
BMI		16.6	18.5	17	17.1	17.5	17.6
Major current illnesses [2]							
father	—	gastric ulcer TB	—	gastric ulcer	—	blind	gastric ulcer
mother	gastric ulcer	gastric ulcer	gastric ulcer, severe anaemia	severe anaemia, acute depression	gastric ulcer	gastric ulcer	severe anaemia, gastric ulcer
Days incapacitated in November 1984 due to sickness:							
father	—	23	0	5	0	0	0[3]
mother	0	0	5	10	5	0	25

Notes

[1]   Weight for height, height for age, weight for age are percentages of NCHS growth standards.

[2]   All diagnosed by a physician.

[3]   Severe tooth pain prevented father from secondary occupation for whole month; family lost half its income.

squared, in metres; it is an indicator of leanness in adults. A level under 20 is considered to have a higher risk of mortality.) If we use NCHS growth standards, 56 per cent of all female children in the case study households (compared with 12 per cent of male children) are either second or third degree undernourished (under 80 per cent of expected weight for height). Sexual discrimination against female children in terms of both malnutrition and mortality have been reported in South Asia, particularly in the north (see, for example, Chapter 2). This survey would lend support to this thesis. Such levels of undernourishment place women at risk of producing infants of low birth weight, and young children at risk of elevated levels of morbidity and mortality. In addition, the prevalence of chronic illnesses among parents is extremely high. Most of these illnesses are related to poor environment, physical and mental stress and inadequate nutrition. They have a direct bearing on

Table 18 Nutritional status of other household members in the sample households

Case number	Sex	Age (years)	Weight for height (per cent)	Height for age (per cent)	Weight for age (per cent)
1	M	12	96	74	46
(Mina)	F	10	64	73	31
	F	7	75	79	49
2	F	15	94	90	66
(Hasna)	F	12	90	96	79
	F	7	84	93	82
3	F	13	85	89	65
	M	8	81	94	75
	F	4.5	91	85	68
4	M	12	85	86	57
	M	8	90	77	55
5	M	7	85	78	54
	F	5.5	74	73	44
6	M	7	83	83	58
7	F	12	93	80	48
	M	9	92	87	69
	F	4.75	84	83	62

Notes: Weight for height, weight for age, height for age are percentages of NCHS standards.

Table 19 Employment profile of case study households – May/June 1984

Case no.	Earner dependency ratio	No. of consumption units (CU)	Occupation of father	Monthly income (taka) value cash and kind	Occupation of mother	Monthly income (taka) value cash and kind	Occupation of other household members	Monthly income (taka) value cash and kind	Total monthly income in taka[1]			
									wage	in kind	other sources	house-hold total	per CU
1 (Mina)	2:3[2]	3.48	(dead)	—	Domestic servant and water carrier (casual labour)	cash = 180 kind = 70	Son bread seller (piece rate)	cash = 120	300	70	—	370	106
2 (Hasna)	2:5	5.47	Fisherman (self-employed)	cash = 166 kind = 200	—	—	Daughter servant (casual)	kind = 224	166	424	—	590	108
3	2:4	4.49	Quilt maker (self-employed)	cash = 800	Match box maker (piece rate)	cash = 90	—	—	890	—	8	898	200

4	1:5	3.6	Crockery seller (dependent labour)	cash = 500	—	—	500	—	500	139
5	2:3	3.58	Tailor (piece rate)	cash = 550	Tutor (casual) cash = 35	—	535	—	535	149
6	1:3	2.94	Beggar	cash = 450 kind = 480	—	—	450	480	930	316
7	1:5	4.17	Labourer (permanent employee), rickshaw puller (casual)	cash = 1379	—	—	1379	—	1379	331

Notes

1. 35 taka = £1 sterling.
2. Two earners to three dependants.

the productive capacity of household members, partly reflected in the number of days' earnings lost through physical incapacity (Table 17).

The economic characteristics of these seven most severely undernourished households are shown in Table 19. They come from the poorest strata within the slum. They own few or no productive assets and no savings and are therefore vulnerable to any crises. All depend on the market for employment and food. They are deeply indebted (to between 65 and 353 per cent of monthly income, with an average of 173 per cent), predominantly from the informal credit market: not money lenders, but landlords, employers, shops and neighbours. As the only productive asset of these households is labour, all adults who are not physically incapacitated do some sort of wage work. Men are employed in a variety of poorly paid activities, most of which fall within the 'informal sector' (Chapter 1), including rickshaw pulling, daily labour and petty trade and hawking. As in the rural areas, employment is highly seasonal; the monsoon months of June to September are the lean months. The number of case study households in which women are contributing financially to the household budget increased from three to five between June and November 1984. In two of these households women were major earners. The women in the other two households were incapacitated from wage work by severe illness and/or full term pregnancy. In the slum economy, work for women consists predominantly of paid domestic work or home-based piece rate work; both involve long hours and extremely low wages, both absolutely and in relation to male wages. The number of women who were forced into illegal black marketing increased substantially during 1984.

Income in cash and kind from the labour of household members was low, unreliable and seasonal. The proportion of total expenditure on food was between 57 and 90 per cent (average 68), the remainder being spent on priorities such as rent, fuel and debt repayments. Food intake (as assessed by dietary recall) provided between 980 and 2240 kilocalories (average 1764 kilocalories) per consumption unit (CU), which is well below the Indian Council of Medical Research's (1981) Recommended Daily Allowance for energy of 2800 kilocalories per CU. (A consumption unit is defined here as the energy requirement of a moderately active male adult. It is used to standardize households of differing demographic composition. It should be noted that Recommended Daily Allowances are a hotly contested issue; the Indian levels are used here for consistency.)

Table 20 Household level responses to insufficient income and insufficient food (November 1984)

Case no.	Credit from shop	Loans for food	Sell/pawn household utensils	Charity or gifts of food	Begging/acquisition of free food	Increase or decrease expenditure on food according to income	Fasting	Use of capital from business	Savings from high season work months	Increase no. of workers/diversify employment	Send family to relatives in crisis
1 (Mina)	Yes			Yes	Yes	Yes	Yes			Yes	
2 (Hasna)		Yes			Yes	Yes	Yes	Yes		Yes	
3	Yes	Yes	Yes			Yes	Yes		Yes	Yes	
4		Yes	Yes			Yes	Yes				
5	Yes					Yes		Yes			
6	Yes	Yes	Yes		Yes	Yes				Yes	Yes
7	Yes	Yes			Yes	Yes				Yes	

The most common responses of households to insufficient income and insufficient food are shown in Table 20. They can be summarized as follows:

1 sending as many able bodied persons out to work as possible;
2 maximizing the diversity of the employment profile;
3 taking loans/credit for food;
4 pawning/selling household assets;
5 begging/gifts from relatives and/or neighbours; and
6 cutting back on food quantity/going without food.

These expedients are struggles for survival rather than solutions to the problem of malnutrition. We need to know how this extreme condition was reached. The two profiles which I have selected, dramatic though they may seem, are representative of households which suffer extreme malnutrition. They illustrate not only the household experiences which result in nutritional crisis, but also the economic options available to women faced with extreme deprivation in a slum economy.

Household profile one

Mina, a Hindu widow, aged about 40, lives with her son aged 12 and her three daughters aged 10, 7 and 27 months (case study 1 on Tables 17–20). Of the seven children to whom she has given birth (five girls and two boys), two (one girl and one boy) died within the first month of life. Mina had no institutional education; her son irregularly attends class 1 of a local free community school. All household members except the son are acutely undernourished. The 27-month-old and 7-year-old daughters are 75 per cent weight for height, the 10-year-old daughter 64 per cent weight for height. Mina herself is only 25 kilograms (see Tables 17 and 18). In addition, Mina has been suffering for the past ten years from a gastric ulcer, and is unable to afford medical treatment. (A high prevalence of gastric and peptic ulcers has been reported in Bangladesh: Chowdhury et al. 1981.) There are two income earners for three dependants in the household. Mina works ninety-one hours a week as a domestic servant and water carrier, and her son thirty-five hours a week as a piece rate bread seller. Total household income in cash and kind is 385 taka (£11) per month, comparing with approximately 1500 taka (£43) per month for an average slum household of the same size (Table 21). (The price of rice in June 1984 was 8 taka per kilogram.) They own no productive assets and their household possessions are minimal.

Table 21   Household one

Household monthly income		Household monthly expenditure	
	In taka		*In taka*
Mina: cash	180	Food: cash	165
kind	70	kind	70
The son: cash	135	Fuel:	45
		Rent:	40
		Debt repayment:	50
Total income:	385	*Total expenditure:*	370

Notes:
The household totals 3.42 CUs (see text, p. 138). Energy intake totalled only 980 kilocalories per CU; the Indian RDA is 2800 kilocalories per CU.

In January 1985, one month after completion of our interviews, the three daughters were admitted to a nutrition rehabilitation centre run by Save the Children Fund. (Here they receive about 600 kilocalories of food daily, and medical treatment.) On admission they were diagnosed as acutely undernourished (marasmic) and having a range of infections (notably of the upper respiratory tract), worms and acute signs of severe micronutrient deficiency diseases associated with lack of vitamins A, B and C and iron.

Household history: the process of impoverishment

Mina's economic circumstances throughout her life have inextricably entwined with those of her father and later, after marriage, of her husband. She was born in the village of Kamarkhola, in Khulna district. Her paternal grandfather was a farmer and owned 4 bhigha (0.54 hectares) of land. Her father was disinherited as a result of protracted family quarrels. After a period of mental illness and vagabondage, he migrated to Khulna when Mina, the youngest of four daughters, was only 2 years old. In Khulna the family survived, her father working as an unskilled labourer and her mother as a servant. As she grew older, Mina, like her older sisters, contributed to the household budget by working as a servant till she was 12, when her marriage was arranged to a distant cousin, Ashok Lal, aged 27. Ashok Lal's financial position was somewhat better than that of Mina's own family. He jointly owned 12 bhigha (1.6 hectares) of land with his two brothers, and worked as a potter in the vicinity of Mina's home village.

But then came the Liberation War, and the family were Hindu. Mina's husband and brothers-in-law sold all the family land for a value far below the market price. They were subsequently robbed and threatened, and finally fled to a refugee camp in Amarcoat district in India. On their return, in 1972, they had lost everything, and their house was occupied by Muslims. The Hindu potter with whom Ashok Lal had worked had also fled. Without any means of livelihood, Mina and her family came to her parents, who were by that time living in the Khulna slum. Ashok Lal worked as a vegetable seller (on a credit basis) with Mina's father, and Mina worked as a servant. They continued to live with her parents for the next eight years, but, as Mina's family grew to eight members, the one room in which they all lived became insufficient. So, in 1979, they rented a plot of land from Mina's employer and built their own thatched hut. By this time it was apparent that Mina's husband had contracted TB. On moving, he changed his occupation and share-cropped a small plot of land adjacent to their home which belonged to the landlord. He did this work for two or three years until his illness compelled him to give it up. He suffered severely for a further two years and died in May 1984. He refused all forms of medication for religious reasons, till the final few months of his life, when, under pressure from both his family and the landlord, he received treatment from a variety of homeopaths, spiritual healers and allopaths including a TB specialist. The cost of this treatment, totalling 3000 taka (£86), was met mainly by an award in a court case, lodged by the landlord in their name, over the death of Mina's father in a road accident three years before.

During this time and since, Mina has been totally dependent on her patron who is both her employer and landlord. He arranged and paid over 200 taka for Mina to have hospital treatment for severe dysentery. He arranged an interest-free loan for the marriage of her second daughter just before her husband's death and occasionally gives them food when the children are importunate from severe hunger. Mina's relationship is deferential: without his help they might not survive. But he pays her less than 50 per cent of the market rate for domestic service. Mina, obviously acutely aware of their shortage of food, cannot obtain loans or credit for food, and has no household assets of value to pawn or sell. The household survives on the earnings from wage work, from gifts from neighbours and the landlord, and from scavenging in the gutters.

How has this chronic condition of acute poverty and stress affected Kohinoor, the youngest child? The data on pregnancy history, nutritional practices, morbidity, allocation of childcare responsibilities, and the use of health services suggest that several processes are at work. First, the mother, grandmother and an experienced Hindu midwife who delivered the child stated that

Kohinoor was extremely small at birth. Mina discarded her colostrum, as is common in Bangladesh, depriving Kohinoor of its immunological properties, and fed Kohinoor sugar water for the first three days of life. From 3 days to 5 months Kohinoor was exclusively breastfed: thereafter she was weaned on to rice, and then family food. Supplementary breastfeeding continued till she was 18 months of age, by which time Mina's milk supply had dried up. This weaning practice is unique among the seven case studies. Normally, infants are weaned very early, from birth or up to two months of age, on to low energy dense gruels. (Low energy dense gruels have been reported as highly contaminated and implicated in cycles of infection and undernutrition: Barrell and Rowland 1979; Black et al. 1982; Watkinson 1981.) Others are exclusively breastfed for prolonged periods of up to eighteen to twenty-four months. (Prolonged exclusive breastfeeding has been shown to lead to growth faltering as nutrient requirements outstrip what is provided by breastmilk: Waterlow and Thomson 1979; Whitehead and Paul 1981.) Direct evidence from Save the Children Fund monthly records shows a history of faltering growth for Kohinoor which indicates illness and/or inadequate intake of food. She has been recorded as severely undernourished from eight months of age. From 8 to 27 months her weight for age as a percentage of NCHS growth standards has fluctuated between 49 and 54 per cent. Her mother confirms high incidence of common illnesses such as diarrhoea, fever, upper respiratory tract infections, and measles. An important point is that Mina did not seek medical treatment when Kohinoor was ill. Before her husband's death the predominant reason for this, according to Mina, was her husband's religious conviction, to which he bound all his household members.

Mina goes out to work from 7 a.m. to 4 p.m. and from 6 p.m. to 11 p.m. every day. In her absence her third daughter (now aged 10 years) assumes responsibility for childcare and domestic work. But her own state of critical undernourishment (64 per cent weight for height, 31 per cent weight for age) makes her physically incapable of discharging the responsibility of the two children forced upon her, and in all our visits the children were found to be ill and unattended. After his morning's work, Mina's son cooks the noon meal of 0.5 kg rice and salt, which is shared by the four siblings. Their only other meal is a small portion of Mina's only meal of 0.25 kg rice and dal, supplied by her employer as charity, which she brings home in the evening to share with her children.

It is clear that the crisis of poverty, malnutrition and ill health threatens the lives of all members of the household except the less severely malnourished son. (This exception may be seen as a desperate struggle to ensure the survival of the household.) 11 per cent of households in the survey were in a similar nutritional state.

Household profile two

Hasna, aged 32, lives with her husband Abdullah Rahman aged 50, and their four daughters aged 15, 12, 7 and 21 months, and their niece aged 17. Hasna has given birth to eight children (seven girls and one boy); two of them (one girl and one boy) died in the first year of life. Only the niece, who has read up to class 5, has had institutional education. The 15-year-old daughter was married 2 years ago. Her husband works in India as a casual labourer and does not remit money. She and her elder married sister, who lives elsewhere, have each given birth to one son; both boys died within the first month of life. The nutritional status indicators (Tables 17 and 18, case study two) show that Hasna and the youngest daughter, Shahanna, carry the main burden of acute undernutrition within this household. Shahanna is 71 per cent weight for height, and Hasna weighs 38 kilograms.

In November 1984, there were four earners to three dependants. Hasna blackmarketed Indian saris, Abdullah was a fisherman, the 12-year-old daughter was a servant in the main market, and the niece helped Hasna with selling saris.

Hasna is the economic and social household head, though she has a husband. He is suffering from suspected TB, chronic gastric ulcer and severe unidentified head pains. In addition, he is acutely mentally depressed. He was able to work for only fifteen days a month in mid 1984, and only six by the end of the year. They have no productive assets and minimal household possessions.

Household history: the process of impoverishment

Abdullah Rahman was born in the village of Pakhimara in Khulna district. His paternal grandfather was originally a large farmer owning 100 bhigha (33.3 acres) of land, but this land was washed away by the river Shesbati. The patriline was rendered landless, and Abdullah's father and grandfather worked as woodcutters in the Sunderban forests. Abdullah was third of his parent's six surviving children. His father's income was insufficient to meet household needs, so Abdullah was sent at the age of 11 years to his uncle in Khulna to work as an unskilled labourer, remitting his wage to the home village. Six or seven years later his father died of diarrhoea, and that had severe financial repercussions for the family. It was at a time of crop failure and hardship in the village. The family responded by migrating to kin in India, where they remained for four or five years, returning after the food emergency in the village had ended. On their return, Abdullah worked as a woodcutter, like his forefathers. His brothers worked as day labourers. At the age of 27 or 28 years, Abdullah married Hasna, who was at that time 10 years old. Two daughters were born. Then in 1968, Abdullah became partially paralysed and they migrated to Khulna in hope of treatment and survival. There, they lived in a squatter settlement and survived for the first year by Hasna's begging with her younger, apparently undernourished, daughter, who subsequently died. During this time Abdullah was treated by a homoeopath, and his paralysis was so far reduced that he was able to start working part time in the wood depot of a Bihari who had given alms regularly to Hasna.

During the Liberation War, Hasna's household went to their home village for safety and food. When they returned to Khulna, the Bihari for whom Abdullah had worked had been killed and his depot looted. (Muslim Biharis, who had fled from Bihar as a result of massacres during the partition of India in 1947, were victimized during the Liberation War as they supported the ruling Pakistanis.) For the next twelve months Abdullah did a variety of casual jobs, but in 1973–4 he started dealing in black market wheat, which at that time had a good market, and the household entered a phase of accumulation. In the three or four years his business grew to a working capital of 10,000 taka (£285). However, in 1976–7 there was a dramatic decline in the black market supply of wheat. Abdullah was forced to disinvest. First, he spent 5–6000 taka of his capital for consumption (to make up the fall in income) and for treatment of Hasna, who was at that time severely ill with her seventh pregnancy and later miscarried. In addition, 3000 taka was stolen from their home. Since this time they have been once again struggling to survive. Abdullah was forced to close his wheat business, and did a variety of casual jobs until he started fishing on an irregular basis five years ago. His worsening health status has meant that he can work for a few days a month. Five years ago, Hasna started working as a servant. She ceased working on the birth of her youngest daughter and her third daughter took her place.

On our first visit in June 1984, the household was under severe economic strain (see Table 22 which is Hasna's budget for June 1984). It spent the final 150 taka of a 1000 taka loan, which accounts

Table 22   Household two, June 1984

Household monthly income		Household monthly expenditure	
	In taka		In taka
Abdullah: cash	166	Food: cash	185
kind	200	kind	424
Daughter: (12 year old)		Rent:	30
cash	—	Fuel:	60
kind	224	Sickness:	30
		Household necessities:	2
		Cigarettes and pan:	20
		Total household	
Total income	590	expenditure	751
		Balance	−161

Notes:
The household totals 5.47 CUs. Energy intake was only 1350 kilocalories per CU.

for the gap between the figures of income and expenditure flows. The loan had been granted six months before by an agency of the Bangladesh government as part of an income generating scheme, but was spent entirely for consumption. The household also cut back on expenditure and on consumption of food; this included fasting for two days per month.

In mid 1984, Hasna responded to her crisis, by entering the black market in a trade which, despite its risks, has become common among women living in the slum. The Indian sari black market is highly differentiated. There are large and small traders, middlemen/women and piece rate sellers, all with different levels of income and risk. The majority of slum women involved in this trade work at the lower end of the scale on a piece rate basis, earning between 2 and 5 taka per sari. Hasna, however, entered the market as a small trader. She borrowed 1000 taka (£28) from three women in the slum at an interest rate of 10 per cent per month. She goes to the Indian border three or four times weekly and buys three to six saris at a time from an Indian woman. Purchase and sales prices vary according to the quality of the sari. The profit margin per piece is between 20 and 50 taka, after deductions for transport and payments of 'bakshish'. ('Bakshish' or bribe was apparently paid to border officials at the rate of 10 taka per sari.) On the basis of transaction prices over two weeks in November 1984, I estimate that her net income during that month was approximately 1000 taka (see Table 23). Hasna understands the risks of illegal merchanting. Four of her women friends known to us have been imprisoned. Indeed, Hasna herself had had 750 taka worth of saris confiscated at the border two months before our interview. This represented her total savings, during the five months that she had been working, after meeting household expenditure and the interest payments on her loan.

The repercussions of the household level stress on Shahanna, the youngest child, were similar to those in profile one, as indeed they were for all seven case studies. Similar indirect evidence pointed to low birth weight. After birth, Shahanna was fed sugar water for the first three days, colostrum being discarded; she was then exclusively breastfed from 3 days to 2 months. Thereafter, she was weaned on to a weak rice flour gruel, as Hasna's breastmilk supply was inadequate – possibly a result of her own poor nutritional status. At 7 months, solid rice was introduced. Supplementary breastfeeding has continued throughout, but this has declined to only once or twice daily since Hasna has been trading.

Evidence from Save the Children Fund monthly records and from Hasna herself again reveals patterns of faltering of growth and of infections from an early age. Hasna did not seek medical help during Shahanna's illnesses. The reason in this case lay in deeply embedded spiritual beliefs. Hasna believed that she had been severely attacked by spirits during her previous pregnancy, and that this was the cause of her miscarriage. While Shahanna was in the womb, Hasna suffered from vomiting, stomach cramps and

Table 23   Household two, November 1984

Household monthly income		Household monthly expenditure	
	In taka		*In taka*
Abdullah: cash	100	Food: cash	442
kind	120	kind	344
Hasna: cash	1000	Rent:	30
Daughter: cash	—	Fuel:	120
kind	224	Debt repayment:	260
		Sickness:	100
		Household necessities:	21
		Cigarettes and pan:	30
Total income	*1444*	*Total expenditure:*	*1347*

Notes:
Energy intake had increased as a result of Hasna's employment to 1960 kilocalories per CU.

dysentery. She attributed this, together with her difficult birth, the smallness of Shahanna at birth and her inadequate supply of breastmilk, to the same spirits. Similarly, her perceptions of Shahanna's ill health and undernourishment revolved around spirits which 'attack young children' (Blanchet 1984). Although these belief systems are held by the majority of slum women and indeed are common throughout the whole of Bangladesh, they may be more heavily relied upon as explanations of misfortune among those who have little or no control over their life circumstance (Hartmann and Boyce 1983). As in Mina's case, no substitute mother was obtainable. In Hasna's absence, Abdullah and Runa (the 15-year-old married daughter) were responsible for childcare, but Abdullah was too ill and depressed, and Runa was nearly always absent, socializing with young adolescents of her own age in the slum, so for the greater part of the time Shahanna was left unattended.

Conclusions

All seven case studies, and these two detailed profiles, illustrate that the processes which generate a chronic condition of acute impoverishment not only cause malnutrition in children, but also in adults and older children, indicating total inadequacy of household level food supplies. Women and young children are the most vulnerable when food is scarce.

Production of malnutrition

The most important factors leading to the process of impoverishment and malnutrition within the two household profiles are both diverse and familiar: serious illnesses and/or death of the chief earners, leading to the sale of assets, and to a deepening entrenchment of poverty through loss of earnings; environmental hazards beyond human control, such as erosion of land by rivers, causing loss of assets; membership of, or economic dependence upon, a religious minority group causing either distress selling of assets or loss of the sole source of employment. Within the household, malnutrition is promoted by being a 'female child'.

Reproduction of malnutrition

The reproduction of malnutrition depends upon the constraints operating at the household level and the household's ability to cope. The two households described, like all the case study households, come from the poorest strata in the slum. Assetlessness and indebtedness, compounded by chronic incapacitating ill health of adult earners, led to inadequate, unreliable and seasonal flows of food. Such is the chronic shortage of food, with the fundamental insecurity that this entails, that households must struggle to survive at all; they cannot possibly solve the problems of malnutrition.

How do female head of households cope?

The two women in these households had no assets, and the few jobs open to them involved long hours of work and sexual discrimination in wage rates. One was forced into heavy dependence on a patron and the other into illegal trading. Both strategies are highly precarious. The inadequate level of existence derived from Mina's patron threatened the lives of all household members, except the less seriously malnourished son. Similarly, the criminal and economic risks of Hasna's selling of saris posed a heavy threat to the long-term viability of her household.

Repercussions of household crises upon young children

Infants were reported as being small at birth, possibly a consequence of the mother's own inadequate nutritional status. Weaning practices are inadequate, possibly as a function of poverty. Avoidance of medical treatment during periods of acute illness is attributed to religious and/or spiritual beliefs.

Adequate caretakers for the children are not available. Child neglect is the inevitable result.

Acknowledgements

Acknowledgements are due to John Seaman, Alex Gray, Ghias Uddin and Bikash Roy of Save the Children Fund (UK) for institutional support in their urban community programme in Khulna; to the Overseas Development Administration (ODA) for academic funding; to Barbara Harriss, David Nabarro, Edward Clay, Hilary Standing and Naila Kabeer for academic supervision and comments on this chapter. The high degree of diligence and dedication of my principal interviewers, Ms Rowshan Are, Anzuman Ara and Runa Shahnaz are gratefully acknowledged; it is less easy to thank the household members from whom data were collected. They gave up their time, often during periods of acute economic and emotional stress: without their co-operation, this study would not have been possible.

Part Three

Agriculture, Gender and Capitalist Penetration

5 Rural women's work in sub-Saharan Africa and the implications for nutrition

Esther Trenchard

Editors' introduction

As agriculture becomes more complex and more differentiated, and spatial divisions of labour become more pronounced, the demand for female labour in agriculture often decreases (see Chapter 1). The upshot in any one place still depends on regional or even local features, particularly where there is substantial mechanization. In Africa, cash crop and plantation work has tended to be male, while in Asia there is an important female presence; in Latin America, work in bananas and sugar is traditionally male, but much labour in new cash crops is female, from the fruit of Chile and central America to the tomatoes and onions of north-east Brazil. This Part will show that gender roles and their outcomes are regional and specific, and so are the forms of change in gender when capitalist penetration reshapes the production process and the organization of space.

Just as women's contribution to agricultural production has no simple, direct relationship to capitalist penetration, so too the implications of change vary from place to place (Chapters 6, 7 and 8). Trenchard, however, inquires into five dissimilar African ethnic groups which share a highly unattractive trend: the woman's mothering role in providing food for her family has been retained, but her previously adequate access to the means of production on the land has been reduced; cash cropping does not support subsistence, but competes with it for land, labour and resources. Trenchard's five case studies include labour reserve, direct production and transitional areas. In all of these women's role in food production both provides cheap labour and is central to nutrition. The relative and absolute losses in women's production and incomes bear immediately on the food crisis of many African countries. It emerges that current policies and recommendations for the African food crisis are likely to fail, because women's work is largely ignored and the situation therefore wholly misunderstood. The evidence is that capitalist penetration has simultaneously both depended on women's food-providing role and undermined it, until the whole system is now in danger of collapse.

Introduction

There has been much talk, especially since the UN Decade for Women, on how women have been excluded from the development process and tend to be among the most disadvantaged of those from the poorer classes in low income countries. ILO labour force estimates for twelve sub-Saharan African countries give crude economic activity rates ranging from 2 to 47 per cent for women and from 46 to 63 per cent for men (ILO 1977). This suggests that African women are less economically active than men. The impression is shattered if one includes women's part in that most essential of activities, the production of food (see Figure 2). The ILO definition of economic activity is activity that produces commodities or services for exchange on the market; by excluding subsistence food production this makes the bulk of women's work invisible.

For a fuller understanding of woman's role and activity patterns it is necessary to consider her position within the household in terms of rights, obligations, exchanges, the allocation of resources and responsibilities, and the division of labour. Furthermore, this should be placed within the context of wider social structures of co-operation, obligations, rights and exchanges.

In this chapter I examine the following hypotheses:

1 That the 'development process' in sub-Saharan Africa has tended to marginalize, demote or downgrade rural women in the subsistence sector. This has reduced their productivity and their control over resources relative to that of men (Boserup 1970).
2 That rural women's total work burden in sub-Saharan Africa has increased (Boserup 1970).
3 That the marginalization and increase in the work burden of women can best be understood as an integral part of the process of accumulation of capital, rather than as meaning that women were excluded from development (Deere 1982).
4 That these changes may have important implications for nutrition, affecting both overall levels of food production and also women's increased work burden, with stress on her social and biological roles.

Figure 2 The importance of women in the food system

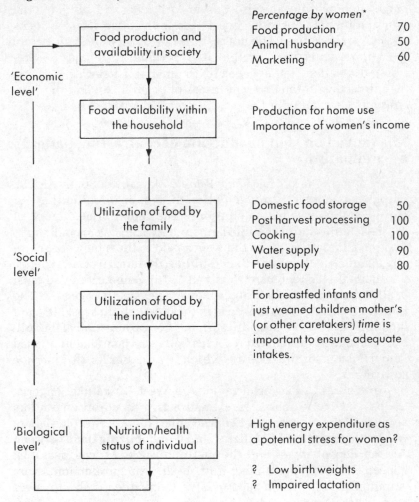

	Percentage by women*
Food production	70
Animal husbandry	50
Marketing	60

Food production and availability in society

'Economic level'

Food availability within the household

Production for home use
Importance of women's income

Utilization of food by the family

Domestic food storage	50
Post harvest processing	100
Cooking	100
Water supply	90
Fuel supply	80

'Social level'

Utilization of food by the individual

For breastfed infants and just weaned children mother's (or other caretakers) *time* is important to ensure adequate intakes.

'Biological level'

Nutrition/health status of individual

High energy expenditure as a potential stress for women?

? Low birth weights
? Impaired lactation

Sources: adapted from Payne 1984;* United Nations Commission for Africa 1974.

I examine these hypotheses on the basis of material drawn from studies of five ethnic groups from different regions.† These show some of the variety in women's roles and work patterns and the different ways in which they have changed. Two points should

†The main sources for these studies are as follows: *Luo*, Pala Okeyo (1980 a and b), Hay 1976; *Kikuyu*, Stamp (1975/6), Kershaw (1975/6); *Ewe*, Bukh (1979); *Kusasi*, Whitehead (1981); *Mandinka*, Weil (1973), Dey (1981).

be noted. First, these examples certainly do not represent the full range of possibilities in sub-Saharan Africa. Second, although the term traditional is used to refer to the indigenous social systems and cultural practices, I do not assume that these were static before the Europeans arrived, or that it is possible to define the pre-colonial situation. Rather I wish to examine, as a historical process, the interaction of the external forces of colonialism and the penetration of capital with the pre-existing social structures.

The impact on food production of contrasting patterns of colonialism

In east and southern Africa (e.g. Kenya, Zimbabwe, South Africa), Europeans adopted a settler policy to exploit opportunities for mining and intensive cash cropping. They appropriated much of the most fertile and accessible land, and Africans were confined to designated reserves. Since the wages paid to the men were generally insufficient to support their families, the burden of subsistence production fell on women (Newman 1970). Some tribes had most or all of their land appropriated and were physically relocated. The Luo and Kikuyu groups looked at in these case studies lost less land than some others, but they still suffered from exhaustion of the soil, because in their designated reserves there was insufficient unused land available for the clearing which is essential for shifting hoe cultivation.

In contrast, the coastal regions of West Africa (e.g. Nigeria, Ghana and Ivory Coast) were unattractive to European settlers because of the climate and malarial infestation. Here colonialism was for the purpose of stabilizing and monopolizing trade between African dependencies and the metropolis. So African peasants, instead of being prohibited from cash crop production, were 'stimulated' by tax and labour laws to produce cash crops for European markets.

The Kusasi in north-east Ghana are in a relatively inaccessible region for cash cropping; since the 1920s the region has served as a source of labour for the cocoa farms and mines in the south. Commercial rice farming, introduced 110–160 kilometres away in the mid 1970s, now requires even more male labour (mostly seasonal). Increasingly, men are growing cash crops (rice and groundnuts) at the expense of the staple, millet.

The Ewe, in the Volta region, south-east Ghana, live just outside the main cocoa-growing region of southern Ghana. Their area initially served as a labour supply zone. A survey in 1976–7 still showed a net out-migration of males (42 per cent of households were under a female head). Early migrants, in the 1890s, brought back cocoa beans, which grew well; but cocoa trees did not become widespread until the 1920s, when they took up much of the best land and most of the attention of men remaining at home.

In the Gambia, by a combination of commercial incentives and taxes around the turn of the century, Mandinka men were generally encouraged to use their dry land to grow groundnuts for cash at the expense of their food crops (millet and sorghum). Men used some of their groundnut revenues to purchase local or (increasingly) imported rice to make up the deficit. From about the 1950s women began to cultivate rice in tidal swamps as well as in rainfed swamps, and so produced higher yields.

Land tenure

The basic feature common to most traditional African land tenure systems was that ownership was by group (lineage or community). A most important point is that *land could not be bought or sold*. In four of the case study regions, inheritance was basically patrilineal. The typical pattern was that male lineage elders controlled the allocation of land among members of the patrilineal descent group, although the Mandinka had a somewhat different system (see pp. 159, 162).

Among the Luo and Kikuyu, women did not receive any allocation of land from their fathers' lineage, but had rights to use the family land until they married. Sons did not receive their allocations of lineage land until they had married, on which their wives had clearly defined rights to farm and to control the produce. Among the Kikuyu there was a second category of land users, the *ahoi*, who were not lineage members, but borrowed lineage land. This land could not be passed on to a descendant, but while land was plentiful the position of the *ahoi* was secure.

A Ewe woman could receive an allocation of land for her own use from either her father's or her husband's lineage; in the case of household fields from the husband's lineage, husband and wife worked together. A Kusasi woman, before marriage, worked on the household farm, the produce of which was controlled by the male household head. After marriage she would work on her husband's household farm, and she would also receive a small allocation from her husband's lineage for private use.

Among the Mandinka there were two main forms of land use. Compound land (dryland and rice-land) was under the control of elders and its produce was for household use. In addition, both men and women had, with the permission of the elders, the right to clear land for individual use. This land could be exchanged or given away (but not sold) and could be inherited. Men tended to pass their private dryland fields to sons and women their private rice-fields to daughters, though this was not always possible if a daughter married into another village.

In all five groups, individuals were not solely dependent on inheritance of existing lineage land, as rights of use could be established by clearing unused land.

Changes in land use

Among the Luo and Kikuyu the colonial reserve system restricted the land available for allocation among lineage members. This led to an increased fragmentation of land holdings and a weakening of lineage elders' authority, as individual household heads assumed autonomy and passed their fallow land to their own sons. The most serious undermining of women's rights to land came with the reform of land tenure, which was initiated by the colonial government in 1955 but implemented after independence in 1963. This created individual ownership of land, with the right to sell it. Land was usually registered in the man's name, and the legal status of women's usufruct rights became uncertain. In practice women continued to cultivate land as lineage wives; but their security was removed, as absent husbands or sons could sell the land from under their feet. Women lost the important role of guardians of their sons' land until marriage.

Pressure on land in West Africa occurred for other reasons. In the main cocoa belt, the value of land increased dramatically and a private land market developed. Migrant cocoa farmers bought up large tracts of land. Among the Ewe there was no significant private land market, but men increasingly took the most fertile forest land for their cocoa farms, thus reducing the land available for women to grow food crops. Male farmers laid claim to land in which they had invested labour, and passed on their fallow land to their sons. The land itself could not be sold, but if a permanent tree crop like cocoa had been planted the trees could be sold. The introduction of claims to ownership of land undermined women's traditional rights of use. Women had previously had the right to cultivate lineage common property; now they had to get permission from individual men to use their fallow land. Also, as many women's husbands were absent and thus not available to assist in clearing land, the women's choice was further restricted to land which was easy to clear – which tended to be the least fertile. The Kusasi, living in a subsistence/labour supply zone, apparently did not experience any serious disruptions of the traditional lineage system of land tenure. Among the Mandinka, women's access to land was in some ways more secure, as they farmed different land from the men and had more control over the allocation of land for rice. As the men's cash cropping used dryland, they did not compete for the women's rice land. However, as the value of rice land increased, especially as more use was made of the higher-yielding tidal swamps, some conflict has been observed between men and women over the rights to allocate rice land. Recent major drainage and irrigation schemes have greatly increased these problems.

The division of labour by gender

Tables 24–28 summarize the traditional division by gender of the main agricultural tasks in the five case study groups. However, it should be noted that, in addition to their agricultural tasks, women in all five groups were also responsible for post-harvest processing, collecting fuel and water, cooking, childcare and other 'domestic' work. Children also helped in many tasks.

Changes in women's work patterns

The pattern of a withdrawal of male labour into the cash economy, and consequently of increased responsibilities falling on women for food production, can be traced in all five cases; but there are

Table 24   Luo (Kenya): division of labour

Land	Female tasks	Male tasks
Household fields	Planting, weeding, harvesting	Clearing fields, some assistance in weeding, (animal husbandry)

Notes:
Crops: sorghum, finger millet, barley, maize (to a lesser extent), sesame, sweet potatoes, yams, pumpkins, beans, green gram, various vegetables.
   Organization of labour: A new wife would initially work with her mother-in-law, and would often continue to help mother-in-law with weeding and harvesting after establishing her own household.

significant variations within this broad theme. At one extreme, among the Luo and Kikuyu of Kenya, there was an increasingly long-term male migration for waged employment. The women in

Table 25   Kikuyu (Kenya): division of labour

Land	Female tasks	Male tasks
Household fields	Planting, weeding, harvesting	Clearing fields
Men's gardens	Assistance	Cultivation (Animal husbandry)

Notes:
Crops: 'household fields' – sorghum, millets, maize, various beans, peas, vegetables, sweet potatoes, cassava, and taro (an exclusively female crop); 'men's gardens' – sugar cane, bananas, yams, tobacco (mainly for social and ritual purposes), sometimes sweet potatoes and cassava.
Organization of labour: Women had a strong tradition of working co-operatively on each other's fields. There was a practice of bringing sufficient firewood to a woman who had just given birth to last until she was capable of collecting again herself. The other women in the new mother's household would cook food for the group providing the firewood.

Table 26   Ewe (Ghana): division of labour

Land	Female tasks	Male tasks
Household fields	Planting (except yam), weeding, harvesting (except yam)	Clearing fields, digging mounds, planting yam, weeding, harvesting yam

Notes:
Crops: 'household fields' – yam planted with maize, cassava, okra, red pepper, beans, groundnuts and cotton. Married women sometimes also had their own separate plots on which they would cultivate any of the above except yam. On forest land, cocoa, yam and plantain were grown and oil palm (from which oil and wine are extracted) grows wild.
Organization of labour: Traditionally, women and men would work together on the same fields.

Table 27 Kusasi (Ghana): division of labour

Land	Female tasks	Male tasks
Household fields	Planting millet, harvesting	Clearing fields planting millet, weeding, harvesting
Men's private fields	Planting (groundnuts and rice), planting millet, harvesting	Clearing fields, planting millet, weeding, harvesting
Women's private fields	Clearing fields, planting, weeding, harvesting	Clearing fields, weeding, harvesting

Notes:
Crops: 'household fields' – millet; 'men's fields' – millet, guinea corn, rice, groundnuts; 'women's fields' – rice, groundnuts.

   Organization of labour: All household members were obliged to work on the household fields; in addition men and women would work on their private plots. The ability to command labour was crucial in determining a household's viability. 'Exchange' labour parties would be provided with food and drink. Men could use the unremunerated labour of their wives (and often of all women in the household) on their private plots, but women had to provide food and drink to obtain male labour.

Table 28 Mandinka (The Gambia): division of labour

Land	Female tasks	Male tasks
Rainfed (and increasingly tidal) swamps	Rice cultivation	
Dryland		Cultivation of millet, sorghum, maize and groundnuts

Notes:
Organization of labour: Women and men worked separately on swamp and dryland respectively. Both women and men worked in labour groups; women's labour groups were also cooking units. Within a household there could be a number of labour groups and cooking units.

these two groups responded differently. The Luo women came to rely increasingly on trade to supplement the family's income. The Kikuyu organized collectively (drawing on traditional support networks) to use modern techniques. After 1953, when restrictions were lifted, they increasingly experimented with a cash crop, coffee.

At the other extreme, the Mandinka in the Gambia experienced very little male migration. Here, men increasingly put their labour into the more profitable cash crop (groundnuts) and neglected the traditional 'male staples'. Thus the cultivation of the 'woman's staple' had to become more intensive. Rice cultivation was extended from the rainfed swamps to the tidal swamps; these gave greater yields, but walking distances were also greater.

The Kusasi and Ewe from Ghana in some ways represent an 'intermediate' position: they experienced both net male out-migration and a shift of male labour at home from the traditional staple towards cash crops. In both these cases, traditionally, men had the greater responsibility for the main staple; among the Kusasi for cultural reasons, and among the Ewe because of the labour needed for yam cultivation. Even when women became more responsible for ensuring the household's food supply, they could not take over growing the main staple. Kusasi women had to intensify their efforts to grow groundnuts to make up shortfalls of millet during the hungry season; they also relied increasingly on income from petty trading to buy other foods. Ewe women increasingly cultivated the less labour-intensive cassava to replace yam, and also relied on petty trading to supplement the household's day-to-day income. Cassava has a higher output of starch per labour hour but is low in protein. The quality of the diet suffers also from the practice of close planting (to reduce weeding), as fewer vegetables can be grown. The processing of cassava is also more time-consuming.

In all the groups, women's work load was increased; but the nature of the extra work depended on the 'traditional' division of labour by gender and the local agricultural system. While, broadly speaking, women were responsible for the household's subsistence needs, the equation of 'male' with 'cash' and 'female' with 'subsistence' is an over-simplification. First, women's unremunerated labour was often crucial for men's cash crops. Second, it became vital for women to have a cash income from trading in order to buy additional food and other household necessities. Women's cash income tended to be smaller than men's, yet it was often more important for the household's standard of living.

Allocation of resources and responsibilities within the household

In all five study areas men and women had separate sources of income (which were not pooled) and different areas of responsibility. Women in the different groups had different degrees of responsibility for the actual *production* of food – but all had ultimate responsibility for food, as it was they who prepared the meals. The general trend was that the changes in work patterns described above gave men greater access to cash, but areas of responsibility did not shift correspondingly.

Among the Luo, a woman on marriage would join her husband's household and help her mother-in-law in domestic and agricultural tasks. After she had had two or three children and had contributed to several harvests, a wife would achieve full status as a woman and set up a separate household, cultivating the fields allocated from her husband's lineage and cleared by her husband. In polygamous marriages, each wife would set up a separate household and have her own granary. After having provided food for her husband and children, a woman had the right to dispose of any surplus. This was frequently traded for small livestock (sheep and goats) which could be exchanged for grain in bad years, thus providing some security. Men had a separate source of income from animal husbandry (mainly cattle) and from trade in iron, poison, shields and headdresses. Among the Kikuyu the pattern was basically similar, but there were minor differences.

In both groups, as male labour was withdrawn into waged employment, men who could afford it might contribute some money to enable their wives to hire assistance in those tasks, notably clearing, for which they were traditionally responsible. Men also often contributed towards children's clothes and school fees. However, assistance in the provision of food was not generally perceived as their responsibility. Also, Stamp (1975–6) observed among the Kikuyu that men now, even if they remained in the homelands, had many places in which they could eat outside their homes, so they were less aware of the predicament of their wives and children. At the same time men's social activities, particularly the consumption of alcohol, became separated from lineage activities and family responsibilities and were frequently reported by women to be a serious drain on household resources.

A Ewe woman also would, on marriage, initially join her husband's compound, but would establish her own cooking pot and become an independent unit of production and consumption.

Husband and wife worked on the same fields, and, as previously noted, Ewe men played an essential role in the cultivation of the main staple, yam. Produce from the household fields was primarily for subsistence; but, in contrast to the Luo and Kikuyu practice, men controlled the disposal of any surplus. Ewe men traditionally played a larger role in the production of food, but women took more of the ultimate responsibility, as it was they who did the processing and cooking. Male migration left 42 per cent of households in 1976–7 with a female head; these women had to take complete responsibility for providing food. As the men turned their attention to the cultivation of cocoa, women became totally or partially responsible for the provision of food even in households with a male head present.

Men were more likely to contribute towards occasional expenses, such as school fees, farm tools and maintenance of the house, than towards food and the day-to-day requirements. Women complained that men spent their money on 'bachelor consumption goods' such as cigarettes, palm wine, clothes, watches and, less often, bicycles and radios.

Kusasi households tended to be much larger than those discussed so far. All household members were responsible for working on the household fields to produce the main staple, millet; but the produce was controlled by the male head of household, and only he was allowed to place his hand in the household granary. Each married woman in the compound was responsible for preparing meals for her husband and children from allocations of millet given out by the household head on a regular basis. Men and women also cultivated private plots, and had complete rights of disposal over the produce from these. Men's fields, however, tended to be much larger, and could provide a substantial personal income. In contrast, much of the proceeds from women's smaller plots (on average less than 0.5 hectares) went towards the purchase of other necessary items in the household diet (for example, salt, fat, vegetables, fish) or was directly consumed. Women's groundnut crops were traditionally viewed as a 'hunger crop' for their children when the millet supplies ran out during the pre-harvest hunger season.

Kusasi women were not allowed to grow millet, and were thus completely dependent on men for the staple food. They were, however, traditionally responsible for supplementing the diet from the produce of their private plots. As it became increasingly profitable for men to concentrate on cash crops, it fell to women to make up for the shortfall in the production of millet. For men, there was a sharp distinction between cash crops, the proceeds of which were for their personal use, and millet, which could not be sold. For women there was no such distinction, and they had more direct responsibility for their children's needs. Again, women's petty trading became increasingly important.

Mandinka households also tended to be large, and could contain a number of separate production and consumption units, but they worked separately, men on dryland and women on swampland. This gave them more equal responsibility for the provision of food, and clearly defined rules applied to both sexes about making up deficits. As men were increasingly drawn into groundnut production, they would usually spend part of their earnings on local or imported rice to make up their household obligations. There was one asymmetry. On both household and private fields, women grew rice, whereas men traditionally grew millet, sorghum and maize. The women's rice was all for household use, but men's crops on their private fields were primarily a cash crop. Once again, as women did the cooking, the final responsibility would fall on them; and their private incomes were used for buying extra cooking ingredients.

Discussion

In order to extract surplus value, necessary for the process of capitalist development, the external forces of colonialism had to break the 'reproductive cycle' of the traditional economic system (see Bernstein 1982, for a detailed analysis of this process). Two particularly significant methods of achieving this were the withdrawal of labour (mainly male) and, in some cases, the withdrawal of land. The relationship of women to the process of commercialization was essentially contradictory. On the one hand, they appear to have been 'left out' of the commercial sector and its benefits; on the other, their being 'left behind' to maintain the traditional food systems was essential for the economical maintenance and reproduction of the labour force needed by the process of commercialization. This has remained true in more recent agricultural development. In the now distorted 'traditional system', women's work and responsibilities are greatly increased; the nature of the increase has varied with differences in the traditional social system and historical context.

Traditional systems of land tenure came under pressure in those areas (e.g. parts of Kenya and southern Ghana) where commercial farming took much of the most productive land. This exposed the weakness of women's rights of access. When land was abundant and women's labour crucial, their rights to use land were well defined and apparently secure. However, these rights were dependent on their relationships to men, and were lost as soon as the men wanted to turn land over to commercial use (for example, among the Ewe cocoa farmers) or when land registration was enforced (as in Kenya). Similarly, the *ahoi* among the Kikuyu in Kenya lost their previously secure usufruct rights. A serious consequence of women's lack of a legal title to land has been that they have been unable to obtain the credit essential for taking advantage of improved agricultural techniques.

The case studies show that the women in the different groups traditionally had different degrees of responsibility for the cultivation of food, and that they coped in different ways with the withdrawal of male labour (and sometimes of land). For example, Luo, Kikuyu and Ewe women had to take on responsibility for clearing land (a 'male' task), although wherever possible they hired male labour to do it. Ewe women changed the cropping patterns to reduce the need for labour. Kikuyu and Mandinka women intensified their methods of cultivation, the Kikuyu to try to maintain yields and the Mandinka to compensate for the reduced production of 'male' staples. Kusasi women were traditionally excluded from cultivation of the staple, and this meant that they had to use their small private plots more intensively and to trade in order to make up the shortfall in staple production. All the women became more dependent on income from trade to supplement their households' basic diet, in contrast to the previous situation when their trading was chiefly for personal use and to accumulate wealth as a security.

To understand why women had to attempt to maintain the productivity of the traditional systems in these ways we must realize that traditionally women's and men's income and responsibilities had been well defined and *separate*. Changes in the division of labour and in access to cash were not matched by corresponding changes in areas of responsibility.

Implications for nutrition

Women's activities are important at all levels of the 'food system' in these case studies (Figure 2). I will now examine some of the possible implications for nutrition of the changes discussed above. Economic implications include both macro-level effects on the availability of food in society as a whole, and micro-level effects on its availability within the household. Social implications include the possibility that a woman's increased burden of agricultural work might conflict with her domestic tasks, especially childcare and nutrition. Biological implications include some possible effects of high energy expenditure on women's nutritional/health status, on their infants' birth weights and on lactation.

Changes in rural women's work

Economic effects

At the macro-level, it is estimated that women contribute 70 per cent of the labour involved in food production in Africa as a whole (UNECA 1974). Using the case studies I have discussed the ways in which women tended to be marginalized in subsistence agriculture during the colonial period. More recently the tendency has been for women's agricultural productivity to continue to be lower than that of men because women have poor access to agricultural extension services and credit. There is also evidence that a number of agricultural development schemes have suffered because they have ignored women's central role in traditional food systems and their experience and expertise in farming. In some areas productivity is declining in absolute terms because of environmental deterioration and because women are often restricted to marginal land. While male labour is being withdrawn into waged employment and the production of cash crops (both food and non-food), the importance of female labour in food production tends to increase. Food crises have become increasingly frequent in Africa; in this context the low productivity of women's food production takes on additional significance.

At the micro-level, in addition to producing a large proportion of the food consumed within the rural household, women earn income from trading which is of vital and increasing importance for the family diet. Increased reliance on petty trading for day-to-day domestic requirements was found in all five case studies and has been noted elsewhere (Obbo 1981). Tripp (1981) in a study of a farming community in northern Ghana, with a millet based cultivation system and pattern of male migration comparable to the Kusasi (see above, p. 162), found that the trading activities of both mother and father were positively associated with higher nutritional status for their children, whereas agricultural variables were of relatively minor importance. Of all the variables tested, the trading activity of the mother was the one most significantly associated with the nutritional status of the child. The profits from women's petty trading were much smaller than those from the men's long-distance trading, but they were directly translated into the nutrition of the children.

From what has been said above and from the five case studies, two main reasons emerge why women's income is often more important than men's for the household nutrition. First, women are traditionally responsible for their own children's food, and it is a common practice for women and men to keep their incomes separate. Second, although women's incomes tend to be smaller, they are often more regular; men's earnings from long-distance trade and sales of cash crops may be received only a few times a year.

Social effects

There is ample recognition of the importance of women's social roles in choosing, buying, preparing and cooking food for the family, and in particular in feeding young children and infants. What I wish to examine is how far a heavy or increasing work burden upon a woman in subsistence farming (and other economic activities) may come into conflict with her domestic duties. It should be emphasized that, in view of the importance of a woman's income for the nutritional status of her children, a woman in a marginal situation might have to balance the costs and benefits of devoting her time to childcare with those of gaining extra income, and that any reduction in the time devoted to childcare should not be perceived as 'neglect'.

The following points emerge from time allocation studies. (The most rigorous and informative research has been conducted in the Philippines, but the few African studies indicate similar results.)

1   Infants take up a significant amount of a woman's time. This becomes less as children grow up, until they become capable of saving time for their mothers. Even so, children's productive and reproductive inputs may be counterbalanced to some extent by their consumption and the consequent need for increased household income (Da Vanzo and Lee 1983). (It is important that there are other people available to help to look after children; the mother's time allocation should not be isolated from its social context.)
2   Is productive work time reduced by childcare? Is time devoted to childcare reduced by productive work? The main reduction

appears to be in the woman's leisure time, with possible implications for her health. The fact that a woman's leisure time tends to give before either childcare or work indicates the importance to her of these two duties.

3 The compatibility of the work with childcare appears to be an important factor determining the woman's time allocation. There is also the problem of whether simultaneous childcare and work can impair the efficiency of either or both (Da Vanzo and Lee 1983). This raises one of the problems with time allocation studies: that equivalence of time units cannot be assumed.

The importance for the children's nutrition of the mother's time devoted to them depends on their ages and on whether adequate help is available. An infant up to 6 months old is usually almost entirely dependent on breast milk; after that supplementary foods reduce the need for the mother's actual presence. Children are, however, commonly at least partially breastfed until about 18 months or 2 years old. During the weaning (which may be gradual or abrupt), the quality of childcare is important to ensure that feeding is adequate, particularly if a bulky weaning food is used (Weisner and Gallimore 1977; Woolfe *et al.* 1977).

Biological effects

Pregnant and lactating women are conventionally considered to be a nutritionally vulnerable group. However, energy requirements during pregnancy are controversial. It appears that in practice the energy intake of a pregnant woman can fall to as low as 1500–1800 kilocalories per day before the growth of the foetus is impaired. In women with low energy intakes, high expenditure of maternal energy may contribute to a low birth weight by decreasing the blood flow to the placenta, particularly if there is a lot of standing activity during the last trimester. The question is how far women doing heavy work, especially during peak seasons, are able by adaptation to reduce their expenditure of energy during late pregnancy and early lactation. Obviously, local cultural customs will largely determine how far the woman is allowed or expected to withdraw from her work, and also whether she is able to eat more.

Studies in the Gambia give somewhat inconsistent findings on whether or not women's physical activity is reduced during pregnancy and lactation (Thomson *et al.* 1966; Roberts *et al.* 1982), but they do indicate a trend for women to be deficient in energy and for birth weights to be lower during the rainy season (Paul *et al.*

1979). In women who are unable to accumulate sufficient sub-cutaneous stores during pregnancy, there is some evidence that lactation may be impaired. But the rainy season is also a time of high energy expenditure, low energy intake and high incidence of infections, so it is difficult to disentangle the importance of these factors. High expenditure of energy is undoubtedly an additional stress for women whose nutrition is already low.

Policy issues

Figure 3 summarizes some of the policy issues arising from women's major, but often neglected, role at all levels of the food system and suggests some possible strategies.

However, any consideration of women's development must take into account the structural bases of women's inequality; a piecemeal approach is likely to have little effect. For example attempting to increase women farmers' productivity by training women extension officers is likely to have limited success unless women's lack of collateral for credit and lack of time to attend training courses are also tackled. Income-generating schemes that ignore the woman farmer's already heavy work burden may benefit only those better off women who have the time to take advantage of such projects. Labour-saving technologies that ignore the power relationships in a community can end up being labour-displacing; they may, for example, induce women to take work in collecting water or processing grain for richer farmers in return for a wage. Technological innovations at one stage in the agricultural process, for example a new high yielding crop, can have repercussions on later stages – which may increase women's work in (for example) weeding, transplanting or harvesting.

Policies are likely to be inadequate if they overlook the rela-tionship between the subsistence sector and the commercial sector and women's roles in each. There may be links between women's essential function in providing food at minimal cost for the house-hold and the function of the agricultural sector in providing cheap food for African society as a whole. The low-price food policies common in Africa have been often criticized as evidence of 'urban bias', and the World Bank Report on sub-Saharan Africa (1984) identifies them as fundamental causes of the food production crisis, because they do not provide adequate incentives to agricul-tural producers. The report advocates radical measures to improve both incentives and the working of domestic markets, and argues that the current crisis in agricultural production should be dealt

Figure 3   Policy issues arising from women's roles in the food system

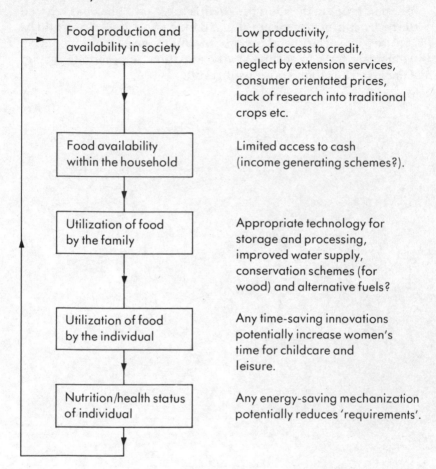

Food production and availability in society	Low productivity, lack of access to credit, neglect by extension services, consumer orientated prices, lack of research into traditional crops etc.
Food availability within the household	Limited access to cash (income generating schemes?).
Utilization of food by the family	Appropriate technology for storage and processing, improved water supply, conservation schemes (for wood) and alternative fuels?
Utilization of food by the individual	Any time-saving innovations potentially increase women's time for childcare and leisure.
Nutrition/health status of individual	Any energy-saving mechanization potentially reduces 'requirements'.

with by increased integration into the world market. A crisis in food production affects women much more than men because they contribute so much to and are so dependent on agriculture; yet this, like an earlier report, appears to ignore the central importance of women's role. The policies advocated do not look very promising for women (see also Allison 1985). The World Bank alleges that African agriculture has a stronger comparative advantage in the world market in the traditional export crops (coffee, cocoa, cotton, groundnuts, palm products, tea and tobacco) than in the food staples. It suggests that African food production should be opened to market forces by more specialization in export crops and more use of purchased inputs – and argues that measures to increase food production should emerge in the long run from increased sale of export crops in the short run. In this the World Bank has ignored the restructuring of gender roles and food systems which would be required by such 'liberalization'. More pressure would be put on women's efforts to secure family nutrition, and serious further damage to nutrition could well result.

6 Women farmers and traders in Oyo state, Nigeria – a case study of their changing roles

Heather M. Spiro

Editors' introduction

State intervention is increasingly important in changing structures of production, whether in building roads (Chapter 8), resettling whole populations (Chapter 7) or recommending development strategies (Chapter 5). Unfortunately, planners are often ill-advised about the activities of the female half of the population and the plans therefore ill-founded. Planners must confront both the importance and the diversity of gender. In West Africa, for instance, the forms of social and economic complementarity of the sexes are extremely varied; in commerce, the ratio of women to men (in officially recorded economic activity) is 1:7 in Niger, 2:1 in Ghana. Given the will to inform themselves on the way gender works in different localities, planners could achieve a great deal by appropriate methods of rapid rural appraisal (Chambers 1981, 1984). More detailed studies are also required.

Spiro's meticulous recording of the time spent by women in different activities in two Yoruba villages yields data of both local and general importance to policy. Yoruba women are regarded as traders *par excellence*, of economic independence and historical political power. Spiro balances and shifts this image by demonstrating that all women, regardless of occupation, spend more time farming than trading. Usually, this is on their husband's land. For all women, domestic activity is the most time-consuming. Policies predicated on a female population which is free to switch from notionally full-time trading into other activities, or at liberty to dispose of time without reference to husbands, would clearly be set to fail. Our image of Yoruba women must be reshaped. Of more general application is the evidence that childcare is regarded as compatible with either farming or trading; it almost appears as if the conventional conflict between fertility and economic activity does not arise (Chapter 1). Andean farmers (see, for example, Chapter 10) and many academics would be equally startled by a daily structure of female domestic tasks in which cleaning and laundry consume little time and childcare almost none. Maybe this is how 'the same women who become the mothers of six or seven children . . . also provide 60 to 80 per cent of the agricultural labour supplied on the continent of Africa' (Ware 1983).

Introduction: the invisible woman

In most of sub-Saharan Africa, much of South-East Asia and some parts of Latin America, women make up between 40 and 80 per cent of the agricultural labour force. They cultivate, weed, harvest, process and store food crops, carry water and fuel, look after animals, go to market and prepare and cook food, in addition to their household and family responsibilities. Yet the long hard hours that rural women work are statistically invisible. Women's work is only marginally reflected in statistics on labour force and income, because economists assume that 'work' is performed for money and exists only in the modern sector. 'In most households throughout the world, the work performed by women is not valued in economic terms, and the same attitudes are reflected in the way that governments define and measure women's work for the purpose of national censuses' (ILO 1975).

The concept of the 'non-economic' role of women is, however, deeply entrenched throughout the world, and the role of development planners (the majority are male) in exporting western models of the 'proper' role of women has further strengthened this and other misconceptions about women. For example, though rural women have received attention from international bodies such as the United Nations, the World Health Organization and the Food and Agriculture Organization, they have been studied as farmers' wives, housekeepers, cooks and mothers rather than as farmers, food processors, traders and entrepreneurs in their own right. Thus their social role as wives and mothers has long been acknowledged, but their economic roles have been *underestimated*, *undercounted* and *undervalued* by rural men and women themselves, and have seldom been articulated or acknowledged by development planners, even though often observed. Consequently women have not been benefiting fairly from development, and in some circles the failure of development itself has been attributed to the failure to involve women in it in a substantial way.

The insistence of the early 1970s that women should be 'integrated into the development process' has given way to the realization that 'the role of women in food and agricultural production is already so pervasive in most countries that exhortations to "integrate" women into rural development run the risk of sounding ridiculous' (Sicoli 1980). Instead, it is now argued that development planning should recognize the part women have traditionally played in their societies, and devise policies that bring their roles fully into account and build on to them, rather than undermining their position. There is still a long way to go: commonly, 'without any individual intention or even thought about women, the overall effect is to exclude them absolutely from development planning, or to categorize them as a special group, with separate welfare-orientated projects that can sometimes be attached to the main development project' (Rogers 1980).

The invisible made visible: a case study among the Yoruba

Method of approach

The data discussed in this chapter were collected in 1977, over a period of twelve months, from Oluwatedo, a traditional unplanned village with medium sized farms, and Ilora Farm Settlement (IFS), a planned government settlement with large farms.

General information on household composition, farming and trading was collected from all adults in households which fulfilled the criteria of the survey. A household was defined for this study as a woman or a group of women, with or without husbands or children, living in a house, eating and sleeping there and with financial or service commitment to the household. Households containing only men were therefore excluded from the survey. This information provided a framework from which women in different occupations could be selected for more intensive study. On the basis of what the women themselves defined as their main occupations, four main groups emerged. Some women farmed only; some farmed and traded; some traded only; and some said they neither farmed nor traded. Within each occupational group women were further divided into four age groups: 15–24; 25–34; 35–44; and 45 plus. With this framework, a stratified random sample was drawn for an intensive study over a period of five months from August to December 1977, to provide detailed data on women's farming and trading as well as on their domestic and leisure ('other') activities, with particular emphasis on time budgets.

The research area

The two villages, Oluwatedo and Ilora Farm Settlement (IFS), are inhabited by people of the Yoruba language and culture. They lie in what used to be called Yorubaland, south-west of Oyo, in the forest savanna-mosaic zone of Oyo state, Nigeria. The area is of gently undulating countryside, and as a result of the use of fire and varying degrees of shifting cultivation and grazing, vast area which were woodland have been converted into savanna. The area lies below 300 m, and it consists of grassland with trees scattered in very variable density, forming gallery forest along the rivers and relict patches away from them. Temperatures are high throughout the year, with a daily mean of 26°C. Four seasons can be distinguished: a cool, dry season (November to March) associated with the Harmattan wind from the north; a hot, dry season (August), and two hot, wet seasons, one from late March/early April to June and the other in September and October. The two rainy seasons allow for double cropping during a total of six or seven months. The rivers and streams are highly seasonal, rising to peak flow in September, but diminishing to a trickle between January and March. At that time, water collection, which is one of the most time-consuming domestic chores for women, becomes extremely arduous. There are wells in Oluwatedo, but they run dry in the dry season.

Oluwatedo was founded in 1926 as a temporary farming camp. It is a traditional nucleated village of mud huts with tin roofs, grouped round a lorry park, with a church, a mosque, a primary school, three stores (a barber/cobbler and two beer parlours) and a grinding machine. A periodic market meets in the village every four days. The population in 1977 was 304 (compared with 466 in 1969), of whom 131 were adults (73 women, 58 men) and 173 children (83 girls, 90 boys). Sixty households were included in the survey: fifty-three were headed by men, with an average age of 58.8 years, and seven by women, whose average age was 71.7 years. The average number of adults per household was 2.18, and the average number of children per household was 2.9.

Farming is the main male occupation; the main female occupation is trading, with some farming (Table 29). Land is held in trust for the benefit of the people by the *Alafin* (king) of Oyo, but it is the village chief who is responsible for allocating land to family heads. Farm land is thus held corporately by the descent groups, and any male member of a lineage has the right to farm on a piece of the land belonging to the lineage. Spouses do not inherit land from each other, but daughters can inherit family property, on the under-standing that this property does not pass to their husbands' lineage. More commonly, wives and daughters are given the right of usufruct of a piece of land at some time during their lives.

Ilora farm settlement, in contrast, was established in 1959 as part of the former Western state 'settlement scheme' (based on the Israeli Moshavei Ovdim) 'which combined individual initiative and responsibility on the one hand, with collective life and work as well as production under close supervision on the other' (Roider 1971). The village is circular with a large central land enclosure, including houses, one or two stores and a market place. Farm holdings radiate out from this centre in all directions; the total area

Table 29 Male and female occupations in Oluwatedo and IFS in 1977

| Males | Number | | Females | Number | |
	Oluwatedo[1]	IFS[2]		Oluwatedo[1]	IFS[2]
Farming only	54	26	Farming only	12	3
Farming and poultry	—	25	Farming and poultry	2	2
Poultry only	—	1	Poultry only	—	9
Farming and other	4	—	Farming and other	2	3
			Trading only	53	26
			Trading and sewing	—	1
			Sewing only	—	3
			Helping husband/ mother	3	9
			Hair dresser	—	1
			Labouring	2	—
			Too old to work	1	—
Total	58	52		73	57

Notes:
[1] from a sample of sixty households; [2] from a sample of fifty-two households.
Source: Field work, 1977.

of 3039 hectares includes 1063 hectares for arable crops. Eighty-nine settler units were initially planned, but this was raised to 102 units in 1960. Each settler was entitled to a holding of 28 hectares (14 hectares for arable crops and 14 hectares in fallow), four poultry units each containing ninety-six birds, and a pig pen. However, because of shortages of staff, it was not possible to lay out all the holdings or provide all the settlers with poultry and pig pens. In 1966, each settler was allocated 10 hectares for arable crops, 10 hectares for pasture, and either a battery cage of 192 layers or a broiler house stocked with 100 broilers. This was the pattern in 1977.

There were seventy-five settler families in 1977, but only fifty-two were included in this study. The total population of these was 264, including 115 adults (fifty-seven women and fifty-eight men) and 149 children (sixty-nine girls and eighty boys). The average age of household heads was 36.5 years (in Oluwatedo it was 59 years). There were no female heads of households, as only men had been considered as settlers. The average number of adults per household was 2.2, and the average number of children was 2.8.

As in Oluwatedo, farming is the main male occupation (Table 29). Among women there is some farming, but poultry keeping and trading are the main occupations. The traditional land tenure system has been replaced by a system whereby male settlers have permanent tenancy of their holdings, as long as they pay a nominal sum of ₦.1.50 per month. (In 1977 a naira was £0.88.) Women are still dependent on their husbands for land.

The farm economy

According to Boserup (1970), 'Africa is the region of female farming par excellence': women produce most of the food crops and do between 70 and 80 per cent of the total agricultural work. Among the Yoruba, however the traditional and contemporary division of labour is that the majority of men farm and the majority of women trade. Women's role in farming is somewhat debatable. Previous work among the Yoruba suggested that women were not directly engaged in farm work, but were primarily responsible for refining agricultural produce for marketing. But studies in the 1970s by Patel and Anthonio (1973), Grant and Anthonio (1973), Osuntogun (1976), Adeyokunnu (1976), Igben *et al.* (1977) and Spiro (1979) found that, though very few women own farms, many of them work on their parents' or husbands' farms. Women play an important role in planting, applying fertilizer, harvesting, carrying and marketing.

The main farming system has been shifting cultivation based on rotational bush fallowing. During the dry season, land is cleared (except for very large trees or those of value) and the debris burned. Seeds or cuttings are then planted; root crops are planted in mounds or ridges. Some weeding may be done in the first year, but rarely in subsequent years. Modern farming methods include the use of fertilizers, herbicides and tractors. Tractors are particularly useful for clearing the land, uprooting trees, preparing land and carrying the harvested crops to store. The survey found that though the proportion of women engaged in farming in their own right was low (only 34 per cent in Oluwatedo and 19 per cent in IFS), the numbers of women farmers had increased significantly during the 1970s. The majority were aged 40 and over; the older ones (average age 45) lived in Oluwatedo and the younger (average age 32) in IFS. All the farmers, except one widow in Oluwatedo, were married and living with their husbands and children or grandchildren. Indeed, most of them were farming on land given to them by their husbands. Distances from house to plot ranged up to 45 minutes walk; the average size was 0.2 hectares in Oluwatedo, 0.5 hectares in IFS.

The main crops of the area were maize, cassava, yam and okra, with some pepper, melon, tomato and vegetable leaf. In Oluwatedo, cassava and maize were the most important crops; in IFS maize was dominant. Crops were grown in both sole and mixed stands. Less than half the women farmers in Oluwatedo used tractors and fertilizer on their farms; but all those in IFS did so. Approximately 75 per cent of all the crops produced in both villages were sold in the market, and some of the women farmers were also engaged in processing and selling agricultural products. Most processed *gari* (from cassava) in Oluwatedo and *pap* (from maize) in IFS. Because women have only recently begun farming in their own right in this area, it was important to find out who decided when farming operations should be carried out. The study found that husbands in all villages tended to make decisions about the heavier farm operations such as clearing, burning, stumping and tractor ploughing; husbands also helped to carry out these tasks, but most of the work was done by hired labour. Women made decisions about hand ploughing, planting, weeding, harvesting and carrying, which they actually did themselves.

Women farmers worked on average four to five days (five to six hours daily) in Oluwatedo and three to four days (two to four hours daily) in IFS, but the actual amount of time spent on farming varied considerably between full-time farmers and farmer/traders. Generally, women farmers in both villages spent the same amount of time in farming, and they also spent more time in farming than farmer/ traders. Farmer/traders in IFS worked longer hours than farmer/ traders in Oluwatedo. Women living in IFS also looked after their own and their husbands' poultry. The amount of time occupied by each farming operation also varied substantially: weeding, harvesting and transporting were the most time consuming activities, followed by the shelling of maize. Very few women sold crops on behalf of their husbands; men preferred to sell to other traders as they were afraid that their wives would cheat them. In IFS, maize was bought directly by wholesalers.

The importance of women among the Yoruba in local farming systems has clearly been established. However, the roles of men and women in farming differ greatly, as women are more likely to help on farms than to own them, and the farms they own tend to produce food, not cash crops. Women also tend to be given farms as gifts from parents and husbands rather than to acquire them by their own efforts. Even as farm owners, women have smaller farms than men and enter production at a later age. Women are also expected to assist on their husbands' farms. Men do reciprocate to some extent on their wives' farms, but in practice most women relied heavily on hired male labour for all farm operations.

The market economy

In many market systems in West Africa, women have traditionally assumed a significant position in market trade, especially in staple foods, and this continues today. Among the Yoruba the role of women as independent market traders has long been highly institutionalized; two-thirds of all adult women are engaged in trading. For half of them, trade is their main occupation; for the rest, trade is subsidiary to agriculture or crafts. This is because within Yoruba society, though it is generally the husband's responsibility to provide basic items of clothing and to pay his children's school fees, many men are unable to do all these things. Women are, therefore, expected to contribute towards the basic upkeep of the family as well as to provide their own clothing, luxury items, etc. In addition, women have separate financial responsibilities to their own kin groups, and must contribute towards birth, death and marriage ceremonies and other religious and cultural festivals as well as providing their own ceremonial funds. In order to fulfil these responsibilities a women needs to earn money, and for an uneducated woman in Nigeria the easiest way to earn money is to trade.

Table 30 Type of trading by women traders in Oluwatedo and IFS

Category	Number of Traders		
	Oluwatedo	IFS	Total
Trading in unprocessed agricultural products			
Cowpeas, peppers, vegetable leaf, kola, ground nut	4	3	7
Trading in self-processed agricultural products			
Gari (cassava porridge), cassava flour, palm oil, palm wine, *asa* (snuff)	12	5	17
Trading in self-prepared ready made food for consumption			
Akara (fried bean cake), beans, *pap*, rice, rice and beans, meat and *gari*, beans and plantain, rice and palm wine	20	6	26
Trading in meat, fish and eggs			
Ponmo (edible cow skin), dried fish, eggs	3	4	7
Trading in local and non local provisions and manufactures			
Provisions, bread, salt, plates, baby wrappers (sling)	11	11	22
Total	50	29	79

Source: Field work, 1977.

Fifty women (75.3 per cent of total women) in Oluwatedo and twenty-nine women (50.9 per cent of total women) in IFS carried on some type of trading in the market places of Oluwatedo, IFS, Oyo and Ibadan, as well as trading at home. The trading of women in the villages can be classified in five categories: trading in unprocessed agricultural products; in self-processed agricultural products; trading in self-prepared ready-made food for consumption; trading in meat, fish and eggs; and trading in local and non-local provisions and manufactures. Table 30 shows that the most important trade was in ready-to-eat foods, with provisions in second place.

The majority of women traders were under 40 in both villages (unlike women farmers, who tend to be over 40), but there was no clear relationship between age and the commodity traded. There was however a noticeable variation in average age between the trading categories: the youngest women in Oluwatedo dealt in meat and fish and the oldest in self-processed agricultural products. In IFS, this was reversed: the youngest women dealt in self-processed agricultural products and the oldest in meat, fish and eggs. An explanation may be that it is the older women in Oluwatedo who are more likely to be farming on their own account and thus involved in the processing and trading of agriculture produce, whereas in IFS it is the younger wives who help their husbands with farming and related tasks, such as processing. The majority of women traders started trading between the ages of 30 and 34 in Oluwatedo and between 25 and 29 in IFS. Before becoming traders most women helped their husbands with farming, but with the birth of their children a large proportion became traders, as their responsibilities towards their families became increasingly financial. The majority of traders taught themselves to trade, using money from their husbands to start their business.

The amount of capital available to a trader was the main factor in determining the type of commodity traded, and most traders had an initial starting capital of less than ₦20. In general, little money was needed to start trading in food commodities, particularly in the cooked food trades. Traders starting with ₦21–100 engaged in bulking and break-bulking activities in products varying from beans to rice and in provisions, plates, salt, etc. Traders with more than ₦100 were relatively large scale dealing in meat provisions, enamelware and sewing.

The majority of traders had only been trading between six months and four years and they tended to specialize in cooked foods, some provisions and unprocessed agricultural products from their husbands' farms. Traders who had been selling between five and nine years tended to specialize in both the processing of agricultural products and cooked food. Traders with more than ten years experience specialized in cooked food, provisions and salt, but those traders who also farmed in their own right tended to specialize in the selling of self-processed agricultural products. Although traders did switch from one commodity to another because of seasonal availability, traders who had been trading for a considerable period of time reported that they were still selling the same commodities as when they first started trading. The exceptions were those traders who acquired farms in their own right as they became older and they tended to turn to self-processing products.

Most traders worked between four and seven days a week. Women who processed agricultural products such as *pap* and *gari* traded the smaller number of days, as these take two or three days to make. Cooked-food sellers traded five or six days a week. Those who dealt in provisions and unprocessed agricultural produce might trade seven days a week, from home: the villages were like big supermarkets, with different commodities stored in different households. Because such goods were always accessible, traders were open for business virtually twenty-four hours a day and no customer was ever turned away. The majority of traders said they were full-time traders, but personal observation revealed much more fluidity than that suggested. Traders left their goods with neighbours and children; in this way they could carry on more than one activity at a time. Women could be farming or travelling while their businesses were being looked after by someone else. All women traders, regardless of commodity traded, followed the home–market–home pattern of trading. This is the most basic of the trader travel patterns; traders take their produce to market either daily or periodically and sell their goods, returning home at night. Traders in Oluwatedo and IFS usually visited one supply market and one retail market. The time devoted to marketing varied widely from area to area, but nowhere featured as a major burden in the week's activities.

The domestic economy

Ethnographic studies of the role of women in traditional societies show that, though the specific details of women's roles vary from culture to culture, there is an underlying denominator that 'in all societies from the past to the present, the breeding of babies and the feeding of humans of all ages is almost exclusively the work of women . . . . Women also grow, process and cook food, provide water, fuel and clothing, build houses, make and repair roads, serve as beasts of burden, and sit in the markets to sell the surpluses' (Boulding 1977).

Due to the absence of domestic water supplies, women in most rural areas still have to walk, often for some kilometres to fetch water, particularly in the dry season. In Oluwatedo and IFS water is mainly obtained from the River Ogun and its tributary streams. In addition, in Oluwatedo there are a village well and a little waterhole nearby which provide water during the rainy season. In

Table 31   Distance and time expended on water collection

Village	Distance, km	Average number of trips/day	Average time (minutes) spent daily
Oluwatedo			
Dry season	1.2	1.6	60–90
Wet season	0.4	2.6	30–45
IFS			
Dry season	2.7	3.3	120
Wet season	0.6	3.3	60

Source: Field work, 1977.

IFS, a piped water system was laid down, but it has yet to be connected to a water supply. The distance to water supplies, the number of trips made and the estimated average time spent on water collection are shown in Table 31. The actual time spent on water collection in August (Table 32) was however much less than expected for the dry season. This was because in Oluwatedo the village well and waterhole continued to provide water and in IFS the water truck for the government poultry farm distributed surplus water to domestic units.

Food preparation is often tedious and time-consuming, as cereals and other staples have to be ground, husked or pounded before cooking. But, because the majority of women in Nigeria are engaged in economic activities outside the home, many women have specialized in the sale of ready cooked foods, providing themselves with a livelihood and at the same time supplying a service to other women who cannot do all their own cooking. Consequently, most Yoruba women only prepare one meal a day, though if there is more than one woman in the household they may take it in turns to do the cooking as well as sharing the routine daily household tasks. Table 32 shows that, of all household chores, food preparation and cooking are the most time consuming.

Cleaning and laundry work do not demand much of a woman's time. The modestly furnished mud huts and forecourts require only sweeping, a task done several times a day. The small amount of time spent on collecting water and wood is due to help from children and husbands. Furthermore, every person from about the age of 6 takes responsibility for washing his or her own clothes. In reality, who does what in the home often departs from the culturally expected norm, as husbands and children often carry out

Table 32 Daily time budgets of women's domestic tasks in Oluwatedo and IFS, August 1977

Tasks	Oluwatedo		IFS	
	h	*m*	*h*	*m*
Sweeping		54		38
Collecting water		43		25
Collecting wood		13		4
Collecting leaves		7		0
Food processing and cooking	5	52	4	11
Washing clothes		16		21
Childcare		1		1
Total average hours on daily domestic tasks	8	06	5	40

Hours per day

Source: Field work 1977.

household chores. The amount of time spent exclusively on child-care is quite negligible. Women carry their babies on their backs until they can walk, and breastfeed them on demand. Nappies are not worn, and mothers only have a few items of baby clothing to wash. Older children and men also look after younger children and babies.

In summarizing the position of women in rural Africa in relation to household tasks, Taylor (ed. 1975) states that 'at present, in the whole of Africa, food processing and preparation and care of the children are almost exclusively women's tasks. In rural areas probably 90 per cent of hand-carried water supplies are provided by women (provision of water supplies in villages is therefore a priority need for women), as are 80 per cent of the fuel supplies. Women do at least 30 per cent of housebuilding and half the house repairs'.

Other activities

The heterogeneous group of activities, vaguely defined as 'leisure activities', includes eating, bathing, resting, visiting, plaiting hair and church going. The time spent on these activities cannot be easily measured, but it is from these that time is taken during peak labour seasons, and often it is women who lose their 'leisure' time to fulfil their other obligations.

Table 33   Time spent on various activities in hours per week for fifty-six women in Oluwatedo and IFS, for a sixteen hour day

| Month | Domestic work | | Farm work | | Trading | | Other | |
	Oluwatedo (hrs)	IFS (hrs)	Oluwatedo (hrs)	IFS (hrs)	Oluwatedo (hrs)	IFS (hrs)	Oluwatedo (hrs)	IFS (hrs)
August	8.1	5.6	2.9	3.8	1.8	2.1	3.2	4.4
September	5.6	6.1	4.9	3.6	1.4	1.7	4.0	4.5
October	5.7	5.2	4.0	3.9	1.6	2.3	4.7	4.6
November	6.1	5.0	3.7	3.2	1.6	2.9	4.6	4.9
December	5.5	4.7	4.3	4.6	1.8	2.2	4.4	4.5

Source: Field work 1977.

Women's weekly time budgets

The amount of time a woman can contribute to farm work and trading depends to a large extent on the number of other things she has to do. Her availability for work can be differentiated between days and between seasons. During any day certain routine tasks occur, no matter what time of the year; other tasks, such as planting and harvesting, recur seasonally.

Table 33 shows that the time spent by all women (regardless of occupation) on the various activities in Oluwatedo and IFS is more or less the same, with some variations between the months and between the villages. For example, the large amount of time devoted to 'domestic' work in Oluwatedo during August, and the comparatively small amount spent in 'other activities', can be explained by an increase in the processing of freshly harvested maize to make *pap* and of palm fruits to make palm oil.

The main variations in time spent are accounted for by the nature of women's occupations. By far the most time is devoted to domestic work, with farm work second. *All women do more farm work than trading*, even farmer/traders and full-time traders. The average time spent on farm work in both Oluwatedo and IFS was 25 per cent of time available and it was greatest for farmers and women who said they neither farmed nor traded – 32 and 38 per cent respectively in Oluwatedo and 32 and 28 per cent respectively in IFS. In Oluwatedo farming occupied about 22 per cent of the time of traders, but only 16 per cent of that of farmers/traders. Traders and farmer/traders spent about 20 per cent of their time farming in IFS. This is because women (particularly young wives) are expected to help their husbands whenever they are asked; women may negotiate a different time for doing the job if they have a business trip planned, but they are expected to do it. The average time spent in trading was 8 per cent in Oluwatedo and 12 per cent in IFS. In Oluwatedo, farmer/traders spent as much time trading (15 per cent) as women who only traded (14 per cent), while farmers and women who neither farmed nor traded spent less than 2 per cent of their time in trading. In IFS, it was the traders who spent most time trading (20 per cent), followed by farmer/traders (18 per cent). Trading took about 10 per cent of the time of women who neither farmed nor traded, but less than 2 per cent of the time of IFS farmers. The time spent in 'other' activities was 29 per cent in Oluwatedo, 30 per cent in IFS. Farmers in both villages spent more time in other activities (33 per cent) than any other group. Women who neither farmed nor traded in Oluwatedo, and traders in IFS,

Table 34   Percentage of time spent on farm and non-farm activities in various areas of Nigeria

| | Eastern Nigeria | | | | Western Nigeria | | |
| | Calabar[1] | | Uboma[2] | | Yoruba cocoa[3] | Oluwatedo | IFS[2] |
Tasks	Male	Female	Male	Female	Family	Female	Female
Domestic work	—	42	2	19	27	38	33
Farm work	31	5	28	20	36	25	25
Harvesting and processing	42	42	—	—	20	—	—
Marketing	—	11	—	—	11	8	12
Other work	—	—	14	14	—	—	—
Other activity	27	—	56	47	6	29	30
Total	100	100	100	100	100	100	100

Sources: [1] Martin 1956, 24–5 and 46–7; average hours per day; [2] Oluwasanmi 1966, 100; average time per twelve hour day; [3] Galletti 1956, 299; average family hours per annum; [4] Field work 1977; average time per sixteen hour day.

had the least leisure: 24 per cent in Oluwatedo and 27 per cent in IFS.

These times can be compared with data from other areas of Nigeria (Table 34), though comparisons are difficult because of the different classification of activities. For example, harvesting and processing products are a separate category of work in Calabar and in the Yoruba cocoa areas, whereas in the research area processing is included in domestic work because of the difficulties involved in distinguishing produce for home consumption from produce for sale. Nevertheless, the table shows that time spent in farming by women in Uboma, Oluwatedo and IFS is more or less similar, while marketing in all areas is the least time consuming of activities. Women in all areas do more domestic work than men, but there is wider variation in the amount of time spent on housework and in the time spent in 'other' activities.

Conclusion

Yoruba culture defines 'ideal' areas of domestic responsibility for both men and women; it was found in Oluwatedo and IFS (and is no doubt true elsewhere) that in carrying out the day-to-day business of living there is considerable overlap in gender roles. Though women carried out almost all the domestic chores, men (and children) were seen to be helping with cooking, washing clothes, water and fuel collection and childcare. In turn women contributed substantial amounts of time to farming on their own and their husbands' farms.

In analysing women's time budgets over a five month period, regardless of occupation, it was found that the amount of time spent on domestic chores was about five hours daily, varying from 33 to 38 per cent of the time available (the work was done in a leisurely manner, with constant interruptions by children and other adults). Of the domestic chores, food processing and preparation took up the most time followed by the collection of fuel and water. Farming occupied 25 per cent of all women's time, and most women took part in planting, weeding, harvesting and carrying. Marketing occupied only a small proportion of women's time (8–12 per cent), even for full-time traders. Time spent on 'other' activities occupied approximately 30 per cent of women's disposable time. *The most significant finding, for women's time and for rural development was that all women, regardless of their main occupation, spent about a quarter of their time on farm work.*

This chapter has shown that women's domestic duties and

their economic activities are not incompatible. Both farming and trading are compatible with simultaneous childcare, and other domestic duties are organized in such a way, with all members of the household helping, that they put no constraints on women's money-making activities. In this way Yoruba women in Oluwatedo and IFS fulfil their domestic and social obligations as well as their financial commitments.

Implications for development

It has been clearly established that Yoruba women play an important role in agricultural production. It is therefore vital to assist women in performing these roles more effectively by teaching them improved farming techniques as well as supplying them with credit facilities and agricultural extension services. Unfortunately, it has been noted that Nigerian agricultural policies, particularly the policies of the extension services, are geared to meet the need of the traditional head of the farming family – the man – to the exclusion of the women (Ighen *et al*. 1977).

Similarly, development policies all too often overlook the significance of women's roles in development projects. Palmer (1985) suggests that opportunities for incorporating women's interests into development projects have been missed due to the combination of ideological bias, lack of information and a desire for expediency among planners and administrators.

The farm settlement scheme of western Nigeria is an excellent example of this. One of the main objectives of the scheme was to attract educated young people of both sexes into viable farming units as an alternative to urban living. Settler selection criteria in the project documents made no explicit distinction on the basis of sex, but settler *de facto* came to mean male settler. Women were referred to as spouses.

The failure to allocate settler status and land to women in *their own right*, plus the absence of an organized market within the local marketing system, meant that women's need for a separate, independent source of income on the settlement was not met. The failure of the settlement to integrate women's economic and concomitantly their domestic and social interests can be regarded as a fundamental weakness of the project and is reflected in the high settlement turnover, particularly among women, and increasingly among men.

The agricultural sector is the area in which rural women play their largest, yet least recognized role. It is astonishing that the fact of women's participation in agriculture – one of the most obvious phenomena of rural life – has had to be proved in almost every country. In Nigeria, with increasing data being made available, this should change and women's role in agricultural development be perceived for what it is: vital to the process of improving productivity and living conditions (ILCA 1984). The crisis in domestic food production may well be the catalyst that gives women this recognition.

7 Carrying heavier burdens but carrying less weight: some implications of villagization for women in Tanzania

Michael McCall

Editors' introduction

Capitalist penetration in the Third World has often brought similar changes to gender in rural areas, particularly the concentration of subsistence production in female hands, the reduction of women's access to the means of production (Chapter 5), and, in the absence of migrant men, the expansion of women's work in social and economic reproduction (Chapters 1, 9). Many governments, as in the Philippines, have paid lip service to the problems resulting from these changes, but most states with a real commitment to solving them are centrally planned economies, in the Second World, from China to Cuba.

Tanzania shows an exceptional recognition by the state of the problems, the importance of women's activities, and the need to better women's lot. Almost two decades of striving for 'African socialism' have seen a theoretical increase in women's property rights and an intensive effort to raise the educational level of women; the *ujamaa* form of collective production was also meant to benefit women. Yet Tanzania remains an exporter of agricultural raw materials, seeking to expand its economy through the growth of the market. African socialism has perhaps merely seen a continuation of the agrarian transition from peasant to capitalist production which began under colonialism.

McCall reports on women's experience under one aspect of this paradoxical process: the physical restructuring of settlement. What has 'villagization' meant for women? He divides their burden into the market economy and their domestic, subsistence tasks and evaluates the effect of villagization on this double burden. Increased distances to fields, to water and to fuelwood are set against real gains in service provision and increased education against the loss of children's work. The effect on women's incomes is assessed through changes in control of land, alterations in the labour process in agriculture, and transformations in women's handicrafts, brewing and co-operatives as well as in village politics. To date, the balance seems negative for women; for the future there are positive policy suggestions, but the outcome is seen to depend on social struggles at many levels.

Villagization

In examining the changing experience of women in Tanzania, the impacts of villagization might seem peripheral. The position of women, their increasing subordination and alienation from the products of their labour, and their increasing resistance, are all features of a historic transformation of the peasant social economy in which villagization is a minor episode. However, this episode has irreversibly altered the spatial organization of peasants, and indubitably affected the functioning of the rural economy through changes in agriculture, pastoralism, access to resources, provision of services, and so on. It has brought revolutionary changes in social relations of production regarding land and labour. The questions here are direct: first, has the implementation of villagization changed the situation of female peasants? Second, in which sectors has the situation improved and in which has it deteriorated? ('Improvement' and 'deterioration' in control of resources, control of their own labour and earnings, autonomy of decision-making, and, implicitly, in legal position, political involvement, and the consciousness of a shared situation.) Little comparative material exists on the impact of Tanzania's villagization programme, and very few writers have explicitly examined the situation of Tanzanian women in villages, though Mascarenhas and Mbilinyi (1983) have produced a critical and stimulating bibliographical review on the 'question of women'.

'Villagization' occurred primarily in 1973–6, when much of the rural population was consolidated into settlements of roughly 250–600 households. (There was also significant movement before this, 1969–72 – see Map 15.) The programme was locally abrupt, sometimes violent; it decisively altered rural space and society, and is having long-term impacts on agriculture and the environment. Villagization was the result of Tanzania's ideology of *ujamaa* (literally familyhood), comprising self-reliance, social and spatial equality, elimination of exploitation, and communal living and production. The ideology was dominant in the single party, CCM (Chama cha Mapinduzi or Party of the Revolution), and was mainly articulated by Julius Nyerere and other activists. The failure to convert the whole of the rapidly expanding state bureaucracy to *ujamaa* values exacerbated the immediate problems of

Map 15   Villagization in Tanzania, by region

Source: McCall 1983   **Note:** Numbers refer to main year(s) of
villagization movement.

implementing the policy of villagization. (Such problems included
the reliance on *ujamaa* ideals as incentives for peasant commodity
production.) Villagization followed a decade of policies directed
towards *ujamaa* goals. Until 1973 the main strategy had been the
voluntary regrouping of scattered farm households into compact
villages. There were several basic aims – provision of services,
promotion of communal agriculture, build-up of communal enterprises in small-scale processing, retail trade etc., increased security, reduced economic differentiation, and enhanced democratic
responsibilities at village and higher levels. (Private plots were
retained, however, and sometimes there was a transitional stage of
block farming.)

Concurrently, farming was to be modernized and economies of
scale achieved, and the resulting rural growth was intended to

stimulate the national economy. The promise and the reality of *ujamaa* villages have generated considerable debate (Hyden 1980).

Before 1973, very few settlements approached the idealistic *ujamaa* goals – of voluntarism, equitable distribution of work and benefits, and democracy. There were however many *ujamaa* village 'shells' dominated by better-off farmers or groups with links to the state bureaucracy. Other villages were ideological show-places where communal production depended on government support. Despite the unequivocal support of the Arusha Declaration (1967) the number of villages grew very slowly till the early 1970s, when the state instigated five large-scale resettlement operations. These were carried out forcibly, if necessary, using extraneous justifications such as flooding, risk of drought, or Portuguese infiltration. In most cases there was some promotion of communal village *shambas* or farms.

Nyerere had never excluded force to achieve short-term material goals. He came to distinguish 'living together' from 'working together' and to emphasize the 'duty' of living in villages to achieve development. The rate of voluntary movement disappointed and disillusioned the party leadership, and on 6 November 1973 Nyerere made the crucial speech demanding that 'all must live in villages by the end of 1976'. Much confusion followed as to whether these were to be *ujamaa* villages. Policy-makers generally agreed that resettlement into villages was compulsory (though some regions created 'village' boundaries around existing high density farming areas), but that communal *ujamaa* farming would develop slowly and democratically. By August 1975 the 'Villages and *Ujamaa* Villages' Act identified two levels of villages. *Vijijini vya Maendeleo* (development villages) controlled all allocation of land and could act as multi-purpose co-operatives. Village buildings and machinery were collectively owned, but livestock and tools remained private. The official authority was the village council of twenty-five members elected by the village assembly, which constituted the whole adult population. *Ujamaa* designation was reserved for villages where a 'substantial portion of the economic activities . . . [was] carried out on a communal basis'. In practice the distinction is not very important; all villages can participate in nearly all government programmes, and aid projects do not differentiate. *Ujamaa* production is now less of a national priority.

During and after implementation, the key factor for Nyerere and the party was spatial concentration, as the essential first step towards 'working together'. But support for villagization came also through very different political objectives, notably the need to modernize agriculture and to gain control over peasant surplus by supervision at the production stage. Some observers (Shivji 1975; Coulson 1982) considered this an underlying rationale for villagization; hence its support from the World Bank and other agencies. Actual implementation relied on widespread promises of social infrastructure, much coercion and some force. The relative lack of resistance suggests that for the majority there was no acceptable alternative. Only guesses have been made of the number of people actually moved; it was at least 5 million, but some guesses top 10 million. It was a massive undertaking. Similarly, there are no national figures for the distances that people had to move. For two villages in Dodoma (Map 16), Thiele (1983) calculated an average of 3 km; for all of Iringa District, Thomas (1984) estimated an average of 5 km, or 1.23 million person-kms in total; for sample villages in nine districts, Maro and Mlay (1976) estimated 'most distances' were below 10 km except in Songea, Nzega and Dodoma districts. In Songea half did not move, but 33 per cent moved further than 16 km.

Most post-villagization rural programmes are premised on the permanence of villages. Policies to consolidate the new villages have included 'operations' for permanent housing and for the elimination of private rural shops, water supply projects, a village afforestation programme, and crop commodity schemes based on the village as the executing and purchasing agent. (A new *Ujamaa* Village Act of 1983 extended the co-operative functions of villages.) Physically, villages have experienced substantial population growth since 1973 (there is a 3.3 per cent national growth rate), at the same time as serious local degradation of the environment, falling crop production (due partly to climatic conditions), and locally high (male) outmigration. Some few oversized villages have been allowed to create satellite settlements.

Initially both sexes suffered from the destruction of houses and stores and the losses of perennial crops and trees. The initial burden fell more heavily on women because of their responsibilities for children and household maintenance. Specifically, women shared in new house building, but were wholly responsible for preparing new 'daily subsistence plots' near the house. (The main crops often continued to be grown in the old fields.) Physical planning of village sites was deficient because access to water, fuelwood and good land was often subordinated to the criterion of road access giving sites on dry ridges (Boesen 1979; Dumont and Mottin 1979; McCall 1983). Water schemes were much delayed in funding and building. There were also local outbreaks of disease

Map 16 Location of districts mentioned

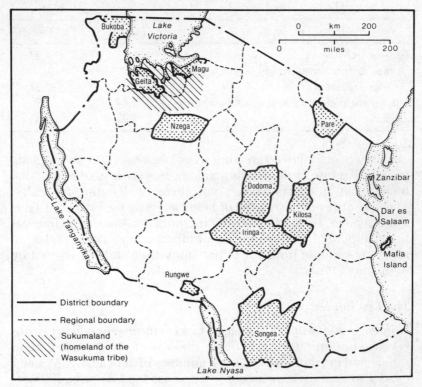

caused by problems of living density and sanitation. Subsistence became problematic in the many female-headed households where males migrated to towns or 'frontier' rural areas. Food production per capita declined between 1973 and 1976, partly because of the disruption that followed villagization. Villages, however, did provide some immediate material benefits for all inhabitants, especially access to road transport, to health services and to shops.

Women's productive and reproductive labour

Whether or not villagization was deliberately intended to direct peasants towards commodity production, its impact cannot logically be separated from the general trajectory of articulation; that is, the continuing transformation of the peasant economy by capital. The Tanzanian peasant economy shows increasing production for markets and reliance on monetary exchange, decreasing use of mututal support systems, decreasing domestic production of

Table 35   Average hours per adult household member per day
(14 hour day)

	Male	Female
Total on-farm work	3.1	4.37
Domestic (food preparation, wood, water, childcare, etc.)	1.16	3.37
Total work, including paid employment	6.44	7.9
'Leisure'	4.83	3.41

essential items, (slowly) growing wage labour, and deepening state penetration into farm decision-making as well as marketing. This transformation affects women both theoretically and practically. They bear the double burden of being not only the primary labour force in domestic production and reproduction but also an increasingly important labour force in production for market. Table 35 gives an example from a detailed study from Bukoba District by Kamuzora (1984).

The first burden

Women's domestic subsistence tasks are inexorably growing because of outmigration by men, the loss of child work time to school and the rapidly increasing numbers of dependants. Women must also earn their own cash to purchase food items and household goods formerly produced at home or exchanged between households. Villagization has exacerbated this domestic burden because soil fertility is declining, greatly increased distances must be walked to fetch wood (and sometimes water), and physical and social problems arise from large concentrations of population. Pressure on women's health in villages has been attributed to increased workloads, deteriorating diets and increased health hazards.

The second burden

Production for market becomes more onerous as commoditization, in Tanzania represented by the parastatal Crop Authorities, requires peasants to produce greater quantities of industrial and food crops. The peasant farmers must also provide surplus food for an urban population growing at a rate approaching 9 per cent p.a.
Increases in yields (or output) in peasant agriculture cannot easily be achieved by increased labour productivity. Even to main-

tain output levels, additional labour is required. Villagization has further led to processes of agricultural involution; increased pressure on land causes less fallow, lower yields and land degradation. These pressures fall on all the productive rural population, adults and youths, but the burden is growing critical for women already carrying the first burden. Historically, because of the specificity of the colonial period, the resource endowments, and the ideology of the post-colonial state, the organization of agriculture has remained mainly on a household basis with very low levels of capital. There has been relatively little farming by settlers, planters or indigenous capitalists, though they can be locally important.

Therefore, with increased state demands, marketed production must come primarily from the peasant sector, and through stepping up the amount of work rather than improving the productivity of labour. The Marxian concept of lengthening the working day to appropriate more value can be applied here to the increasing burden on peasant women: the working year is lengthened by new crops, double cropping, etc.; the working day is lengthened by longer hours and more extensive farming which means longer walking times; more elements of household labour are incorporated into production of commodities (children do less work so the only additional source is women); women also replace male peasants as they outmigrate or enter capitalist agriculture, commerce, etc.; and the intensity of labour increases as more tasks and higher quality work are needed in modern farming. A relatively smaller working population has been subjected to (world) market pressures to increase the quantity and quality of marketed crops. At the same time women peasants have been further subordinated – economically, culturally, legally and physically. Women have been unable to resist further involvement in the market economy, but they have had no corresponding amelioration of the domestic burden and have not received the material rewards of the market.

Why has the second burden on women grown without diminishing the first? The historical experience of industrialized countries was very different. The fundamental reason in Tanzania is, as Mascarenhas and Mbilinyi (1983) and others have maintained, the particular (colonial) form of the capital penetration into specific peasant modes. The concept of 'superexploitation' of peasants as commodity producers and also as workers responsible for their own maintenance and reproduction has been amplified by Bernstein (1977). Thus, the exact nature of the peasant economy and the position of female producers before the advent of capitalism significantly affect their present ability to control resources and their own labour. However, the economic rationale of the (some-times) extreme division of labour remains problematic. As White-head (1981) argues, there are analogies but not isomorphisms between gender hierarchies and economic classes with regard to labour and its product. Female peasants do not function simply as a proletariat *vis-à-vis* a male bourgeoisie.

How have the two burdens been increased?

Peasant women have had very little material, economic or political capacity to resist an increase in their burdens. First, the monetiza-tion of the rural economy and the deteriorating conditions for household production of necessary domestic items have meant that women must earn cash to purchase, for example, clothes, utensils, medicine, and food items like sugar, salt and kerosene. School costs and most children's needs are frequently the respon-sibility of mothers. Women cannot simply opt out of the cash economy. Second, there are degrees of cultural, ideological and ultimately physical pressures on women to assist husbands in the fields, usually with little recompense in cash, kind or reciprocal work by men. Modern farming requires more and higher quality labour, much of it in 'traditionally' female tasks, especially weed-ing, picking, headloading, and sorting and cleaning. The tendency has been for only the 'traditionally' male tasks, especially prepara-tion of the land, to be mechanized. Third, women are perhaps now more involved in wage labour, the state having promoted 'modern' skills through adult literacy, education and the mass media. Universal primary education has helped, although only margi-nally, to relieve parts of the burden of childcare. There is a growing market for wage labour, and rural women may take it as a chance to escape from their subordinated village life (cf. Bryceson 1980).

Villagization has played a significant part in increasing the second burden. The programme had a variety of purposes and reflected the sometimes contradictory policies of different groups. However, spatial concentration did create conditions under which women could more quickly be involved in commodity production, most obviously through extension and marketing legislation. Easier mobility for *bwana shambas* (agricultural extension agents) and other agents allowed them to supervise women farmers more closely. To some extent the provision of basic needs, especially water, freed women's time for field work. Of greater importance have been legal and cultural changes in land holdings, which have often deprived women of their traditional rights to land and its utilization, and left them to become dependent on household males and the village leadership. They have also suffered relative losses in the power to make political decisions as senior males are designated as official 'heads of households'; and a 'model' image of the family has developed in the bourgeois tradition, i.e. male head with female and child dependants.

There has been some breakdown of the semi-autonomous men's and women's functional sub-units of peasant farms. There are, of course, considerable regional–cultural differences between 'traditional' farming systems, but they all show some independence of male and female farm activities. Husband and wife not only do not share all resources, work and proceeds; frequently they work distinct (though interlinked) sub-systems, making separate management decisions. Traditionally, the peasant household is not a nuclear family farm with convergent interests, but a complex of blood and marriage ties, and contractual and interpersonal relations; indeed, husband and wife often show a degree of ignorance of the other's sub-system. Villagization, with its associated legal and political changes and state penetration, is altering this complex system, mainly by reducing the autonomy of female producers, separating them from the fruits of their labour, and making them dependent on males for access to most resources. Ideologically, too, the increasing need for, and participation in, the cash economy 'devalues' women's unpaid reproductive labour.

Specific impacts of villagization for women

The chief ways in which villagization has affected women's daily activities and their social–political situation can be illustrated from a range of empirical studies.

Distance

The salient effect of villagization was to locate farmers farther from existing fields, thus reducing their 'effective working day', i.e. time available for field labour. The programme assumed that peasants would prepare new fields closer to their new homes, and many villages demarcated individual plots. Land clearing and house-building were immediate heavy tasks for the men; and since 'homeplots' growing daily foods such as vegetables, bananas or tubers are essential to household survival, their preparation and manuring were a first extra burden for women, already working on the main plots. There are no national data to show how far peasants continued with old plot sites or prepared nearer ones. Where pre-vious sites were maintained, in addition to the increased travelling time there were problems of field protection, transport of seeds and of crops, care of children in the field, and so on. There is very little information on the difference in distance to fields. In a Dodoma village, Njelango (1981) found that pre-villagization it averaged 0.25 km and after, 1–3 km. Women do most of the headloading of inputs and products, even from fields primarily cultivated by men; in Kenya, such physical burdens cause many injuries and chronic back problems (Carr 1983). Where new fields were created the problems are longer term. No provision was made for the growth of population, and some villages have now outstripped their avail-able resources. Former techniques of medium- to long-term fallow cannot continue where there are populations with headloading as the only mode of transport. Without additional resources of land or fertilizer, only further inputs of labour can maintain adequate production. Again, this burden falls mainly, though not solely, on peasant women.

Water and fuelwood

All water is fetched by women and girls. The provision of water was one of the key incentives for villagization but there were cases where the new villages were even further from clean water than the old house sites. Maro and Mlay (1976) found this was generally true in two of the nine districts they studied. Often the main criterion for the site of a village was access to a road; and in Geita and in Coast Region, for instance, this meant that villages were placed along dry ridges rather than in valley bottoms. Water pro-vides an example of technology-dependent problems in Tanzania. The infrastructure and machinery may be there, but they are not operational because there are no spare parts, fuel, special equip-ment, expertise, or incentives for operators. Reliable provision of water is always a top priority in 'needs surveys' of village women. When the system breaks down, they must walk. In 1970, 10 per cent of the rural population met the target of clean water within 400 metres; by 1980 it had reached 25 per cent, but, taking into account broken equipment and defunct schemes, probably less than 12 per cent had reliable access (Hannan-Andersson 1982). Maro and Mlay found that, in seven of the nine districts, 70–100 per cent of villages had water sources within 5 km. Magu had only 40 per cent within 5 km, and in Kilosa 23 per cent of villages had water more than 16 km away. In twenty-nine villages in Iringa, Mbeya and Ruvuma regions, a recent and probably more accurate survey found that 45 per cent of households had regular water within 0.5 km, but 11 per cent (20 per cent in Iringa) had to go more than 1.5 km (Schultheis 1982).

Hannan-Andersson (1982), studying a village in Pare district with a reliable central supply, found that women still lacked essential elements of control over the water system – over household water consumption, investment in containers, the site of the houses, and the whole planning, maintaining, and managing of the water scheme. She found very little health improvement over comparable villages, and the time freed from porterage was devoted to additional domestic tasks or to preparing sugar-cane juice for *pombe* (traditionally brewed beer). On the other hand, collection of water, as of firewood, had been a communal activity, with social rewards which should be balanced against the physical effort.

Fuelwood is universally an even greater problem, as wood is being depleted in expanding radii around villages. Wood is by far the most important rural fuel for cooking, for lighting, for heating in upland areas, and for many small village industries, especially brewing, brick-making, pottery, blacksmithery, and charcoal for urban markets. Wood is used by 96 per cent of households for cooking, and by 45 per cent for crop drying/processing (Nkonoki 1983). Current estimates of domestic fuelwood consumption in rural Tanzania are about 1 cu metre per person per annum, or about 5 cu m per household (Skutsch 1983; FAO 1984); though earlier estimates were much higher. Including wood used for other activities, consumption reaches about 7.5 cu m/household/year (1.3 cu m per capita). Almost everywhere women must now walk further for wood, normally 3–5 km two or three times a week. Usually one woman or girl carries for each household, though in some areas women, or men, use donkeys or carts, or purchase from lorry supplies. Headloads are 20 to 30 kg, although headloads up to 60 kg have been found. The time needed is considerable – several studies give estimates of 4 to 12 hours per week (partly depending on the difficulty of collection). As with water, the journeys often have some social value. Responses to local wood shortages (apart from local depletion and 'desertification') include the use of less efficient biomass such as grasses and crop wastes or the use of manure, cutting down productive trees, such as cashews or fruit, less cooking of hot food, less home heating, and less hot water for washing. The shortage causes the double impact of less fuel and less time for women, so that cash-earning potential is lost, child-care sacrificed and school time diverted, especially during peak labour seasons (Cecelski 1984). Alternatives to biomass are out of the question; they are too dear and too scarce. The development of individual or communal fuelwood lots has by no means solved the problem. Individual lots are curbed by local land shortage, uncertainty over land tenure, and political discouragement; communal ones by similar reasons plus the difficulty of deriving long-term communal rewards from intensive individual inputs. Both also have technical problems. Most efforts to date have been ineffectual (Skutsch 1983).

Services

Villagization has probably been most successful in providing social services and an infrastructure for welfare. Access to services was the main incentive for relocation, and over the past decade rural dispensaries, community centres/party offices, and especially primary schools have been built with a combination of government investment, self-help (including much women's input) and aid from donors. Maro and Mlay (1979) found in a sample of eleven districts that all large villages (over 500 adults) had primary schools, and that only one district had failed to increase primary school provision by 25 per cent or more during the villagization period. Eight of the districts in the sample also showed at least a 30 per cent increase in the number of dispensaries per 1000 population. These services must have improved the daily life of women and the welfare of village girls. For example, the government has taken practical steps towards universal primary education for girls as well as boys, despite patriarchal and religious hindrances. Mother and child health is also, theoretically at least, a priority in rural health care, which Tanzania seeks to emphasize along with preventive and social medicine rather than specialized hospital care. However, rural areas face a serious deficiency in birth control services, which have a very limited presence even in towns. The national family planning agency, UMATI, had only 50,000 members in 1975, nearly all urban. Women bear on average more than five children, and there is often a high but unsatisfied demand for contraceptives. Overall, the services existing in villages have helped villagized women. However, the existence of schools and clinics is by no means synonymous with the provision of adequate, motivated staff, and even less with operational equipment, drugs, books, beds or desks. Testimony on village 'needs' always stresses 'functioning' and 'reliable' services rather than mere infrastructure (Maro and Mlay 1976; Kleemeier 1983; Nyerere 1977). Educational

facilities also increase women's burdens by reducing the customary participation of their children in a whole battery of tasks.

Land

Legal, or physical, possession of land is now the prerequisite for
control over the products of the land and for linkages with the
modern market economy, such as co-operative membership or
access to credit (and also for dealing in land, although there is no
official market for land in Tanzania). In peasant systems with
labour intensive, low-yielding cultivation, reinforced by an ideology of 'attachment to the land', the lack of either legal title or
physical control is perhaps the most fundamental cause of the
subordinate position of women. A practical example of this can be
seen in Kilimanjaro and Bukoba (two highly market-oriented farming regions), where 98 per cent of economically active women are
small-scale farmers on land not theirs by legal right (Swantz 1977).
In the whole country 0.4 million smallholdings, out of 2.4 million,
were 'owned' by women.

Before the *Ujamaa* Village Act, customary land law was complex but not static; there were significant regional differences between patrilineal and matrilineal systems of (land) inheritance.
Many tribes had been matrilineal; inheritance was through the
female line and women held independent and unconditional
rights to land, or there were cognate inheritance lines through both
husband and wife. German and British authorities effected changes
in several areas towards more 'rational' male inheritance, easier to
administer for land tenure, marketing, and indirect rule; this
legal–administrative component of subordination has continued
despite *Ujamaa*. Brain (1976) found that in the Village Settlement
Authority schemes (the 1960s 'improvement approach' precursors
to villagization) women lost the rights to land they held under
matrilineal custom. The loss of their material base subordinated
women to their husbands (and sons), as they had to leave the
schemes if divorced or widowed. Many women therefore refused to
work on these schemes, and this helped bring about their collapse.

Villagization itself accelerated this deprivation of rights. The
Ujamaa Village Act called for plot allocation (and subsequently
official registration) to be made separately to all 'members' of the
village. Women are entitled to be village members in their own
right, but they are rarely allotted their 'own' land by the village
authorities. In practice allocation of plots is by 'family', and thus,
by elision, to male 'heads of households'. Legally, the only land

rights that peasants have is usufruct. Land is owned by the state and allocated by the village council, and people have the right to use it and own its produce so long as they are working it productively. In practice, however, the council gives *de facto* continuous entitlement (and *de jure* usufruct) to the male 'family heads'. The usufruct rights of women over their fields (i.e those they continually work on) thus depend on the goodwill of the male head. Women can determine the use and management of their land so long as this meets household (male) needs for food and market crops; having separate plots does not imply separate or equal decision-making. Independent women now receive their own plots only when they are indisputably household heads. Widows, divorcees and unmarried mothers may be allocated plots, and others, such as traders and retired prostitutes, may purchase their own rights to land and be full village members. (Bukoba is particularly known for this.) But generally, whereas previously women had some customary rights they are now much worse off. Caplan (1981) shows how, on Mafia Island, this reduced economic and property status curtails women's access to land, their ability to move, for example, following divorce, and their whole standing in the community. (The changed tenure also restricts the mobility and freedom of old people and adolescent boys.)

Income

Agricultural income

Villagization created physical opportunities such as road access and input supply for expanding market production. It also facilitated control over the whole labour process – supervision of husbandry practices, bye-laws concerning minimum farm size, purchase of produce by state organs, etc. The gender division of labour has changed. Women now help considerably with formerly 'male' cash crops on land owned (and usually managed) by their husbands. The control of land provides the basis for male control of the income from the produce. Official crop sales must be to parastatal crop authorities or regional multi-product co-operatives through the intermediary of the village, which acts as a co-operative buying agent. Co-operative membership is usually limited to recognized 'heads of households' and cash payments for crop sales are paid to these male 'heads'. In the illegal *magendo* market system, too, males predominate – they have contacts with middlemen and transporters and can pay off officials. In legal private trading, e.g. in fruit and vegetables, women are involved but do not dominate as in West Africa. With milk products, for instance, women sell the surplus above household needs – provided they have mobility and access to markets. Bryceson and Mbilinyi (1978) stress that income from female marketing is expended on household reproduction needs, whereas surveys show that male income is likely to be spent on bicycles, radios, beer and women.

Agricultural wage labour

Casual, and sometimes permanent, female agricultural wage labour is growing under the the twin pressures of monetization of subsistence needs (including health and education) and the increase in female-headed households. Virtually all economically active women are in agriculture, but only 5 per cent are in official agricultural wage employment. There is some hired female labour on plantations and state farms; and more women go to work on the larger peasant farms, usually seasonally, especially for weeding, harvesting, and post-harvest processing. A significant proportion may be on richer, larger, female-headed farms where males are absent, as in Rungwe. Farm-to-field porterage may also provide a small cash income for many women; such is the case in Kenya (Carr 1983).

Small industries

More women are engaged in small rural industries and marketing – in pottery, fish drying, poultry, handicrafts, tailoring, charcoal, and, the most significant, brewing. Other sources of income, for which there are no empirical data, are porterage, domestic work and childcare for other women, traditional medicine, midwifery and magic. For all these rural enterprises, villagization has generally been helpful, by expanding the market, allowing economies of scale and outside inputs, disseminating skills and facilitating the set-up of female co-operatives. Unfavourable effects have included the replacement of local crafts by cheaper manufactures and the physical separation of craft workers from essential inputs and fuels. There are also some restrictions not specific to villagization. The current situation in Tanzania is hardly conducive to new enterprises beyond small, often illegal, service activities. Businesses need co-operation with the administration (for numerous permits, licences, and backhanders), and here female entrepreneurs are often discriminated against. Restrictions on women's mobility, access to credit and finance, and land rights, and overall resistance to female financial independence, are also hindrances (Mbilinyi ed. 1984).

Brewing (and distilling) forms an economic subsystem, and holds a prime function in the circulation of rural money. Brewing is significant in resource decisions and in the sale and consumption of maize, millet, bananas, and locally of bamboo, sugar-cane and fruits. Brewing is also a large user of fuelwood. There are variations with different types of brew and of wood used, but a rough estimate, taking into account brewing for home use and ceremonies and larger-scale brewing for sale in village bars, is that between 5 per cent and over 30 per cent of annual village wood consumption is for *pombe*. FAO figures (1984) suggest that brewing consumes 300 to 400 cubic metres per village per annum, which is roughly equivalent to 150–200 hectares of *miombo* (dry, thorny woodland) on a sustained basis. *Pombe* can be a significant component of normal energy intake for adults, especially men (up to 60 per cent for men and 16 per cent for women) (Schultheis 1982). In many parts of Tanzania *pombe* sales are a major direct source of cash for rural women to spend on domestic essentials and chidren. About 55 per cent of women have said that brewing is their main source of income, at least in the slack season (Cecelski 1984), and FAO (1984) found 25 per cent of households said they brewed regularly, one to four times a month. Villagization has probably brought about considerable increases in per capita and total consumption. Spatial concentration allows people to drink socially in larger groups, although still in specific tribal/age/kin/ gender sub-groups. A considerable amount of time (and money) is available for drinking – in villages in Mbeya, from 3 p.m. to 10 p.m. Monday to Saturday, and all day Sunday, although in Usukuma following villagization drinking was restricted to the weekend – there is no other recreation.

The concentration of population has allowed informal groups and co-operatives of village women to build up regular brewing businesses with economies of scale which can reach high levels of turnover and are relatively profitable. Small groups, two to four women, will brew between four and ten 4 gallon containers known as *debes* at a time (80–200 litres), usually once, but maybe twice, a week. Most are settled peasant women; for the bigger producers it has replaced farmwork. Very rough estimates suggest profits of 250 to 420 shs per drum (200 litres). There are also linkages to markets for finger millet, bananas, etc., for firewood, for water where necessary, for making utensils, for hiring *askaris* (night watchmen), and so on. Some income goes into productive activities, to hire tractors or ox-ploughs, or for casual farm labour. Brewing also illustrates how, with commercialization, women's projects tend to be 'hijacked' by men. In peasant societies, wives prepared *pombe* and food for *ngomas* or parties to celebrate events and to feed communal 'working groups'. Women continue this brewing function, but the growing trend is the insertion of male middlemen who purchase direct from brewers and sell for themselves in the *vikao* (*pombe* bars). They and the bar owners create a monopoly market to force down the price, often in collusion with the village licensing committee. Orders are agreed but payment is made on delivery, and as there is some probability that the beer will turn sour during fermentation the risk is the brewer's who could lose an investment of 700 shs or so per drum.

Most small-scale industrial enterprises of village women are heavily fuel-intensive. Pottery-making requires 1 cu m of wood per 100 large clay pots, fish-smoking about 0.8 cu m per tonne of fish, and brick-making about 5 cu m for an ordinary two-roomed house (FAO 1984). Small industries take up to 10–50 per cent of village wood consumption. The direct impact is the extra distance to walk, not only in these businesses, but for all village women. Charcoal for the urban market is fast developing as a male business or a registered village enterprise. Since charcoal is made from natural woodland without any replanting, in areas with market access the charcoal business is indirectly adding to women's resource burden by reducing accessible reserves of village fuels.

Women's co-operatives

Many women's co-operatives have been started up in villages, some 'spontaneously', many instigated by UWT or missions. A large proportion are small farming projects, others are brewing, tailoring, handicrafts, and running bars and lodgings, and some are welfare services such as crêches and nutrition projects. Case studies have found various levels of failure (Mbilinyi, (ed.) 1984). The immediate causes have been identified as the low levels of female experience and training in managerial, commercial and technical fields; but 'male' and 'village' co-operatives also have a very low success rate; moreover, women do have successful businesses, especially in petty trading and marketing. The essential problem is the double burden on the ordinary co-operative member's time; successful projects frequently include a high proportion of older women without family dependants. A second obstacle is patriarchal attitudes and resentment of women's economic independence (on top of bureaucratic suspicion and endeavours to control any projects even slightly independent of party and government). Third, there are the internal economic and social struggles. Many case studies have shown how the organization, and thus policies, management and appropriation of surplus, are taken over by richer female peasants or traders or by educated leaders with connections with the bureaucracy (Mascarenhas and Mbilinyi 1983; Mbilinyi ed. 1984). Villagization nevertheless has had a positive impact in creating opportunities for women's cooperatives and the potential to learn from each other, and generally to raise their consciousness of the triple facets of their 'exploitation' as poor, peasant women.

Village government and decision-making

A declared intent of villagization was to extend democracy and decision-making to the lowest levels, and mechanisms were laid down for this in the Village Act and in government directives. The extent to which economic and political power has been brought to the masses is debatable. The institutions exist, and may sometimes thwart richer peasants or promote popular proposals, but village studies generally have not found increased mass control. The assembly allows broader discussion over political topics, and village plans are widely debated; but the resettlement and its associated economic changes have actually reduced peasants' discretion and subjected them to more external direction.

Women are largely underrepresented both in elected posts and in village debates. (Since this is also true for appointed decision-making offices, there is little direct female contribution to village planning except through the official women's political organization, the Ushirika wa Wanawake ya Tanzania (UWT). An official survey by the prime minister's office in 1979 found in 514 sample villages no woman chairman or secretary and only thirty-two village managers. Another sample found an average of three to five women among the twenty-five village council members. However, other studies have found more women taking part in politics, and some tendency for women to hold finance posts because they are 'less likely to be corrupt'. The specific reasons for women's lack of representation are: restrictions on party membership; the failure of UWT to mobilize women or articulate the needs of the poorer strata; unfamiliarity with Kiswahili; illiteracy; discouragement or hostility from menfolk; and historico-cultural passivity (especially in Islamic areas) when confronted by male visiting officials and aid workers. Behind these lie the two primary causes. First, in the eyes of the law women only exceptionally 'own' land or are 'heads of households', and thus village leaders see no reason to involve women in planning. Women's work in agriculture and domestic maintenance is discounted: 'Women have been as brainwashed about the worthless nature of their work as men have, thereby devaluing themselves as well as their own skills and knowledge' (Mbilinyi 1984). The second cause is the large amount of work done by women. Women simply do not have time to attend the voluble debates of village government and lengthy harangues of visiting dignitaries (though they are more likely to attend technical addresses). Village meetings are usually scheduled for late afternoon, when farmwork is finished but women are fetching water or cooking. Thus the burdens are exacerbated by the lack of opportunity to alter the inequalities through political decision-making. Women who do take part tend to be wives from richer households, or older women without dependants, who may have personal and class interests in conflict with those of village women in general.

Village communal activities

Communal projects as a step towards *ujamaa* life include village *shamba* work and self-help building of schools, clinics, teachers' houses, CCM offices and so on. Construction projects are usually more popular and successful because they lead to concrete results with some benefit for all. Communal *shamba* work, however, conflicts with peasants' peak labour demands and is not expected to provide any personal benefits except to the village leadership. Lack of motivation coupled with poor organization and management, leads to low outputs and yields, and extremely low returns to labour time in communal farming. Moreover, *ujamaa* farm output is sold at the lower, official prices. Communal farmwork is usually so unpopular that it must be enforced through sanctions and fines, and wives may be pressed to do their husbands' shares (Dumont and Mottin 1979). Since women are already doubly burdened, and since they have little control over the planning and output of village projects, it is not surprising that they sometimes refuse or somehow avoid their 'share' of *ujamaa* labour. Women may then be criticized for a negative attitude towards *ujamaa* and classed as reactionary; this reinforces their exclusion from village decision-making.

Villagization and the double burden – what will women do?

It is difficult to distinguish between the effects on women's status of spatial concentration and the broader effects of the continuing transformation of peasant production. The problem is compounded by the lack of evaluation of the results of villagization. The immediate assessment would be negative – there are few material benefits except physical access to primary education, health and, often, water. Access to water, which should bring a significant saving of drudgery can have little effect on women's activities and life-style unless their fundamental workloads, lack of education, restricted mobility and subordinate position are remedied. Improved water supplies, too, have often only created opportunities for more domestic work, such as collecting the now less accessible fuelwood, or for more beer-brewing.

The drawbacks of villagization can be summarized as increased pressures and greater risks for all peasant producers: more pressures to produce for the market; new pressures on the carrying capacity of farmland and the surrounding environment; and pressures falling on labour because the effective working day is reduced by travelling time and often by inefficient participation in *ujamaa* activities. These pressures directly endanger the survival of peasants. State services and technology are insufficient to counter the new risks to health and to the environment; and peasant households lose their self-sufficiency in becoming dependent on an inefficient, overstretched parastatal marketing system. At the same time they become more dependent on the state in crises, e.g. for famine relief. Women are more acutely affected because they are primarily responsible for household maintenance. Concomitantly, the double burden weighs more heavily on them as they are drawn further into expanding commodity production.

Villagization, by reducing the physical separation of women, has perhaps enabled them to recognize their situation and has encouraged social analyses of it. Their range of contacts has been enlarged and this has generated a new awareness. More concretely, real opportunities occur for forming women's co-operatives and informal groupings for productive and welfare activities, although, at the same time, 'traditional' reciprocal groups based on kinship and neighbourhood have often faded because of the suspicion and mistrust caused by the influx of strangers and the actual layout of the new villages. Probably more significant is the demographic and social change caused by male outmigration, which leaves a significant number of households headed (permanently?) by women. In some villages these women already have rights to their own land, and the demand for this will surely increase. A shift in the perception and acknowledgement of women's responsibility for the household may follow and allow some resolution of the conflicts over women's co-operative membership, marketing, and so on. Continuing psycho-cultural changes should also follow as village women develop their skills in management, trading, and mechanical handling tasks. These changes will not come about without a struggle and hardship for all the rural population.

In the short run, some specific reorientations of policy would alleviate parts of the double burden:

1   moves towards legal protection for personal land holdings and co-operative membership in villages for non-'independent' women;
2   easier CCM membership for women, and institutional mechanisms to ensure greater participation in decision-making;
3   (rapid) resource assessment of village sites and environments to determine actual workloads in farming, etc. Physical planning of villages with respect to resources, population and needs could considerably lighten women's load (even without mechanization, but, for instance, through developing 'satellite villages');
4   identification and introduction of appropriate technology (this involves the complex conceptual and methodological problems of what village women recognize as 'appropriate' for themselves, and subsequently how they can adopt it, retain it and sustain it to alleviate their own situation).

The future for village women depends on the outcome of social struggles at many levels: subordinate women against dominant village women, women against men, small peasants vs emerging large-scale farmers, private vs communal farming, rural vs urban needs, the masses vs the state bureaucracy, and, over all, the contradictions of Tanzania's underdevelopment. It is crucial to determine whether patriarchal dominance in the rural economy is a necessary part, or whether it is somehow independent, of class relationships in the capitalist arena. Will women reduce their own burdens through deeper involvement in the market economy, though as full participants (with 'wages' in accordance with their input)? Or will they succeed only through creating new forms of co-operative organization – mutually supportive, less competitive and presenting a united front to capital and the state?

Glossary

askari   guard, night watchman
baraza   village meeting
bwana shamba   agricultural extension agent
CCM   Chama cha Mapinduzi (Party of the Revolution): Tanzania's sole political party
debe   gallon container (usually for kerosene)
magendo   'blackmarket', 'alternative' market, 'parallel' market (also connotes sometimes illegal activities such as bribery)
miombo   dry thorny woodland, mainly Brachystegia–Isoberlinia
ngoma   traditional dance party (as a social occasion)
pombe   traditionally brewed grain beer
shamba   cultivated farming plot, or the whole farm area
ujamaa   (literally: familyhood); communal village living and production units (and the philosophy behind it)
UWT   Ushirika wa Wanawake ya Tanzania – official women's political organization, one of five affiliates to CCM.
vijiji(ni)   village(s).

8   A decade of change in the Lake Titicaca region

Jane Benton

Editors' introduction

Capitalist penetration in agriculture is widely seen as having adverse effects on women relative to men (Boserup 1970; Chapter 1). Chapters 5 and 7 have illustrated such situations, as does Agarwal in Part Six. But advocates of the 'modernization' view that women gain both relatively and absolutely from capitalist penetration also draw on empirical examples. The truth is that women do not and cannot constitute a homogeneous category; their situations vary on several dimensions, including place, class and life-cycle. At specific times and places, some women undoubtedly gain from capitalist penetration in agriculture, although it remains our view that it is more common for life options to be reduced.

The women whom Benton studied on two occasions, a decade apart, are a modernization paradigm. Perhaps given unusual opportunities by their locality, many of them seem to a considerable extent to have gained control of their income and their bodies, achieving education and independence and escaping violence and oppression. They remain poor. Benton concurs with Domitila (Barrios de Chungara 1978), a Bolivian feminist from the mines, that the Third World reality is of the economic and social subjugation of both sexes, which they will have to combine to overturn; the traditional oppression of women is but a facet of this.

Theoretically, this is perhaps the least feminist chapter in this book. All the more interesting that it is this chapter which most consistently annoys male chauvinists, for a significant number of these women who have so significantly improved their lot are willing to dispense with men, save briefly for the begetting of children. For women to be good only for the begetting of children is a familiar theme; for men to be viewed in the same light is clearly heresy.

Recent changes in the domestic lives and economic activities of Aymara *campesinas* (peasant women) in Bolivia's Lake Titicaca region have been dramatic. This chapter will discuss these changes in communities that were studied in 1971 and again in 1981. It is encouraging to have a contrast to the general Third World trend of a gradual deterioration in the socio-economic situation of women. Any former division of labour in the traditional crafts of weaving and knitting has been effaced as men and women alike capitalize on the ever-expanding tourist industry; campesinas, whatever their marital status, are not discriminated against as entrepreneurs because campesinos have come to appreciate, albeit reluctantly, the superiority of the women's marketing skills and are obliged to rely on them for their livelihood; additionally, teenage girls and married women with few dependants are extremely mobile, and many of them spend weekdays on field tasks by the lakeside and the weekends (the peak marketing period) with relatives in the city of La Paz.

The Lake Titicaca region is in the forefront of change; if not unique, it is by no means typical of highland Bolivia. Life in more isolated rural communities has changed insignificantly over the thirty years since agrarian reform; many communities on the altiplano still await better communications, housing improvement, electricity, secondary education, marketing facilities and consumer goods. Even along the lakeshore, it would be misleading to create the impression that all is well. Weather hazards (floods in 1981, drought in 1983), lack of reliable drinking water and sanitation, abysmal health standards, national political instability and sudden, drastic devaluations of the currency are problems that beset lakeside and remote communities alike.

Buechler (1980) reports that, 'the division of labor according to sex is very pronounced among the Aymara. Men undertake the more arduous tasks, such as plowing, while women do the lighter work in the fields' (i.e. strenuous weeding and clod-breaking with crude, heavy tools!). In the early 1970s the lot of campesinas was excessively harsh, in this and every other respect. Teenage girls viewed marriage as an inescapable means of acquiring some measure of security and protection; it either came about through rape or was arranged by fathers or other male relatives, with land or livestock prospects uppermost in mind – emotions were not considered. Of an average of ten children born per family, only three or four usually survived 'the dangerous years' (to the age of 5), and girl twins, representing 'a curse of the gods' were still being suffocated at birth. Women interviewed by the author in 1971 stated that their most acute problem, apart from food shortage and male physical violence, was the difficulty of watching over several children while engaged in field work. Few girls received much formal education; fathers, always the undisputed heads of households, believed girls' education to be 'a waste of time and money'. Enrolments at secondary schools were rare. For girls whose fathers were either landless or in control of insufficient land for cultivating cash crops, domestic service in La Paz (usually for a pittance) provided the only escape. Girls from traditionally free holdings (never subject to the injustices of the *hacienda* system), where the pressure on land was less intense, had begun to sell onions in city street markets – an experience which has since proved invaluable in fostering more ambitious business enterprises.

According to Figueroa and Anderson (1981), one of the 'survival strategies' adopted by Andean women enduring subordination in a male-dominated society is 'their intense relationships with female friends and relatives', which 'compensate women for their frequently troubled relationships with their male *compañeros*'. Such was not the case in 1971 in the lakeside area where women, often sexually abused, were personally withdrawn and accustomed to suffering alone in their adobe homesteads, while fear compelled them to remain loyal to their household heads.

However, women's lives in this region have been transformed. Marriage patterns have become remarkably flexible: girls meet their partners at secondary school or when visiting La Paz – 'arranged' marriages are now rare occurrences. A growing number of young wives within the study area come from other Bolivian cities, partly because local girls refused to accept the proposals of lakeside boys before they had completed military service. Amazingly, half the teenage girls interviewed in 1981 were adamant that they would remain single in order to preserve their independence and to avoid becoming victims of wife-beating. Despite a Roman Catholic tract (1975) urging *campesinos* 'to denounce and personally resist all forms of birth control and to submit to the will of God and the needs of Bolivia', none of the young couples interviewed in 1981 planned to have more than two or three children – 'life and education are dear'. The stigma attached to illegitimacy, resulting previously in countless deaths from attempted abortions to escape ignominy, has receded. Indeed, several young women remarked that although they had no intentions of marrying, they would like a child 'for company'.

Since 1977 an ever-increasing number of girls from lakeside communities have been completing secondary school courses. For the daughters of landless *campesinos* secondary education now provides the means of entry to teaching, nursing and the police force – welcome alternatives to economic, often sexual, exploitation in domestic service in urban *blanco* ('white') establishments.

Girls from *comunidades* (free communities) have similar aspirations; they can speak Spanish fluently and dress *a la moda* (western style). Generally speaking they are more cash-oriented and eager to begin their commercial careers at the earliest opportunity (i.e. when proficient in Spanish and elementary bookkeeping). Selling onions for their fathers is regarded as a useful preparation for selling products for their own financial benefit. In recent years marketing activities have greatly increased in both volume and variety. For example, by 1981 a number of young *campesinas* from Compi community were regularly visiting the Yungas (the valley region east of La Paz) to sell lake fish, dried meat and vegetables purchased from lakeside markets; others from Compi and Huatajata had lucrative businesses raising and selling pedigree pigs. Women were running the majority of general stores in lakeshore communities, obtaining their stock mainly in La Paz. Women from Llamacachi, in addition to other ventures, were buying liquid gas for cooking from the national oil company, to sell by contract in their home communities. One aged *campesina* displayed remarkable skill and initiative by setting up and successfully running a bakery, employing four men and supplying local markets and general stores along the lakeshore (bread was formerly distributed from city bakeries, over distances of up to 110 km).

The women themselves regard the ready access to machinery, especially bicycles and sewing machines as one of the greatest achievements. These were previously denied to them on the grounds of their alleged 'clumsiness'. Several women have dealt a strong blow to *machísmo* (male pride) by fishing on the lake, traditionally a male prerogative.

Such unprecedented changes have been accompanied, not surprisingly, by modifications in attitudes and behaviour patterns. Women have become more 'open', more self-confident, politically aware and assertive; they are only too willing to discuss domestic affairs, such as financial difficulties and physical abuse, even with strangers – despite the obvious resentment of their *compañeros*. As they frequently remark, 'there is strength in numbers'. They are critical of the freedom enjoyed by men, who have no domestic responsibilities, and have for several years been demanding the right to attend community meetings and participate in making decisions which affect their lives – they are particularly vociferous about the need for reliable supplies of drinking water.

What accounts for the greatly improved social position and

economic strength of women in what has been from time immemorial a patriarchal society?

Geographical factors are obviously of tremendous significance: while not determining the shape and pace of changes, clearly they have greatly facilitated it. 'Proximity to La Paz has countless inextricable implications in terms of, for example, rural–urban migration, marketing activities, educational opportunities leading to government employment, the influx of consumer goods and the high degree of politicization of the lakeshore' (Benton 1984). The lakeside zone benefits from more amenable climatic and soil conditions than those prevailing elsewhere on the bleak, windswept *altiplano*. Furthermore, lakeshore communities are strategically located for the dramatic development of tourism within the Lake Titicaca region. Despite an age-old hostility towards outsiders, *campesinos* and *campesinas* alike appear to have welcomed the advent of tourism because of the commercial opportunities it presents. Women are now accustomed to haggling with individual visitors about prices for woven articles, and many *campesinas* sell items by contract to city tourist shops, thereby frustrating the endeavours of unscrupulous middlemen. Moreover, communication has been considerably eased by the paving and re-routing of the main thoroughfare, thus halving the average journey time between Llamacachi and La Paz, a distance of 105 km. Many *campesinas* regard the replacement of open trucks by rural buses for passenger transport as one of the most beneficial innovations over the last decade.

Unquestionably, education has played a vital role in raising the status of lakeside women. 'Education can challenge the subservient role of women, giving them wage-earning potential, confidence, status, independence and new possibilities. Educated women pose a challenge to male authority' (World University Service 1984). Certainly, in the study area education has had its effect on marriage patterns, family size, greater respect for women on the part of young men, and women's newly acquired confidence and assertiveness. Not surprisingly, education is highly prized by women of all ages: many schoolgirls are teaching their mothers to read and write, and some mothers admit to hoarding hard-earned cash to finance their daughters' secondary education. In many parts of Bolivia fathers deny their daughters access to secondary schooling; in the Lake Titicaca region the feelings of *campesinos* are, understandably, ambivalent. Fathers strongly resent the fact that their daughters are better educated than themselves, but have come to accept secondary education, especially instruction in Spanish and mathematics, as essential for profitable marketing. The girls have learnt to manipulate the system to serve their long-term aspirations.

Women feel that these improvements have been greatly facilitated by their gaining access to a cash economy and an ever-expanding network of marketing facilities, denied to them in pre-agrarian reform days (before 1953). Smaller families place fewer strains on them, enabling them to take full advantage of rewarding openings. Many campesinas enjoy the social aspects of marketing – travelling in company, chatting in the street markets and staying with friends or relatives; others allege that they have assumed financial responsibility for their families from sheer necessity. The reasons are multifarious, and vary from the illness, death, laziness, or drunkenness of spouses, to desertion and the temporary migration of family members to seek work. In some situations, where the husband and male children are absent, a heavy burden is placed on the wife; unless she can afford to pay for casual labour, she is obliged to undertake heavy farm work in addition to employing her skills and resources in entrepreneurial activities. On the other hand, it appears that an increasing number of the young wives of government employees working elsewhere in Bolivia prefer not to join their husbands, remaining instead with the people they have always known by Lake Titicaca, where, away from the noise and pollution of cities, they are able to plan their field tasks round their visits to market. Women so placed are obliged to act for most of the time as household heads and to take family decisions.

Through generations of struggle against alien forces, Aymara women have acquired the courage and determination to fight against the odds and survive; an astuteness, fostered by adversity, has equipped them to take advantage of changing circumstances and to gain control over their own lives. Several stalwart women entrepreneurs from the lakeshore have, within the last few years, held positions of leadership in women's city market syndicates, defending their own rights and protecting other campesinas from the malpractices of the city police and other government officials.

The militancy of the wives of Bolivian miners, especially Domitila, has also had an impact on peasant women throughout Bolivia. Lakeside men have tended to withdraw and regard their neighbours with suspicion – a suspicion arising from land claims, political intrigue, contraband and cocaine smuggling – but their women have drawn ever closer together for their mutual benefit (Figueroa and Anderson's statement, discussed above, is becoming true). Lakeside campesinas were well represented at the First

National Congress of Bolivian Peasant Women, held in La Paz in 1980. As an encouragement to *campesinas* congress leaders drafted a sixty-four-point manifesto, calling for improvements in their social, economic, political, cultural and education position. 'Women are beginning to discuss, to ask questions, to talk about their needs. If we work well together, maybe we can even make the government listen to us. But if we stay in our houses, we have nothing. No one is going to take any notice of us' (the words of a *campesina* delegate to the congress, quoted by Bronstein).

It is to be hoped that the achievements of the women in the Lake Titicaca area will withstand the test of time and will become commonplace within the next few years both in Bolivia and throughout the Andean region.

Part Four

Labour Reserve Regions

9 Women, migration and work in Lesotho

Clive Wilkinson

Editors' introduction

Many nations and regions of the world function in the spatial division of labour as labour reserves. They reproduce labour for distant markets, where the workers will not necessarily receive a wage that will cover the subsistence costs of their families at home; labour reserve areas subsidize workers' wages at the migrants' destination. Migrant labour was part of the international trading economy before the industrial era and has been an important factor in the development of the international economy, but the world market in labour is still growing. Migrant labour, remittances and split households (within or even between nations) are all increasingly important features of Third World social and economic geography. Whether as a cause or effect of their labour reserve role, the development of the productive forces in such areas is always inadequate to the population: many labour reserve areas suffer ecological imbalance and resource depletion. These include mountainous areas (the Himalaya, the Atlas, the Mexican sierras, Indonesia and the Philippines) and drought-prone regions (India, Pakistan, north-east Brazil and much of Africa), but by no means all source areas are rural. One modern feature is the scale of restrictions of migration as the state increasingly intervenes.

The greatest polarization is found in southern Africa. Controls on migration here introduce the most dramatic distortions. Most studies examine the migrants, the remittances, or both; Wilkinson reports on the life options of the women left behind – left behind not just because of the statistical preponderance of male migration over female so common in Africa and parts of Asia (Chapter 1), but because of the banning of female migration to South Africa, the frontier being sex-selective.

Introduction

Migration provides a dramatic and highly visible response to socio-economic change, a response which carries the seeds of yet further change in both the sending and receiving areas. Female migration in Lesotho is one such 'further change' which contains unexpected features. In southern Africa, one of the most enduring and fundamental facts of life is the migration of labour between core and periphery. The core is represented by the large urban industrial complexes of South Africa, particularly that centred on Pretoria–Witwatersrand–Vereeniging; the periphery includes the 'Homelands' in South Africa and such states as Lesotho, Swaziland and Botswana. Labour migration was initially a response to European intervention in the nineteenth century, and it has continued virtually unabated to the present day. Its impact on the receiving areas of South Africa has been profound, forcing the authorities to resort to legislation to limit cross-cultural contact between racial groups and thus to avert the possibility of social transformation. The impact on the sending areas of the periphery has been equally far-reaching. Of all the southern African states, Lesotho is the most heavily dependent on labour migration, with about 33 per cent of the total labour force employed in South Africa, compared with approximately 5 per cent in formal employment inside Lesotho (Colclough 1980). Lesotho is a classic example of a peasant economy that has been transformed into a spatially specific labour reserve. Basotho labour migrants, as elsewhere in southern Africa, are typically male, giving rising to high masculinity indices in the reception areas, notably the mining regions, while in the sending areas the population is predominantly feminine. Lesotho may aptly be described as a land of gold widows: most of the able-bodied men are absent, and the women, children and old men are left to make of life what they can. Basotho women, therefore, live in a society in which most of the burden of agricultural work and social reproduction falls on their shoulders; the burning issue is the way in which society is structured in order to keep them in subordination. Yet the subordination is not complete, for Basotho women are on the whole better educated than the men and have considerable autonomy born of a long tradition of managing and maintaining home and land. It is against this background that we may examine the role and position of women, the personal conflicts inherent in their situation, and the possible ways in which these conflicts may be resolved. We shall focus on the movement of women to the towns of Lesotho, especially Maseru, and relate this to the way they respond to the constraints and opportunities brought about by social and economic change.

General features of female migration

It is not always clear how sex acts as a basis for selectivity in migration; the pattern changes over time and varies from region to region. In nineteenth-century England females migrated more than males, especially over short distances. Grigg (1977) attributes this to the lack of employment for women in rural areas, the demand for domestic servants, and the tendency for women to move on marriage. It has also been suggested that the preponderance of women in short moves in Europe was due to the fact that women tend to follow 'more institutionalized and less risky migratory streams' (Simmons 1976). Men, it is alleged, move when the economic risks are greater, and their wives join them later when prospects become less uncertain. In more recent years the predominance of women in migrant moves in the United Kingdom has decreased considerably, and Lewis (1982) suggests that in the western world generally males are now more migratory than females.

In the Third World men far outnumber women in rural-to-urban migration. There are, however, exceptions. In Latin America the majority of rural-to-urban migrants are women, and a similar situation is to be found in the Philippines. In Asia and Africa, however, such migration is typically more masculine than feminine. It is usual for women, particularly in Africa, to take responsibility for working the land while men move to town on a permanent or recurrent basis. Thus, it is the young males who dominate most African migration streams, and when women do migrate it is usually to join husbands already working in town. It is also true, however, that the proportion of women moving to African towns is increasing; as a result, the urban sex ratios (males per 100 females) are decreasing. For Ghana's internal migrants, for example, the ratio fell from 129 in 1960 to 120 in 1970, while for the 15–24 age group the decline was from 121 to 107 (Zachariah and Condé 1981). By and large, however, the urban sex ratios in Africa still remain consistently masculine; Gugler (1981) reports for twenty-two African countries in the period 1965–71 an average urban sex ratio of 109. The increased flow of women to African towns may be the result of one or more of several factors. Little risk is incurred when women move to join their husbands as economic dependants, female labour is in increasing demand, there is a growing tendency for economically independent women to move to town, a trend already well established in Latin America and the Philippines. In the specific case of Lesotho it will be seen that all these factors are at work.

Female migration in Lesotho

Broadly speaking, it is true to say of Lesotho that men are more mobile externally and women more mobile internally. A questionnaire survey of urban and rural residents in 1978, for example, revealed that of the 269 respondents who had worked in South Africa, only 23 per cent were women; of the 421 who had migrated to the capital, Maseru, on the other hand, women accounted for 54.7 per cent. Moreover, within the rural sector, which contains over 90 per cent of the population, it is normal for a woman to move to her husband's home on marriage. In a survey of 130 households in three villages in the foothills, for example, 84 per cent of the males, but only 48 per cent of females, were born in their place of residence. Of the total rural–rural moves recorded, females accounted for 80 per cent. In the rural areas of Lesotho, therefore, there is a tradition of female movement on marriage, while the typical rural male moves to and from the mines of South Africa. This dual pattern of migration pervades rural life. Women too have sought and found work in South Africa, and in 1956 women constituted 27 per cent of the total Basotho working in the republic. Since the early 1960s, however, there has been a marked decline in female absenteeism as a result of the plethora of measures introduced by the South African government to control entry. Those women who had work experience in the republic were generally employed as domestic servants or in the manufacturing sector.

In recent years another pattern of mobility has been emerging, that of migration from the country to towns inside Lesotho. A survey, conducted by the author, of 533 households in two peripheral areas of Maseru, Thamaes and Qoaling, found that 78.5 per cent of the resident population were migrants. Over a third of these migrants had been in residence for three years or less, and over two-thirds for nine years or less. Maseru grew from a population of just 5739 in 1956 to 21,400 in 1966 and to 45,700 in 1976. It is now growing at over 11 per cent per annum. This can only be the result of massive urban migration, for natural growth rates are in the region of 2.8 per cent per annum. Like urban migrants elsewhere in the Third World, migrants to Maseru tend to be relatively well educated and young (see Tables 36 and 37). However, what is surprising, even in the context of an increasing proportion of migrant females in Africa generally, is the large number of young women among the urban migrants. For Maseru, the data on age at time of move give a sex ratio for the under-24 group of 48.8 males per 100 females and for the migrant population as a whole 83.0.

Table 36 Internal migrant status and education

Years of full-time education	Rural residents		Maseru migrants	
	No.	%	No.	%
7 or more	62	47.7	338	80.9
6 or less	68	52.3	80	19.1
Total	130	100	418	100

Source: Urban and rural surveys, 1978 (3 missing cases).

Table 37 Age of Maseru migrants at time of move, by sex

Age	Males		Females	
	No.	%	No.	%
24 or less	60	32.8	123	55.7
25–34	60	32.8	55	24.9
35–44	42	22.9	27	12.2
44+	21	11.5	16	7.2
Total	183	100	221	100

Source: Urban survey, 1978 (17 missing cases).

Women also move when very young: 56 per cent of the female migrants were aged 24 or less at the time of move, compared with 33 per cent of the males, and over 70 per cent moved before the age of 30, compared with 55 per cent of the males. The unusually high proportion of young women among the urban migrants in Maseru reflects similar sex ratios reported elsewhere. The data of Monyake (1973) yield a sex ratio of 66.21 for the 20–29 age group, and so low are the ratios in the lowland townships generally that he concludes, 'large numbers of females in the age range 15–39 years (but more especially 15–29) are flooding the towns, presumably to take up employment, or alternatively perhaps in pursuit of the urban limelight'. In the urban areas of Lesotho there is what Monyake calls a 'grotesque imbalance' between the sexes. Teyateyaneng, for example, has a sex ratio of 34.34 for the 25–29 age group and 37.89 for the 30–34 year olds. These ratios are too low to be accounted for by male absenteeism alone. Using census data to compute expected sex ratios (i.e. ratios which take account of absenteeism in South Africa) for the Maseru district for the three critical age groups of 20–24, 25–29 and 30–34, it is possible to compare expected with observed values for the number of males in each group (Table 38). It

Table 38   Difference between observed and expected number of
males in Maseru survey (252 persons)

Age group	Males oberved as per cent of those 'expected'
20–24	19
25–29	82
30–34	87

Source: Based on census and urban survey data.

is clear that the surplus of young females must be accounted for by
factors other than male absenteeism in the republic.

Why do women move to town?

Why do so many women move to town in Lesotho? One explanation, reflecting trends elsewhere in Africa, is that a growing
number of women are moving to town with, or to join, their husbands. Sabot (1979), for example, showed that in Tanzania 66 per
cent of the women who moved to town did so to be with their
husbands as economic dependants. In Lesotho, however, only 28
per cent of the female migrants stated that they had moved to
Maseru 'to be with my husband'. (A total of 38.9 per cent of the
migrant women in Maseru cited domestic reasons for moving,
compared with 3.2 per cent of the males.) Another possible explanation may be the increasing tendency for independent women to
move to town as a direct response to growing prospects for employment there, and as a result of a changing social climate. Sabot
(1979) detected a growing female involvement in the Tanzanian
urban labour market and noted that this increased with the length
of full-time education. The opportunities for women to gain a
better education, the improved economic prospects resulting from
this, and the changes in women's perception of their social role,
may all be reasons why there is an increased flow of independent
women to African towns. Gugler and Flanagan (1978), in their
work on West Africa, also stressed the importance of social and
psychological factors in the movement of independent women to
town. They cite barrenness, which places women in the rural
community in a weak economic and social position, marital instability, and education, which often renders young girls 'dissatisfied
with the prospects that marriage in the rural community offers', as
push factors.

Comparison with Tanzania again highlights the distinctive-ness of Lesotho. The increased flow of independent women to town in Tanzania is evidenced by the growing proportion of female urban migrants who are unmarried on arrival; this has risen from 13 to 33 per cent in recent years, while the proportion of single male arrivals has remained fairly steady at between 58 and 64 per cent (Sabot 1979). The evidence for Lesotho, however, shows that more independent women than men are moving to town. Thus, in Maseru 38 per cent of the female migrants were single, compared with 19 per cent of the males. In addition, it must be remembered that, of the 62 per cent who were married at the time of the survey, a large number will have had little or no contact with their husbands for a long period because of the separation imposed by the migrant labour system. Many will have lost contact with their husbands altogether and may, therefore, be regarded as 'independent'. Furthermore, 49 per cent of the women stated that they had moved to town for economic reasons, while in Tanzania only 9 per cent said this. By comparison with Tanzania, then, fewer women moved to town in Lesotho to join their husbands, more were single or of independent status on arrival, and more moved specifically to participate in the urban economy rather than as economic dependants. In other words, a much larger proportion of independent women are moving to town in Lesotho than in Tanzania and perhaps in the rest of Africa.

The position of Basotho women

To understand why this is so it is necessary to appreciate the pressures which surround Basotho women in a migrant labour economy. First and foremost among the constraints on role and status are the severe limitations imposed by male absenteeism. 'The absence of the majority of the male population is a striking feature' (Agency for Industrial Mission 1976); 'a woman left alone is the norm in Lesotho' (Gordon 1981). According to Safilios–Rothschild (1985) 60–70 per cent of rural households are headed by women. However, only about half of these have migrant husbands and receive remittances; the rest are widows (this is attributable to the high mortality rates associated with mining in South Africa and to the fact that rural husbands are usually much older than their wives). Gordon (1981) not only refutes the view that the absence of men is so normal that families adjust to it without its being significantly disruptive, but finds evidence that the hardships involved become increasingly intolerable over time. A reasonable level of agricultural output becomes difficult to maintain: 'I have problems with work in the fields, because there is no one to help me in ploughing. Another problem is theft of cattle, crops or farming implements. Our headman has tried to stop it. But it still goes on' (Agency for Industrial Mission 1976). Yet extra work on the land must be performed, and this is, of course, in addition to the responsibilities of home and children.

It is true that men tend to be at home at the time of the most critical agricultural operations, the spring ploughing and the planting of maize. Yet they are of little help to their wives and spend most of their time tending livestock or relaxing. Where they do help 'once the subsistence crop is in, men at home feel they have done their agricultural duty and are free to take up a new mining contract towards the end of the calendar year' (Wallman 1969). Nor are men always present even for ploughing. Some indication of the strain placed on wives may be gained from the fact that even in the period of ploughing, October and November, 63 per cent of households in a village near Butha Buthe in 1974 had no male present aged 17 years or over. So important is the role of women in taking responsibility for rural households and agricultural tasks that Murray (1981) finds it necessary to distinguish between the roles of household 'head' and household 'manager', arguing that about 70 per cent of rural households are effectively managed by women.

Women also face the uncertainty of cash remittances from absentee husbands, and frequently outright abandonment. The following quotation typifies the predicament of many women: 'My husband left four years ago and has never contacted me since. . . . To care for my children I have to work in other people's fields and I knit jerseys and bake cakes to sell' (Agency for Industrial Mission 1976). Many women are under intolerable economic strain with little or no secure income from migrant husbands; others, the widows who head 30–35 per cent of all rural households, receive no remittances and often, because of traditional land tenure practices, have diminished access to land. Severe strains are imposed on family and personal relationships by long periods of absenteeism in South Africa. 'When I was married my husband was already employed at the mines . . . since we were married we never stayed for a year together enjoying life. He only comes home on leave for about three weeks a year' (Agency for Industrial Mission 1976). The absence of men, dependence on uncertain cash remittances, heavy domestic and agricultural responsibilities, and broken or fragile relationships make it hardly surprising 'that women's experience ranges from relative security to bitter frustration, acute personal stress and emotional desolation' (Murray 1981).

At one time women had the possibility of work in South Africa and thus of some measure of economic and personal independence. Since the 1960s, however, this has been extremely difficult. Basotho men have work permits arranged for them by the labour recruiting organizations inside Lesotho; women, if they are desperate enough, resort to illegal border crossings to seek work. This blocking of female labour migration is the second severe constraint on women. In South Africa, the political economy of apartheid demands a *temporarily* resident black urban labour force. Recent legislation, therefore, ensures that 'the number of Africans legally in the cities is increasingly composed of men, men who are on limited time contracts', and 'the law is used to maintain and intensify the pattern of oscillating migration' (Wilson 1972). The disruption of Basotho female labour migration is part and parcel of this process. It imposes severe constraints on women who might otherwise have been able to establish independent lives for themselves.

A third constraint is imposed by male attitudes in Africa to female migration to towns. As Obbo (1980) shows, 'the subject of female migration is controversial throughout Africa generally'. In East Africa, for example, both the urban authorities and migrant men have always regarded females who migrate to town alone as a problem, so much so that in Kampala in the 1950s there were laws 'requiring the repatriation of all single women found loitering in town' (Obbo 1980). Obbo reports that the prevailing attitude in East Africa is still that 'urban migration is bad for women because it corrupts their virtue, leads to marital instability and erodes traditional norms. This leads to the weakening of family structure, an increase in juvenile delinquency and violent crimes'. Obbo's own research on female urban migrants in Uganda and Kenya, however, indicates that the towns, far from being morally corrupting, offer an opportunity for women to improve themselves and their children socially and economically, especially by enabling them to earn enough money to pay for their children's education. In Lesotho similar attitudes prevail. It is a male-dominated society in which men expect women to play a subservient role, to remain in the rural areas when men are absent working in the Republic, to perform their allotted tasks and to obey their husbands. The vehemence with which these views are expressed, even by educated men in the presence of educated women, is a stark reminder of the rigidity of certain attitudes in a rapidly changing society. From these attitudes springs the hostility to female emancipation and the consequent deep suspicion towards the migration of women to town. So strong are these attitudes that rural women are thwarted in their attempts to improve their status and to promote their economic and political interests through self-help groups. Safilios–Rothschild (1985) states that there are powerful structural and normative obstacles to the official registration of these groups as co-operatives; without official status these groups are ignored for administrative and development purposes, despite their proven ability to function as productive units. It is not surprising, therefore, that many rural women seek a solution to their problems by moving to the towns of Lesotho, especially Maseru, in search of work and independence only to be forced into starting a shebeen (where illicit beer brewing takes place) and into the prostitution which so often accompanies this activity.

Positive factors

Constraints on the role and status of Basotho women are severe; yet there are encouraging factors which help us to understand female migration to the towns. Foremost among these is what Murray

Table 39   Women and education in Lesotho

Whole of Lesotho, 1966

Education	Males		Females	
	No.	%	No.	%
No schooling	214,687	58.7	178,068	37.0
Some schooling	150,970	41.3	303,086	63.0
Total	365,657	100	481,154	100

Source: 1966 census, Vol. I.

Rural sample, 1978

Years of full-time schooling	Males		Females	
	No.	%	No.	%
7 or more	11	19.6	51	68.9
6 or less	45	80.4	23	31.1
Total	56	100	74	100

Source: Rural survey 1978.

(1981) refers to as the remarkable 'strength and resilience of women as managers of most rural households'; by contrast, he suggests, many men are 'transient visitors, strangers even, in their own communities'. One aspect of this resilience is the significance of informal networks for mutual support among women. Elderly women play a particularly important role in these support groups, helping younger women to cope with personal and domestic problems and teaching them how to supplement their incomes. 'My friends are the women with whom we share the worries and difficulties. We also go to Church together' (Agency for Industrial Mission 1976).

Second, women in Lesotho are generally much better educated than men. This is borne out by census data for as early as 1966 and by a rural survey conducted by the author in 1978 (Table 39). These data indicate a strong association between sex and education in favour of women. Boys are expected to take up herding at an early age, and this disrupts their education. It is common for them to commence herding as early as 8 years old and to continue until they are old enough to engage in migrant labouring at 18. So fundamental is this to Basotho society that the sex inequality in favour of women persists throughout every sector of education, as shown in Table 40. Even in primary school the male drop-out rate is high, so that in grades 6 and 7 the ratios of boys to girls are respectively 1:1.8 and 1:1.9 (Ngwenya 1978). This massive over-representation of women in Lesotho's educational system is unusual in Africa. Among African women generally there is a considerable lag in education; the ratio of girls to boys in primary schools ranges from a quarter to two-thirds (Little 1973; Gugler and Flanagan 1978). Furthermore, the high rates of attrition for girls account for an even more serious under-representation in secondary and higher education. Women's education in Lesotho provides a sharp contrast with the rest of Africa.

Table 40 Ratios of boys to girls in schools and colleges in Lesotho

Primary schools	1:1.52
Secondary schools	1:1.10
Teacher training	1:1.79
Technical and other vocational	1:1.87

Source: Based on data in Williams (1971).

Education is, of course, closely bound up with personal status, opportunity and self-image, and the increasing opportunities for women to gain an education in Africa in recent years have heralded changes in their place in society. Sabot (1979) shows how, in Tanzania, formal education has been a powerful tool in changing a woman's perception of her social role, and for West Africa Gugler and Flanagan (1978) show that western ideology, mediated largely through mission schools, 'has been a potent factor in changing the position of women'. Women have found new aspirations and, with increased education, have taken advantage of new opportunities. This new-found confidence has enhanced the already existing self-assurance found among African women generally. 'Unaccustomed to relying on anyone but herself, the African woman will have no need to acquire a feeling of self-confidence, since she is already rarely without one' (Paulme 1963, quoted by Gugler and Flanagan 1978). It is not difficult to see how this independent and confident spirit has been greatly strengthened by the new-found freedom given by education, and most women probably find much better relationships with men in town. If this is true of Africa generally, how much more true is it of Lesotho, where the subordination of rural women is maintained by the migrant labour economy, but women's aspirations are aroused by superior education?

This has clear implications for female migration to Lesotho's towns, but a final trigger sparking off the decision to move may be what McLoughlin (1970) refers to as the 'frustration gap'. This is felt by an individual, family or even community where exposure to modernizing influences has brought a desire for an increased standard of living but there are few or no opportunities for satisfying this want. In Lesotho, Wallman (1972) refers to the gap 'between what is known to be possible [in the city] and what is [at home]'. She describes the intense frustration experienced by people who are denied the outlet of permanent migration to the towns of South Africa, yet are exposed to the industrial complex of Johannesburg and the Reef and thus acquire the 'tastes and preferences of a full-time urbanite'.

It has been suggested elsewhere (Wilkinson 1983) that the 'frustration gap' among the better educated labour migrants is so strong that it triggers off the decision to move to Maseru as a substitute for permanent residence in the towns of South Africa. The 'frustration gap' is generally strong among the Basotho, but it is particularly so among women, and it may be expected that this will have a powerful effect on migration. Gay (1980) refers specifically to the 'deep sense of frustration' which many younger rural women feel because they are denied the opportunity of taking their place in the life of the modern industrial world; they are restricted by the traditional male-controlled society, but are prevented from leaving that society by the 'influx control' measures. 'All that most of them can now do is to remain on South Africa's periphery, reproducing its labour force, doing unpaid domestic work, cultivating impoverished fields, seeking low-paid local employment, providing a market for South Africa's products, and becoming increasingly dependent on undependable male wage earners' (Gay 1980).

Figure 4 summarizes the dynamics of male and female migration and the significance of the political boundary. For male migrants the boundary is permeable, since movement through it is possible under strictly controlled conditions; this movement is usually through an urban gateway which, by familiarity, provides an additional attraction. For women, however, the political boundary has become impermeable, even though the attraction of work in South Africa is kept alive by tales told by the older women (Gay 1980). This impermeable boundary, and the impossibility of achieving an independent, urban life-style in South Africa, deflect would-be female labour migrants away from the republic to

Figure 4 Migration and the political boundary

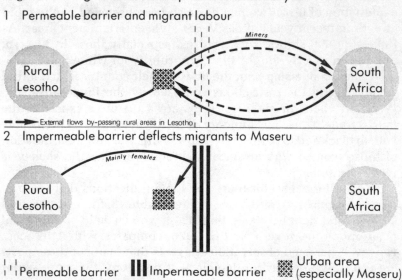

1 Permeable barrier and migrant labour

2 Impermeable barrier deflects migrants to Maseru

Permeable barrier   Impermeable barrier   Urban area (especially Maseru)

Source: Based on Wilkinson 1983.

Maseru, or to other urban areas inside Lesotho. This may account
for the fact that women are more committed than men to a permanent life in Maseru – 43 per cent of female migrant respondents
stated that they would never return home, compared with 30 per
cent of the males. It seems that Basotho women find in Maseru a
degree of freedom and independence not possible in the rural
areas. In other parts of Africa 'many women do eventually find a
measure of economic independence in town' (Gugler and Flanagan
1978); in Lesotho it seems that urban independence is more highly
valued and sought after because of the strength of the 'frustration
gap'.

   Yet in the urban areas independence is often illusory. Indeed,
in some respects, female subordination is more complete in town
than in the country. There is a great deal of urban unemployment,
particularly among women, many of whom eke out a meagre living
by engaging in informal sector activities. Employment data, collected by the author in 1978 for a randomly selected sample of
Maseru household managers (293 women and 232 men), showed
that 53 per cent of the women were unwaged, compared with 17
per cent of the men (Wilkinson 1985). Large numbers of women
therefore take to petty trading in the town centre and, in the suburbs, to selling home-brewed beer. Prostitution also exists, largely,
as noted above, in association with the shebeens. This has not been
studied and no data exist, but it is thought to be widespread. This
exploitation of urban women has also been hastened by the rapid
growth in recent years of Las Vegas style entertainment areas. As
Rubens (1978) shows, such centres, especially those in Maseru,
provide an eagerly sought after opportunity for white South African males to side-step both the laws of their country which forbid
gambling and the restrictions imposed by the Immorality Act.
Weekend visits for such purposes are a lucrative aspect of the
tourist trade. Thus, the boundary depicted in Figure 4 is permeable
both to black and to white males, and in this way the subordination
of those women who are most vulnerable in Basotho society is
made absolute.

   In the formal sector there are some indications that the position of women is rather more favourable. Safilios–Rothschild
(1978), for example, states that 3314 women held professional
positions in the government in 1976, compared with 2152 men.
However, personal observation suggests that many of these posts
are probably inferior, routine clerical positions, the more senior
positions being held by men. Some support for this view is again
provided by the 1978 urban survey (Wilkinson 1985). This showed

that 13.8 per cent of the waged women were in professional, technical, managerial and administrative positions, compared with 16.1 per cent of the men, and 36.2 per cent were in clerical and retail jobs, compared with 19.2 per cent of the men. The majority of the men (54.9 per cent) were in jobs such as construction, driving and engineering, while 39.8 per cent of the women were in some form of domestic service. The concentration of women in the unwaged and informal sectors and, within the waged sector, in retail, clerical and domestic work, is surprising when seen against the background of their high educational status and their numerical supremacy in Maseru. It must clearly be explained in terms of the same kinds of structural and normative obstacles which inhibit their economic and political progress in the rural areas.

Nevertheless, there are powerful forces for change in Africa, in the context of which the increasing proportion of women, especially independent women, in the rural–urban migration stream must be understood. So powerful are these forces that women are prepared to break through the hostility and disapproval aroused by their decision to move to town, and to assert their right to a life of dignity and independence. How far they will succeed, given Lesotho's political economy and social structure, and what the implications will be for the future, remain to be seen.

10 Gender roles in colonization of rainforest: a Colombian case study

Janet Townsend and Sally Wilson de Acosta

Editors' introduction

Spatial divisions of labour are always being reworked, with dramatic effects in particular places. Such reworking may include a redefinition of gender roles and sexual divisions of labour, but this does not always occur. We do not argue any direct economic determinism for this, for social and spatial structures re-form and 'regions and localities are themselves constantly being formed and re-formed, constructed and disintegrated' (Massey 1984), not as a simple function of the requirements of capital, but as the outcome of a complex social process. We have seen sharp changes in the meaning of gender (Chapter 8); we have seen facets of gender held relatively constant, with unexpected effects, while other social phenomena change (Chapters 5, 7, 9).

What happens when people move in to an unoccupied area, in which new physical conditions will require a new farming system? They are incorporating new space into the spatial division of labour; how far will they need to restructure their divisions of labour by age and sex within the household? Such areas usually have a very masculine sex ratio: is time heavily biased towards 'productive' tasks? Townsend and de Acosta describe a frontier society classic in its sex ratio (150 males to every 100 females in their survey!), but it transpires that this ratio is not simply produced by the sex structure of in-migration, or reinforced by higher female mortality. It is reproduced by the sex structure of out-migration, in which young girls leave for the cities. This labour reserve function is common to many Latin American localities of otherwise highly disparate character, as is the differential migration by gender (Chapter 1). As in the Mexican Sierra, girls are redundant: there is employment for them in the cities, but not here. Their life in this frontier area is also extremely exacting: the labour involved in raising healthy children is painfully illustrated by the condition of the undernourished. To the researchers' surprise, this small case study of gender roles on the forest frontier found reproductive tasks to receive a very substantial commitment of time. They not only take up almost the whole of women's time but involve considerable male participation. Men who have moved to this frontier from areas where such tasks are never performed by men now take them on and give them high priority: frontier living has actually raised the status of reproductive against productive tasks.

From Mexico to Paraguay, the lowland forests of Latin America have been falling to the axe and the bulldozer as farms, ranches and new landscapes are created. The settlers must adapt to new farming systems, new ways of living in a new environment, but little is known of the adaptations they make in gender roles in constructing these new lives. There is a vast literature on this 'colonization', but only one field study on gender roles: this was carried out in Brazil by Lisansky (1979) in Santa Terezinha (Mato Grosso). Is the pattern of gender roles she found general across the continent? We tried to develop general hypotheses from her work and our own field experience, and tested them in a small survey in Colombia. The results were unexpected: we describe them here for their own merits, and to encourage other case studies so that a deeper and more comprehensive understanding may be achieved. We had expected to find women engaged in agricultural production and processing: we found them fully occupied in domestic tasks, in reproduction. Was the small area we studied atypical? Or is women's role in Latin American colonization confined to reproductive activities, to the stereotype of the 'domestic' duties?

Colonization in Latin America

If we include the cities, perhaps 25 million people now live in regions of Latin America which only a generation ago were sparsely settled tropical forest. Few of them are on the land. The World Bank (1978) estimated that official, planned colonization schemes had, over two decades, absorbed a minute 2 per cent of the natural increase of the rural population, and spontaneous colonization perhaps another 20 per cent. These small numbers of people have disproportionate effects on the environment and the political economy; they in turn have perhaps attracted an extravagant amount of attention from geographers. Colonization is, on the whole, a depressing topic since the destruction of the forest leads to such poor results in human welfare. The colonization is now very rarely for subsistence. Usually, it begins with crop farms (petty commodity production), which are displaced in time by cattle ranching of low productivity and very low employment, supporting sparse populations at low incomes. Often the ranching is associated with land speculation. In a few cases there is agro-industrial production: this is often highly exploitative and depends heavily on casual and seasonal labour, but after a fashion it does offer livelihoods.

Colonization and gender

Townsend had previously examined colonists' survival strategies in Colombia (1977), Bolivia and Brazil (1984, 1985). She had observed that farm households without a woman are even rarer on the 'frontier' than in settled areas. Why? Is the woman indispensable there in her directly productive role? She and her children are to be seen helping to clear undergrowth, to burn, to sow, to weed, to harvest. Are they essential as a labour reserve for seasonal work? Or is it that the women's labour is required to reproduce the conditions of production, to cook, to clean, to nurse? Or are women needed for biological reproduction: is the labour or the earning power of children needed? Is women's direct production primarily of use values or exchange values? Frontier women produce, reproduce and sustain: which activity is critical? Our survey sought to ask these questions for one small area. We also have specific expectations of gender roles at the different stages of colonization, which we tested:

1 *Before colonization*, there may be low-density occupation by Amerindian groups, or these may already have been destroyed or displaced by disease or by violence. There will have been direct exploitation of the forest by transient groups, often exclusively *male*, in search of timber, skins or minerals. There may also have been very low-density shifting cultivation for subsistence, by family groups of incomers.

2 *The agricultural frontier* is commonly composed of *families*, attempting to create permanent farms by producing for the market. There is usually a preponderance of males: each holding needs at least one woman, particularly to process and cook food, but can use all the men it can obtain and sustain for the heavy labour of clearing forest. Molano (pers. comm. 1984) postulates that the woman in colonization is in an exceptionally strong position, so essential is she to the survival of the enterprise. At this homesteading stage, we expect to find family farming systems. That is, we expect women to be involved in direct agricultural production and particularly in

processing, and to play a significant role in agricultural decision-making.

3 *Capitalist penetration* may bring low-density cattle ranching or agro-industrial production: in either case, the family farms are destroyed and replaced by a wage labour force with, we expect, scant opportunities for women.

Serranía de San Lucas

In 1984, we sought to test our hypotheses in the Serranía de San Lucas, Colombia. A pilot survey of seventy-five households compared the household division of labour by age and sex in an established agricultural village (Papayal) with that in a colonization area a day's walk away. Our survey was designed to yield findings on gender roles which could be compared with those of Lisansky (1979) for a colonization area of Brazil, and those of Deere and Leon (1982) for long-settled rural areas of the Andes. Leon (ed. 1980) organized a research project on gender roles in Colombian municipalities with very different farming systems and physical environments (see Map 17). These included a ranching area in the northern savanna lowlands (Sincelejo), a mountain coffee area (Fredonia), an irrigated lowland area of agro-industrial production (El Espinal), and a highland peasant area with heavy outmigration (García Rovira); surveys were carried out in El Espinal and García Rovira. The survey data were later compared (Deere and Leon 1982) with Deere's findings for Cajamarca, Peru (another highland peasant area, with more capitalist penetration than García Rovira). Deere and Leon (1982) concluded that the northern Andes are characterized by *family farming systems*, not male farming systems as census data would suggest, and that *social class* is important to gender roles; women's participation in agriculture being inversely related to the peasant household's access to land. We wanted to see whether these conclusions applied also to a colonization area, and to compare the Serranía de San Lucas with García Rovira.

García Rovira is a labour reserve and a source of cheap wage goods: these are often functions of colonization areas, as shown for Brazil by Foweraker (1981) and for Colombia by Samper and Ladrón de Guevara (1981). Would similar functions in the spatial division of labour yield similar gender roles, under very different farming systems and physical environments?

We selected the Serranía de San Lucas not as an ideal type, but because, at the time of the survey, it was peaceful. In Colombia, the

Map 17   Location of this and comparable surveys

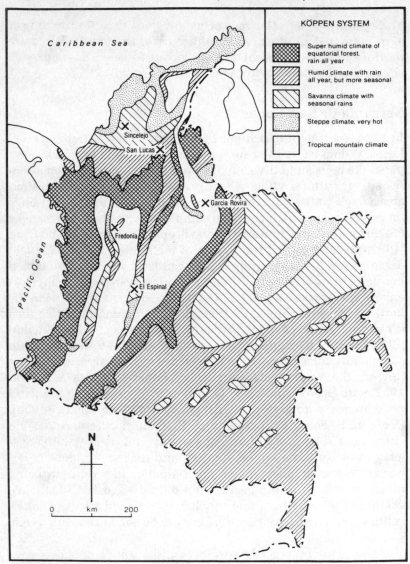

KÖPPEN SYSTEM

Super humid climate of equatorial forest, rain all year

Humid climate with rain all year, but more seasonal

Savanna climate with seasonal rains

Steppe climate, very hot

Tropical mountain climate

Caribbean Sea

Pacific Ocean

Sincelejo
San Lucas
Garcia Rovira
Fredonia
El Espinal

N

0   km   200

isolation of colonization areas and the distress occasioned there by exploitation and injustice are turned to account by guerrillas and by dealers in illicit drugs. Military and paramilitary action often renders the situation of the colonists harrowing, and effectively precludes survey research. Since the survey, some of our respondents have died violently.

Surveys were carried out in 10 per cent of households in the riverside village of Papayal, and in all households (except the gold mining camp) along a hill trail into the Serranía, from Norosí to La Pacha. Deere and Leon (1982) had concentrated mainly on agricultural and income-generating activities; we extended our inquiry into gender roles, to maintenance or domestic activities (Table 41), and recorded the weights and heights of children under 5. The first concern was to establish women's share of agricultural activities; the second, to scrutinize the household division of labour in production and reproduction.

The Serranía de San Lucas forms one northern tip of the Andes, isolated between two major rivers. Colonization is 'blocked' or, in the local phrase, 'bottled up': the trail from Norosí to La Pacha was cut in 1951, but no roads have been built in the area, which remains mainly in the 'agricultural frontier' stage. Ranches exist, but have not taken over, and even some secondary forest services; there is limited capitalist penetration in agricultural production, which is still mainly of a petty commodity nature. All farmers are deeply involved in the market, and transport costs are everyone's first concern, whether for sale of produce, for purchase of goods or for access to services such as health care. Most transport of produce to the rivers is on mules or donkeys, which are expensive; river transport onwards to market is also costly. Profits accrue to traders rather than farmers. The colonists campaign for roads and credit, although they know that when these come, so will land speculation, depriving many of their land and livelihood. Although this part of the Serranía has been relatively peaceful, illicit activities have been significant. Between 1976 and 1981 there was, for once, a profitable crop: marijuana, grown illegally for export to the United States, but always at risk of discovery. One respondent was reported to have invested marijuana profits in his children's education: they had indeed been supported in distant cities through secondary and even professional training. Another reported marijuana grower had achieved a piped water supply; another, two tractors, a chain saw and a large ranch. Losses were more common, as traders blackmailed producers and, eventually, crops were officially destroyed. More recently, the airstrip at the gold mine had been closed because cocaine smuggling was suspected.

Conditions of production

All sectors combine simple and advanced technologies. In

farming, crops still predominate, with forest fallow; cattle yield better returns but call for higher investment; and neither can achieve the profitability of marijuana. Townsend first visited the area in 1986, and the most notable change since then, apart from the area of forest cleared, is in the improvement of the health of the cattle. These (unlike the people) are managed with vaccines, mineral supplements and antibiotics. Weedkiller, and, more rarely,

Table 41   Participation in tasks, by sex and age

Task	Respondents over 13 years old (women:men = 114:216)			5–13 years (girls:boys = 61:69)	
	Always participate women/men		Sometimes participate women/men	Always participate girls/boys	Sometimes participate girls/boys
	Ratio	Numbers	Numbers	Numbers	Numbers
Cooking for labourers	—	42/0	5/0	2/0	3/1
Make clothes	15.0	30/2	0/0	3/0	2/0
Bath children	11.6	81/7	7/19	8/3	12/5
Mend clothes	11.4	91/8	5/8	8/0	10/2
Wash clothes*	10.1	91/9	9/19	12/0	20/4
Iron clothes	8.7	26/3	1/1	0/0	2/0
Nurse sick children	7.2	79/11	3/22	8/2	8/2
Clean house	6.4	96/15	6/39	20/3	27/10
Cook	5.7	97/17	10/50	18/0	18/12
Childcare	5.3	85/16	4/40	13/3	10/8
Wash up	5.2	94/18	9/36	23/3	25/10
Teach children	4.6	79/17	5/19	8/2	8/0
Gathering	2.9	26/9	3/4	0/0	5/2
Care of poultry	2.7	76/28	8/18	14/4	14/4
Care of pigs	1.1	41/36	5/18	8/5	7/9
Fetch water	0.9	60/69	17/38	26/16	17/25
Process produce for sale	0.9	11/13	1/4	4/1	0/1
Salt fish	0.5	24/47	8/13	3/6	3/2
Clean fish	0.4	26/64	9/13	3/6	3/2
Shopping	0.3	28/90	13/21	22/22	8/12
At school	0.2	9/36		39/37	
Work in vegetables*	0.2	5/21	3/3	0/2	0/0
Sell produce	0.18	9/51	0/8	0/3	1/3

Table 41 Continued:

Task	Respondents over 13 years old (women:men = 114:216)			5–13 years (girls:boys = 61:69)	
	Always participate women/men		Sometimes participate women/men	Always participate	Sometimes participate
				girls/boys	
	Ratio	Numbers	Numbers	Numbers	Numbers
Work in garden	0.17	4/24	1/1	0/3	0/1
Fetch firewood	0.16	21/129	13/33	15/16	9/25
Threshing	0.15	17/111	8/13	4/6	2/9
Chop firewood	0.13	17/131	14/26	7/11	3/17
Make nets	0.09	3/23	0/4	0/2	0/0
Work in beans*	0.08	3/40	1/5	0/4	0/2
Work in sugar*	0.07	2/27	3/4	0/3	0/1
Work in fruit*	0.04	3/76	4/10	0/5	0/3
Milk cows*	0.04	2/62	2/10	0/0	1/2
Transport produce	0.03	2/69	0/8	0/5	0/7
Harvest*	0.02	3/135	3/16	0/4	0/7
Work in rice*	0.02	2/94	3/10	0/6	0/4
Work in plantain	0.02	2/95	3/6	0/6	0/6
Weed pasture*	0.018	2/110	4/13	0/5	0/4
Sow pasture*	0.018	2/110	3/12	0/5	0/3
Weeding*	0.016	2/128	3/19	0/4	0/9
Sowing*	0.013	2/130	3/17	0/4	1/11
Work in yuca*	0.014	2/135	4/17	0/7	0/8
Work in maize*	0.014	2/136	3/16	0/7	0/8
Prepare for sowing*	0.014	2/140	4/20	0/5	1/8
Repair house	0.013	1/75	2/9	0/1	4/3
Build fences*	0.011	1/69	1/12	0/5	0/3
Fell forest*	0.009	1/110	2/15	0/3	0/4
Clear undergrowth*	0.008	1/127	2/19	0/4	1/9
Treat sick cattle	—	0/33	0/11	0/0	0/2
Build own house	—	0/36	3/1	0/0	8/2
Care of cattle	—	0/65	0/15	0/9	0/2
Catch fish		0/87	2/11	0/9	0/3

Note:
*Tasks which are carried out elsewhere for a wage as well as for the household enterprise.

tractors, are used more for cattle than for crops; the hoe and machete are still the main tools. By comparison with García Rovira and El Espinal (Map 17) farms are large: 64 per cent of the households surveyed had over 10 ha, as against 7 per cent in El Espinal or García Rovira. Reserves of land and forest are commonly ample, but even these physically large farms can rarely meet basic needs because they combine high market orientation with poor profitability. Almost all real economic opportunities are in *commerce* and in sawmills. Chain saws, tractors, outboard motors, speedboats, storage capacity – and diesel generators for chilling beer – these are the profitable investments. Gold panning, timber and fishing are important ancillary activities, but male *temporary migration* is important, and is mainly to nearby areas of agro-industrial production. Increased mechanization threatens this resource, for labouring 'skills' are in wielding a machete.

Survival strategies

The first decision here in the household division of labour is who is to constitute the household and who is to migrate, for how long and how far. Crudely, for most of the households surveyed, the land is the main source of income. Women do almost no agricultural work. Migration is high (almost all households have family members living elsewhere) and is sex-selective: adult males outnumber females by almost 2:1 (Figure 5), which is remarkable even in this continent of female-led urbanization. How does this structure come about?

For those who remain, livelihoods come mainly from the land. Even in the village of Papayal, the main source of income for eleven of the twenty-four households surveyed was their own farm, and for four more it was agricultural labour. On the trail, in the Serranía, thirty-one of the fifty-one households depend primarily on their own farm, and another twelve on agricultural labour. Wage employment is scarce, but so are the resources to work one's own land: four households on the trail owning over 10 ha depended on agricultural labour.

The real product of the area is labour. Only eight of the seventy-five households ever receive any form of remittances, but family members elsewhere

1   cease to call on household resources;
2   are a route to employment, health and education for other members of the household;

Figure 5   Demographical structure of the survey populations

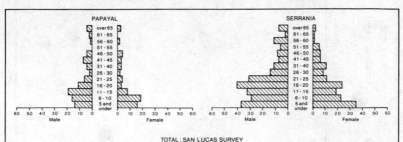

3   may bring substantial gifts in kind when they visit, or earnings when they return.

Yet labour is also an asset in the region, particularly in the Serranía where fifteen of the fifty-one households had more than ten members (the size of the largest household interviewed in Papayal). Through the recruiting of labour, household structures are intricate; including distant relatives, adopted children, employees and sometimes the offspring of migrant children. Women in the Serranía had also borne more children.

Many individuals migrate, but the majority who leave permanently are girls. By age 15, there is a large discrepancy between the sexes even in Papayal (Figure 5). The initial colonization and subsequent inmigration and outmigration have all served to select men into the area and women out, from a very early age. Among the first colonists and perhaps later inmigrants, adult males predominated; among their children and grandchildren, girls have tended to leave. Males are now dominant not only among inmigrants, but among the children of the household, resident relatives and employees. Young (1982) has documented a similar outmigration of young girls from Copa Bitoo (Oaxaca, Mexico), but that appears to have been produced through the collapse of domestic manufacturing in a long-settled peasant area. In San Lucas, a 'relative surplus population' of young girls is leaving at the same time as inmigrant male labour is being recruited: the female surplus population is

Table 42   Participation rates in agricultural field tasks by sex and region

Tasks	García Rovira (non-capitalist)		El Espinal (advanced capitalist)		Cajamarca (predominantly capitalist)		San Lucas (colonization)	
	Women (per cent)	Men (per cent)	Women (per cent)	Men (per cent)	Women (per cent)	Men (per cent)	Women (per cent)	Men (per cent)
Field preparation	10 (n = 229)	89 (n = 253)	14 (n = 281)	29 (n = 301)	24 (n = 140)	74 (n = 151)	5 (n = 96)	77 (n = 161)
Seedling preparation	29 (n = 180)	91 (n = 195)	21 (n = 101)	43 (n = 97)	NA	NA	NA	NA
Planting	30 (n = 229)	93 (n = 253)	16 (n = 289)	39 (n = 305)	48 (n = 139)	74 (n = 150)	6 (n = 95)	81 (n = 182)
Transplanting	7 (n = 136)	93 (n = 163)	32 (n = 298)	78 (n = 311)	NA	NA	NA	NA
Weeding	4 (n = 252)	93 (n = 281)	31 (n = 309)	82 (n = 325)	47 (n = 139)	80 (n = 151)	5 (n = 99)	78 (n = 189)
Cultivating	4 (n = 206)	93 (n = 230)	20 (n = 285)	57 (n = 308)	24 (n = 112)	79 (n = 110)	NA	NA
Harvesting	46 (n = 227)	94 (n = 251)	52 (n = 309)	85 (n = 325)	62 (n = 135)	81 (n = 140)	6 (n = 101)	77 (n = 196)
Threshing	NA	NA	NA	NA	66 (n = 102)	83 (n = 117)	31 (n = 87)	77 (n = 161)
Processing	51 (n = 354)	93 (n = 381)	36 (n = 358)	82 (n = 367)	NA	NA	44 (n = 29)	33 (n = 51)

Notes:

n = number of persons 13 years of age or over residing in households in which at least one person participates in the task; NA: Information not applicable or not available; Participation: those who sometimes or always participate.

defined as surplus by gender roles in which women do not work on the land. Girls can obtain employment in domestic service in the coastal cities and cease to be a cost on the household, although their contributions under points 2 and 3 above are much less than those of males. Domestic servants often live with their employers; they can seek work for their kin, but cannot offer them accommodation which might make possible school attendance or hospital treatment. Women are also less likely to save to return and invest in the farm. The advantages to the household of female outmigration are therefore limited, but females still leave, many of them at such an early age that the initiative must come from their elders. How do gender roles define females as having so little value to the household?

Women's work

The participation of women in an array of farming and reproductive tasks in the San Lucas area is set out in Table 41. (The tasks are ranked from highest to lowest female participation, using the ratio of women to men who 'always participate' in each task.) Unexpectedly, this proves to be a male farming system. Women's role in direct production is very limited. Those who 'always participate' in agricultural field tasks are all the same three women (out of 114). On most farms, women were found to be ill-informed about production and ill-equipped to participate in decisions about production (unique in Townsend's experience). They even engage little in agricultural processing for sale, although a few make cheese. Table 42 and Figure 6 provide comparisons. For agricultural field tasks, female participation rates were found to be lower in San Lucas than in García Rovira, El Espinal or Cajamarca. Women's main direct contribution to production, as in García Rovira, is in cooking for labourers: farmers provide food in lieu of a third of the wage. This can be demanding at certain seasons, with women rising at 2 a.m. to start the day's cooking, although San Lucas women regarded the demands as less than in other areas. In highland García Rovira, women predominate in milking, but in San Lucas it is said that lowland cattle are men's work – only four of 114 women milk – and the care of cattle is an even more male occupation than felling forest. In Amazonia, cattle are also men's work, so that the expansion of ranching displaces women from direct production. In San Lucas, children engage in direct production but are hardly a labour reserve: boys (not girls) of 13 and under are engaged in farming to a greater extent than women, but the numbers are still not large.

Figure 6   Participation rates in agricultural field tasks by sex and region

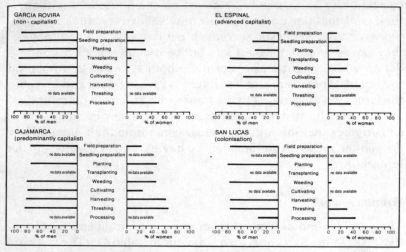

Note: see also Table 42.

Wage labour in farming is almost entirely male. Other male activities include trade, transport, carpentry, timber, gold panning, religion, herbal cures and teaching.

Women's dominance is in reproducing the conditions of production and in social reproduction (see Table 41). They cook, wash, clean and make income-earning possible. Apart from cooking for labourers, all the tasks in which more women than men 'always participate' fall into these categories (even the poultry and pigs for which women primarily care are for household consumption rather than sale). The difference from El Espinal, Cajamarca and García Rovira is that in San Lucas, men perform more of both the productive and the reproductive tasks. Men and boys participate in cooking, cleaning and the washing of clothes and in childcare; they bring wood and water and daily subsistence items from the farm. (Children of both sexes participate more in reproductive than productive activities.) In García Rovira, by contrast, men's contribution to maintenance activities is minuscule. Even schooling depends on maintenance. In the Serranía, rich families send their children to live in a village or city to attend school: three of the fifty-one households maintain separate establishments in a village where the mother lives in term time, caring for her school-age children. Female earning in San Lucas is limited to domestic work, cooking food items for sale, washing clothes, making clothes, teaching, and one productive activity: panning for gold. Few women earn.

The household division of labour here is highly spatial. Women perform tasks in and around the house; men help in many of these, and carry out tasks away from the house. Exceptions for women are washing clothes and bathing children (usually carried out at the stream or river), gathering herbs and fetching water. Vegetable plots and gardens are small and rare, but commonly close to the house; they can be tended by women, but many are not (Table 41). The main exceptions for men are the building and repair of the house itself and the making of fishing nets, which is done in the house. Taking food out to family or labourers is not common, and it is as often a male as a female task (in contrast to García Rovira). The use of space relates to the company of small children: 103 females and eighteen males always have small children with them when engaged in household chores, while only small numbers of either sex take them on farm work or errands. There is a massive spatial bias here in the household division of labour, in strong contrast to the high Andes where babies and children are taken to where adults are working. The bias is even more extreme than in the areas from which the colonists come.

Biological reproduction

In these households, biological reproduction must be regarded as successful. Twenty women had had more than ten pregnancies, six had more than ten living children, twenty-seven out of the ninety-three women aged 15 to 50 were pregnant or lactating. 'The boys are our labourers', and the girls can migrate. Given the state of health and nutrition, the survival rate is surprisingly high. Of seventy-five children under 5 weighed, twelve were severely malnourished (less than 80 per cent of the expected weight for age) and twenty mildly malnourished (80 to less than 90 per cent expected weight for age) (NCHS standards). Explanations are not simple. The colonists have focused their efforts on commercial rather than subsistence crops, and food security is not good. Food value is perceived narrowly in terms of animal protein, particularly that from cattle; some pigs and poultry are kept and fish is caught, but fruits, vegetables and legumes are relatively neglected. Only the herbalist has a large, diverse self-provisioning plot – but he is also relatively wealthy. More malnourished children do occur in land-less families, but only two of the four worst cases are in such families, and malnutrition occurs in households with over 100 ha. Some explanation may lie within the household; of the severely malnourished children, none was the child of the head of household.

Women as caretakers of health

Reproductive activities include a great emphasis on visible personal cleanliness, as is usual in lowland Colombia. There is, however, almost no faecal-oral hygiene in the Serranía, and little in Papayal. Most water is drunk raw (and dirty, especially in Papayal, where most comes from the river Magdalena, the nation's main sewer), latrines are few, sanitation is left to the pigs, and children are not taught to wash hands after defecating. Only 13 per cent of respondents have access to latrines. None have water filters. All children have parasites, many to an acute degree. Diarrhoea and dehydration are common, faecal-oral diseases are endemic, helminth infestation is widespread, so are amoebiasis and anaemia. Members of three households were reported to eat earth. The level of parasitism and infection can only be combated by outstandingly good nutrition. Child-rearing therefore becomes an onerous task: only by heavy labour do other households avoid the plight of the four children who are less than 70 per cent of the expected weight for age.

State support for health is highly centralized and is in practice still a commitment to high-technology medicine. The exceptional mother who had taken her child to a doctor had been prescribed expensive vitamin injections, and had not been advised to buy or grow the appropriate (much cheaper) food. Malaria is traditionally endemic, but spraying of dwellings was withdrawn from the countryside some years ago on the grounds of danger to operatives; explosions of mosquitoes, cockroaches, bed-bugs and other arthropods followed. Confirmed cases of malaria were encountered. Most respondents live under thatched roofs (chagas is a real possibility) on dirt floors, and more than half live between stick or dirt walls, so that insect control is taxing. Much health care (for childbirth, broken limbs, etc.) is supplied by relatives and neighbours. Unfortunately, there is a destructive intrusion of quacks making inappropriate use of high-technology medicine.

Case studies

The household division of labour mirrors both gender roles and migration, while confronting the difficulties of production and reproduction. The complexities of response are perhaps best illustrated by case studies.

A successful senior colonist

In 1951, Justo (now 65) was one of the team which first opened the trail through the Serranía. After several trips to Venezuela, in 1967 he returned 'with only a machete lent by my brother' and with Etilda, his present *compañera*, and two small boys by a previous union. He now has 199 ha colonized and titled, 100 ha purchased and thirty cattle. Nine sons, including Etilda's eight, live and work on the farm, as well as a granddaughter and nephew; one son and family live nearby, and work on the farm; and a daughter lives nearby. Of the other children by previous unions, one has died, the others live in coastal cities: one daughter is in domestic service, one son is an ambulant vendor, one son is a small landlord, and one son is a landlord who has built ten houses to rent out. None of these children visit, but Justo is to stay with one for cataract and hernia operations. On the farm, Etilda has some help from Justo and the 7-year-old granddaughter around the house – cooking, cleaning and washing for thirteen. Many features in Justo's life and household are characteristic of other respondents: the migration (particularly to Venezuela), the migrant progeny, the predominantly male household, the migrant children as a health resource.

A failed senior colonist

Ana came here from an old village nearby in 1950, aged 16, but her household has only achieved 20 ha and most income is from wage labour. Her *compañero* has been sick for two years. In a household of sixteen, one daughter and one son have basic literacy; the rest are illiterate. She has borne twelve children, and eleven have survived; six in the household, five on nearby farms. (None live outside the area.) The four grandchildren in the household are all under 5, and achieve 50, 55, 75 and 94 per cent of the weight to be expected for their age. A 23 month boy weighed 6.2 kg, scarcely more than his 6 month sister at 5.5 kg; their 39 month cousin reached only 8.0 kg. This family illustrates a whole complex of failures, impoverishment from illness, illiteracy, malnutrition, failure of the younger women to retain partners. The household is exceptionally female (50 per cent) and the women do process crops in the house, but do not engage in field tasks. Despite family failings and failures, Ana did raise eleven of her twelve children.

An abandoned family

Ricarda's *compañero* went to Venezuela three years ago and has not communicated since. The main household income comes from her two sons, now 9 and 11, who engage in agricultural labour and work a subsistence plot. Ricarda has never worked in agriculture. Even in this extreme situation, the social construction of gender holds.

In each household, familiar threads are crossing and recrossing to and from an individual web at a specific moment in time. Each mesh, web or case study yields information on the threads.

Conclusion

This survey sought to compare the household division of labour by age and sex in the riverine agricultural village, Papayal, and a nearby colonization area, the Serranía, in terms that would permit further comparison with other published surveys. It was expected that women's input in agricultural production would be much lower in Papayal than the Serranía, that there would be a high incidence of female heads of households, particularly in Papayal, and that female earnings would therefore be important in strategies for household survival. Experience from other colonization areas predicted an important role for women in agricultural decision-making and in seasonal agricultural activity, with 'family farming systems' dominant. Unexpectedly, the household division of labour proved broadly similar in Papayal and the Serranía: only 'male farming' systems were encountered, the nuclear family dominated, and female heads of households were rare. The outstanding feature of the household division of labour is the remarkable imbalance between adult females and males. Most adults have migrated, but the outmigration of women has been much greater than of men. Adult males outnumber females by almost 2:1; a high value is set on reproductive activities, and men participate in them to an unusual degree, while few women participate in direct production and almost none in agricultural field tasks, which is most unusual for the Andes.

 Women's work is primarily in reproduction, biological and social. It is carried out under highly adverse circumstances; despite women's best efforts, severely malnourished children are found in families with access to considerable areas of land. In conversation, women's work is described as of great value; in action, men define it as valuable by participating in it, yet females leave the area as if their labour were surplus to requirements. Why have gender roles not shifted to give them access to income-earning activities, making them an asset instead of a liability to their household?

It is likely that the area will prove exceptional, but these findings stress the need for further empirical work of a comparative nature. Time budget studies are ideal, but require a heavy input of research time over an extended period to achieve worthwhile results. This survey has shown again that the salient features of the household division of labour may be established by a questionnaire survey on participation in specific tasks. But those features may very rightly lead to further questions; in this case, how may we adequately explain the construction of gender in the Serranía de San Lucas? Demography and gender roles interact strongly: how may we account for these gender roles?

11 Non-farm employment and female labour mobility in northern Thailand

Anchalee Singhanetra-Renard

Editors' introduction

It is essential that the stereotype of the Third World farm family as self-sufficient, independent and immobile be dispelled. Such a model is commonly inapplicable, and can have disastrous effects in planning practice, yet it remains all too widely implicit. The role of farm labourers has long been admitted, but non-farm employment, diversified household enterprise, occupational multiplicity or polyvalency in rural areas, rural–urban commuting and high overall rural mobility all still tend to be thought of as exceptional. In reality, all save commuting may be the norm rather than the exception, and commuting may prove common wherever there is an appropriate urban area. In this study of rural people's movements, Singhanetra-Renard has encountered all these phenomena, not in the vicinity of a capital city but deep in northern Thailand.

In Chiang Mai, it is essential to the existence of the agricultural community that married female villagers supplement their families' incomes, usually through urban construction work. Conversely, city construction companies can pay extremely low wages since these manual labourers either commute to work or have free accommodation at the construction camp. Commuting reduces the rate and problems of urbanization. In Thailand, 14 per cent of construction workers are female. Local gender roles permit the sexes to work side by side in construction, moving materials and equipment, digging, hauling dirt, mixing cement etc. Skilled female workers are preferred for tasks calling for patience or detail, such as tying steel rods, polishing cement floors or laying bathroom tiles. In Chiang Mai city, female workers comprise about a quarter of the construction workforce; two-thirds are single, and almost half are under 20. Most single girls commute daily. The construction industry, unlike the traditional agricultural economy, has created incompatibility between motherhood and income-generating activity: construction workers tend to delay motherhood and to space their pregnancies. Commuting has exposed women to an urban environment and created high educational aspirations for their children (Singhanetra-Renard 1984).

In this chapter, this gender structure is linked by mobility to the multiplicity of strategies in the rural household. An examination of the mobility extracts a remarkable array of rural complexities.

Introduction

Most people in Third World countries live in rural areas and are engaged primarily in agriculture. Yet to view the rural economy in these countries as agricultural is simplistic, and often overlooks underlying structural changes in the economy. The rising proportion of the non-agricultural rural workforce in Thailand, for example, suggests that non-farm employment has become increasingly important to the rural economy, particularly to the landless and land-poor. Economic growth in the 1960s and 1970s among ASEAN countries, Thailand included, was rapid, exceeding the average of both industrialized and developing countries. This led to a corresponding increase in female participation in the labour force in all ASEAN countries. Much attention has been paid to the female workforce in urban centres (Jones 1984), but not in rural areas. The conventional notion that women's work is subordinate to that of men and less essential for the functioning of the economy has impeded any study of the rural women's workforce. Academics and planners have been preoccupied with agriculture, and women have been stereotyped as unpaid family workers.

For more than a decade, many village studies have documented the changing Third World socio-economic structure: the large numbers of landless households, the uneven distribution of holdings among those who own land, the extreme multiplicity of occupations, and a highly flexible division of labour among household members in rural areas. For urban areas, there has been good description of the growth of secondary cities and transport networks, the expansion of informal sectors, and the circular mobility of labour between rural and urban areas. Yet there is little understanding of how these changes have transformed the role and position of the female workforce in the rural economy. The nature of the mobility of female labour, and the access women have to non-farm employment, are of crucial importance and have implications for those formulating development policy.

Non-farm employment and types of the rural workforce

Thailand's 1980 census reports that about 4.4 million people live in the eight provinces of northern Thailand, covering 89,484 km². The region thus has a population density of 53 persons per square kilometre, making it the least populated region in the whole country. However, this is quite misleading since over 40 per cent of northern Thailand is mountainous. Limited land resources in the narrow river valleys have been one of the main problems for people in this region, where 80 per cent of the people live in rural areas. (The very rapid decline in the rate of population growth in the north during the last two decades could very well be attributed to population pressure; it is now, at 1.0, the lowest in the country.) The average land holding is very small, only 1.2 hectares per household; many farming families are not able to achieve self-sufficiency in rice production. Every year about half the agricultural households face rice shortages; their rice silos are empty for periods ranging from one to ten months. These households must supplement their income, even to meet very basic needs. In addition, about one-third of northern Thai villagers are members of non-agricultural households, and depend almost entirely on purchased rice. Non-farm employment has become such an important source of cash income for both farm and non-farm households that the rural workforce spends about half its time on non-farm jobs, and income from non-farm jobs constitutes about 49 per cent of the income of rural households (Chulasai et al. 1983). This shows the importance of non-farm employment, particularly wage-labour, in the northern Thai economic system. Paradoxically, it is noted everywhere that opportunities for non-farm employment are very limited in most rural areas and have been almost wholly neglected in rural development, because planners have been preoccupied with agriculture. The result has been the movement of large numbers of the rural population seeking employment outside their home villages. Labour mobility has become essential for the rural workforce in northern Thailand.

In an effort to make ends meet, villagers move in and out of agricultural work and in and out of the village to engage in a variety of jobs. 'Occupational multiplicity', or the necessity for individuals or households to combine several economic activities in order to subsist, is not restricted to northern Thailand, but characterizes many Third World rural societies (Comitas 1973; White 1976; Long and Roberts 1984). In northern Thailand, it seems that village

Table 43 Sources of village household cash income in Mae Sa

	Number	Households Per cent of total (N = 226)
Agricultural products: cash crops, rice	170	75.2
Trade: market merchant, forest products	89	39.4
Business enterprise: general/food store, poultry farm, rice mill, nursery, mini-bus, marketplace	16	7.1
Wage labour: farm, construction, stablehand	116	51.3
Skilled labour: craftsman, seamstress, hairdresser, barber, traditional doctor, spirit medium, musician, driver	42	18.6
Monthly salary: teacher, soldier, police, village official, juvenile home officer, housemaid, salesgirl, janitor	41	18.1

Note:
Households may have multiple sources of income.
Source: Singhanetra-Renard 1982.

households derive their cash income from the various sources detailed in Table 43 for Mae Sa, a lowland village about 13 kilometres from Chiang Mai city. The village workforce itself can be divided into three groups according to workplace and mobility: urban-based, rural-based, and bi-local (see Table 44).

Urban-based workers

Some villagers, Group 1 in Table 44, work full time in urban centres. They can be separated into three sub-groups according to their socio-economic background. First are the better educated villagers from well-to-do families. The number of those who have secondary, vocational or college education has been increasing, particularly in villages near the urban centres, such as Mae Sa. Villagers of this group engage in clerical work at middle level in governmental or private enterprises as well as in professional jobs in education, the police or the army. Most commute to work, apart from the few who find jobs in other provinces or live beyond the commuting distance (about 15–20 kilometres in northern Thailand). These usually engage in long-term circulation, many for the length of their civil career.

Table 44 Types of rural workforce

Group	Major socio-economic characteristics of labour	Type of work in home village (Mae Sa)	Type of work in other rural areas/district centres	Type of work in city (Chiang Mai)	Type of wage	Type of circular mobility
1	Secondary school education and above Landlord family/village non-farm family	—	—	Middle level, clerical work in government, private enterprise Professionals, e.g. teachers, policemen	Monthly salary, fixed scale	Daily commuting, circulation
2	Above compulsory education*, apprenticeship training Average-holding family	—	—	Lower level, semi-skilled in government/private enterprises, e.g. guards, janitors, hotel maids, foreman, nursing aides	Monthly salary, fixed scale	Daily commuting, circulation
3	Compulsory education Small farm/landless family	Periodic agricultural wage labour	—	Employees in family/small-scale business, e.g. garage, shops, restaurants, etc. Household maids	Monthly salary, no fixed scale	Circulation
4	Compulsory education Large/average-holding farm family	Rice farming/cash cropping	—	Trading	Family/self-employment	Periodic commuting

| 5 | Compulsory education Small farm/landless family | Agricultural wage labour | Agricultural wage labour Tobacco factory worker Collecting/gathering Foothill gardening | — | Daily wage/ no fixed scale, (often receive in kind) | Seasonal/ periodic commuting |
| 6 | Compulsory education Small farm/landless family | Periodic agricultural wage labour | House construction | Construction workers in building industries | Daily wage/ negotiable and no fixed scale | Daily commuting |

Note:
*Compulsory education: sixth grade primary.

Members of Group 2 also work full time in the city, but are less well educated than the first group. They usually have only a lower secondary education because their families' economic conditions preclude them from continuing any further. Most of them secure semi-skilled, lower level jobs in government or private enterprise. They work as guards, errand boys, janitors, garage helpers, hotel maids, or nursing aides.

Group 3 are mainly of children of landless or land-poor families. Equipped with only a sixth grade compulsory primary education, they can only find low-paid non-skilled jobs, perhaps as housemaids or waiters/waitresses, and these usually in family or small-scale enterprises. Since most of them are too poor to afford the costs of commuting, they find jobs where the employers provide housing. So, unlike most of the workers in the first two groups who commute to work outside the home village, they nearly always engage in circular movement.

All urban-based workers share three characteristics: full-time urban employment; monthly salaries; and regular, circulatory movement between village place of residence and urban workplace. This differentiates them from the following two groups.

Rural-based workers

The majority of the village workforce are probably rural-based. They are basically farmers (owners/labourers) who supplement their income through other activities, mostly in rural areas. Patterns of employment differ between rich and poor families. The rich, Group 4, farm their own land in the village and trade in the city market, or operate minibuses running between the village and the city. Some engage in small enterprises such as rice milling, poultry farming, or running a village general store. Poor families (Group 5) make their living from farm or non-farm wage work in their home villages and in neighbouring rural communities. Many are too poor to afford transport to work, and thus can only find jobs within walking distance. They are usually hired on a daily basis and paid in kind. Some jobs, such as handicrafts, are paid on a piecework basis. They form the economically least secure group in the rural areas. When unable to find work, they resort to collecting forest products, hunting, or fishing. The rural-based workforce commute daily or move periodically or seasonally outside their home villages.

Bi-local workers

Members of Group 6 earn their living primarily from wage work, particularly in construction, both in rural areas and in urban centres. Unlike those in Group 5, they are full-time wage workers and commute regularly to work. They are usually trained on the job and often become highly skilled, some being foremen. They are often recruiters of other workers from their home villages. Although most prefer to work in nearby villages to save on the cost of commuting, they are usually obliged to move to the cities, where most construction opportunities can be found. Their usual work-places and type of employment make this group of village labourers essentially bi-local. They form the larger part of the village workforce in the city.

Bi-local workers are almost always hired on a daily basis, and their job turnover rate is high. On construction sites, 200 workers are commonly hired in one day, but, just as frequently, only fifty are called the next day. Many factors contribute to this dynamism. First, the building industry is characterized by different phases in the work, calling for different skills and widely differing numbers of labourers. Taking advantage of the readily available rural labour supply, construction companies only keep a handful of permanent technicians and executives on the payroll. The companies hire the rest, skilled and non-skilled labourers, on a daily basis for each phase of the construction work. Workers are dismissed when their labour is no longer needed. The workers, therefore, have to be searching continually for new jobs at other construction sites.

A second factor is that the casual hiring system, the minimum of educational requirements, and the flexible working days attract many villagers newly entering the urban labour market. Some try out construction work for a couple of years before moving on to other city jobs; some remain and acquire skills, making construction their life work; many others return to rural work.

Third, the movement of labour for construction jobs, perhaps more than other forms of population mobility, is determined by the stages of the worker's life-cycle. For example, female workers will find that raising children is incompatible with construction work. Substitute mothers are becoming scarce; day-care centres have been recently introduced in many villages to help solve the problem, but they are too costly for this group. Many married female workers, therefore, leave construction work and turn to agricultural wage work or small-scale trading in their villages. Thus, bi-local women workers who become pregnant and start a family, are apt to become rural-based.

The three groups of village workers described here are by no means mutually exclusive, as the case of female construction workers illustrates. The situation found among the Indonesian rural workforce by White (1976) parallels what is happening among rural northern Thais: 'Each household's income is derived from a great variety of sources which constantly change in response to available opportunities according to the season, the state of the market and even the time of day; and each individual household member has normally not one or two occupations, but a great number in which he/she engages in differing combinations and for differing lengths of time in response both to his own opportunities and those of the other household members.'

Occupational multiplicity and sex differentials

A detailed investigation of the rural occupational structure un-covered a very complex situation. As noted earlier, most villagers cannot subsist on any single occupation (the exceptions are a few rich farmers and salaried government officials and professionals). Many, therefore, have second and third jobs (Table 45). About 67 per cent of 654 economically active individuals in Mae Sa held second jobs, and 25.9 regularly engaged in third jobs. 'Unemploy-ment' or 'underemployment' is a luxury that the poor cannot afford. It is in this context that the multiple occupations of many rural workers make sense.

Despite the generally held assumption that all rural dwellers are farmers, only just over half the rural workforce in northern Thailand, male or female, has agriculture as a main occupation. Among non-farm jobs, wage work is the most important. Almost a quarter of the men are wage workers, the second largest group after farmers. The main occupations among female workers have a traditional pattern. The few jobs in the modern sector requiring formal education and training, such as governmental and profes-sional occupations, are still amost entirely closed to women.

The occupational composition for secondary jobs generally follows the same pattern as for main jobs, except that, after agricul-ture and wage work, males resort to collecting/gathering in an effort to make a living. When we compare farm and non-farm occupations across the three categories, the highest proportion of farm jobs is in fact as a secondary occupation. The usual reasons are:

Table 45   Occupational composition of the economically active population of Mae Sa (per cent)

	First job		Second job		Third job	
	M	F	M	F	M	F
Agriculture	57.4	57.6	72.1	68.9	12.3	9.2
Non-agriculture:						
wage labour,	24.3	15.2	15.3	9.6	47.9	26.8
governmental/						
professional	9.6	3.2	2.6	1.0	1.4	—
Trade	2.3	15.2	0.9	14.8	4.4	57.7
Skilled labour	2.0	2.6	3.1	0.5	1.4	1.0
Handicraft	2.0	0.3	—	—	2.7	—
Business enterprise	1.5	3.2	0.9	—	2.7	—
Collection/gathering	—	1.0	5.2	3.8	26.0	5.2
Others	0.9	1.6	—	1.4	1.4	—
Total	100.0	100.0	100.0	100.0	100.0	100.0
N	345	309	229	209	73	97
Per cent	(52.8)	(47.2)	(52.3)	(47.7)	(42.9)	(57.1)

1   A surplus of family farm labour. Small holdings mean that only some household workers, e.g. heads of household and their wives, are needed to work the farm. Their children, then, often become wage workers and turn to farm work only when there is high demand for labour, for example, during planting or harvesting.
2   Small-scale cash cropping by villagers without rice land. These people find land on river bars or in foothills or rent rice fields from large landowners for cash cropping after the harvest season. Vegetables, tobacco and soy beans are some of the more popular crops grown. At other times of the year these villagers take non-farm employment.

Among third occupations, it is clear that petty trade for females and collecting/gathering for males cushion village families and enable them to subsist. More females than males have a third occupation, suggesting that they are taking jobs with low returns to free the men of the family to participate in jobs with higher returns, which are usually not available to women. This, together with the traditional practice of emphasizing the son's education or training above that of the daughter's, leaves no choice to rural female workers but to engage in low paid jobs.

Labour mobility

Both sexes not only engage in several occupations but move from place to place. Studies of labour mobility in Chiang Mai city among a broad sample of construction workers and rural employees (Singhanetra-Renard 1981, 1982) show a highly mobile workforce. Labour mobility in northern Thailand is confined to two types of population movement: commuting and circulation. Most movers, however, are commuters.

Of 161 respondents in a stratified random sample of rural employees in Chiang Mai city, about 65 per cent journey to work daily. The rest are circulators: 23 per cent move to live in city housing provided by their employers, and 12 per cent either live with relatives or have rented rooms. Most circulators come from villages more than 40 km away from the city. Daily travel becomes inconvenient at about that distance, or less for those who do not live close to routes regularly served by cheap public transport. The mobility pattern of the construction workers studied closely resembles that of rural employees working in Chiang Mai.

An intensive investigation of labour mobility from Mae Sa (Singhanetra-Renard 1982) illustrates the age and sex structure of the rural workforce moving out of that village for work. Their destinations include Chiang Mai city but also smaller urban centres, upland tea picking villages and foothill gardens. The following analysis, based on that study, shows the nature and characteristics of village circulators and commuters.

Labour circulation

Data from villages confirm those collected in urban destinations about the proportion of rural labourers circulating and commuting. Some 13.8 per cent of the villagers in Mae Sa reside temporarily outside the village, for the purpose of employment. The majority of both females and males have salaried jobs, but this figure includes two groups: the better educated, engaged in government jobs such as the army, the police, and teaching; and children of poor or landless families working as housemaids, sales clerks and in factories.

Labour commuting

Of the 654 economically active individuals in Mae Sa, no less than two-thirds work outside the village. Half of all females in the village aged 10 and over commute to work. In the age group 15–19, which is the most mobile of all age groups, a higher proportion of females commute than males. Female villagers enter the labour market earlier, at an age when their male counterparts are continuing their education beyond primary school. This high female mobility, however, is halved in the age group 20–24 when females tend to be married and having children. With the exception of the 20–24 age group, over 60 per cent of the female population in all age groups between 15–54 years travels to work. Among certain age groups the proportion of female movers is higher than for their male counterparts, particularly those in the 10–19 and 30–39 age groups. Women over 20–24 usually resume working once their children are old enough to go to school, and continue to work until their 50s.

For most rural people who enter the labour force at age 15 or over, mobility seems to have become part of the way of life. This runs contrary to the impression widely expressed in migration studies and implicit in the census definition of 'move', i.e., that rural people are immobile. Wage labour alone accounts for slightly over half of all movement to work. The other objectives are (in this order) foothill and upland gardening, trading, government/ professional employment, skilled work, agricultural wage work, and collecting and gathering. Each of these comprises not more than 17.5 per cent of all movement for work; ranging from foothill and upland gardening (17.5 per cent), through trade (10 per cent) to collecting/gathering (0.5 per cent).

Moves for wage work

Wage work is the most important means of supplementing cash income among the rural population, employing the largest number of people and attracting the largest numbers of moves. Wage work covers such activities as construction, fruit/tea picking, and factory work as well as jobs as housemaids, waiters and waitresses, sales clerks, and stable hands. Two-fifths of those moving for wage work are female. Most find jobs as construction labourers, factory workers, housemaids, or waitresses in the city. After marriage they usually turn to other jobs, such as trade or agricultural wage work, which allow them to take care of their families at the same time. Most, however, do not leave their city jobs until the first child arrives. This explains the drastic decrease of female participation in wage work by members of the higher age groups. Informal sector jobs, with no security, provide the only work available to villagers with little formal education who want to work in the city. Similarly, although the flexible hiring and firing conditions characteristic of the informal sector enable villagers to continue working seasonally on the land, the insecurity also characteristic of the informal sector prevents them from depending on non-farm employment in the city for their whole livelihood.

Moves for foothill and upland gardening

As agricultural land has become increasingly scarce in northern Thai villages, ever large numbers of people have been moving in order to cultivate nearby foothill areas for subsistence or to supplement lowland farming. In foothill agriculture, which involves daily walks of 5–8 km to the plots, the cultivators depend almost entirely on family labour. Exchange labour is usually practised in rice cultivation, but is rarely extended to cash cropping in the foothills. Since the family has to pool its labour for clearing and cultivation, all those aged 15 or over are involved. The most numerous foothill workers, however, are middle-aged parents with teenage children.

As with wage labour, 40 per cent of all those who move to the foothills are females. Females, however, make more total moves than males, not only because some households consist of only a widow or have more teenage daughters than sons, but also because wives and adult daughters take responsibility for guarding plots and carrying out other tasks on them. This frees their husbands and sons to work in construction or other jobs for cash income. Some landless families go to live temporarily at their gardens, but most travel daily except during the harvest when they stay in the gardens at night as well.

Moves for trade

Females undertake 90 per cent of all the moves for trade, buying and selling in the Chiang Mai markets. One study (Singhanetra-Renard 1982) counted 713 such moves during four months, accounting for 10 per cent of all Mae Sa mobility. They were made mainly by seven women aged between 30 and 39. Market trading was their main occupation and they were prepared to travel to Chiang Mai on any day. However, they maintained a flexible schedule and did not go if the supply of vegetables was known to be slight, or at times of village activities, family business, or illness. They would leave together, between 3 and 4 in the morning, to buy from villager wholesalers in the city and would then separate to resell their vegetables in one of four large retail markets. During December and January, at the peak of the harvest, many more women take fresh produce grown in Mae Sa to the city because they receive more money by selling directly than they do by using the vegetable wholesalers who travel throughout local communities.

Men make only 10 per cent of the trading moves from Mae Sa, but they are absent for longer periods than the women. Men trade in various items, including cattle and buffalo, tea, fruits, and home-made balm and herbal medicines.

Moves for government/professional employment

Males outnumber females moving to take up employment in the government or professional sectors by more than two to one. Whereas female movers are from the younger age groups, between 20 and 35, male movers are aged 20–54. This reflects the development of a new employment opportunity for rural female workers.

Moves for skilled work

People moving to take up skilled work account for only 8 per cent of all movement for employment. There is little opportunity for women to obtain the modern skills that would open many employment opportunities to them. The women who do learn hairdressing and dressmaking open shops in the village. For men, there are opportunities to work as carpenters, traditional doctors, spirit mediums, and musicians; and besides practising these crafts in their home communities, they may also make occasional trips in response to specific requests. In the study area all movers were male, except for one woman who is hired to teach folk dancing in the youth club of an upland village.

Traditional skills of village women have lost their economic importance. Manufactured goods have replaced the home products traditionally made by women, such as clothes, pottery, sweets and bedding. Midwifery, another traditional skill, has almost disappeared.

Moves for agricultural wage work

As with other types of wage work, little agricultural wage work is available locally. The practice of exchanging farm labour and the characteristically small holdings of the north mean that landless villagers are hired only by a few large landowners who have insufficient family labour. The tasks, mainly ploughing, preparing the soil, planting, harvesting, weeding and watering, provide seasonal employment, mainly for females. Family connections are important in finding this work, and they largely govern the inter-district flow of agricultural labourers. Most of these are aged 25 and over, generally older than those who move for construction jobs.

Moves for collecting and gathering forest products

In the nineteenth and early twentieth centuries, people in the north depended on forest products for many facets of their life-style. Most households continue to use firewood for cooking, and wood and bamboo are used for housing and the thatch for roofing. Villagers also collect bamboo shoots, mushrooms and other edible plants. There was a forest on the edge of Mae Sa village until it was felled for timber in 1960. Thus, whereas it was formerly convenient to gather forest produce, it now requires trips of 5 to 12 kilometres. As more people converge on the smaller and smaller remaining forests, shortages arise, particularly of bamboo. Collectors of produce from forested land are predominantly men (88 per cent). They travel in groups of between two and four, leaving before dawn and returning at midday. Most belong to landless or poor households, and the materials and foods gathered are mainly for domestic use, although some are sold at local markets. To the poor, gathering forest products is easier than taking up wage work because there is no transport cost.

Concluding remarks

Non-farm employment has become very important to the rural economy of northern Thailand. This is not generally recognized by rural development planners, and there has therefore been little interest in developing non-farm job opportunities in the rural areas of northern Thailand. One programme sponsored by the Thai government, the Rural Job Creation Project, does offer some short-term assistance by providing local government funds to create temporary work; but little has been done to build stable solutions. The result is a workforce that is highly mobile because of the rural need to engage in the non-farm employment available in the informal sector of urban centres. This mobility has slowed the urbanization and its attendant problems, but village movers still face uncertainties.

Longer-range planning will have to take into account the changes that are taking place in northern Thailand's rural society in jobs, education, the role of women, and mobility patterns. These changes are bringing new needs for which innovative solutions must be found. The promotion of rural jobs and careers outside the farm sector – particularly for women among whom the need is greatest – will give northern Thais the opportunity to work nearer their home villages. This will encourage the building of a stronger economic base in the non-urban areas and will allow community development to emerge from within according to local needs and desires.

Part Five

Industrial Change and Divisions of Labour

12 Family structure and female labour in Querétaro, Mexico

Sylvia Chant

Editors' introduction

Women in Latin America are excluded from 'direct production' and 'economic activity' (Chapter 1) to a degree which is exceeded only in the Middle East and North Africa. They are also highly segregated in particular occupations and activities in both the 'formal' and 'informal' sectors (Chapter 1), with a considerable bias to 'informal' activities. Industrialization has offered stable employment to some young and educated women. Many others need access to income, but are excluded from many activities. This may be by socio-cultural factors which define 'women's work', by the demand or opportunity for work, by supply factors such as their own education or their husband's income, and by demographic factors such as their age, size of family, age of youngest child and family type. Thus, at the micro-level, a whole array of social and economic factors affect the economic options of an individual woman.

Women's access to income-earning activities is limited in Latin America, especially in cities like Querétaro, Mexico, where the economic base is heavy industry. Chant explores the shape of economic opportunities for the women of Querétaro's 'irregular settlements'. She has elsewhere (1984a, b) delineated their exacting reproductive role, which involves a continual fight against harmful living conditions to shield their families from discomfort, disease and insecurity. Yet, despite the onerous nature of domestic labour she found that earning money is highly valued by women, and extra-domestic work is an important source of power and prestige, even if it results in a 'double day' of labour. The man's supremacy in the family is largely based on economic power, and, although women work very hard in the home, domestic labour is considered to be menial and is therefore undervalued. Female entry into the labour market represents a challenge to male domination in the home. Many western feminists and Marxists question the advantages of the nuclear family for women; Chant has established that domestic work bears less heavily on women in extended households in Queretaro since other family members, including men, help more with housework. In this chapter she questions the role of household structure in access to employment, and the household circumstances that facilitate income-earning among women.

Introduction

Mexico has one of the lowest rates in the world of female participation in the labour force, only 19 per cent in 1970. By 1979 this figure was nearer 25 per cent in larger Mexican cities. However, this is still low by comparison both with other developing nations (which have an average of 26 per cent of women in the labour force) and with advanced, industrial nations – for example, in the UK women make up 40 per cent of the national labour force. Of working women in Mexico, over two-thirds are involved in semi- or unskilled occupations. In 1970, 45 per cent of working women fell into the lowest income group, compared with only 19 per cent of men. Thus, women not only make up a smaller proportion of the labour force than men, but they also seem to be concentrated at the lower end of the labour market. This is often attributed to two factors which are external to the household: first, the structure of demand for labour, which is biased towards men on the assumption that they will play the main role in supporting their families; and second, discrimination by employers. Women have a lower level of education, their work may be interrupted by pregnancy, and the cost of employing women is high where protective legislation requires paid maternity leave, the provision of factory crêches, and so on. However, there are also equally important factors at the household level. The nature and extent of female employment is strongly influenced by cultural norms, by prevailing ideologies of female status, and, in particular, by the role that women play within the family.

This chapter seeks to show the specific effects on female employment of household-related factors in the case of three shanty towns in Querétaro – an industrializing city in Mexico. The data are derived from a 1983 survey of 244 low-income households selected randomly from lists of owner-occupiers. Part of the analysis will examine the utility of conventional explanations centred on culture, marital status and fertility. The remainder will introduce an idea that has only recently emerged in the literature: the effect of family composition on female employment (García,

Muñoz and de Oliveira 1982; Gonzalez de la Rocha 1984b). This focus on family factors permits us to examine the constraints perceived by women on their employment prospects. Indeed, the composition and organization of the household unit may often determine whether a woman will attempt to enter the labour market at all. It is suggested in the present study that a non-nuclear family structure maximizes her opportunities to participate in economic activities outside the home. However, before we commence our discussion of the influence of these factors on working-class women's paid work in Querétaro, it is necessary to outline briefly the employment structure in the city.

The labour market in Querétaro

Rapid industrialization, much of it due to the investment of foreign capital, has fundamentally altered the nature of Querétaro's labour market. Founded in 1531, the colonial city had hardly changed in appearance prior to the arrival of the first multi-national corporation in 1956. But it is now five times as large as it was then, and in 1983 its population was about 350,000.

In the early 1960s the primary or agricultural sector was the most important employer in Querétaro, occupying 40 per cent of the economically active population. Since then Querétaro has become a key centre for industrial location under a nationwide programme of economic decentralization. By subsidies and other incentives the state has attempted to divert industry away from Mexico City towards provincial centres. Querétaro, being relatively close to the capital and having abundant natural resources, was an attractive location. Foreign investment created new factories and gradually broadened the industrial base, so that by 1970 agriculture had lost half its importance, and occupied only 19 per cent of the workforce. By 1980 this figure had fallen to 8 per cent. Industry, on the other hand, employed 25 per cent of the workforce in 1960, 32 per cent in 1970 and 38 per cent in 1980. This high rate of industrial employment is impressive for a Third World city, as usually most jobs are in services. Indeed, it has been estimated that in general only one-seventh of the population of urban centres in developing countries is engaged directly in productive activities (Hackenberg, Murphy and Selby 1981).

The marked growth of 'formal' industry in the city has tended to favour the employment of men rather than women, although in the last decade women's employment has increased significantly. In 1970 women made up only one-tenth of the industrial labour

Table 46 Occupations of household heads and spouses

Branch of work	Independent worker	Employer	Employee (white-collar)	Category of work: Manual worker (blue-collar)	Domestic servant	House person	Unemployed
Agriculture, hunting, fishing	M[1] —	—	—	4 (1.9%)	—	—	—
	F[2] —	—	—	—	—	—	—
Manufacturing	M 1 (0.4%)	—	11 (5.2%)	45 (22.0%)	—	—	—
	F 1 (0.4%)	—	—	3 (1.2%)	—	—	—
Electricity, gas, water	M 1 (0.4%)	—	—	7 (3.3%)	—	—	—
	F —	—	—	—	—	—	—
Construction	M 1 (0.4%)	—	1 (0.4%)	35 (17.0%)	—	—	—
	F —	—	—	—	—	—	—
Retail/wholesale commerce, restaurants, hotels	M 14 (6.6%)	2 (0.9%)	1 (0.4%)	17 (8.0%)	—	—	—
	F 32 (13.1%)	—	1 (0.4%)	8 (3.3%)	—	—	—
Transport, storage, communications	M 3 (1.4%)	—	1 (0.4%)	12 (5.6%)	—	—	—
	F —	—	—	—	—	—	—
Finance, banks, real estate	M —	—	1 (0.4%)	—	—	—	—
	F —	—	—	—	—	—	—
Other private services	M 4 (1.9%)	—	1 (0.4%)	9 (4.2%)	17 (7.0%)	—	—
	F 7 (2.9%)	—	—	—	—	—	—
Other public services	M —	—	6 (2.9%)	12 (5.7%)	—	—	—
	F —	—	4 (1.6%)	1 (0.4%)	—	—	—

	M	F		M	F			M	F
Housework	—	—		—	—	169 (69.2%)		—	22
Unemployed (10.4%)	—	—		—	—	—	17	—	22
Total	64	2		27		153	17	169	22

Notes:

1 Male household heads. Figures in brackets give the percentage of the total sample of male households heads (N = 211).

2 Female household heads and female spouses. Figures in brackets give the percentage of all female heads and female spouses (N = 244).

force in the state of Querétaro. In 1980 it is estimated that perhaps one-quarter were women (Meza 1982). However, women tend to figure more prominently in 'informal' occupations than in industrial employment. 'Informal' employment is a term used widely in the literature on Third World urban labour markets to describe economic activities which are small scale, which operate outside the law, which are labour intensive, which use rudimentary technology and which are characterized by low and irregular earnings (Bromley 1982; Gugler 1982; Lailson 1980; LACWE 1980; Moser 1978, 1981). The 'formal' sector is the converse of this, being distinguished by large-scale enterprises, foreign capital inputs, mechanized production and social and labour legislation. The informal sector itself is highly differentiated, and the term often merely acts as a catch-all for a wide variety of non-institutionalized employment; but it has often been seen as inferior to 'formal' sector work and to be closely associated with female activities (Arizpe 1977; Connolly 1981). As we proceed to discuss in detail the employment structure in three of Querétaro's shanty towns, the differences between the two types of employment should become clearer.

Employment patterns in the study settlements

The workforce in the study settlements is engaged in a wide variety of income-earning activities. In the sample, nearly one-third of all male and female household-heads are in manufacturing, and a slightly smaller proportion in the retail and restaurant trades. The remainder are mainly in private services, construction and transport. Of all male and female household heads, 9 per cent are unemployed, 11 per cent are self-employed, 10 per cent are white-collar workers, mainly low-level clerks in factories and in the public sector, and 65 per cent are employed either as shop assistants or as manual labourers in industry, construction, transport and services. Men figure prominently in manufacturing (30 per cent of all male household heads in employment) and construction (20 per cent). Among women, if we discount the 169 (69 per cent) who are full-time housewives, only 6 per cent of the female household heads and spouses at work were in manufacturing, 32 per cent are domestic servants and the overwhelming majority (55 per cent) are in commerce or in the hotel and restaurant trade (see Table 46). Traditionally these occupations have been associated with informal employment. If social security protection is taken as an indicator of the 'formality' of employment, many more men than women tend to be employed in formal activities. In Querétaro, two-thirds of the working male heads of household in the study settlements were in 'protected' employment, but only one-quarter of female workers. Although factory work was considered desirable by both men and women in the interviews, it was not the main occupation of working-class females. While 27 per cent of all employed male household heads in the study settlements worked in formal manufacturing enterprises, only 2 per cent of employed female household heads and spouses do so. Additionally, men in factory employment earned an average of 3586 *pesos* a week as manual workers, whereas women earned only half this amount (see Table 47).

In the study settlements informal employment is most common in two branches of activity – commerce and private services – in which women outnumbered men. For example, 8.4 per cent (sixteen) of all 'working' male heads are independent workers in commerce, compared with 43 per cent (thirty-two) of all 'working' female heads and spouses. Half the men engaged in informal commerce have their own family business, such as a small shop or stall, which frequently used the unpaid labour of other family members: the rest are *ambulantes* (self-employed itinerant tradesmen). Within this informal commercial sector, women do not own their own businesses as such, though a woman fortunate enough to possess a refrigerator will sometimes sell soft drinks from her front room as a sideline activity. On the whole, however, women produce goods and foodstuffs and sell them to personal contacts either within the neighbourhood or nearby. The most common form of female commercial enterprise is the making and selling of *tortillas*, the Mexican staple foodstuff. In about one-third of these cases the wife makes them and the man sells them, otherwise women produce and sell direct to a specific clientele that they have built up over time, either within the settlement or close by. Women also produce other types of cooked food, such as fudge, decorated individual jellies, and peeled *nopales* (cactus leaves), or engage in small-scale manufacture of plant pots, dolls and soft toys. Net income in informal commerce for men amounted to an average of 3232 *pesos* a week, whereas their wives and female heads of household make an average of only 1741 *pesos*. This is most probably because women spend more time producing items than trading and thus earn less. Furthermore, women are more restricted by time and space in their choice of market locations. Women, therefore, are not only heavily involved in unprotected, non-unionized employment; they also rank low in the hierarchy of informal sector

Table 47   Average weekly earnings of household heads
according to sex and branch of work

Branch of work	Male household heads		Female household heads	
	Average weekly earnings in Mexican pesos 1983	Percentage of total male heads (N = 211)	Average weekly earnings in Mexican pesos 1983	Percentage of total female heads (N = 33)
Agriculture, hunting and fishing	3050.00	1.9	—	0
Manufacturing	3961.40	27.0	1866.70	9.0
Electricity, gas and water	3250.00	3.8	—	0
Construction	2932.40	18.0	—	0
Retail and wholesale commerce, restaurants and hotels	3055.90	16.0	3600.00	21.2
Transport, storage and communications	2775.00	7.6	—	0
Finance, banks and real estate	6500.00	0.5	—	0
Services (public) not included above	3288.90	8.5	—	0
Services (private) not included above, e.g. domestic service	2485.70	6.6	1100.00	48.5
Housepersons	—	0	Unpaid	21.2
Unemployed	—	10.4	—	0

jobs, being in the worst paid activities with least status. Why do fewer women work than men, and why are they concentrated in different forms of economic activity?

Undoubtedly, this pattern in Querétaro derives in part from the demand side. Querétaro industry is heavy, it produces many high-technology goods and parts for export, it is subject to state legislation, and it does not commonly employ home-based piece-workers. Thus there is little opportunity for women to work in manufacturing, so they take up informal employment because there is nothing else. On the supply side, however, low levels of education, high fertility and a cultural formation emphasizing domesticity also decrease women's chances of getting out of the home.

Household constraints on female labour

The household factors normally invoked to explain women's participation in the paid labour force include age, education and family size. We shall discuss briefly these concepts with reference to the data from Querétaro, and then analyse at greater length the effects of household composition.

Age

Most studies have found that women's rate of employment is highest when they are young. Employment among females is at a peak around the age of 23 in Mexico City (Pedrero and Rendón 1982), and also in Querétaro (Selby 1979). The explanation is that women are likely to be married by their mid 20s and married women here are less able and less likely to be employed. They do not have time to balance a dual role of worker at home and worker outside, and factories usually have additional obligations to married women employees, and therefore find it is cheaper to employ either men or single women. In the study settlements, the correlations between age and female employment accord with the results of previous studies – among women of working age and under 25 (mothers and daughters) a total of 49 per cent are in paid work or self-employed; this is a much higher proportion than in any other age group. However, when these figures are controlled for marital status different results emerge: 66 per cent of unmarried daughters of all ages are in paid work, but only 10 per cent of married mothers. Among married mothers the highest rate of participation in the labour force is in the age group 40–44; about half the married women of that age work. The highest rate of employment for female heads of households (i.e. mothers who have been widowed or deserted by or who have left their husbands) is between the ages of 30 and 34, when children are probably too young to work and the mothers have no other option. So, although age is important, it is very much interlinked with marital status: where there is a high frequency of marriage break-up, for example, women are far more likely to enter the labour force.

Family size

Another factor put forward to explain varying rates of female participation in the labour force is family size. Findings are often contradictory, but it is generally thought that women with smaller families are less bound to the home and more likely to engage in paid work. This is especially true in advanced industrial nations. However, in the Third World, the prevalence of part-time, informal, home-based jobs for women means that frequently there is very little connection between the two variables. In her study of Mexico City, Elú de Leñero (1980) found that working women had slightly fewer children (3.8) than non-working women (4.1), but there is usually very little relationship between fertility and female work-patterns in less-developed countries. This is probably because many low-income women work in home-based employment, so that family size is not affected greatly by women's involvement in paid work. In fact, in the study settlements in Querétaro, women working outside the home in paid employment had the largest average number of children (5.4), compared with full-time housewives (4.1), and female workers in small family businesses (3.4). Logically this would also be affected by the age of the children, but no significant differences between age groups were found for the Querétaro sample.

Education

Education is a highly valued and highly marketable resource in urban areas in Mexico, and a significant supply constraint on female labour. This is because women's access to education appears to be far more limited than that of men. In the republic as a whole in 1980, only 16.7 per cent of all men were recorded as illiterate compared with 21.3 per cent of all women. In the study settlements in Querétaro the discrepancy seems even more marked. One-quarter of the 211 male household heads had no education whatsoever, and the proportion rose to more than half for the thirty-three female heads. Only three female heads had completed more than four years of primary education. This disparity between the sexes is now narrowing, since most boys and girls receive at least three years' primary schooling, but on the whole women still have far lower levels of literacy and educational achievement than men. This is often a key to the understanding of differences in the nature of employment and earning potential.

Educational requirements even for manual work in the formal sector, for example, generally exclude at least half the workforce from protected employment. In the study settlements, male and female factory workers had an average of six years' education (i.e. they had completed primary school). The men with least education worked in construction and agriculture (average of two to three years' schooling), the women with least education in commerce and private services. Most domestic servants had no education whatsoever. Although urbanization has had the effect of raising levels of education generally, women are still relatively disadvantaged, and this is a significant criterion when employment patterns are considered. The difficulties associated with education and fertility are compounded by the influence of culture and of the family.

Culture and the sexual division of labour

A strong constraint on wage earning by women arises from cultural factors and the general position of women within the social formation. Latin America is

characterized normatively by a social order noted for its strong familism, patriarchalism, cultural tradition of male supremacy and the sanction of a religion [Spanish Catholic] . . . which reinforces the subsidiary position of women in the social structure. The criterion of family esteem depends largely, if not exclusively, upon conformity to behavioural norms that are conceived as having to do with male honour (Youssef 1972, p. 143).

In general there is a sharp division between the sexes in Mexican society. Men are encouraged to be aggressive, dominant and 'manly'; while women are supposed to be passive, retiring, and devoted to their homes, their children, and the church. The cult of *machismo* embodies the idea that males are superior to females in many ways, and ordains that 'men are for the streets and women are for the home' (de Barbieri 1982). The family is an arena where these cultural norms can be observed in play. The prevalent ideologies of womanhood give few Mexican women the opportunity to participate in activities outside the home. Mexican women are often not allowed to enter the labour force, or if they are, they perform their paid labour within the household, either because their working elsewhere would be a threat to the authority of the husband–father or because the menfolk are afraid that women who go out to work will be suspected of being prostitutes. At the same time, men are often very unreliable as economic contributors to the family budget; many retain their wage packets for themselves, which further worsens the position of women as non-earners. Fieldwork in Querétaro, in accordance with these explanations, indicated that men had three main reasons for not wishing their wives to work. First, the wife might earn more than her husband and 'get ahead', though this is quite unlikely to happen in practice. Second, it might suggest to other families that the husband is unable to fulfil his role as breadwinner and to other men that he is failing to exercise his will and authority over his wife: in other words, that he is weak. And third, the greater freedom of movement accruing to working wives is viewed suspiciously by their husbands, who fear it may result in their spouses being unfaithful (Chant 1984a). This last explanation also means that women are less likely to be allowed to apply for jobs where they will be working alongside men, and it may account for the concentration of women in occupations noted for their isolation, such as domestic service.

The effect of family structure on female employment

At this point it is useful to discuss the influence of different family structures on women's role, for the cultural ideal of female domesticity seems less rigid in some types of families than in others. Within the settlements, nuclear families represented 68 per cent (167) of the total sample of households. Single-parent families (headed by women) represented 9 per cent (twenty-two) of the total. Extended families (families residing with kin) constituted 23 per cent (fifty-five). (Four-fifths (forty-four) of this group were headed by males and one-fifth (eleven) by females.) Other studies on low-income urban communities in Mexico have also shown that nuclear families form between two-thirds and three-quarters of the total (García, Muñoz and de Oliveira 1982; Ward 1976). One interesting feature emerging from the Querétaro data is that the prevalence of the nuclear family may be related to male authority. In-depth interviews on household composition with a sub-sample of forty-seven families revealed that many women would welcome the opportunity of introducing a relative into the house, but there was much male resistance to this. As many as four-fifths of the male heads of nuclear families were unwilling to share their homes with a relative, for fear of losing exclusive ownership of the family's property, or because they feared lack of privacy, or were jealous that another man, even a brother-in-law, would share the same house. As men often had the final word in decision-making, it is probable that more families remained nuclear than otherwise would have been the case.

The structure of the nuclear family lends itself most easily to a strict sexual division of labour, the male partner earning a wage and the woman in the home doing the housework and looking after the children. The facts that women bear children, and that men earn more in the Mexican labour market combine to favour the man's position as breadwinner, quite apart from cultural influences. This rigid division of male and female labour often results in a marked imbalance of power within the domestic unit, with female subjugation to male authority reinforced by economic dependence. In as many as half the nuclear families in the Querétaro study, men regularly withheld half their wage packets from their wives and children. The amount and regularity of family privation varied according to the strength of the husband–father's commitment to his dependants, but there appeared to be very little inherent in the nuclear structure to ensure equality of resource allocation. The husband's economic support was often negligible, yet if his was the only wage in the family and he was opposed to the idea of his wife working, she was on weak ground if she wanted to earn a wage of her own and thus raise the level of household well-being. In single-parent families and in extended families where there may be several male and female adults under one roof, not only is it functionally more possible (or more imperative) for women to enter the labour force, but also, possibly as a result of these work patterns, the cultural norms may be sufficiently diluted to allow greater equality within the household and thus improve the women's status. The exigencies of life in low-income communities have been seen in the past as forcing certain families to seek alternative roles in order to survive (Nalven 1978; Lomnitz 1977): this appears in Querétaro to apply most to non-nuclear families. In 'unconventional' family structures, albeit often through economic necessity, women have more freedom both to enter the labour force and also to choose the kinds of jobs they are going to do.

Only one-third of the female spouses in nuclear families have paid work, compared with nearly half of the women in male-headed extended families and four-fifths of female heads. What kinds of factors explain this variation? Several authors assert that the rise of the nuclear family in industrializing economies is accompanied by an improvement in the status of women. This is attributed partly to the increase in employment opportunities outside the home, and partly to a trend towards egalitarian relationships within the household (Bridges 1980; Das and Jesser 1980; Goode 1963). These authors see nuclear families as removing the vestiges of male status traditionally associated with extended family hierarchies and eliminating obstacles to individual improvement, and thus as conducive to liberation of women from domestic subservience. This is not borne out by the data from Querétaro. There it appears to be the women from non-nuclear households who gain access to work opportunities in urban areas, and not those from nuclear families.

The organization of housework is one of the most important factors explaining why women in some families are more likely than others to take paid employment. Domestic work is often seen as women's main obstacle to entering the labour force. Nowhere is this truer than in the study settlements, which lack many basic urban services such as piped water, sewerage, rubbish collection and paved roads, and where housing is of poor quality. Deficient housing and servicing make the domestic workload much greater for women in shanty towns than for their counterparts in more consolidated neighbourhoods, and it is therefore probably far more difficult for them to take up paid work in addition to their domestic chores. For example, the provision of water alone confronts housewives with several time-consuming tasks each day. Water is delivered to the settlements by tankers, which deposit it in oil-drums provided by the residents. As many 'roads' in the settlements are impassable, the women must do much fetching and carrying with buckets, often up and down hill. The tankers are often unreliable, so women sometimes have to find water elsewhere – for example, by taking their washing to a stream or to the house of a friend in a more central part of town. Furthermore, as the water is contaminated, the women have to boil it for longer periods to get rid of parasites and bacteria. Essentially, the less consolidated the settlement, the greater is the burden of domestic labour.

Family structure may reduce some of these problems by allowing housework to be shared. Two things are important here: first, the number of family members available to carry out domestic work, and second, the frequency with which household tasks are divided up among the members. In nuclear families the frequency and amount of help is considerably lower than in non-nuclear households, and often housework is done by the female spouse alone. The reasons are as follows. First, because the woman has no other role except her domestic one, it is assumed that she can manage that labour in its entirety, so she is nearly always left to carry it out single-handed. Second, even where her husband actively encourages the children to help, they may be too young to do so. Third, there may only be male children, and in a culture which discourages male participation in 'female spheres', boys should not be seen to help their mothers in this way. In non-nuclear families the situation is different. The active help of both sons and daughters in single-parent households (motivated by the fact that often their mothers have full-time jobs), and of female relations in extended families, means that there are often two, if not three, people to shoulder the burden of housework.

Another factor influencing female work-roles is the relative need for women to work. In many single-parent families, women obviously have to take up paid work, especially if their children are young. In extended households, because the housework is shared and because there are more people to support, there is less pressure on women to be in the home on a full-time basis and a greater need for them to earn money. In nuclear households women not only find it far more difficult to balance the two work-roles, especially if they have no daughters to whom they can delegate some of the domestic tasks and if they are rearing young children, but also, if the husband is earning, there is less apparent need for them to enter the labour force. They conform to a cultural pattern whereby the man alone provides for his wife and dependants.

However, what is also important, as we explained previously, in deciding whether women will enter the labour force is the attitude of the male and his commitment to his family. Nuclear families frequently have only one wage-earner – the husband–father – whereas both single-parent and extended families generally have at least two paid workers in the home. In single-parent households, sons and daughters (if they are old enough) help financially because women's earnings are often low and need to be supplemented. In extended families, the greater number of adults allows more people to enter the labour market. A notable finding of the Querétaro study was that in families where wage-earning was divided between two or more people there was a greater tendency to pool all earnings in a collective family budget and to allocate finance more equitably among the dependants (Chant 1984a). The built-in checks to egoism caused by the sharing of earnings in single-parent and extended families could mean that the family (and its male head where relevant) has a vested interest in sending as many members as possible out to work and maximizing potential income. In one in two of the nuclear households the family does not function as a cohesive unit with the husband– father co-operating responsibly with the rest of his family and sharing his earnings: and he feels he has nothing to gain if his wife goes out to work.

Among less direct influences, it is significant that male author- ity is modified in non-nuclear structures. In single-parent house- holds the absence of the male leaves to the woman the status of primary decision-maker and allows her the freedom to decide whether to take up paid work (though she often has to). In extended households, the presence of several earners means that no man has the position of sole provider and arbiter of expenditure. Women who are not dependent on one wage-earner alone are in a stronger position to press for the right to employment outside the home. Furthermore, the sharing of work-roles, both paid and unpaid, appears to spread an ethic of equal participation in the strategies and benefits of family life: it makes it less easy to justify the division of labour on the basis of sex. For example, if one adult woman in the family has taken up paid employment, it is difficult to substantiate an argument that another woman may not.

A final influence on the entry of women into the labour force is the support gained through having other women resident in their homes. For example, there is often more than one adult woman in the home in male-headed extended families; this contributes to female solidarity and strength and so helps women to challenge male authority. This probably explains why not only a greater number of women from non-nuclear families enter the labour market, but also why their jobs tend to be of a higher status and to occupy more time than the jobs held by women from nuclear families. More women tend to be engaged in full-time activities of a formal nature, such as shop work and factory employment, in non-nuclear structures. But the sample is not large enough to enable significant comparisons to be drawn in this area.

Conclusion

We have discussed in this chapter the way in which a variety of aspects of household type and composition influence women's involvement in the labour force in three shanty towns of Querétaro, Mexico. These 'supply' constraints include cultural norms, age and fertility, and (perhaps most important of all) the predominance of the nuclear family, in which few women are allowed by their husbands to enter the labour market. The nuclear family, as an 'ideal' model, is highly conducive to a strict segregation between male and female roles, whereas other family patterns not only make it functionally more feasible for women to work, but also allow a certain degree of deviation from the standard ideology that a woman's place is in the home. Female heads, by virtue of their status and authority, have the freedom to determine how they will organize the family's earning strategies. Female spouses in male-headed extended families enjoy a reduction in their housework burdens if these are shared by other family members, they have greater support for their claim to work from other female members, and the sharing of decision-making and finance between several adults means that the male head has rather less of a prerogative in dictating what his wife will do and more of a vested interest in maximizing the total earning potential of the household.

These data derive from a city where a large-scale export-oriented industrial sector creates a greater demand for male than for female labour. We need to look at other Third World centres with different types of labour markets in order to establish more clearly how the economies of the household and of the city inter-relate. For example, in Guadalajara, a Mexican city whose economy is based upon small-scale workshop production geared to providing cheap consumption goods for the domestic market, a larger number of young wives in nuclear families are employed in industry. This may be a result of greater opportunities for outwork – much paid labour may be performed in the home – or because women's work does not challenge male authority in the same way as it may do in Querétaro. But the implications of this for the functioning of the nuclear family are as yet unexplored. In Querétaro, there is little opportunity for outwork, and in the shanty towns several women have been prevented by a lack of services and physical difficulties from taking up part-time flexible jobs. The economic condition and work-roles of many women are therefore totally dependent on their husbands. This is especially true for women in nuclear families. It suggests that we should consider family structure as a contributory factor in the analysis of female employment in less-developed countries.

Acknowledgements

The author wishes to thank Priscilla Connolly of the Centro de la Vivienda y Estudios Urbanos, Mexico City, for her comments on an earlier draft of this paper.

13   Gender and industrialization in Brazil

Susan Cunningham

Editors' introduction

Women's recorded share of the labour force of manufacturing industry in the Third World varies from zero in Kuwait, 4 per cent in Malawi and 5 per cent in Egypt to 56 per cent in Singapore (Chapter 1); commonly it is between a quarter and a third. Industrial production more than any other is now organized internationally, in a complex articulation of national and international capital and markets. Most aspects of this production have been heavily researched and described, from investment structures to the labour process, yet little has been done to account for these discrepancies in female participation, save for recent attention to the feminization of certain export processing which characterizes the New International Division of Labour (Fröbel *et al*. 1980). Striking though this feature may be, it rarely dominates the labour markets of newly industrializing countries. Heavy employment of young women in border areas of Mexico (Christopherson 1983) has little effect on national female participation (Chapter 12) and almost none on women in shanty towns of Querétaro.

Female shares in the labour force in different sectors of manufacturing have nevertheless altered considerably in the newly industrializing countries – and not only in 'export processing'. The 'background' socio-cultural determinants of women's economic activity which are so often taken as given are themselves changing, being reshaped. Cunningham here begins an elucidation of the process in one country: Brazil. In a sense, Chapters 12 and 13 are counterposed, since they use Latin American case studies to examine influences on female participation at very different scales. Given a specific level of female participation, which women will be able to enter the labour market (Chapter 12)? Conversely, given that women can be excluded from or drawn into the labour market, how is the level of participation altered – and in whose interests (Chapter 13)?

Introduction

This chapter explores some aspects of the changing pattern of women's paid work in a rapidly industrializing country, Brazil. The emphasis is upon women's growing role in a variety of formal, waged and essentially urban occupations, and particularly in manufacturing industry. Recent census data and related evidence are used to show the scope and the scale of women's paid work, both at the national level and in further detail for the most industrialized region, the state and metropolitan area of São Paulo. Relevant data for other areas are given as appropriate. The objective, however, is not the study of women's work as an end in itself. Rather, it is essential to consider employment patterns for women in conjunction with those for men. A basic contention is that differences in gender can be used by capital, especially in labour-surplus societies, to contain production (and other) costs. So, in addition to the well-known role of women's work inside the home in defraying the costs of reproducing and 'maintaining' the labour force, their 'productive' labour is extensively exploited by 'modern' industrialization.

Growth of the labour force and changing occupational patterns

Brazil's workforce has grown rapidly during recent decades (roughly 1940 to 1980, a period when industrial expansion has been virtually uninterrupted). Over this period, too, the population increased almost threefold, from 41 to 119 million, and became more heavily urbanized; the proportion classified as urban rose from 31 per cent in 1940 to 45 per cent in 1960 and 68 per cent in 1980. It is against this background that more women have been incorporated into the growing urban workforce, across a diversified range of activities (see Table 48). While the population over 10 years of age classified as 'economically active' and constituting the EAP grew from 14.7 to 43.7 million, the female share in this category grew from 19 per cent (2.8 million) in 1940 to 27 per cent (almost 12 million) in 1980. If agricultural labour is excluded, the female share is even higher, at 33 per cent in 1980 (10.2 of 30.6 million).

But even this statistical growth of the 'active' female workforce profoundly understates the numbers and role of the full complement of women of working age. To the almost 12 million women shown as being within the EAP in 1980 must be added no less than

Table 48   Brazil: employment structure of the economically active population by gender, 1940–80

Sector	1940		1960		1980	
	Male (per cent)	Female (per cent)	Male (per cent)	Female (per cent)	Male (per cent)	Female (per cent)
Agriculture	70.3	46.8	58.8	30.1	35.8	14.4
Industrial	10.2	10.6	13.2	12.5	27.9	14.8
Retailing	5.8	1.8	7.2	4.3	9.2	9.7
Personal services	3.9	34.3	6.9	35.5	9.8	33.0
Social services	0.7	4.1	1.4	10.6	2.8	17.9
Public administration	3.1	0.8	3.1	2.0	4.8	3.1
Other	2.2	1.1	3.8	3.9	4.5	5.9
	100.0	100.0	100.0	100.0	100.0	100.0
Totals						
Male	11,958,968		18,597,763		31,392,986	
Female	2,799,630		4,054,100		11,842,726	

Sources: IBGE 1974 for 1940 and 1960; IBGE 1981, 1983 for 1980.

32.6 million women over the age of 10 (compared with only 11.9 million males) who are classed as being 'economically inactive'. The non-economically active population is defined for census purposes as those who during the previous twelve months were exclusively occupied in one or more of the following: housewives, students, retired, sick or invalid, could not find work, or did not want work. In fact the majority of women so classified, and thus relegated to invisibility in the occupational data, are housewives engaged not only in their own domestic work and family obligations, but frequently also in informal self-employment (cf. Moser and Young 1981). As we bear this in mind, we recognize that the census data on which we must depend in the analyses which follow fail to convey the real fluidity of Brazilian labour markets, notably the shifting balance between formal and informal work as individuals of both sexes and, indeed, whole families, adapt their living and working arrangements to rapidly changing economic circumstances. The failure of official data to recognize a large sector of female workers as 'active' testifies to the inferior status generally accorded to women's unpaid work inside the home. As we shall see, this neglect of the 'invisible sector' of women workers is a prelude to the undervaluation of women's work even in the 'visible sector'.

Occupational segregation by sector of activity

Table 49 shows the proportions of women employed within the main sectors of non-agricultural activity in 1980 in Brazil as a whole and in three metropolitan areas: São Paulo and Rio de Janeiro (both in the south-east), and Recife, the capital of the state of Pernambuco in the impoverished north-east region. The figures show a tendency towards specific sectors dominated by males or females with a 'middle ground' in which males predominate but women contribute a significant proportion of the total workforce (20–30 per cent). For Brazil as a whole, the construction and transport/communications sectors are shown to be almost wholly male preserves (98 and 92 per cent respectively), while personal and social services are strongly female areas (women account for 56 and 71 per cent of the respective totals). Occupations in manufacturing, retailing and public administration are all male dominated (over 70 per cent), but with a substantial female share (24, 27 and 21 per cent). Overall, even at this aggregate level, it is clear that in the sphere of paid work women's role in most sectors is essentially a

Table 49 Brazil: female shares in the employment structure, 1980

Sector	Economically active population, million		Female share, per cent			
	Total	Female	Brazil	São Paulo MA[3]	Rio MA[3]	Recife MA[3]
Manufacturing	6.9	1.6	24	26	24	20
Retailing	4.0	1.1	27	29	29	29
Public administration	1.7	0.37	21	28	17	22
Personal services[1]	7.0	3.9	56	52	52	59
Social services[2]	2.9	2.1	71	68	64	67
Construction	3.1	0.06	2	3	3	3
Transport and communications	1.8	0.14	8	10	11	9

Notes:
[1] Personal services are mainly domestic service and portering;
[2] social services comprise predominantly teaching and nursing;
[3] total numbers of the female EAP (over 10 years of age) in each Metropolitan Area in 1980 were: São Paulo 1.7 of 5.3 million; Rio de Janeiro 1.1 of 3.3 million, Recife 247,000 of 724,000.

Source: IBGE, 1983.

Table 50   Brazil: employment status of female and male economically active population by sector of activity, 1980

| Sector and gender | Employment Status (percentage share of each gender) | | | |
	Employees	Self-employed	Employer	(Subtotal)
All non-agricultural				
Female	74	15	1	(90)
Male	62	28	3	(93)
Manufacturing				
Female	91	7	1	(99)
Male	90	6	3	(99)
Social services				
Female	95	3	0.5	(98.5)
Male	87	8	2	(97)
Public administration				
Female	99			(99)
Male	99			(99)
Retailing				
Female	72	21	4	(97)
Male	58	33	8	(99)
Personal services				
Female	73	23	1	(97)
Male	63	30	5	(98)

Note:
Construction and transport sectors (which are virtually all male) are excluded.
Source: IBGE, 1983.

minority one, subsidiary – and, indeed, subordinate – to activities mostly organized and staffed by men.

Women's subsidiary role is further borne out when gender differences in employment status are examined. Within the formal sectors of activity which we are primarily considering here, Table 50 shows that women are far more likely than men to be employees rather than self-employed or employers. It is interesting that in three important sectors – manufacturing, social services (predominantly a public sector activity) and public administration – the proportions of both women and men classed as 'employees' are similarly high (87–99 per cent). It can perhaps be inferred that the productive core of the economy, concentrated in private hands, and the public services and bureaucracy, run by agencies of the state, harness both sexes as wage slaves. (The industrial ownership structure in Brazil is divided roughly into three sectors of about a third each: private domestic, foreign enterprises and state enterprises. For public sector employment, see Rezende *et al.* (1976), ch. 2.)

It is only in retailing and personal services that women appear to enjoy some scope for autonomy through self-employment (between a fifth and a quarter of women formally registered in these activities were self-employed in 1980). Yet it is precisely in these sectors that job status and incomes tend to be lowest. Within personal services, for example, female domestic service is the largest single category; census data show that there are over 2.3 million women in a total of 2.47 million workers. Some 52 per cent of these 2.3 million women earned less than one minimum wage in 1980, a minimum wage being much less than basic subsistence.

Paid work and marital status

In most sectors of paid, urban employment, 50–60 per cent of women workers are single and some 30–35 per cent married; the remainder are separated, divorced or widowed (1980 census). It is only in social services (including teaching, nursing, etc.) and, to a lesser extent, in public administration that the experience marriage brings in the domestic realm (servicing and caring for the family) confers some employment advantage for work outside the home. For the most part it is younger, single women, largely free of domestic ties, who will be preferred by employers (the majority of whom are men).

This picture of women in paid employment – and, in particular the predominance of single women – contrasts sharply with that of men. Indeed, whereas married women are a minority of the women in waged work, the opposite is true for men. Some 60–75 per cent of waged male workers are married and only 25–35 per cent are single.

Taken together, these observations confirm that, in the world of paid work, women's family role and the particular stage reached in their life-cycle shape their employment prospects much more strongly – and in the opposite way – than for men. To reinforce the point made earlier, although the majority of women of working age are classed by the census as 'economically inactive', and some two-thirds of them (almost 17 million in 1980) are married, it does not follow that this large sector of the population fails to occupy a work role outside the domestic sphere. On the contrary, as other researchers have found (Moser and Young 1981; Schmitz 1982), these women make up a large part of the workforce in informal activities.

Gender and manufacturing industry

The growth of employment in manufacturing industry was quite substantial during the period 1960 to 1980. The net increase in jobs was almost 2.9 million, raising the total from 1.75 million in 1960 to 4.65 million in 1980. Some 2 million jobs were gained in the 1970s alone, although the ratio of women to men remained at about 1:4, much the same level as it was decades earlier. In any case, it should be noted that the growth in industrial employment did not keep pace with the labour force, which in the two decades almost doubled in size, from 22.5 to 43 million.

To underpin this increase in manufacturing employment there was both an expansion and a restructuring of Brazil's industrial base. Successive governments, especially since the mid 1950s, have sought to diversify and increase industrial capacity, using a variety of policy and planning measures (Cunningham 1979). At the leading edge of the strategy of industrialization was the promotion of newer or 'dynamic' sectors (often harnessing new technology to Brazilian needs and often with a large presence of foreign companies or of the state). More traditional sectors were modernized. In the process, the industrial structure changed; the main products were no longer basic consumer goods (particularly foodstuffs and textiles), but a range of consumer durables from the transport, electrical–electronic and chemicals industries. These changes had a particular impact upon the employment opportunities for women. At one extreme, the decline of textiles – an industry traditionally employing a large proportion of women workers – and the reorganization of production not only reduced jobs but altered the gender balance in favour of men. By contrast, the rise of some dynamic sectors, including the electrical–electronic and pharmaceuticals industries, provided new areas of employment for women. But the changing pattern of female employment in manufacturing, and of the division of labour between the sexes, is more complex than this simple outline suggests.

Gender typing by sector of manufacturing

It should be emphasized that data are not available for a com-

Table 51 São Paulo state: female employment shares by sector of manufacturing industry 1960, 1970 and 1980

Sector	Percentage share of total employment in production			Total females 1980
	1960*	1970	1980	
Non metallic				
minerals	13.6	11.7	13.0	14,733
Metallurgical	8.0	7.0	8.5	22,143
Machinery	3.5	3.4	3.5	10,149
Electrical-electronic	19.0	26.5	37.4	54,234
Transport goods	3.6	4.7	8.5	13,328
Timber	3.0	4.7	9.3	2,356
Furniture	3.9	4.8	12.2	6,695
Paper and				
cardboard	22.2	22.0	24.1	11,900
Rubber	12.9	12.8	14.5	4,905
Leather/hides	8.8	16.9	36.9	3,805
Chemicals	19.0	9.5	8.7	5,532
Pharmaceuticals	67.6	53.7	56.9	8,522
Perfumes, soaps	41.3	35.1	42.5	4,478
Plastics	34.3	26.7	32.6	21,167
Textiles	57.3	52.6	48.4	82,175
Clothing/shoes	48.4	61.4	68.5	116,587
Food products	17.3	18.8	29.3	38,778
Beverages	15.5	8.1	13.1	1,746
Tobacco	47.0	54.6	56.5	961
Printing and				
publishing	17.8	16.5	20.4	9,784
Miscellaneous	28.2	34.5	40.6	22.844
All manufacturing	25.7	22.8	23.9	439,094

Notes:
*Figures for 1960 include workers and foremen only; for 1970 and 1980 they also include technicians.
Sources: IBGE, 1984; Humphrey, 1984.

prehensive analysis of the changing balance between male and female employees by industry over time. (Relevant statistical sources and methodological points are discussed in Cunningham 1983 and Humphrey 1984.) It is, however, possible to throw some light upon the evolution of female employment in Brazil's most industrialized state, São Paulo, over the period 1960 to 1980.

Table 51 summarizes the trends in the proportion of females in employment in each industry in each of the three main census years (1960, 1970 and 1980). While the average proportion of women employees in manufacturing industry as a whole has not changed much over the period (hovering between 23 and 26 per cent of the total and tending to decline slightly), there have been some remarkable changes in particular sectors. First, in 1960 there were only two sectors with a predominantly female workforce: pharmaceuticals (68 per cent) and textiles (57 per cent). A further four industries had between 30 and 50 per cent females (perfumes, plastics, clothing and tobacco), while in the electrical, pulp/paper, and chemicals sectors the female share was about a fifth of the total. By 1970, there were some important differences. Proportions of women in both pharmaceuticals and textiles had declined (though in both they were still in the majority), but two new predominantly female sectors had emerged: clothing/shoes and tobacco. Substantial proportionate increases in the female share were evident in the electrical and leather goods industries, but there was a marked decline in chemicals, plastics and beverages. In 1980 the pharmaceuticals (57 per cent), clothing (68 per cent) and tobacco (56 per cent) sectors still predominantly employed women, but the largest proportionate growth in female employment from 1970 to 1980 (continuing the trend from 1960 to 1970) was in the electrical and leather sectors, and there was also substantial growth in the food and miscellaneous industries. The female share in plastics and furniture was increasing more sharply than in the previous decade; and it should be noted that, although their share in the motor industry remained small, it grew from 4.9 per cent in 1970 to 8.5 per cent in 1980, when total employment in the sector had reached 281,272.

Over the period 1960 to 1980 as a whole there was some decrease in the proportion of female employees in six industrial sectors, particularly in chemicals, pharmaceuticals and textiles; in one sector (machinery and equipment) the proportion remained the same; in all other sectors it increased.

Explaining shifts in the gender division of labour

It is clear from the evidence for São Paulo state that by 1980 the proportions of women employed in the dynamic sectors of manufacturing, consumer durables, capital goods and chemicals had been contained at or below their 1960 levels. (The main exceptions to this were the electrical–electronic and, to a lesser extent, motor industries.) Of course, since employment grew in all these sectors from 1960 to 1980, the absolute numbers of women employed in them also rose. However, the fact remains that the proportion of women in the seven principal dynamic sectors (taken together) changed little between 1960 and 1980, from 13.2 to 13.7 per cent of all women in employment. (Metallurgy, machinery, electrical equipment, transport equipment, chemicals, pharmaceuticals and plastics together employed 40,411 women out of 305,369 in 1960, and 135,075 out of 988,072 in 1980). By contrast, employment of women increased in both numbers and shares across the range of basic consumer industries, excluding textiles but including those generally falling within the 'traditional' category, notably clothing/shoes, leather/hides, wood products, furniture, foodstuffs and tobacco. Indeed, although female participation in textiles declined, this was more than offset by the growth in the clothing sector, so that the female share in employment in these seven industries (taken together) rose from 37 per cent in 1960 (134,000 of 359,134) to 44 per cent in 1980 (252,140 of 575,200). In other words, from 1960 to 1980 it was the restructuring of established consumer industries (in addition to the expanding numbers of female workers in the electrical–electronic industry) which produced the largest proportional shifts in the gender balance. Restating the changes in the sexual division of labour hardly pinpoints the reasons why women workers were substituted for males (or vice versa in the case of textiles), but it does clarify what we principally need to explain.

Suggestions made by Hirata (1981) have been followed by Humphrey (1984), who has used detailed analysis of trends in female employment, particularly 1970–5, to explore a number of hypotheses which may provide more specific explanations. Their analysis drew attention to the rising shares of female production workers in all sectors of industry, except textiles, over the relatively short span of five years marked by an economic boom. Humphrey's conclusions favoured the explanation that shortages of male labour led to replacement by female labour. On the supply side, there was evidence that larger numbers of women were entering the labour market during the 1970s. It is implied that the erosion of wage levels through the policy measures (including those taken to curb trade union action on wages) of post 1964 military governments was an important factor in driving more women to work outside the home. These causes may well account for much of the observed change in the gender composition of industry during the first half of the 1970s.

Taking the longer-term perspective spanning 1960–80, the hypothesis of a shortage of male labour is rather difficult to sustain, since both the male and the female workforce grew rapidly through migration, as well as by natural increase, especially in urban areas (and in São Paulo state in particular). Here we need to consider another explanation, which takes account of the changes in industrial structure (including associated technical changes) wage and income differentials, and patterns of consumption.

Gender and labour costs in manufacturing

In Brazilian manufacturing the proportion of the cost of labour in total costs of production has fallen progressively during recent decades. The author has calculated labour costs from the industrial census data. In 1960 labour costs averaged almost a fifth (18 per cent) of total costs, ranging from 8 per cent in the food sector to 36 per cent in non-metallic minerals; by 1970 there had been a small reduction to 16 per cent. Between 1970 and 1980 there was a sharper comparative fall in labour costs, to 11.5 per cent, and the range narrowed to between 6 per cent in food and 28 per cent in machinery.

This trend towards reduced labour costs over a period when marked gains were registered in productivity reflects a number of changes taking place within Brazil itself and in the international economy. First and foremost, it was only for a brief span, from roughly the mid 1950s to the early 1960s, that, under democratically elected governments, labour unions were permitted to be fairly active and thus able to campaign for better wage increases. From 1964, when the military took over the reins of political control, government efforts were channelled into containing wage levels, and, as an essential element, union activity was impeded. These efforts were not relaxed until the late 1970s, and indeed available evidence suggests that real wages during the period from 1964 to 1979 were held below those achieved from 1955 to 1963 (Tavares and Souza 1983). To the general climate of government-imposed wage restraint can be added two further main factors affecting the trend of labour costs. One is the process of industrial modernization and automation which started as long ago as the later 1940s. It is linked, at least in part, to the dissemination of new technology through the changing international organization of production spearheaded by the expansion of multinational enterprises. Growing investment in plant and equipment by domestic as well as foreign firms, and the increased volumes of raw materials used in larger-scale production, diminished the relative costs of labour. Second, the sharp rise in petroleum-based energy costs resulting from OPEC price rises in 1973–4 also worked through to price rises in capital goods (whether produced domestically or imported) and increased other costs of production.

It is against this broader background that shifts in the gender balance of particular manufacturing industries need to be considered. In sectors such as the electrical–electronic, which are predominantly owned by large, foreign multinational enterprises, the growing share of female employment in Brazil tends to reflect the international uptake of female labour in such industry. In other words, the international division of labour in this industry holds important clues as to why women are employed rather than men. At the same time it should be emphasized that in any industry, increased (or decreased) proportions of females employed can be produced either through gender substitution within the existing employment structure, or through the creation (or, conversely, destruction) of specific areas of work. Over the 1960–80 period there was a substantial increase in direct manufacturing employment associated with the expansion of dynamic industries and with the restructuring of traditional industries. This suggests that it was the creation of 'new' areas of work with significant proportions denominated (or gender typed) as female which accounted for the rising proportions of women employees observed in some sectors. Further research is required on this point, but there does appear to be some evidence that employing more female workers gave employers an extra opportunity to contain wage costs. Table 52 presents relevant wage data for female and male workers in the main industries of São Paulo state in 1980.

It is clear from Table 52 that the remuneration of female workers in any industry is weighted towards the lower end of the wage scale. Indeed, over 80 per cent of females employed in the sectors shown (except in textiles) earned less than two minimum wages in 1980, compared with 30–60 per cent of males in the same industries (except leather). Moreover, in the traditional industries where the proportion of women has been rising, twice (or even three times) as many females as males earned less than one minimum wage. Even male wage levels are far from satisfactory. Nevertheless, at least 50 per cent of the male workforce in most sectors earned more than two minimum wages. These comparisons take no account of the varying categories of work performed, or of work time. But a separate analysis of hours worked indicates that 90–98 per cent of each sex worked a week of more than forty hours, so part-time working by female employees was not a primary reason

Table 52   São Paulo state: gender distribution of minimum salary by industry 1980

Sector	Percentage of workforce earning minimum salaries				
	Under 1	1–2	2–3	3–10	Subtotal
Machinery/metals					
Female	8.3	76.0	12.0	2.4	(98.7)
Male	5.9	24.5	23.0	44.5	(97.9)
Electrical					
Female	6.5	74.7	15.5	2.9	(99.6)
Male	5.5	23.2	22.0	46.2	(96.9)
Textiles					
Female	13.9	63.9	17.0	4.2	(99.0)
Male	6.9	38.7	30.3	23.2	(99.1)
Clothing					
Female	31.1	53.9	9.7	4.0	(98.7)
Male	17.2	38.7	21.2	20.5	(97.5)
Leather					
Female	2.8	65.6	6.4	3.3	(98.1)
Male	14.2	50.3	19.3	14.2	(98.0)
Wood/furniture					
Female	28.1	58.1	9.5	3.0	(98.7)
Male	9.2	33.6	28.5	27.1	(99.0)
Food/beverages					
Female	27.5	56.8	9.4	5.1	(98.8)
Male	10.1	40.1	27.9	20.5	(98.6)
Other industries					
Female	14.3	69.4	11.9	3.6	(99.2)
Male	7.3	32.9	23.4	33.6	(97.2)

Note:
Separate figures are not given in the demographic census for all individual industrial sectors, and the occupational data are not fully comparable with the industrial census.
Source: IBGE, 1983.

for the much lower female wages. It is difficult to transpose these general observations into a coherent explanation of shifts in gender balance on a sector by sector basis; and decennial census data are unlikely to be sufficiently sensitive to intra-industry conditions. Yet the evidence shown here lends some support to the argument that wage discrimination by gender provides an additional tool for trimming production costs.

Women's work and the growth of a consumer society

The degree to which feminization of production is also bound up with changing patterns of consumption and consumer power in what is a very rapidly industrializing, urbanizing society, should not be overlooked. A necessarily brief outline of the development path followed by Brazil during the past forty years or so provides the context for this. Above all else, the country's industrialization strategy has been primarily geared first to the opening up, then the deepening, of the domestic market. Hence, the expansion of manufacturing capacity and the range of goods produced have been accompanied by the spread of waged work and by increased income differentiation. Market growth was achieved in two main stages. First, the growth of a highly acquisitive middle-income sector (to add to the small upper elite) was spurred on by, among other factors, the activities of the state itself. The state encouraged ever larger cadres of public sector employees at all levels of government and in the numerous state enterprises, and it made available ample credit facilities. This provided the bedrock on which a modern domestic market was built until about the early 1960s. From then on, in the second stage, emphasis shifted to the creation of a mass consumer market for a vast range of domestic appliances and other sophisticated goods, through the progressive incorporation of the low-income majority. The increased presence and market power of multinational enterprises, again encouraged by the Brazilian state, was integral to this shift. Related developments were the use of mass advertising, hire purchase credit and the observed fall in relative prices of goods as economies of scale in production were achieved.

The progress of this latest phase of market expansion is charted for the 1970–80 period by a World Bank study (1983). The study shows, among its other findings from census data, the widespread penetration (even to impoverished parts of the north-east rural interior and remote, frontier regions) of a range of consumer durable goods including televisions, refrigerators and gas stoves. This reinforces the evidence provided by Wells (1983) concerning the disproportionately high level of expenditure by low income families on consumer durable goods. As a further point, it needs to be emphasized that for the majority of Brazilians, incomes remain very low, while those for women are usually among the lowest. Even in the comparatively wealthy metropolitan region of São Paulo, census data showing the distribution of monthly earnings in 1980 reveal that some 38 per cent of the workforce (3.7 million) were classified as without income (sem renda) and a further 18 per cent (1.8 million) had very low incomes from a quarter to one and a half minimum wages. Female workers accounted for three-quarters of those without incomes and over half those with very low incomes. (It is likely, however, that the 'no-income' category can conceal informal earnings.)

An equally interesting point not brought out by these studies is that women are a vital link in this whole process of market expansion. In the first place, through their domestic role in reproducing and servicing the family it is they who can most effectively press the case for the acquisition of new products ranging from household cleaning materials to labour-saving devices which often also improve hygiene, efficiency and comfort. At the same time, it is women who, through their formal and informal earnings represent a large sector of growing consumer power. Not surprisingly, companies recognize this potential and target the housewife in their advertising campaigns. (These are increasingly conducted on television: in 1980 some 55 per cent of all Brazilian households had a TV compared with only 24 per cent in 1970.) Women are a central focus of the fashion business of clothing, shoes, cosmetics, jewellery, diet products; an area of the economy where Brazilian designers and entrepreneurs are especially active.

Conclusions

Against the background of an expanding product matrix in a society which is predominantly composed of low (and a substantial proportion of no) income dwellers, and where, moreover, for the greater part of the past twenty-five years there have been severe constraints upon wage growth, there are clear pressures for more women (and often children too) to take up paid work outside the home. Their growing participation in the urban labour force is driven by the necessity to survive and shore up family incomes. Yet at least as important to the dynamic of expansion is women's apparent desire to improve material well-being, by the acquisition of durable consumer goods, and other trappings of the urban dweller. In manufacturing, employers are able to exploit female labour doubly, capitalizing on women's desires both for survival and for material improvement. The employment of female rather than male labour provides an opportunity to contain labour costs as well as performing a socializing role upon a key sector of potential consumers.

14 Women's issues and men's roles: Sri Lankan village experience

Rex A. Casinader, Sepalika Fernando and Karuna Gamage

Editors' introduction

The industrial structure of Sri Lanka is rather different from Latin America, and women form a larger part of the industrial labour force. Yet in both areas women provide much of the labour for agricultural processing and the food industry. The processing of cashew nuts is a particularly unpleasant operation as the edible nuts lie in a hard outer casing protected by a mildly corrosive acid. In Brazil the industry is factory based and dependent on the labour of young female migrants from rural areas who generally lose their jobs if they marry or become pregnant. In Sri Lanka, cashew-nut processing is based on a system of women home workers organized by middlemen. In both countries the women are poorly paid and have little security of employment for their vital contribution to the production of a high-value commodity.

Access to credit can revolutionize the lives of poor women workers. In 1977 the Grameen Bank was founded in Bangladesh specifically to lend money to poor rural women. Today over 99 per cent of its loans have been repaid and studies have shown that borrowers have been able to increase their real incomes by an average of 35 per cent within two years of obtaining a loan (Madeley 1985). Village-based credit schemes organized by a non-governmental organization have been equally successful for the cashew-nut processors of Sri Lanka. Casinader et al. show how credit allowed these women to free themselves of the middlemen and to set up as independent, petty commodity producers. This sudden expansion of women's economic power, at a time of declining opportunities for male employment, provoked adjustments in the gender division of labour in the household. The authors describe the polarization of male reactions, with some husbands taking refuge in alcohol, violence and the denigration of women, while others choose to work with their wives in cashew-nut processing or take over traditional female chores such as childcare and housework in order to free their wives for income-earning activities. Like Benton's paper on Bolivia (Chapter 8) this chapter provides an optimistic view of the effect of capitalist penetration on the economic position of women. But economic change can lead very rapidly to social change, not only in the gender division of labour, but also, as in Bolivia, in household structure with women rejecting unsupportive husbands and deliberately choosing to establish female-headed homes.

This chapter documents the experiences of two Sri Lankan villages in a village improvement programme undertaken by a non-governmental agency or organization (NGO). The importance of these experiences is that they centre on changes in women's roles, and on some of the consequences for gender relations, an aspect often neglected in village studies. The Non-Governmental Organization, in activating the village improvement programme, was not primarily concerned with women. Its objective was to improve some aspects of the village economy, and it was the nature of the village economy that led to gender roles becoming a central issue in the village improvement programme.

It should be stated at the outset that the two villages, Ralahamywatta and Pannagoda (both pseudonyms), which adjoin one another, are dependent on small holdings of rubber or coconut with negligible, if any, paddy land. The small holdings in rubber or coconut are invariably insufficient for the subsistence of households and there is thus dependence on wage employment in the rubber plantations, coconut fibre mills, and the tertiary sector, as well as in the incipient industrial sector in the urban centres of the region. Pannagoda is one such village, dependent on coconut production and wage employment, mainly in the tertiary sector in Colombo and its suburbs. There are 153 households at Pannagoda with a population of 548, of which females number 285. Although this area has coconut plantations, such plantations have a low labour requirement at 0.25 persons per hectare (i.e. 1 person for 4 hectares). This compares unfavourably with the other two plantation crops in Sri Lanka, tea and rubber, which have labour requirements of 3.1 and 1.0 per hectare respectively. Thus, the labour absorbed by the coconut plantation is negligible. Except for a few isolated pockets, there are no tea plantations in this area of Sri Lanka.

Ralahamywatta, though in this same broad category, has significant variations. It was a village born out of the village expansion programme of the Sri Lanka government in the 1960s. This programme, whose origins can be traced to the 1930s, was set up in the context of population increase and consisted of the government alienating state lands adjoining villages, for the use of villagers with no land. The lands so alienated were in blocks of 1000 to 2000 m² and mainly served as land for housing, though villagers did plant cash crops (such as rubber and coconuts) in whatever space was left after putting up their houses.

Obviously it was the poorer sections of the villages that opted for and were, indeed, eligible for these blocks. Often these sections of the village community had social characteristics typical of their poor economic status, for example, low educational attainment, unemployment, substandard housing, and low nutritional standards. These characteristics quickly conferred low prestige on such villages. The new villages also exhibited less social cohesion than the older villages. The high incidence of crime, juvenile delinquency and bootlegging, as indices of social disorganization, support this image of the new villages. Ralahamywatta is one such village. Its residents had previously been residents of surrounding older villages, including Pannagoda. The population of Ralahamywatta is 343 with 167 males and 176 females. The households number seventy-three.

As would be apparent in the description of the two villages, they were, like all villages of this region and elsewhere in Sri Lanka, subsumed within colonial and post colonial social formations which are dominated by commodity production in plantation and peasant agriculture. Of significance in the economy of the two villages was the petty production of cashew nuts. Cashew fruits and cashew nuts are a minor cash crop, and although these villages are not in the cashew producing area, they are close enough to such areas to engage in the processing of cashew nuts for domestic and export sales. Traditionally in these two villages, cashew processing was carried out by the petty bourgeois and middle bourgeois of the village, employing the women to do the processing manually for a wage. A few women, who had enough capital to purchase raw or unprocessed cashew nuts, did their own processing on a petty production scale. The women augmented their family income either in this manner or by the wages earned by working for the larger petty producers of processed cashew nuts.

At some stage occupational segregation occurred and processing of cashew nuts has, at least for the last few decades or more, been viewed as women's work. This type of division of labour by sex, where the women are engaged in petty production, is suggestive of Carmen Diana Deere's argument that in peripheral capitalism such division of labour is crucial to the extraction of surplus labour, for subsistence agricultural production and petty commodity production by women allow the wage (to the men) to be less than the cost of production and reproduction of labour power (Deere 1976). Some can see embedded in this the notion that women contribute to the low male wages that prevail in colonial and post colonial plantation and peasant economies. The allied notion that the man's wage should be adequate to support his wife and children is also a divisive issue in women's studies (Barrett and McIntosh 1980). Hence one has to be cautious in interpreting the role of petty production in cashew processing within the hypothesis put forward by Deere. Yet the division of labour by sex does appear functional to capitalism and, as Jane Humphries (1976) states, women's 'usefulness must be seen as clearly dependent on their adherence to established roles within the occupational structure. Once women step outside these roles then they are not only no longer supportive of established hierarchy but are a direct threat to it'. These ideas are a useful background within which to explore the problems of gender roles that emerge in these two villages. We shall draw upon these ideas where necessary.

The crystallization of occupational segregation, by which cashew processing became women's work, occurred a few decades ago. Significantly, women's participation in economic activities was relegated to petty production, while men participated in the more dominant and prestigious sections of the economy. This reinforced the hierarchy in occupational segregation and also constrained the development of class consciousness, driving a wedge between men's and women's experience. At the time the occupational segregation occurred, the characteristic inability of a colonial economy to absorb the available supply of labour was apparent. Recently it has become a more acute problem, with an increasing number of men and women entering the age group that aspires to be economically active and yet not all able to find ways of achieving this. The consequences are seen in the rate of unemployment in these two villages. At Ralahamywatta 32.4 per cent of those between 15 and 55 years of age are unemployed, while at Pannagoda the rate is 25.3 per cent. Most of the unemployed are young, with 77.4 per cent at Ralahamywatta and 69.9 per cent at Pannagoda aged between 15 and 30, and, significantly, 77.5 per cent at Ralahamywatta and 58.7 per cent at Pannagoda of the total unemployed are male.

These figures need some comment. Men seek employment in the dominant mode of production, and the increasing numbers seeking such employment and the incapacity of the economy to absorb them results obviously in unemployment. Women, on the other hand, are engaged in petty production, and increasing male unemployment pushes the women further towards this as a survival strategy. This explains the different unemployment rates for men and women.

But within this context the different rates for the two villages are significant. We noted at the outset that Ralahamywatta belongs to a category of villages newly created for the resettlement of the more economically depressed sections of the older villages. In this situation women seek income in petty production, and do so increasingly when male unemployment rises, as a survival strategy. On the other hand, at Pannagoda, which is relatively better off, there are many women who, because of their economic and social class positions, do not need to engage in petty production activities. Their labour is confined to housework. Such labour is enumerated within the typical sexist paradigm of demographic data collection and census as unemployed; hence the apparently higher rate for female unemployment at Pannagoda.

The Gampubuduwa Movement in its work at Ralahamywatta and Pannagoda shares many common features of the NGO phenomena in Sri Lanka, notably the marked involvement of the Christian clergy and the access to international funds; yet, it has exhibited features much less common and more noteworthy. Among these the following may be identified:

1   The joint involvement of the Christian and Buddhist clergy. This combination is not a common experience in Sri Lanka.
2   The courage and capacity to identify and tackle problems central to the village economy, in this instance cashew processing, rather than indulge in the characteristic concern of most NGOs to tinker with problems peripheral to the village economy, such as digging of wells, building roads etc. whose benefits and beneficiaries are both dubious.
3   Use of the funds obtained from international sources as security to a bank that agreed to release loans to the villagers for petty production in cashew-nut processing.
4   Use of voluntary labour, a former characteristic of Sri Lankan NGOs that has now almost disappeared.
5   In relation to other NGOs far less dependence on a costly central, often monolithic organization and infrastructure to push, service and sustain the village improvement programmes.

The village development programmes of this NGO, the Gampubuduwa Movement, largely emerged out of the participation of the villagers and the Gampubuduwa Movement leaders in a long process of discussion and work. The ideology of the movement is to encourage the villagers to identify their problems and needs and set priorities for action. At Ralahamywatta and Pannagoda the village society, formed under the guidance of the Gampubuduwa Movement, identified their major problem as being the lack of capital for householders to process cashew nuts on their own. Processing cashews in their own households would give a substantially greater income, they argued, than working for a wage.

This demand came mainly from the women because it was they who were engaged in cashew processing. It is not clear whether the men, too, identified themselves with this demand or had different opinions as to what should be the priorities in the village development programme. While the mechanics of how the Gampubuduwa Village Societies at Ralahamywatta and Pannagoda arrived at the decision on a programme that would enable the women cashew producers to process cashews on their own are not clear, the fact remains that such a decision was arrived at and became the central thrust of the village development programme. Using some of the international funds available to the Gampubuduwa Movement as partial security, the Gampubuduwa Village Societies at the two villages were able to obtain loans from a bank for their members for the purpose of cashew processing.

In spite of such loans being inadequate and purchasing and marketing problems acute, this programme brought a remarkable increase in income for the women processors. The women found that for 1000 nuts purchased, processed and sold, the profit or income was nearly three or four times the wage they earned for processing a similar quantity of nuts for the petty production entrepreneurs. The quantity of nuts processed also increased, partly because the greater return acted as an incentive to produce more. Also when done at home, longer hours of work split up into a number of sittings were possible, for in between their cashew-nut processing work, the women attended to domestic chores as well. All this helped to increase production. The labour of other women family members was a further contributory factor.

When many women joined the Gampubuduwa Village Society, obtained bank loans and processed cashews on their own, it led to a labour shortage for the cashew processing *mudalalis*, or middle men, in these two villages. This resulted in a rise in the wages of the women who continued to work for them. Such increases in income and wage rates did not mean that poverty was completely eliminated. Surplus extraction continued through the exchange system, both in the purchasing and sale of raw and processed nuts respectively. Yet, the remarkable increases in income were clearly manifested in improved living conditions, particularly in housing.

All this was happening in the context of a high level of male unemployment. This has pushed women towards greater petty production. What were the consequences of this for the women's position and role in the family and in decision-making? We noticed that even prior to the entry of the Gampubuduwa Movement, the women had to contribute to the family subsistence. Thus there already existed a tradition of an economic contribution by women and a share in family decision-making. Obviously, increasing incomes, particularly in the context of some families where the men were unemployed, would have had an impact on the women's position, role and status. These changes are now explored through illustrative case studies which reveal some of the problematic consequences for gender relations and the social and cultural tenets of male dominance.

Changing household strategies

Mallika is 52 years old and is the mother of eight children, five sons and three daughters. Six of the children are now married and live away from the parental family. The youngest two, both sons who are now in their late teens, live with the mother. The father lives with one or other of the married children. The relationship between Mallika and her husband does not appear to have been a happy one and she now does not like him to return and stay with her. They were married in 1949. The husband was a resident of Pannagoda while Mallika was from Lagonna a village a few miles away. They had both been unemployed at that time and their source of income was the wages they earned in doing any odd jobs in the village or villages close by. Mallika states that with her parental family's help she purchased 500 m² of land at Pannagoda to put up a house in which she continues to reside with the two youngest sons.

Mallika, from being a casual worker doing odd jobs about the village, shifted quite a number of years ago to cashew-nut processing on a wage basis. This was for the cashew processing entrepreneurs or *mudalalis* in the village. Later Mallika, along with such cashew-nut processing work for a wage, had, as a supplementtary source of income, started to process cashew nuts on her own. She bought raw cashew nuts with some money borrowed from village money lenders, and then processed the nuts for sale. This helped to increase her income.

Mallika is a good example of the women in this village who by their petty production in cashew processing had been keeping the family going. The credit facilities introduced by the Gampubuduwa Village Society brought some changes to Mallika's working arrangements and increased her income substantially. With the aid of the money she could borrow under this scheme, she opted to process cashew nuts entirely on her own and stopped working for a wage for the cashew-nut processing *mudalalis*. She also gradually increased the amount of cashew nuts processed. The initial loan of Rs 1000/- she obtained under the credit scheme thus increased to Rs 5000/- because of the expanding nature of her activities. The physical manifestation of her increased income can be seen in the improvement she had made to her house. Recently she spent Rs 3000/- in replacing the *cadjan* roof of her house with a tiled roof. Cashew-nut processing is now identified as a 'woman's job' and a rationale of women having the manual dexterity to do such a job has been put forward. For instance, villagers state that while a woman can process 2000 nuts a day a man cannot even process 500 nuts. Obviously with long association, cashew-nut processing has acquired the status of being a woman's job, and men will not engage in it because it would not be in keeping with their masculine status in sociocultural terms.

What is interesting in this context is that with the introduction of the credit scheme of the Gampubuduwa Village Society the income generated by cashew processing has increased. This has put more income into the hands of the women and they wield much greater economic power in the home than before. This is very apparent in Mallika's case. She has throughout been the breadwinner of the family and the recent increase in her income has given her an even greater economic strength.

One result of this is that she does not want her husband to be with her anymore and she has the economic power to keep him out. She states that her husband does not want to help her in cashew-nut processing, nor is he capable of doing it. Her husband consumes liquor heavily and would, in her view, be more interested in using her income to buy liquor rather than to help her. According to her, having him with her will be more a problem than a help.

What is significant in this case study is that Mallika's husband is not positively oriented to helping her even in the purchasing and selling of cashew nuts, let alone the manual processing of the nuts by decorticating the outer skin. This case study shows how when a husband has to face up to a situation in which he is not the breadwinner, a role socially and culturally expected of the men, it can lead to a situation where his status and role, his masculine identity and self-image are threatened. In such stress situations, the husband seeks to exhibit or indulge heavily in behavioural practices which are strongly masculine, such as drinking liquor, and spending time in places where liquor is served or consumed. This invariably leads to further conflict between husband and wife and given the situation where the wife has the economic power, the husband may have to leave the home.

What appears to be happening is that the women, from a position of contributing to the family subsistence by petty production in a context of an inadequate wage for the men in their prescribed economic activities, are now the dominant, if not the sole contributor to family subsistence. This is basically because the stagnant economy is incapable of providing adequate employment even at a low wage rate. But the impetus given by the credit facilities of the Gampubuduwa Village Society has accelerated the disparities in the expected and actual roles of men and women.

The heavy consumption of liquor is an allegation that many women in these two villages make against their husbands. The authors did not have the opportunity to verify empirically the truth of the allegation. Nor was it possible to measure whether the consumption of liquor at these two villages was heavier than in other Sri Lankan villages. The fact that it is repeatedly alleged is significant. The conflict role situation for the men also suggests that they may be attracted to consume liquor and to spend time at places where liquor is consumed because these are in Sri Lankan culture identified as masculine behavioural practices, and indulgence in such practices is a necessary and satisfying experience in the context of the decline in the role and self-image of the men.

The first case study presented described features within the family of importance to women's roles. The second case study, of Malini, shows many of these features, but also illustrates some village attitudes which are of relevance to women. Malini is well known in the village as the most skilled cashew-nut processor. She can process nearly 5000 nuts per day giving her an earning capacity under the Gampubuduwa Scheme of Rs 150/- per day. Malini, as is the case with most women in the two villages, works only four days a week. One day is spent on purchasing raw nuts and/or selling processed nuts. Another half day is spent on the weekly Gampubuduwa Village Society meeting. The other one and a half days which coincide with the weekends are usually spent on domestic chores and with the family, as school children and working members of the family are at home. Yet for most women even working for only four days under the Gampubuduwa Scheme has substantially raised their income. The main avenues of expenditure of the increased incomes are in settling old debts, improvement to housing, purchase of consumer durables and pilgrimages.

Malini is 38 years old and the mother of five children aged 3 to 17. Before marriage she was living with her brother at Ralahamywatta. During this time she had a love affair with Gamini, a mason by vocation, who was from a distant place but temporarily resident in the village in connection with some work. When she realized she was going to have a baby by Gamini she asked him to marry her but he was not keen and in fact left the village. She made a very determined effort to trace him and indeed tracked him down to Colombo. They were married at a simple legal ceremony at the Marriage Registrar's Office in Colombo. She states that he consented to the marriage because he was concerned about the legitimacy of the child, rather than out of any affection or love for her.

Soon after the child was born he left her but returned a year later, and Malini had three more children. He left again after a stay of nearly five years. He once again returned eight years later, and they had another child. The relationship between Malini and Gamini was not a happy one though she accepted his return on two occasions. Malini alleges that Gamini was very cruel to her from the very beginning of their married life. There seem to have been frequent quarrels and physical assaults right from the start, although she states that he is a little better since his last return. This according to her is because she has threatened to strike back if he assaults her any more. Her attitude is ambivalent for although she had accepted him back on two occasions, she contemplates seeking legal separation. Her experiences appear to have hardened her and she is reputed to be tough and authoritarian.

It is significant that soon after marriage Gamini attempted to encourage his friends and other men in the village to have close relationships with Malini and even have sex with her. She contends that this was contrived by Gamini so that he could divorce her under the ruse of infidelity, which Sri Lankan laws permit as grounds for divorce. This was years ago, but many men in the village today attempt to make out that Malini was and still is a woman of easy virtue. Some quite pointedly describe her as a prostitute. The women in the village, on the other hand, categorically refute this and describe it as a baseless allegation concocted partly by her husband.

What is of interest here is that it demonstrates some village attitudes towards those women who, having been forced into a situation of being the sole breadwinner of the family, have in fact raised the family's economic standing. This is manifest in their improved or improving life-styles and living conditions. When this occurs it earns the displeasure of the men and psychological underpinnings are apparent. This displeasure is often expressed in deprecating such women. And it is extremely significant that they deprecate a woman by calling her a prostitute, or a depraved woman. For in describing a woman as a prostitute the association with women as the property of men, a commodity that they purchase for pleasure, is strong. And the sexual act in a forced or 'purchased' context is also seen by the men as a conquest, as an act of aggression degrading the women. It would then seem that in describing Malini as a woman of easy virtue, a prostitute, these undercurrents may be present. Even in the identification of Malini as tough and hardened, a subtle negation of the culturally valued 'feminine' characteristics, such undertones appear operative. Equally significant is the rationalization of Gamini's behaviour by some villagers. They state that Gamini was a good man, and it was because Malini was not an obedient and faithful wife that he developed into a cruel person.

Interestingly, a recent study of women workers in the Sri Lanka Free Trade Zones (Casinader 1983), identifies a similar syndrome operating in some attitudes to the Free Trade Zone women workers. The Free Trade Zone and its environs are described as 'Isthiripura' – which in Sinhala literally means 'Women's City', but with the subtle connotation of it being a city of women of easy virtue. There is an attitude of hostility to the women workers because they seek employment and economic independence, are away from their homes living in boarding houses, and are not fulfilling the culturally venerated roles of mother and wife attending to domestic chores. This hostility is expressed in terms of sexuality.

The case studies presented, while highlighting the positive effects of the Gampubuduwa Village Programme by way of increased family income, adding economic strength to women's position and enhancing the principles of equality between the sexes, also bring out the negative responses of men and the ensuing problems both at the family and the village level. It also appears that these male responses are largely consequences of the Sri Lankan social system, which prescribes a dominant role for the men in the family and village society. However, empirical data also suggest that it is possible for families and individuals, both women and men, to break through these structures. A dilution of the socially dominant internalized state of values appears to be taking place. We shall now present a case study where such trends appear.

Sita is 40 years old and is the mother of five children, three sons and two daughters. Her husband Merril is employed at a government department in Colombo as a storeman. He is on the permanent cadre. Merril is from a village close by and obtained a land allotment or block at Ralahamywatta in the 1960s under the village expansion scheme.

Soon after marriage they built a small house on this block and moved in. When the first child arrived, Merril and Sita found that Merril's monthly wages were inadequate and, as in many other cases, Sita began working in cashew nut processing to supplement their income. Later, with some money she borrowed from her mother, she processed cashew nuts on her own as a supplementary activity. Subsequently, she expanded this with the help of a loan obtained from the rural bank in the area and stopped working for a wage. With the advent of the Gampubuduwa Village Society she joined the society and utilized the loan facilities available to its members. This has resulted in further expansion of her cashew processing work, and a substantial increase in income. Her family life is without any serious conflict or friction.

Merril has a positive attitude towards Sita's work and activities and helps her in cashew processing when he returns from work and at weekends. The income they get from cashew processing is entirely in the hands of Sita and she manages to meet the subsistence needs of the family with this. Merril keeps what he earns from his job in Colombo for his expenses and for little odd needs of the family. Their compatibility is strengthened by their common desire to improve the living standard of their family and to help their relations, friends and other villagers.

Sita is very active in the Gampubuduwa Village Society work and is the president of the society. Most villagers respect her social awareness, and the capable way she runs the society. One may conjecture that some of her own experiences in obtaining loans from the rural bank for cashew processing have acted in some way as a catalyst for the thinking behind the work of the Gampubuduwa Village Society in the village. Here, too, her desire to share her knowledge with others is apparent.

It appears that the improvement in the material conditions of Sita's life and her accompanying economic and social independence has led, along with the transmission of the social work ideology, to the enhancement of her solidarity with and participation in village level activities. There is a social awareness and willingness to be involved in activities that are beneficial to the village or larger society, although within a reformist framework. Her husband, Merril's, positive attitude has been very supportive in her development. What is significant, in comparison to the earlier case studies, is that such positive attitudes free Sita from being trapped in a family conflict situation which would have burnt up her energies, and also constrained her participation in village activities.

Conclusion

The first two case studies have shown the problems of male dominance, where economic emancipation of women has occurred, and the conflicts experienced by both men and women. The last case study, on the other hand, is illustrative of a situation where a peaceful dilution of male dominance is occurring and indicates ways in which such dominance may be overcome. In the two villages there are many more such situations and a number of intermediary types.

Petty production in cashew-nut processing, which emerged as a poverty survival strategy, had the potential and capacity to enhance women's status. But it also contained within it the seeds of conflict between women's and men's objectives and roles as well as between their subjective reactions to change. This, we observed, is because they are both trapped in the wider matrices of social values and systems, which conflict with the emerging new patterns.

The Gampubuduwa Movement village development programme at Ralahamywatta and Pannagoda has activated these various responses, although gender relations were not the concern of the movement either at an ideological level or in the programme that formed the basis of its work in these two villages. But women's issues have now emerged as strikingly important and crucial to the programme.

This study, while focusing attention on the sexual division of labour and gender roles within the family, has also sought to recognize the vital importance of women's incomes for family survival. This implication lies embedded in the experiences of the women in the two villages described in this chapter.

Acknowledgements

This paper is extracted from a much longer article which appeared in the *Sri Lanka Journal of Social Sciences*, **5** no. 2, December 1982, pp. 73–91.

Part Six

Research Directions in Gender

Editors' introduction to Part Six

We are beginning to appreciate the complexity of the geography of gender, but have made little headway in identifying the order within the complexity, still less in explaining or understanding it. Survival proves a multifaceted problem (Part One); no single explanation accounts for the geography of the sex ratio in India (Chapter 2). Capitalist penetration in agriculture has often had adverse outcomes for women (Chapters 5, 6 and 7) but individuals may benefit (Chapter 8) and there is no model sequence of events in space or time; outcomes are highly specific, having been influenced by a range of social and economic factors. Similar disparities appear in labour reserve regions (Chapters 3, 9, 10 and 11): contingent factors make women's worlds very different in Nepal, Lesotho, Colombia and Thailand. In industrial situations (Chapters 12, 13 and 14) there is perhaps a stronger comparability, but regional contrasts remain pronounced.

For a geography of gender, we need more systematic studies and more regional studies at a range of scales. Our data are still too uneven and our hypotheses too many. In this section, we include reports on current research, and calls for new research, all of which will take us closer towards our goal. We begin also to redress a balance. A disproportionate amount of the research on the geography of the Third World to date has come from advanced industrial economies: we need more work from indigenous researchers, such as the majority of contributors to this section.

Bagchi calls for an examination of technology appropriate to women's needs in the face of the desperate Third World shortage of domestic fuels: her present research consists in interviewing Indian women about their own needs (Chapter 15). This is an issue which bears immediately on the lives of Third World women (and particularly the poor), and on the decisions of policy-makers. Agarwal reports a sequence of research projects through which she has moved in seeking to identify systematic effects on women's lives through examining spatial patterns in South Asia: starting with the impact of the Green Revolution, moving to the differential impact on the sexes of agricultural growth and then seeking to map the underlying feature of women's access to land (Chapter 16). Beshara, looking for ways to reconstitute gender in Egypt to achieve a more complementary relationship between the sexes, looks back as well as forward, to highly regarded queens and goddesses of Ancient Egypt; she seeks to ground a way forward in a feminist interpretation of Egyptian history (Chapter 17).

Henshall Momsen summarizes her research findings over more than two decades on women farmers in the Caribbean. She has progressively identified them as a distinct group and become aware of their changing problems with shifting structures of migration and remittances; she reformulates the research problem (Chapter 18), and, like Trenchard (Chapter 5), she encounters an explanation for a regional food problem in an institutional bias against women farmers. Young and Salih argue for a world systems approach to the changing structure of the Malay family; like us, they identify the importance of changing spatial divisions of labour in the constitution of gender (Chapter 19). McGee advocates research not on components of the system, such as the family, but on a single, under-researched process in the system: the creation of consumption needs (Chapter 20).

This group of research reports illustrates the need to reconcile not one, but two intersections: the macro and the micro, the systematic and the regional. We have seen the South Asian phenomenon of discrimination against women examined at the sub-continental scale (Chapter 2), and described at the level of the human individual (Chapter 4). Rural women's energy problems similarly are a global and a local feature (Chapter 15). The creation of consumption needs is a universal aspect of capital, the international division of labour is a worldwide phenomenon; yet for each of these, our authors advocate study within a single country, Malaysia (Chapters 19 and 20), both to improve understanding of that country and to advance knowledge of the phenomenon. This crossroads is a familiar feature to geographers, who might wish to extend it into a further dimension by including the people–environment relationship (Chapter 15). It is only by such familiar approaches to new knowledge that we shall arrive at a satisfactory geography of gender. We leave it to our contributors to make the points without further editorial intervention: we have no glib conclusions, we have found no easy answer, but must continue to seek for a way forward.

15 Rural energy and the role of women

Deipica Bagchi

Introduction

Since the OPEC oil embargo of the 1970s, the unstable price structure of fossil energy has placed unprecedented stress on rural systems that are struggling to achieve agricultural modernization through integrated rural development. A crucial aspect of the rural energy issues in the developing world is the high proportion of energy use in the domestic sector, and it is believed that over a billion of the world's poor, of which the vast majority are rural dwellers (Table 53), are now living in a state of acute fuelwood scarcity. The impact of this shortage is most severe on those

Table 53 Populations involved in fuelwood deficit situations (million inhabitants)

Region	1980 Acute scarcity		1980 Deficit		2000 Acute scarcity or deficit	
	Total	Rural	Total	Rural	Total	Rural
Africa	55	49	146	131	535	464
Near East and North Africa	—	—	104	69	268	158
Asia Pacific	31	29	832	710	1671	1434
Latin America	26	18	201	143	512	342
Total	112	96	1283	1053	2986	2398

Note:
The table indicates the total population and the population with a predominantly rural type of energy consumption (total population less urban centres over 100,000 inhabitants); these are the estimated populations living in the areas under the identified fuelwood situations.
Source: FAO, *Map of the fuelwood situation in the developing countries:* explanatory note (FAO, Rome 1981), p. 8.

members of the household on whom rests the responsibility of collecting domestic fuel, usually the women.

Rural energy requirements

The major traditional energy sources in the domestic sector are charcoal, firewood, crop waste and dung in addition to animal and human power. Of these, the single most important source for fuel is firewood. According to one estimate, 16 per cent of the world's population in a total of forty-eight countries use firewood to meet 50 per cent of their energy needs. In all, 38 per cent in sixty-one countries draw 25 per cent of their energy requirements from fuelwood, and a total of 41 per cent (sixty-seven countries) use firewood for 20 per cent of their energy needs (Table 54).

The search for fuelwood, however, has been one of the primary causes for deforestation in the developing world. According to a World Bank report, 15–20 million hectares of forests are being consumed annually in developing countries, especially in the semi-arid regions of the world. In many regions, the rural population has simply outgrown the carrying capacity of the forests. In

Table 54   Firewood consumption related to commercial energy

| Region | Firewood Use as per cent of Total Energy Consumption | | | | | |
| | 50% | | 25% | | 20% | |
	No. of countries	Population (millions)	No. of countries	Population (millions)	No. of countries	Population (millions)
Africa	32	279	35	292	37	317
Asia	9	363	14	1095	15	1172
Latin America and the Caribbean	6	23	10	168	13	181
Oceania	1	30	2	3	2	3
Total	48	668	61	1558	67	1674
Per cent of world population (4.1×10^9)	16		38		41	

Source: Tinker, Irene. Energy Needs in Rural Households, Working Paper #4, Women in International Development (WID) Series, Michigan State University, East Lansing 1982, p. 24.

others, the concentrated demands of urbanized industrial consumers have depleted firewood supplies for kilometres around the cities.

The shortage of fuelwood manifests itself in several ways in rural lives: in increased requirements of time and labour to procure fuelwood, and through changes in dietary or cooking habits. In India, as fuelwood supplies grow scarce, dependence on animal and crop waste increases. The villager is faced with a dilemma as the use of organic waste as farm manure is vital in view of the escalating costs of chemical fertilizers; yet the household must also satisfy its energy needs with available animal waste (Table 55).

Most of the energy consumed in the rural areas of the Third World is used for the preparation, production, processing and transport of food. The major users of rural energy are women. A study by the International Labour Organization (ILO) on gender divisions of labour in Africa revealed women working longer hours than men in collecting water and fuel, caring for domestic animals, harvesting, transporting, processing and storing food, all of which are energy intensive operations. In the semi-arid nomadic societies of the Middle East, women spend approximately half the day collecting just firewood and water. A study on the south Asian paddy system finds water and fuel collection as women's major workload in association with the tending of livestock and the processing of rice (Whyte and Whyte 1982).

The work burden of poorer women has undoubtedly increased in more than one way as a consequence of widespread deforestation and the extension of agricultural lands into forested areas. Longer distances have to be travelled and greater time must be allocated to the collection of firewood. Substitutes must be found for the diminishing firewood supplies. Cooking methods and family nutritional needs have to be adjusted to firewood availability. Finally, all of these responsibilities have to be accommodated with equally pressing needs for extra-domestic, income generating work (Table 56).

There is often a trade off between the time spent in collection of fuels and the time that must be devoted to preparing food or tending to fires. Dung and crop waste are normally considered inferior fuels due to their smokiness and need for constant tending. They are, however, preferred if they are more easily available than firewood. In India, cow dung processed into cakes is a more acceptable fuel supplement than firewood. In Burkina Faso (Upper Volta), millet and stalks are preferred because of their ready availability and standard sizes which leave women time for other activities.

Table 55   Domestic fuel use by land groups, Madhya Pradesh, India

Land groups	n	Firewood %ofn	Cow dung %ofn	Crop residue %ofn	Kerosene %ofn	Electricity %ofn
1 Landless	33	97.0	68.8	31.3	100.0	12.1
2 Small holders	19	100.0	94.7	52.6	100.0	15.8
3 Medium holders	9	88.0	77.8	66.7	88.9	44.4
4 Big holders	8	100.0	71.4	62.5	100.0	62.5
Total	69	66	52	31	66	16

Notes:
Small holder: 3 hectares or less; medium: greater than 3 to less than 8; big: over 8 hectares.
Source: Survey data by author, 1983–4.

On the other hand, women would sometimes rather spend more money and time on higher quality fuel in order to minimize cooking time. In the case of Peru, women prefer to walk further in search of better fuel rather than use bushes available close at hand which when burned smell and smoke (Skar 1982). Coconut husks and bamboo are not preferred fuels, although plentiful in the rural areas of the Philippines. As quality of fuel decreases, more time is required for preparation and tending of the fire. Time is thus an important factor in consumer choice of fuel, and women often save fuel or consume more of it to save time. In a study of Ghana, management of cooking fires was directed more to save time than fuel, although women were also found to be devising ways to save fuel (Steckler 1972). Similarly in Tanzania, a charcoal stove pro-gramme found households in favour of such stoves in order to reduce cooking time. In Senegal, a programme for improved mud stoves had similar findings. The fuel stress thus has repercussions on women's time, work and life that deserve careful attention in alternative energy plans.

Rural energy strategies

Responses to the rural fuel crisis have moved in more than one direction. Those that are relevant in the context of this chapter are both the afforestation projects and also efforts to develop new technology for renewable energy and fuel-efficient cooking media.

As new programmes are designed to involve community leaders in fuel afforestation projects, the important fact to remember is that a good number of such projects have failed because the needs of the most affected group, women, were overlooked (Super 1980). Hoskins (1979) and Tinker (1980) argue that any successful agroforestry programme must be tied to incentives for women and their perceived benefits from such a project. Hoskins (1979) has gone further, stressing the need for prior gathering of information on items such as local demand for fuelwood, women's roles, social taboos and customs and land-use practices.

Women who have been hardest hit by the fuelwood crisis are

Table 56 Rank order of activities performed by rural women in Madhya Pradesh, India (sample size = 69)

Activities	A number	B % of total	C1 at home	C2 near home	C3 far from home
	Women reporting activity		Locale (per cent of A)		
Cooking	63	91.3	100	—	—
Collection of water	61	88.4	1.4	26.2	72.4
Collecting firewood	56	81.2	3.6	5.4	91.0
Preparing cow dung cake	56	81.2	100	—	—
Collecting cow dung	50	72.5	48	24	28
Wage related work	44	63.8	—	20.5	79.5
Crop processing	38	55.1	68.4	23.7	7.9
Collecting fodder	30	43.5	—	32.3	67.7
Grazing livestock	30	43.5	3.2	29	67.8
Marketing	28	40.6	21.4	14.3	64.3
Work on own farm	26	37.7	7.7	53.8	38.5
Craft work	13	18.8	100	—	—
Voluntary work	7	10.1	85.7	14.3	—
Other	6	8.7	33.3	50	16.7

Note:
Activities reported under 'other' are construction, dairying and marketing of vegetables.
Source: Survey data by author, 1983–4.

now becoming involved in community forestry plans. In a community forestry programme in India, women were demanding fuel and fodder trees for planting, while men were in favour of fruit and timber species. The New Delhi based Gandhi Peace Foundation, which has been responsible for organizing eco-development camps in northern India, has encountered, to their surprise, a marked divergence of attitudes to forestry between men and women (Sharma 1982). In India women have provided much of the motivation and energy for the 'Chipko' (hug the tree) movement that grew as a protest against commercial exploitation of forests in the Himalayan foothills. Since women had to walk 4 to 6 km, two to three times a week, in search of fuelwood, they were willing to volunteer their efforts for fertilizing and tending the saplings. As life's basic resources of firewood, fodder, water, wild roots, fruits and nuts appeared to be at stake due to large-scale ecological interference, the economic nature of the conflict turned into an ecological one, awakening consciousness in the local female population. Yet again, protesting against plantings of eucalyptus, women in Burkina Faso (Upper Volta) could speak with authority on advantages of other species over eucalyptus.

Another form of response to the fuel crisis has been in the form of technological intervention in two significant ways: in the development of energy efficient food processing devices in adaptation to the changing fuel situation, and in the substitution of available energy by abundantly available renewable sources such as sun, wind, water, and biomass. Both of these strategies tend to overlap into women's work sphere.

Technological interventions, so far, have had differential impacts on men and women. Changes in technology, leading to modernization, have been sex specific, generally benefiting only the male population. For the female population the results have, on the whole, been translated into a loss of control over means of production, a loss of access to resources, and longer hours of manual work for poorer returns to labour.

Several new tools and devices, however, are being developed and tested that might effect a revolution in women's lives in India. Thin-walled cement tanks are being introduced for water storage; simple hand pumps are being designed for water lifting chores which normally tax women's time and energy. Additional provisions for transporting water by pipe to fixed points in the village will be one more step in easing the chore. Energy efficient stoves (chulas) have now been devised, and these considerably ease women's work burden. Chulas are cheap home-made clay stoves, used by millions of Indian housewives, who are resigned to the attendant irritation of smoke, tearful eyes and blackened kitchens. An enterprising woman architect in northern India, disturbed by the plight of local housewives, designed a smokeless chula, containing rectangular asbestos dampers which could be lowered or raised to control heat, flames and smoke with the help of an exhaust pipe. A 40 per cent fuel saving is claimed on this device. It also eliminates the customary use of a second chula for thickening milk which can be done with ease on this stove which can retain heat more easily.

Appropriateness of the technological choice to the physical environment is just as crucial as its affordability by the common people. In south Asia, wherever biogas technology is being introduced, women have benefited by the advent of a clean, readily available and irritant-free fuel source. But these benefits are restricted to the haves and are rarely accessible to the have-nots. Poor women have traditionally collected and processed the bio-waste for fuel and they may now be double losers, being denied the technology as well as the traditional raw materials.

Conclusions

The social burden of large-scale deforestation has fallen heavily on the rural poor and especially on the female population, who now spend longer hours in search of fuelwood, and have to adjust to inferior fuel sources, changed dietary and cooking modes and a decreased quality of life. The domestic sector, as the largest consumer of rural energy, should receive most attention from the planners. The most feasible approach seems to be the provision of energy through wind, sun and biogas aided by village plantings of fast growing trees suitable for firewood – preferably through community efforts. Simple, appropriate technologies, constructed from local materials and skills are preferable to large-scale, capital-intensive technological choices. Women figure prominently in the rural energy crisis and so should be included in both the planning and implementation of projects. Women's needs must be kept in sight in the development of energy efficient devices, particularly for cooking, lighting, and the transport of water. In the total rural energy balance, women must be regarded as one of the key elements.

16 Gender issues in the agricultural modernization of India

Bina Agarwal

In the vast body of literature on the socio-economic implications of the new agricultural strategy in India, there is little gender analysis. This neglect reflects an uncritical acceptance of the assumption that the household is a unit of converging, perhaps even homogeneous, interests and that all its members will share equally in the benefits and burdens of technological change. This assumption must be questioned. Also women of the poorest households require special consideration because they are often the primary or sole income-earners in their families, and their access to employment and income is crucial for their own and their families' survival.

In order to investigate the gender implications of technological change in Indian agriculture, the author undertook two studies. The first (Agarwal 1984) examined the effect of high yielding varieties of rice on women's work burden in the fields and the home, and on their income and consumption, by drawing upon data from three major rice growing States: Andhra Pradesh, Tamil Nadu and Orissa. The effects on labour use in the fields were disaggregated by sex, category of labour (family, permanent and casual), and farm size (used as a proxy for class). The analysis indicated that women, especially those employed as casual labourers, contributed a substantial proportion, and often the greater part, of the labour used in rice cultivation. The adoption of HYV rice increased the total labour used on the farm. Much of this increase was in terms of female and male casual labour, implying an increase in the available agricultural wage work. The effect on the use of female family labour on the farm was found to vary between states, being the net effect of two contradictory tendencies. On the one hand, HYVs increased the labour needed; on the other, as they raised family income, prestige considerations dictated the withdrawal of family women from manual work in the fields.

However, the study emphasized that all these effects must be seen in a wider context. Women of poorer households already have heavy workloads, often higher than those of men; cash income is usually controlled by men and often spent by them largely on their own needs; the intra-household distribution of food favours men over women; and the health of women working in the rice fields is exposed to more hazards than is that of the men who generally perform a different set of operations. Thus, the increased demand for female casual labour may not benefit the women of agricultural labourer households unless, first, there is an increase in daily real wages, which in fact have declined in all three states studied, and, second, there is equal intra-household access for all members to income and consumption items. Where the women of small cultivator households now work longer hours in the fields, their workloads have increased without necessarily any compensatory improvement in their standards of living. These findings underline the need for special consideration of the gender implications of the income and employment impact of technological change.

The second study (Agarwal 1986) which covered all major States in India, examined the interrelationships between gender, poverty and agricultural growth, cross-regionally. It was shown that women and female children in poor, rural households bear a disproportionately high share of the burden of poverty. A systematic bias against females is noted in the intra-household distribution of food and health care, especially, but by no means exclusively, in poor households. However, significant inter-regional variations were found in the extent of discrimination against females, with the bias being much less in the southern states than in the north-western ones; due to economic social and historical factors, including differences in women's labour force participation and marriage expenses. Separate consideration was given to the special survival problems faced by women in female-headed households which were found to be much more poverty-prone than male-headed households.

This study also looked at the characteristics of poor, rural households and the factors underlying the agricultural growth processes which may lead to the further impoverishment of this section of the Indian poor. Data from the Rural Labour Enquiries for 1964–5 and 1974–5, spanning the period during which the new agricultural technology gained a foothold in India, was used to study the effects of this technology and the associated agricultural growth, on the employment and earnings of male and female agricultural labourers. For each state and by sex, the author assessed changes in the average annual days of agricultural wage employment, involuntary unemployment, daily and annual real earnings and male/female differentials in the earnings of agricultural labourers. In addition there was an examination of the association between the changes in these economic variables and other variables such as the incidence and amount of dowry payments among the poor, and the impact of all these changes on rural women in different regions.

On the whole, the picture emerging from these studies of the implications of agricultural growth for poor, rural women is complex, mixed and rather pessimistic. It is believed that unless counteractive measures are taken, the burden of poverty for these women is likely to increase in most regions of India. However, there is a note of hope in the growth of women's organizations and groups through which the concerns of women are beginning to be articulated.

17   The role of women in integrated development in Egypt

Aida Beshara

Since ancient times, Egyptian women have had a higher status and more independence than women in other parts of the Arab world. This unique tradition provides the foundation on which is based the contribution of women to the development of modern Egypt.

The role of women in Egyptian society since the ancient Egyptian period

Most students of ancient Egyptian history have noted the remarkably high status of women during that period. Durant (1935) thinks that 'the position of women was more advanced than in most countries today'. Nazir (1965) also says that 'the Egyptian woman enjoyed full rights, she also contributed considerably to work in the home, field, and factory, she played important roles in religion, politics, and government, as well as in reigning the country'.

Between the unification of upper and lower Egypt in 3100BC and the death of Cleopatra in AD30, Egypt had more than one queen who ruled in her own right, most famous of whom was Queen Hatshepsut (1503–1482BC). Much has been written about Hatshepsut and her achievements. Perhaps Durant (1935) summarizes these achievements best by saying that 'for twenty two years the Queen ruled in wisdom and peace', and 'she became one of the most successful and beneficent of Egypt's many rulers'. Other queens became famous as wives and mothers of reigning kings, and indirectly influenced the governing of the country. In fact, when Bibi II from the sixth dynasty (around 2500–2420) came to the throne, he was still a boy, and his mother became regent. Her great influence in governing the country is portrayed through the many inscriptions that date back to the first years of the rule of this king. Nefertiti, the principal queen of King Akhenaton's dynasty (1370–1352BC) had a dominant role in the royal family. Queen Tiye was the wife of King Amenhetep III, and his partner in directing the policy of the country. She was also the mother of the great King Akhenaton, and Kemp mentions that she 'though a commoner's daughter, was evidently a woman of forceful personality' (Kemp 1983).

As for the status of women outside the royal family, there is much evidence that women were well respected and often held high positions. Nazir (1965) mentions a lady called Bisesht from the period of the Old Kingdom, (2780–2280BC), who was the chief physician of the kingdom. Women were not only recognized for their curative skills but were generally not discriminated against in education. Some women were highly cultured – for example, a lady by the name of Nefru-Kapith who had a large library at Dendera, for which she appointed a special librarian.

As for women's marital status, Durant (1935) says that 'for the most part the common people contented themselves with monogamy. Family life was apparently as well ordered, as wholesome in moral tone and influence, as in the highest civilizations of our time. Divorce was rare until the decadent dynasties. If a husband divorced his wife for any other reason than adultery, he was required to turn over to her a substantial share of the family property.' Women also held and bequeathed property in their own names; one of the most ancient documents in history is the third dynasty will in which the lady Neb-sent transmits her lands to her children. In modern Egypt women retain this financial independence and even keep their maiden names after marriage.

Women's contribution to the economic activities of ancient Egypt must have been substantial. Durant (1935) says that 'the monuments picture them eating and drinking in public, going about their affairs in the streets unattended and unharmed, and freely engaging in industry and trade'. Nazir (1965) mentions that factories were full of women who spun and wove linen well. He also speaks of women going to the village market to sell poultry, butter and fabrics, a job which women still carry out today. Diodorus Siculus describes the old men and women washing the dirt away from the gold that was mined in the eastern desert of Egypt (Durant 1935). Moreover, many murals portray women taking part in a wide variety of urban and rural activities. For all these reasons the author endorses the belief that women's substantial contribution to social and economic activities in rural areas in modern Egypt has been consistent since the ancient Egyptian period.

The role played by women during the urbanization and modernization process

This process started at the beginning of the nineteenth century, but really rapid urbanization has occurred only during the twentieth century, and especially since 1950. During the modernization process in an agricultural country such as Egypt, the overall contribution of women to economic activity diminishes with the declining contribution of rural areas vis-à-vis urban areas to the economic development of the country. This is because many women, previously contributing to economic production in rural areas, and migrating to urban areas, are unable to find urban employment. In the case of Egypt, however, a substantial proportion of the migrating women peasants in the nineteenth century obtained employment as household servants and washerwomen. Eventually, women started to contribute more widely to jobs associated with urban development. The first school for training midwives was established as early as 1831, and the graduates of this school, all women, were employed in Cairo and the Egyptian ports of Alexandria, Port Said and Al-Suez. At the same time, as a result of the development of education, increasing numbers of women were recruited as teachers, especially for primary schools. In 1898 a section was established at one of the first secondary schools for girls for the training of teachers. Later on it was developed as an education training college for women.

One of the economic activities that was growing at this stage of Egypt's development was modern manufacturing. Women, who had always contributed to the production of handicrafts, gradually became employed in modern factories, especially in the textile industry, which was one of the first modern industries to be established. Another modern industry to which women made a major contribution from the outset was that of clothing. The report on women presented to the Egyptian senate in 1984 believes that the government played a role in encouraging girls to work in manufacturing industries as early as 1874. In that year the regulations for a public girls' school at Siyufiya in Alexandria stated that 'graduates of the school are welcome to work in the government-owned factory that is being established for the making of ready made clothes for government servants and other individuals' (Magles El-Shoura 1984).

At present, women's overall contribution (as a proportion of the total numbers employed in the formal sector) is at only 4.7 per cent, and therefore is not substantial, although women workers are numerically important in a few occupations. According to the most recent population census (1976), in the nine occupational groups listed women's contribution was largest in that of professional, technical and related occupations, with 25.1 per cent of all employment in this sector. As in ancient Egypt, women today make a major contribution to the health-care occupations. Women in modern Egypt monopolize two occupations: nursing and midwifery. They provide more than half of the workers in two other caring professions – nursery school teachers (88.4 per cent) and social workers (58.1 per cent) – and between 24 and 50 per cent for six further occupations. For these six occupations the proportions were as follows: librarians (47.3 per cent); primary school teachers (42.9 per cent); pharmacists (36.1 per cent); preparatory school teachers (34.5 per cent); staff of universities and colleges for higher education (24.6 per cent); and physicians and surgeons (24.6 per cent). Significantly, teachers at all levels formed 12.9 per cent of all employed women and 49.8 per cent of all women employed in the sector of professional, technical and related occupations.

Women constituted one-third of those employed in the personal services occupational group. They were particularly concentrated in domestic service, making up to 86 per cent of those working as household servants and nannies. These occupations employed 4.9 per cent of all economically active women. In the manufacturing sector, only two industries had considerable percentages of women employed compared to men; these were dressmaking and embroidery working with 38.3 per cent, and the manufacture of knitted garments with 33.0 per cent. It is therefore evident that while women continue to contribute considerably to traditional occupations such as nursing, midwifery, teaching and dressmaking, they have gained access with various degrees of success to most other occupations.

Women's role in the political life of Egypt is not at present comparable with their contribution to the economy, but it is of some significance, especially if compared to the contribution of women to this activity in most developing, and even in many developed countries. The real beginning of women's contribution to political activities in Egypt started with the onset of a strong national movement after the end of the First World War, in which women took an active part. Women also took part in the famous revolt of Egyptians against Britain in 1919, and this was followed by the establishment of the Egyptian Women's Union, whose first leader was the internationally known Hoda Sharawy.

In 1956 women finally acquired full political rights, including the right to take part in political elections, both as candidates and voters. Another improvement in women's political status came in 1972 when an amendment to the law of the house of representatives (Magles El-Shoura) decreed that for the thirty-one constituencies of Egypt, each list of candidates must include at least one woman. Women, meanwhile, continued to be granted the freedom to stand for office outside this obligatory representation. Furthermore, in 1979 a new law for local government was issued, which stipulated that there must be obligatory representation of women at all levels of local government, namely in each precinct of a big urban centre, in each provincial borough or 'markaz', in each town, and in each village. On the basis of data collected in the province of El-Giza, near Cairo, in December 1984, women now constitute about 10 per cent of representatives on local political bodies in urban areas, and about 15 per cent in rural areas. While it is too early to assess fully the results of this increased representation of women, it is expected that it will have positive results that will benefit Egypt's political, economic, and social development.

The role that women can play in the revitalization of the rural sector and in achieving integrated urban–rural development

It is clear that the role of women was very considerable in ancient times, while in the modern era, it continued to be substantial in rural, and is increasing in importance in urban areas. Yet, unfortunately women's contribution to economic activities in rural areas appears to have diminished considerably in the last three decades. According to the 1976 census, although 55 per cent of all women over 6 years of age were still living in rural areas, women working in rural areas formed only 24 per cent of all employed women. However, a considerable percentage of those economically active in rural areas belong to the informal sector, which has not been included in Egyptian censuses, except in the 1947 census. In 1947 women made up 50.1 per cent of the total employed population (only 4.7 per cent in 1976), and 51.6 per cent of those employed in agriculture (only 3.2 per cent in 1976). But as the 1947 and 1976 censuses are not really comparable, in order to give a more valid picture of the deterioration of women's contribution to economic activities in rural areas, one must compare the 1976 census with that of 1937, as both these censuses omit the informal sector. In 1976, in absolute numbers, the total of women employed in agriculture was very close to that of 1937, but as a percentage of total employment in agriculture, there was a very big drop from about 55 in 1937, to only about 22 in 1976.

The author thinks that since the ancient as well as the most recent history of Egypt has shown a considerable and consistent contribution of women to economic, social, and political activities in rural areas, the chances are that, if sound means are found to curb the present decline, and enhance their contribution once more, this would revitalize the rural sector, help in bridging the gap between urban and rural living standards, and encourage integrated urban–rural development.

A gender division of labour has always existed in Egyptian agriculture. Traditional female tasks are planting, weeding, hand removal of pests, and the harvesting of many crops, such as cotton, vegetables and fruits. Women also are responsible for the primary preparation of some crops after harvesting, such as the removal of cotton seeds from raw cotton, the removal of seeds from marrows and cucumbers for replanting and the blowing of the husk off some seeds. Women share some jobs with men, such as the cutting of clover which is used as fodder for the animals, or taking the animals to the field. Milking cows is a woman's job, as is the making of butter and cheese. According to the 1937 census women employed in the preparation of dairy products constituted 36.6 per cent of women employed in the agricultural sector, and 28.7 per cent of total employment of women in all sectors. In the 1976 census there was no mention of this occupation at all, but there is still evidence of its existence, although there has definitely been a sharp decline in its employment, because of a decrease in the ratio of milking cows to population, and the transfer of a major part of the dairy products industry from the farm to the factory. Women have also traditionally played a major role in the marketing of agricultural products. If one compares women trading in products associated with rural areas, in 1937, with women enumerated as working in trade in rural areas in 1976, one finds a great drop – from 39,966 in 1937 to 11,827 in 1976. Yet trade is still a more important job for women in rural than in urban areas. Trade is another economic activity where the informal sector is quite substantial, especially in rural areas. For instance, it is well established that women nearly monopolize trade in butter and cheese, as well as in poultry. They also do most of the retail selling of vegetables and fruits, either in village or town markets, or as street vendors in small towns and big villages, or moving from one small village to another. In a recent study of markets in Sharkiya province in the Delta (Suleiman 1983), in the weekly market of the big town of Abu Kebir, it was found that 83 per cent of all vendors were men and 17 per cent women. Suleiman also mentions that 'most vendors of dairy products and poultry are women'. Rural women also take part in many cottage industries and small-scale manufacturing. Besides making butter and cheese at home, they contribute to such crafts as spinning, weaving and dyeing of clothes, the making of clay products, the making of sun-baked bricks, and the weaving of baskets and different products from palm trees. With the establishment of modern factories in rural areas, many women have been recruited to work in them, especially in the spinning, weaving and clothing industries. Women, together with men, build their houses out of sun-baked mud bricks, and they also build baking ovens, silos for grain, and pens for breeding of small poultry, all out of mud and straw. Even though some peasants have started to build their houses out of bricks and cement, women still take part in construction, especially in the carrying of bricks and cement.

It is evident that the modernization and mechanization of activities in rural areas is the major culprit behind the decline in women's contribution to these economic activities. In order to overcome the problems that result from the modernization process, and make possible the training and adaptation of women to this inevitable, and in many ways beneficial change that is taking place in rural areas of Egypt it is suggested that:

1 Girls should be encouraged to attend primary and preparatory schools, especially agricultural preparatory schools.

2 More agricultural secondary schools should be established. In these schools girls should be given courses with boys, including simple mechanics and farm management, but they should be offered other specialized courses in poultry breeding, the making of dairy products, the making of jams and preserves, and handicrafts.

3 Extension service units in each village should be prepared to offer advice to women peasants concerning their specialized jobs.

4 Village banks should expand giving loans to women for agricultural activities, or for starting small businesses.

5 Women should be encouraged to work in social and public services in rural areas.

6 The political role of women should be enhanced, and they should play an increasing role in decision-making and in planning for the development of their villages. In this way women would regain their traditional position as major contributors to rural economic activities. This would help to revitalize the rural sector, and curb migration from rural to urban areas.

18   The feminization of agriculture in the Caribbean

Janet Henshall Momsen

Contemporary small-scale agriculture in the Commonwealth Caribbean has its origins in the cultivation by slaves of provision grounds on the marginal lands of the plantations. Often the slaves were allowed to own livestock, sell their produce and keep the profits from their trading. These practices provided the foundation for a post-emancipation 'proto-peasantry' for whom semi-subsistence agriculture was a part-time occupation to be combined with plantation labour. During slavery women worked side by side with men in the fields with little apparent division of labour by gender. When their legal ties to the plantations ended, women were quick to move into alternative occupations. Where possible they sought the status of full-time housewives and mothers, but when they needed to earn money they turned to craft work and the retailing of farm produce. Yet many women were forced to remain as agricultural labourers and it is still the most common off-farm job for women from small-farm families.

Differential migration patterns since emancipation have led to a female majority in the population of most Commonwealth Caribbean countries. In 1970, 35 per cent of all households in the region were headed by women. This regional total blurs many intra-regional variations which reflect ethnic differences in family structure and contrasting levels of migration. The proportion of female household heads varies from 50 per cent among the highly migratory Afro-Caribbean population of St Kitts–Nevis to only 25 per cent in Trinidad and Tobago where there is a sizeable East Indian population.

Female members of Caribbean farm households may play three economic roles related to agriculture. They may be the decision-maker on their own farm, they may market the production of their own and other farm enterprises, and they may work as paid or unpaid agricultural labourers. These roles are not mutually ex-clusive and any one individual may fill all three at the same time or at various stages in her life-cycle. In particular communities one of these occupations may predominate, but from time to time the emphasis may change as a result of exogenous factors.

The role of women in Caribbean agriculture is closely linked to the importance of the matrifocal and matrilocal family so often described in studies of the region. Both Smith (1956) and Clarke (1957) feel that matrifocality is related to the economic marginality of men in many Caribbean societies. Solien (1959) suggests that migrant wage labour of the recurrent type which is found in so many societies of the region produces an excess of adult females over males and thus forces households into matrifocality. Male marginality is most common among the poorest families many of which are dependent on small scale agriculture.

In questionnaire surveys of 1307 small-scale farmers in seven Eastern Caribbean territories, carried out by myself and others over the period 1963–79, it was found that the proportion of farmers who were female varied from 56 per cent in Montserrat to 16 per cent in St Vincent. This variation between the islands does in part reflect real differences, but it is also indicative of varying classifications and attitudes on the part of the investigator, and of the type of farming being studied. In a survey of 212 small farms in Barbados (Henshall 1966) women declared themselves to be the farm operators on 30 per cent of the farms, but further detailed questioning revealed that women were the decision-makers on an additional 22 per cent of the farms, in most cases because the nominal male farm operator had a full-time job, sometimes overseas, and had little interest in agriculture (Henshall 1964).

If it can be demonstrated that farms operated by women are distinctive then it becomes imperative to consider gender in any analysis of Caribbean agriculture. The multivariate statistical technique of principal components analysis was used to test the stability of gender differences in agriculture across the broad cultural and environmental spectrum represented by the islands of Grenada, St Vincent, Barbados, St Lucia, Martinique, Montserrat and Nevis (Henshall 1981). In most cases the variance attributable to gender was split between a land-use vector and a social structure vector.

The land-use factor revealed a link between female-operated farms and subsistence production of root crops on poor quality land in most of the islands surveyed. Farms on which women are the decision-makers tend to be smaller, more isolated and have less fertile soils than those operated by men. Women appear to view the farm as an extension of their household responsibilities, concentrating on subsistence production of food crops and small stock rearing, rather than on the export crops and cattle preferred by men.

The social structure component indicated that the female farm operator is most commonly, though not exclusively, found in households headed by women. Generally, women farmers are less likely to have off-farm jobs than their male counterparts. In the Barbados survey, 73 per cent of the women agricultural decision-makers had no off-farm work compared to 34 per cent of the men. However, this does not mean that women farmers spend more time working their land than men, as the majority of women are either too old and/or too busy with children and housework to expend much energy on the farm. Despite this double burden, women farmers hired fewer labourers than men farmers because of the cost of such labour and also because few agricultural labourers wished to work for women farmers.

Migration has also led to gender based differences in Caribbean agriculture. Migration is an institutionalized aspect of Caribbean societies. Over the last three decades most territories in the region have lost at least 10 per cent of their population to migration. It was generally the men and young women who moved to the opportunities offered by Europe and North America leaving behind a rural population dominated by elderly women and children. Fieldwork (1973, 1977) in the Leeward Islands of Montserrat and Nevis, where migration levels have been unusually high, revealed that among small-farm families men were more likely to be return migrants than women. On the other hand, a smaller proportion of men than women farmers received remittances from family overseas, although previous work (Zuvekas 1978) had shown that these two islands had the highest per capita levels of remittances in the eastern Caribbean. Of those receiving remittances, women more than men farmers were dependent on these sources for the major part of their income. In Nevis (in a sample of ninety-nine farmers) 44 per cent of the women farmers surveyed, but only 16 per cent of the male farmers, received more than half their income from remittances, while in Montserrat out of 115 farms, 23 per cent of the female but none of the male small-scale farmers obtained more than half their income in the form of remittances. Statistical analysis showed a strong correlation between high dependence on remittances and under-utilization of land.

Today the unskilled, rural populace is no longer able to find large-scale migration outlets and in some cases a reversal of the previous direction of population movement has become apparent (Stinner et al. 1982). Farmers who had come to rely on remittances as a major source of income are finding that this source is becoming less dependable as migrants become unemployed and sterling remittances, in particular, are affected by exchange rate fluctuations. For Jamaica, remittance income in 1970 was over five times the net inflow of public external capital, but by 1980 the level of remittances was only two-thirds that of net public capital inflow (World Bank 1983). Comparable figures are not available for countries with populations below 1 million, but it seems probable that the economies of the smaller islands of the Caribbean have been even more severely affected.

My research project on gender differences in Caribbean small-scale farming is now focusing on the impact of return migration and declining remittance income. It will look at the changing role of remittances in household economies, the effect of return migration on the gender division of labour and on productivity on the farm and the role of return migration in the transfer of labour from agriculture to the service sector. Regional disparities in the trends towards both 'depeasantization' and 'repeasantization' of the small-farm sector, as they affect the geography of gender, will also be considered.

The feminization of agriculture without concurrent institutional support has led to declining productivity in the small-farm sector, an increasing proportion of uncultivated land and a retreat into subsistence agriculture by women forced to feed their children from the land without extension or credit. Chaney (1983) sees a clear link between the food problem in the Caribbean, and the plight of women left behind by migrants to support their families from the farm. There is some evidence that return migration is leading to a decline in the proportion of women farmers. The 1972 agricultural census in Montserrat ascertained that women operated 44 per cent of the farms of less than 4 hectares but by 1983 this figure had fallen to 23 per cent. How widespread this 'defeminization' of agriculture is and the nature of its effect on gender roles in rural areas has yet to be determined.

19   The Malay family: structural change and transformation – a research proposal

Mei Ling Young and Kamal Salih

We propose that research be undertaken into recent transformations of the Malay family. Powerful social forces, pulling in opposite directions, are threatening its very character and basic structure. The tremendous changes of the last twenty-five years in Malaysian society have surpassed the evolutionary processes of previous centuries.

Structural change and development: sources of transformation of the Malay family

What are the main recent changes in Malaysian society to which we can attribute the transformation of the Malay family? We may highlight as crucial the progressive integration of Malaysia into the modern world system; the dramatic surge towards industrialization in the 1970s, narrowly-based and distorted though it was, as the world economy redeployed capital to the periphery; the rapid though concentrated urbanization engendered by that industrialization; the concomitant creation of a more permanent Malay urban community; the new presence of single women workers in the urban economy, and the wider participation of women in the labour force; the rise and expansion of a Malay middle class with industrialization, urbanization and the expansion of the role of the state; the restructuring of society associated with state policy (e.g. the New Economic Policy and the 70 Million Population Policy); and the re-emergence of Islam as an important force in everyday life and public affairs.

An analysis of the Malaysian economy in the present conjuncture requires understanding of its historical articulation within the world system. It will remain for us to specify more precisely how this translates into a determinate structuring and reconstitution of the Malay family.

Before the colonial period the economy, except for a little trading, was based on subsistence agriculture with rice as the dominant crop. With the integration of the Malayan economy into the world system and its monetization, Malay peasants began to grow cash crops such as rubber. At this stage, work within the family was no longer solely for subsistence. But Malays were kept in the subsistence economy, or at least in limited cash cropping, by colonial policies such as the Padi Enactment Act and the Malay Reserve Land Act which prevented Malays from leaving padi or selling their land except to Malays. There was also an attempt to incorporate Malays into the colonial bureaucracy, as civil servants, through education policies and the formation of the elite Malay schools. The main occupations of Malays during this period were in agriculture and, for those who were educated, in the civil service. Very few Malay women were civil servants.

Change has been dramatic since independence in 1957. More recently, significant and lasting repercussions for the Malay family have come from the rapid urbanization associated with the particular mode of industrialization adopted in the 1970s. A feature of colonial urbanization in Malaysia was the exclusion of the indigenous population.

In the early twentieth century the towns of Malaya were comprador cities serving the needs of the colonial government. They were peopled mainly by immigrant Chinese and Indians, rather than Malays who mostly remained in the rural sector. It was not until independence in 1957, and more specifically after the implementation of the New Economic Policy in 1970, that Malay urbanization became important. In the past there was a tendency for Malay civil servants to return to their rural *kampungs* on retirement; now they remain in urban areas. The pace of urbanization in certain areas also provides a focal point for youth in-migration. The development of the new Malay urban families must certainly affect Malay education, occupation, mores, socialization and demographic characteristics.

There have been pivotal changes in the nature of recruits to the labour force. Previously, few Malay women entered the formal labour market; those who did so were mainly teachers or clerks in the civil service. However, as a result of increasing intervention by the state and the establishment of the Free Trade Zones (FTZs) for multinational companies, the number of Malay female workers in the manufacturing sector quadrupled between 1964 and 1970. This has tremendous implications for the role of women in the family. For the first time a substantial number of young women, especially school-leavers, are earning a wage. For the first time, too, a large proportion of young Malay girls have become migrants, residing away from the direct control of the family, in house-groups, boarding houses, or company hostels (see Salih *et al.* 1985 for a discussion of these female Malay workers in Penang). The fact that daughters in many rural households are now earning good wages has meant a revision of thinking for parents who have traditionally married off daughters soon after they left school.

There is evidence that the decline of fertility among Malays in recent years is mainly due to a rise in the age at marriage of Malay girls (Jones 1981). One reason is likely to be the increase in their participation in the labour force. This has implications for the formation of Malay families and for individual and family life-cycles. The decline in fertility may also be partly due to changing attitudes to work, mobility and migration, marriage, family formation and size of family, and the intricate processes associated with the family as a social unit. These new attitudes apply also to the socialization of children, and to the value of children; new intergenerational flows such as wealth, obligations and services between parents and children may in turn lead to new norms in fertility (Caldwell 1976, 1978).

The increasing numbers of Malay women in the labour force raises the whole question of their proletarianization, especially those employed by the multinational companies in the FTZs. Is the migration of these girls permanent? What happens when employers resort to retrenchment? Do they return to their villages? There is already a cohort of female workers who have been employed for ten years. In the new urban milieu, do the women workers marry men from the urban areas or the rural areas? Who are these men? What happens to the families they form? Do they withdraw from the labour market when children are born, or do they retain their jobs? Who looks after their children when these women go to work? What is the current impact of the Islamic revival on the Malay girl who is on the one hand responding to industrialization, and on the other, under pressure from fundamental Islamic principles? What are the repercussions of all these forces on the Malay family? In short, does the contemporary urban Malay household have a family wage economy?

The state is central to the transformation, or conservation, of the Malay family. The rapid incorporation of women in the industrial workforce, engendered by the outward-oriented industrialization pursued by the government in the 1970s, has given rise to severe contradictions in the overall position of women in the domestic domain, the factory, the new urban milieu, and the larger society. In other spheres of economic and social development, changes in family structure are brought about by the state through policies affecting the maintenance or demise of the informal sector, the conversion of small holdings into mini estates, and the extension of the peasant family through the promotion of federal schemes initiated in the early 1960s under which poor families were settled on vast tracts of newly opened land. The New Economic Policy (Malaysia 1970), which is intended to correct structural imbalance and to eradicate poverty, provides new opportunities for Malays in the educational and economic spheres. These new developments will affect the Malay family and will be reflected in generation gaps in outlook, attitudes, behaviour and family relations. The declining trend of fertility among Malays will be under pressure from the recent population policy statement on the 70 million population and the incentives given to women in the form of extended paid maternity leave. These will be reinforced by the fundamental Islamic ideology which maintains that the role of the woman is in the home.

The state has also been a significant factor in the recent emergence and expansion of a Malay middle class. This may be said to consist of the professional and administrative class, the higher civil servants, some in the middle administrative level, and teachers. This group has expanded greatly as a result of Malayanization in the public and private sectors since independence, increasing industrialization and urbanization and a near universal schooling system with an increasingly available tertiary level.

The tension between the role of women in the domestic domain and in the public domain can perhaps only be resolved by an ideological transformation of gender relations and the sexual division of labour within the Malay family. But this resolution is threatened by cultural and religious revivals such as the recent resurgence of Islamic fundamentalism. Thus, at the moment the increased participation of women in the labour force does not really represent an emancipation but is mainly a reconstitution of women's role within the sexual division of labour. This may lead to a powerful conservative tendency in the constitution and reconstitution of the Malay family in the future; it may perhaps be further reinforced by such policies as the 70 Million Population Policy, unless the state also acts to promote a dual role for women.

We have so far considered material changes impinging on the structure and functioning of the Malay family. But there are other, equally important influences – ideology, cultural norms and practices, and socialization – which all operate through the household as a social unit. We have already referred to the impact of Islamic values on the definition of women's role in the private and public domains, and the role of the state through the education system in inculcating values which seek to reproduce the family unit, while at the same time material forces such as capitalism, the organization of work, the media and technology, tend to reduce the family to the elemental units of labour.

Dimensions of change in the Malay family

Historical demographic studies on the family in Europe have shown that changing economic and social structures in any country lead to drastic changes in the structures and processes within the family. Recent work by Hareven (1978, 1982) on families in New Hampshire showed how the constraints of the family cycle and life course were adapted to the rapid changes of industrialization. This research has highlighted the critical importance of the household economy and household adaptive strategies, either directly (Hareven 1982) by showing how families allocated labour, investment and resources to cope with changing industrial needs and families socialized their members into an industrial environment, or indirectly (Tilly and Scott 1978) by examining the changing functions, and consequently, types of family over time. The interlocking forces of the household as a unit of production, consumption, accumulation and socialization, determine the form and state of the household.

These theoretical and empirical findings enable us to suggest the manner in which the Malay family has been transformed. It has evolved from a basically subsistence family economy to one of production, and now consumption. In Europe, the wage economy family and the consumer economy family can be clearly defined; but we feel that in Malaysia, and probably in most Third World countries, the line between the family wage economy and the family consumer economy is less clear-cut. The main reason for this is the enormous impact of modern technology in the form of mass media (see, for example, Chapter 20).

Contributions to the study of the Malay family

A survey of published material on the family reveals four important deficiencies that need to be remedied. First, there is a dearth of studies undertaken specifically on the Malay family (Young 1983). There is little research into such areas as family decision-making units, the allocation of labour and resources, relationships between siblings and between generations or the socialization of children.

Second, the overwhelming majority of the studies (except for Djamour's 1959) were carried out in peasant societies. Third, coverage of regional variations in the geography of gender relations in the Malay family is most uneven. Five regional groups may be suggested:

1   the north, covering Perlis, Kedah, and north Perak, which has been influenced by Sumatra, specifically Acheh;
2   the north-east, consisting of Kelantan and Trengganu. Kelantan is an exceptional area, having a very high participation of women in the labour force and the highest divorce rates in the country (Jones 1981);
3   the urban areas of Penang, Kuala Lumpur, and Singapore;
4   the central-south, covering south Perak, Pahang, and Selangor, where the Javanese, Bugis, and other Indonesian immigrants have settled (Wilson 1967); and
5   Negri Sembilan-Malacca (Moubray 1931; Maeda 1978; Selat 1970, 1976; Swift 1954, 1965).

Fourth, the legal and customary system in Malaysia incorporates the following components: pagan/animistic, Hindu, *adat* (customary) Islamic, and secular-western. Local and class expression of these components yields a variety of outcomes which require study.

Conclusion

We advocate a study of the Malay family focusing on the impact of structural change within a multi-level analysis of social phenomena. Malaysia has undergone tremendous changes over the past two decades or so, reflecting the dynamic forces which are occurring at the national as well as at the world level. The articulation of these internal and external forces produces particular forms of change in the family about which our knowledge is still inadequate.

A multi-level and historical framework of analysis is required. What we mean by a multi-level analysis is a study of the family ranging from the household level to the village, region, national, and international levels, to see how the different forces operating at these various scales impinge on the household. The household must be conceptualized as a unit not bounded by the convenience of census enumerators, whose definition of a household is limited to co-residence and eating out of the same pot. The household is a social unit of production, consumption and accumulation, a microcosm of forces at the family level, a reflection of the broader society. In this way, the processes operating within a family in response to societal changes may be untangled and understood as part of the larger processes.

20 Mass markets – little markets: a call for research on the proletarianization process, women workers and the creation of demand

Terry McGee

The usefulness and values of most things depend, not so much on their own nature as upon the number of people who can be persuaded to desire and use them [An Advertiser's Guide to Publicity (1887)].

Introduction

'Mr. Tang's Girls' (Lim 1982), is a story of dramatic intensity, written round the efforts of Mr Tang to arrange a marriage for his eldest daughter with one of his employees. The daughter seems to be accepting the marriage, but she is eventually driven mad and kills her father. (The clash between tradition and modernity epitomized by attitudes to arranged marriages is now a rather hackneyed theme in Asian literature.) The point of the story is that Mr Tang's older daughters live in a world that is full of dreams of fashion and beauty. The growing insanity brought on by the trauma of the arranged marriage is displayed in the use of cosmetics:

When he came back next Friday, Kim Li had gone through a total change. 'I'm a woman now,' she had said to her sisters and began using Kim Mee's make-up every day. She pencilled her eyebrows crudely, rubbed two large red patches on her cheeks and drew in wide lips with the brightest crimson lipsticks in Kim Mee's collection. After every meal she went to her room and added more colour. Blue shadow circled her eyes, and her clumsy application of the mascara stick left blotches below her lids like black tear stains. She teased her short hair into a bush of knots and sprayed cologne until it dropped down her neck.

The realm of images, fantasy and dreams is shaping young women's attitudes in Asia today. This cannot be simply summed up under theoretical frameworks such as modernization or westernization; frameworks ignore the important role played by the creation of consumption 'needs' in inducing women and men to enter and to remain in the wage labour force.

Proletarianization, export zones and women workers

In the last few years a considerable number of studies have described the development of export processing zones in Asia. These studies fall into three broad categories. First, the macro-studies, which analyse the emergence of the Free Export Zones at the level of the international economy. Second, documentation of the conditions and features of the workforce of these zones; the workforce is often female, rural-born, and aged between 16 and 30. Finally, a smaller number of studies have begun to focus upon the lives of workers in these zones at a micro-level, using detailed ethnographic studies (e.g. Salaff 1981).

The broader aspects of the process whereby women enter the labour force of these export zones have perhaps been hidden by too narrow a concentration on labour relations. Recent Marxist work has greatly enriched the analysis of capitalist expansion and non-proletarian incorporation in the Third World, but it has not yet provided fully comprehensive theoretical frameworks. For instance, how do we accommodate the complicated problem of a country such as Malaysia? In Malaysia, state policies which, in collaboration with international capital, are designed to increase peasant (non-proletarian) productivity and ensure peasant control of land, are being subverted by the activities of multinational capital in liaison with national capital. This in turn is creating needs for commodities which can only be purchased with increased monetary income. As farm income is insufficient, the peasant's response is increasingly to seek off-farm employment. Thus these capitalist sectors set up contradictory processes at the non-proletarian level.

I would argue that in many parts of the Third World it is from consumption that the greatest dislocation is being generated for the non-proletarian populations. The considerable technological improvements in transport, which facilitate the movement of commodities and labour, together with the growth of information flows (television, education, improvements in literacy, etc.), have greatly increased the ability of the international and national capitalist sectors to create felt needs for people in Third World countries (see Lagbao and Pa 1981). There is a class dimension to this process. The styles and patterns of consumption of the national bourgeoisie, which imitate those of the advanced capitalist countries, are held up as models of the life-style which Third World populations wish to emulate.

The essential qualities of consumption and circulation are

becoming similar throughout the Third World. This similarity is most obvious in the built environments, transport and life-styles of the cities, but is also increasingly a feature of the countryside. Changes in circulation, producing greater 'speed' of goods and information are crucial to the changes occurring in consumption.

Historically, four components have been necessary to bring about the increase in demand which makes these mass markets possible. Hamish Fraser (1981) has shown how these components operated in Britain between 1850 and 1914. First, between 1850 and 1914 the market was expanded by increasing the numbers of customers. Second, there was growth in disposable income. Third, customers became more literate and better educated. This, together with organizational changes in the structure of retailing, credit, distribution and production facilitated the mass production of commodities for the growing population. Finally, the growing differences between the bourgeoisie and the working classes created an ideological environment in which advertisers would place the emphasis on status in creating demand for the mass products.

Underlying this growth of the mass market were two essential changes. The first was the large increase in wage workers concentrated in urban centres. The second was the creation of a new family form, separated from the production process. The emergence of industrial capitalism led to a restructuring of the family as a consumption unit within which new needs began to take shape. The reconstitution of the family did not take place quickly or evenly, but by the twentieth century the family in countries such as the United States and Britain became the main market for mass produced goods.

Mass production forced the capitalist class to cultivate and extend that market, just as it forced it to look abroad for other new markets. . . . Working people now see consumption as an end in itself, rather than as an adjunct to production, and as a primary source of both personal and social [i.e. 'status'] identity [Zaretsky 1976].

Now while I would not wish to argue that these changes took place in Asia in exactly the same way as in Britain and in the United States, it is surely no coincidence that the countries in which the principal export processing zones have emerged (Republic of Korea, Taiwan, Hong Kong, Singapore, Malaysia and the Philippines) have also been the countries in which the changes just outlined have been greatest.

Historically, using European examples from the eighteenth century, Scott and Tilly (1981) have argued that 'traditional families employed a variety of strategies to promote the well-being of the family unit', and off-farm deployment of labour was common. They argue, therefore, that in response to important structural changes the deployment of women and children in factory labour in the nineteenth century involved no great change in family strategies of off-farm employment. The model they use 'posits continuity of traditional values and behaviour in changed circumstances. Old values coexist with and are used by the people to adapt to extensive structural changes'. I find these arguments very helpful in explaining why parents of young single Malay women allow them to take up factory employment. The creation of consumption needs is a no less important a factor in inducing these young women to enter the labour force. The process is accelerated by new technological means to create these consumption needs (television, etc.) so the dreams of the young women workers are no less important than family strategies.

Of course, changes at the production level in rural areas (increased mechanization, etc.) are at the same time reducing the need for female labour on the farm. Equally, the changes could not be occurring if jobs were not being created in the export zones as a consequence of the New International Division of Labour.

Conclusion

If these speculative arguments have merit, the research agenda is obvious. Instead of studies of the labour conditions of women workers in the export zones of Asia, we need more research at the household and individual level into the motivations and commitment of women workers. This must be set in the context of broader structural research which analyses the changes in production relationships in both rural and urban areas, and in particular the growth of the mass market in Asian countries. Existing studies have tended to concentrate on production and to ignore the spheres of circulation and consumption save in a few micro studies of 'little markets'. Mass markets are not only invading and destroying the little markets and perhaps diverting expenditure from basic needs to non-essentials, they are reconstituting the household and altering labour force formation. An understanding of the consumption 'needs' of 'Mr Tang's Girls' may well be crucial to the broader understanding of the increasing numbers of women 'workers' in Asia and the formation of a female proletariat.

Annotated list of suggestions for further reading

Bibliographies

Buvinic, M. (1976) *Women and world development: an annotated bibliography*, Washington DC: Overseas Development Council
Over 400 items classified by subject categories and geographic area. In the introduction the author presents a critical review of the concepts of status and role.

Jacobs, S. E. (1974) *Women in perspective: a guide for cross-cultural studies*, Urbana: University of Illinois Press
Dated but useful bibliography, classified by continent and topic.

Lee, D. (1985) *Women and geography 1985: a bibliography*
This is the most recent of an annually up-dated bibliography on women and geography. The first was published in 1976 as *Women and geography: an annotated bibliography and guide to sources of information*, by Bonnie Loyd, Exchange Bibliography 1159, Council of Planning Librarians, and *Women and geography: a resource list* by Bonnie Loyd *Transition*, **VI** (4), winter 1976–7, 1–9. Additional listings appear regularly in *Transition*. Requests for copies of these bibliographies should be sent to David Lee, Department of Geography, Florida Atlantic University, Boca Raton, Florida 33431, USA.

Rihani, M. (1978) *Development as if women mattered: an annotated bibliography with a Third World focus*, Washington DC: Overseas Development Council, Occasional Paper no. 10
Contains annotations for 287 items organized by sector and region with the emphasis on development programming, papers by Third World women and finally unpublished documents which can be made available to readers through a publication retrieval system.

Stuart, B. A. C. (1979) *Women in the Caribbean: a bibliography*, Leiden, Netherlands: Royal Institute of Linguistics and Anthropology
651 items annotated and cross-referenced by topic and area.

Tomecek, M. (1983) *Third World women: A select bibliography*, Manhattan, Kansas; Kansas State University
Some 350 citations mostly referring to works from non-commercial publishers, arranged by topic and cross-classified by region.

Townsend, J., Barraclough, R., and Henshall Momsen, J. (1984) *Women in developing areas: A preliminary bibliography for geographers*, Durham: Women and Geography Study Group of the Institute of British Geographers

Approximately 1700 items subdivided by topic and region. Available from the Administrative Assistant, Department of Geography, University of Durham, South Road, Durham, DH1 3LE, UK.

UNESCO (1983) *Bibliographic guide to studies on the status of women, development and population trends*, Paris: UNESCO, Bowker, Unipub
Highly selective but fully annotated bibliographies of world regions.

Vavrus, L. G. and Cadieux, R. (1980) *Women in development: a selected annotated bibliography and resource guide*. East Lansing, Michigan: Non-formal Education Information Center, Michigan State University
Includes some 150 items subdivided by region and major topic. It also provides lists of relevant bibliographies, journals and organizations.

General

Anker, R. (1980) *Research on women's roles and demographic change: survey questionnaires for households, women, men and communities*, working document for restricted circulation, Geneva: ILO
Shows how long questionnaires must be to achieve useful data on these topics. Very instructive model questionnaires.

Anker, R., Buvinic, M. and Youssef, N. M. (eds.) (1982) *Women's roles and population trends in the Third World*, London: Croom Helm
A collection of papers prepared for the International Labour Office focusing on the interaction of women's productive and reproductive roles.

Beneria, L. (ed.) (1982) *Women and development: the sexual division of labour in rural societies*, New York: Praeger
Case studies sponsored by the ILO.

Black, N. and Cottrell, A. B. (1981) *Women and world change: equity issues in development*, London: Sage Publications Ltd.
Contains 13 chapters of which 8 relate to the Third World. Focuses on the following themes: a feminist critique of development theories, women and the world economic system, the impact of governmental policy on women and finally women's collective efforts to influence policy.

Boserup, E. (1970) *Women's role in economic development*, New York: St Martin's Press
The major pioneering survey of women's participation in various economic sectors in developing countries. Changes brought about by economic development are analysed in terms of their effect on women's social and economic status.

Boulding, E., Nuss, S. A., Carsons, D. L. and Greenstein, M. A. (1976) *Handbook of international data on women*, New York: Sage Publications, John Wiley and Co.
Indicators of the condition of women in a large range of countries collected by national governments at the request of the United Nations.

Buvinic, M. and Youssef, N. (1978) *Women-headed households: The*

ignored factor in development planning, Washington, DC.
International Center for Research on Women
Uses data from 74 developing countries to examine the reasons for the
increasing number of households headed by women.

Caplan, P. and Bujra, J. M. (eds.) (1978) *Women united, women divided*,
London: Tavistock Publications
Reports on women's solidarity in a wide range of societies: the strength
of solidarity is explained by the degree of sex segregation.

Cecelski, E. (1984) *The rural energy crisis, women's work and family
welfare: perspectives and approaches to action*, Geneva: ILO
A comprehensive and contemporary review of many studies on women
and biomass energy, both domestic and market-related.

Dahlberg, F. (ed.) (1981) *Woman the gatherer*, New Haven and London:
Yale University Press
Contributions from several disciplines on women's role as gatherer
over 3 million years; includes lessons from chimpanzees and from
current human foraging societies to demonstrate the significance of the
female role to the evolution of the species.

Davies, M. (ed.) (1983) *Third World – Second sex: women's struggles and
national liberation. Third World women speak out*, London: Zed Press
Contributions from women's organizations and individual women
from over 20 Third World countries.

Dixon-Mueller, R. (1985) *Women's work in Third World agriculture*,
Geneva: ILO
Summarizes a large number of studies in an effort to construct
indicators for monitoring changes in women's status. Focuses on the
division of labour, use of time, productivity and employment of
women. Sample questionnaires are provided.

Edholm, F., Harris, O. and Young, K. (1977) 'Conceptualising women',
Critique of Anthropology, **3** (9–10), 101–30
Seeks to clarify the concept of reproduction, starting from Meillassoux.
Distinguishes social reproduction, the reproduction of the labour force
and biological reproduction.

Gallin, R. S. and Spring, A. (eds.) (1985) *Women creating wealth:
Transforming economic development*, Washington DC: Association for
Women in Development
A retrospective overview of the Decade for Women with papers on
women in relation to human, natural and capital resources.

Giele, J. Z. and Smock, A. C. (eds.) (1977) *Women: roles and status in
eight countries*, New York: Wiley
Argues a relationship between societal complexity and sexual equality.
Explores women's status in Egypt, Bangladesh, Mexico, Ghana, Japan,
France, the United States and Poland.

Hrdy, S. B. (1981) *The woman that never evolved*, Cambridge: Harvard
University Press
A sociobiologist reports on female primates and woman's condition.
Provocative and informative.

International Rice Research Institute (1985) *Women in rice farming*,
   Aldershot: Gower
   The 30 papers reflect the variety of women's experience in rice farming
   in Asia and Africa: cultivation, post-harvest processing and marketing
   deploy female labour.
Kuhn, A. and Wolpe, A-M. (eds.) (1978) *Feminism and materialism*,
   London: Routledge and Kegan Paul
   A collection of papers which attempt to confront the theoretical
   problems in providing an explanation of women's position; particular
   reference to the family and the labour process.
Leghorn, L. and Parker, C. (1981) *Women's wealth: sexual economics and
   the world of women*, London: Routledge and Kegan Paul
   Documents the economic position of women around the world,
   comparing 'tradition' and 'modernity' for the position and status of
   women.
Mair, L. Mathurin (1986) 'Women: a decade is time enough', *Third World
   Quarterly*, **8** (2), 583–93
   A review of the political and attitudinal changes which have occurred
   during the UN Decade for Women particularly in terms of equality,
   development and peace.
Molyneux, M. (1979) 'Beyond the domestic labour debate', *New Left
   Review*, **116**, 3–27
   Much of the domestic labour debate assumes that the labour of the
   housewife is a functional consequence of capitalism. This important
   critique calls rather for historical and cultural specificity.
New Internationalist (1985) *Women: a world report*, London: Methuen
   Reviews women's worlds, through academic analysis, women writers
   and a series of statistical tables on women's situation in most countries
   of the world.
Ortner, S. B. (1974) 'Is female to male as nature is to culture?', in Rosaldo
   and Lamphere (eds.), 67–87
   Argues that woman appears closer to nature than man, and is allocated
   a symbolic status which devalues, circumscribes and restricts her.
Palmer, I. (1979) *The Nemow case. Case studies of the impact of large
   scale development projects on women: a series for planners*, New York:
   The Population Council
   Uses a hypothetical case study to illustrate how failure to consider
   women in project design may lead to unsuccessful implementation.
Reiter, R. R. (ed.) (1975) *Towards an anthropology of women*, London:
   Monthly Review Press
   A collection of essays which consider theories of the origin of gender
   relations and the need to overcome male bias in anthropological
   studies.
Rogers, B. (1980) *The domestication of women: discrimination in
   developing societies*, London and New York: Tavistock
   Shows how planners relate to women: examines western male
   ideology, the planning process and the discriminatory impact of the

planning process. Readable, provocative introduction to Third World women and the planners.

Rosaldo, M. Z. and Lamphere, L. (eds.) (1974) *Woman, culture and society*, Stanford: Stanford University Press
  A pioneering collection of original insights by anthropologists.

Schlegel, A. (ed.) (1977) *Sexual stratification: a cross-cultural view*, New York: Colombia University Press
  A collection of papers mainly by anthropologists which looks at sexual stratification in several Third World societies.

Seager, J. and Olson, O. (1986) *Women in the world: an international atlas*, London: Pan and Pluto Press
  A provocative set of maps, diagrams and tables on women's lives around the world. Invaluable, despite some dubious data

Sivard, R. L. (1985) *Women . . . a world survey*, Washington: World Priorities
  Seeks to present comparable statistics for 140 countries, 1960 to 1985. Necessarily relies on projections. Accessible, abbreviated factual information.

Standing, G. (1978) *Labour force participation and development*, Geneva: ILO
  A synthesis of the available evidence on labour force participation patterns and their economic determinants; concentrates largely on the changing economic role of women.

Standing, G. and Sheehan, G. (eds.) (1978) *Labour force participation in low-income countries*, Geneva: ILO
  A collection of case-studies of the socio-economic determinants of participation (mainly female): provocative and individually impressive, but lacking comparable data or hypotheses.

Tinker, I. and Bramsen, M. B. (eds.) (1976) *Women and world development*, Washington DC: Overseas Development Council
  Proceedings of a seminar organized by the American Association for the Advancement of Science to mark the beginning of the Decade for Women.

Tinker, I. (1979) *New technologies for food chain activities: The imperative of equity for women*, Washington, DC: Agency for International Development, Office of Women in Development
  Discusses the effects of recent development policies and new technologies on poor, rural women's participation in the production, processing, preservation and preparation of food.

Whyte, M. K. (1978) *The status of women in preindustrial societies*, Princeton, NJ: Princeton University Press
  Cross-cultural variation approached by comparing 93 cultures on 52 variables: little association between different variables found.

Women and Geography Study Group of the IBG (1984) *Geography and gender*, London: Hutchinson
  An introductory text for students of feminist geography. Demonstrates the feminist approach to geography with particular reference to four

aspects of geography: urban growth, industrial location, accessibility and Third World development.

World Development Report (1984) 'Population change and development', pp. 51–206. Published for the World Bank. New York: Oxford University Press
Argues that population growth is a development problem, that there are appropriate public policies to reduce fertility, and that policy makes a difference.

Young, K. (ed.) (1979) 'Special issue on the continuing subordination of women in the development process', *Bulletin of the Institute of Development Studies*, **10** (3)
Reports a historic conference.

Young, K., Wolkowitz, C. and McCullogh, R. (eds.) (1981) *Of marriage and the market*, London: CSE Books
Socialist–feminist critique of development and woman's subordination.

Youssef, N. H. (1974) *Women and work in developing societies*, Benheley: University of California
Focuses on the non-agricultural labour force in six Latin American and seven Middle Eastern countries: seeks to explain the contrasts with the European experience.

Zeidenstein, S (ed.) (1979) 'Learning about rural women', *Studies in Family Planning* **10** (11/12), New York: Population Council
A special issue containing 22 case studies focusing on time use, economic contribution and health care of Third World rural women.

Zelinsky, W., Monk, J. and Hanson, S. (1982) 'Women and geography: a review and prospectus', *Progress in Human Geography* **6** (3), 316–66
A major review article by three geographers working in the United States on the geographic dimensions of women's lives and the most useful directions for future work by geographers.

Africa

Ardener, S. (ed.) (1981) *Women and space: ground rules and social maps*, London: Croom Helm
A compilation of work by participants in the Oxford Women's Social Anthropology Seminar. It includes two papers on Africa: one on women's space in the Yoruba home, patrilineal compound and city; and one on non-white women in Capetown showing how women in the face of racial and economic oppression may use the home as a base for dominance.

Bryceson, D. F. (1980) 'The proletarianization of women in Tanzania', *Review of African Political Economy*, **17**, 4–27
Concerns women in mainly urban wage employment in Tanzania and explains the pre- and post-colonial differences in female labour force participation rates. There are now many more 'single' females in urban employment. It is argued that rural–urban migration for women is

partially a positive choice to evade patriarchal controls and attitudes in villages.

Carr, M. (1983) 'The long walk home', *Appropriate Technology* **10** (1), 17–19
Brief review of transport-related problems of Third World women using much evidence from Kenya where the women surveyed headloaded 90 per cent of the water and fuelwood.

Himmelstraud, K. and Bickham, N. (1985) *The peripheral centre. Swedish assistance to Africa in relation to women.* Stockholm: Swedish International Development Authority
Reviews the degree to which Swedish assistance to Africa is in accordance with the basic needs of women. Reports on the situation of women and Swedish supported development programmes in Ethiopia, Mozambique, Angola, Guinea Bissau, Cape Verde, Zimbabwe, South Africa, Lesotho, Botswana, Zambia, Tanzania and Kenya. Provides maps, basic statistics and photographs for each country.

Kershaw, G. (1975/6) 'The changing roles of men and women in the Kikuyu family by socio-economic strata', *Rural Africana*, **29**, 20–9
Describes gender-based changes in the decision-making roles among the Kikuyu of Kenya using data gathered between 1955 and 1962. Finds that women's status and autonomy in decision-making are related to landholding rights.

Kruks, S. and Wisner, B. (1984) 'The state, the party and the female peasantry in Mozambique', *Journal of Southern African Studies*, **11** (1), 106–27
Looks at changes in the position of rural women from oppression under Portuguese colonialism to limited improvement under post-independence socialism. Suggests that a prerequisite for any resolution to the crisis of peasant production is for FRELIMO to focus on women as producers as well as reproducers.

Little, K. (1973) *African women in towns*, Cambridge: Cambridge University Press
While analysing the migrational, economic and political roles of women the author puts particular emphasis on their search for new relationships with men and stresses their desire for a significant place in the new urban societies.

Mbilinyi, M. (ed.) (1984) *Cooperation or exploitation? Experiences of women's initiatives in Tanzania*, Geneva: ILO
Seven field studies of female income earning activities in Tanzania – co-operative, individual, rural, ruban.

Mickelwait, D. R., Riegelman, M. A. and Sweet, C. F. (1976) *Women in rural development: a survey of the roles of women in Ghana, Lesotho, Kenya, Nigeria, Bolivia, Paraguay and Peru*, Boulder: Westview Press
A composite report on the current and potential roles of African and Latin American rural women based on field research in seven countries.

Nelson, N. (ed.) (1981) *African women in the development process*, London: Frank Cass

A collection of studies mainly concerned with the effect of development on patterns of female labour.

Obbo, C. (1980) *African women: their struggle for economic independence*, London: Zed Press

A case study of social change in East Africa focusing on women, especially rural–urban migrants. Presents a detailed analysis of the attitudes of rural and urban women to their relationships with men. Examines their occupations and survival strategies. Emphasizes the changes women are bringing about in their own lives.

Palmer, I. (1979) 'New official ideas on women and development', *Bulletin of the Institute for Development studies*, **10** (3), 42–53

A review of the implications for women of ILO country mission reports and urban studies with a critique of their recommendations.

Safilios-Rothschild, C. (1985) 'The persistence of women's invisibility in agriculture: theoretical and policy lessons from Lesotho and Sierra Leone', *Economic Development and Cultural Change*, **33** (2), 299–317

Strong institutional mechanisms maintain the invisibility of women's work and income contributions. Makes a powerful plea for a full and proper recognition of the agricultural work of women for development planning purposes.

Stamp, E. (1975/6) 'Perceptions of change and economic activity among Kikuyu women of Mitero, Kenya', *Rural Africana*, **29**, 173–94

Cash crops and land consolidation disrupted subsistence activity but despite an increased work burden on women due to the withdrawal of male labour, there were also benefits in terms of increased female autonomy.

Staudt, K. A. (1978) 'Agricultural productivity gaps: a case study of male preference in government policy implementation', *Development and Change*, **9** (3), 439–57

An allegedly successful irrigation project failed to take into account the division of labour and responsibilities by gender and thus had detrimental effects on women.

Wilkinson, R. C. (1983) 'Migration in Lesotho: some comparative aspects, with particular reference to the role of woman', *Geography*, **68** (3), 208–24

Examines the spatial features and gender differentiation of flows of internal and external migrants and suggests a functional link between them.

Youssef, M., Buvinic, M. and Kudan, A. (1979) *Women in migration: a Third World focus*, Washington DC: Women in Development Office

Analyses migration in east, north, central and southern Africa. Women between the ages of 50 and 54 are found to outnumber male migrants everywhere except in southern Africa but little attention has been paid to autonomous female migration.

Asia

Bagchi, D. (1981) 'Women in agrarian transition in India: impact of development', *Geografiska Annaler*, **63B**, 109–17
Looks at the impact of agricultural modernization on the status and roles of rural women in India.

Beck, L. and Keddie, N. (eds.) (1978) *Women in the Muslim world*, Cambridge: Harvard University Press
The 33 papers cover legal and socio-economic change, status, fertility, the historical perspective, case studies, ideology, religion and ritual; material ranges from Morocco to China.

Binswanger, H. P., Evenson, R. E., Florencio, C. A. and White, B. N. F. (eds.) (1980) *Rural household studies in Asia*, Singapore: Singapore University Press
Case studies of population and employment in South-East Asia: develops the New Household Economics.

Clark, A. (1983) 'Limitations on female life chances in rural central Gujarat', *Indian Economic and Social History Review*, **20** (1), 1–26
A historical analysis of changing social structure in rural Gujarat, India. Female survival is linked to the hierarchical marriage system, caste endogamy and economic security which are in turn related to family status.

Croll, E. (1979) *Women in rural development: the people's republic of China*, Geneva: ILO
Examines the improvement in the lives of Chinese women brought about by the revolutionary changes in China's politics and rural economy. Despite Mao's dictum 'What a man can do, a women can also do', there is still discrimination in the labour market.

Dyson, T. and Moore, M. P. (1983) 'Kinship structure, female autonomy and demographic behaviour', *Population and Development Review*, **9** (1), 35–60
Seeks an explanation for regional variation in the sex ratio in South Asia by examining fertility and mortality rates within their socio-cultural context. Sex ratios are presented as a function of female autonomy.

El Saadawi, N. (1980) *The hidden face of Eve: women in the Arab world*, London: Zed Press
An Islamic analysis, ascribing class and sex dominance to historical developments.

Gough, K. (1981) *Rural society in south east India*, London: Cambridge University Press
Studies political and economic change in two villages in Thanjavur, Tamil Nadu. Examines the sexual division of labour and the type of work open to women at different ages from different social groups. The means by which women are politically represented and the part they play in the political process are also analysed. Women's economic and political situations are reinforced by forms of oppression and the changing marriage and inheritance systems.

Kahn, S. A. and Bilques, F. (1978) 'The environment, attitude and activities of rural women: A case study of Jhok Sayal', *Sociologia Ruralis*, **XVIII** (2/3), 177–96
A detailed case study of women's daily and annual work patterns.

Levinson, J. F. (1971) *Morinda: an economic analysis of malnutrition among young children in rural India*, Cambridge, Mass.: Cornell/MIT International Nutrition Policy Series
Important nutrition study in Morinda, Punjab, examining malnutrition from a socio-economic perspective in the high caste and wealthier Jats, compared with the low caste, and generally poorer Ramdasias. Nutritional status of males and females in each socio-economic group was related to differences in food intake and local beliefs about weaning.

McGee, T. G. (1985) 'Women workers or working women? A case study of female workers in Malaysia', in Armstrong, Warwick and McGee, T. G., *Theatres of accumulation: case studies of Asian and Latin American Urbanization*, London and New York: Methuen
Looks at the development of Free Export Zones in Asia where young, rural women make up 70 per cent of the employees. Suggests that an appreciation of consumption patterns may be essential to a broader understanding of the formation of a female proletariat in Asia.

Manderson, L. (ed.) (1983) 'Women's work and women's roles: economics and everyday life in Indonesia, Malaysia and Singapore', *Development Studies Centre Monograph* **32**, Australia National University
Two themes run through these papers: the variety of women's situation (according to country, religion and class, for example), and the consistency with which most non-elite women tend to be increasingly marginalized and circumscribed in economic life.

Miller, B. (1981) *The endangered sex: neglect of female children in rural north India*, Ithaca, New York: Cornell University Press
A cross-sectional, regional analysis of the sex ratios from the 1961 census of India data. Female social status is inferred from the sex ratio and linked to the nature of agricultural production, inheritance practices, and the demand for female labour.

Nelson, N. (1979) *Why has development neglected rural women?*, Oxford: Pergamon
The purpose of this review of South Asian literature on rural women is to encourage a widening of research in order to convince planners that the potential of women is largely untapped in rural development projects. It focuses both on existing knowledge and literature and on the question to be asked in the future.

Omvedt, G. (1980) *We will smash this prison: Indian women in struggle*, London, Zed Press
Documents the conditions of different groups: agricultural labour, college students, street sweepers.

Papanek, H. (1971) 'Purdah in Pakistan: seclusion in modern occupations

---

for women', *Journal of Marriage and the Family*, **33** (3), 517–30
One of the best theoretical statements available on purdah, which is characterized as a system of separate worlds and symbolic shelter.

Sharma, U. (1980) *Women, work and property in north west India*
London: Tavistock
Examines the subordination of women in Himachal Pradesh and Punjab, India by looking at local concepts of morality and immorality, honour and dishonour. Describes these concepts as they are manifested in society through, for example, spatial perceptions of territory, the sexual division of labour, and exchange relations between males and females, both within and between households.

Whyte, R. O. and Whyte, P. (1982) *The women of rural Asia*, Boulder, Colorado: Westview Press
Focuses on gender divisions of labour and women's time budgets.

Zeidenstein, S. and L. (1974) 'Observations on the status of women in Bangladesh', *World Education Issue*, **2** (July), New York: World Education Inc.
Reports on a 1973 study of rural and urban women in Bangladesh. Reviews private and government efforts to improve women's status through literacy programmes, health and family-planning services.

Latin America

Arizpe, L. (1982) 'Women and development in Latin America and the Caribbean. Lessons from the seventies and hopes for the future', *Development Dialogue*, 1–2, 74–84
The lessons are that neither independence nor socialism automatically improves the position of women, the hopes that there are practical policy issues which can be addressed.

Barrios de Chungara, D. with Viezzer, M. (1978) *Let me speak. Testimony of Domitila, a woman of the Bolivian mines*, New York: Monthly Review Press
Domitila, a Bolivian Indian woman, recounts her life story and her role in the struggle of the tin miners for better working conditions and wages.

Berleant-Schiller, R. (1977) 'Production and division of labour in a West Indian peasant community', *American Ethnologist*, 4, 253–72
Describes the gender division of labour in the traditional agricultural community of Barbuda.

Bronstein, A. (1982) *The triple struggle: Latin American peasant women*, London: WOW Campaigns Ltd
Uses the life stories and comments of individual Latin American women to describe the triple struggle they face to free themselves from the dependence of underdevelopment, the poverty of the peasant and finally the oppression of being a woman in a male-dominated society.

Christopherson, S. (1983) 'Female labour force participation and urban

structure: The case of Ciudad Juarez, Mexico', *Revista Geográfica*, **97**, 83–5
Examines the position of young female workers in the industries established in the Mexican border zone.

Clarke, E. (1957) *My mother who fathered me*, London: Allen and Unwin
Identifies several family types in three communities in Jamaica. Looks at the mother–child relationship in female-headed households.

Cunningham, S. (1983) 'Labour turnover and women's work: evidence for Brazil', *Bulletin of Latin American Studies*, **2** (2), 93–103
Shows how women occupy the lowest paid jobs in modern Brazilian industry and have a high turnover rate.

Deere, C. D. (1977) 'Changing social relations of production and Peruvian peasant women's work', *Latin American Perspectives*, **IV** (1/2), 48–69
Evidence from a historical case study is used to illustrate the way in which the development of capitalism affects the economic participation and social status of women. Concludes that the passage from the hacienda system to capitalist development is a dialectical process of social transition, based on the resolution of contradictions, in which the socio-economic condition of women both improves and deteriorates. Although exploited as wage earners, women were also oppressed under servile relations of production.

Elmendorf, M. (1977) 'Mexico: the many worlds of women', in Giele, J. Z. and Smock, A. C. (eds.) *Women: roles and status in eight countries*, New York: John Wiley, 127–72
Overview of the position of women in Mexico from pre-Columbian times to the present, embracing cross-class and cross-cultural perspectives.

Harris, O. (ed.) (1983) 'Latin American women', *Minority Rights Group Report*, **57**
A short, popular collection of high quality.

Henry, F. and Wilson, P. (1975) 'The status of women in Caribbean societies: an overview of their social, economic and sexual roles', *Social and Economic Studies*, **24** (2), 165–98.
Reviews a wide range of literature on female roles in the Caribbean and concludes that a double standard of sexuality exists.

Henshall, J. (1984) 'Gender versus ethnic pluralism in Caribbean agriculture', in Clarke, C., Ley, D. and Peach, C. (eds.) *Geography and ethnic pluralism*, London: George Allen and Unwin, 173–90
Compares the roles of Afro-Caribbean women in Nevis and East Indian women in Trinidad working in small-scale agriculture.

Holt-Seeland (1982) *Women of Cuba*, Westport, Connecticut: Lawrence Hill and Co. Inc.
A review of the pre- and post-revolutionary position of women illustrated by life histories of six Cuban women.

Horst, O. (ed.) (1981) *Papers in Latin American geography in honor of Lucia C. Harrison*, Muncie, Indiana: Conference of Latin American Geographers

Includes five research papers on Central America and the Caribbean focusing on migration, farming, national parks and folk medicine. It also has two commentaries on the role of women in the development of Latin American geography.

Latin American and Caribbean Women's Collective (1980) *Slaves of Slaves*, London: Zed Press
Based on meetings held in Paris between 1972 and 1977. In the first part of the book a historical summary of the women's movement in Latin America is provided and this is followed by case studies from 12 countries of the region.

Leon de Leal, M. (1979) 'Women and agrarian capitalism', *Signs*, **5** (1), 60–77
Suggests the analysis of female labour in the productive unit highlights the importance of the participation of women. Links changes in the regulations of production and in class formation to the sexual division of labour in the production and reproduction processes of the peasant household.

Lisansky, J. (1979) 'Women in the Brazilian frontier', *Latinamericanist*, **15** (1), 1–4
Focuses on the impact of land conflicts in the Brazilian Amazon on women over the last two decades. As peasant families make the change from farming to life in a frontier town economic pressure contributes to increased instability of all types of marriage unions.

Martin, L. (1983) *Daughters of the conquistadores: women of the viceroyalty of Peru*, Albuquerque, University of New Mexico Press
In 1498 the first 30 women were licensed by Queen Isabella to join Columbus's third voyage. This book shows that from the beginning women played a significant role in the colonial history of Peru. Shows the great popularity of seventeenth- and eighteenth-century nunneries which gave women more power and independence than those allowed under the system of male control by father and husband of the secular system.

Moser, C. (1981) 'Surviving in the suburbios', *Institute of Development Studies Bulletin*, **12** (3), 54–62
Case study of a low-income *barrio* in Guayaquil, Ecuador, discussing the nature of women's economic and domestic survival strategies, and their implications for reinforcing the class structure.

Moser, C. and Young, K. (1981) 'Women of the working poor', *Institute of Development Studies Bulletin*, **12** (3), 54–62
Shows how structures of capital accumulation and patriarchy are mutually reinforcing and calls for recognition of class and gender inequalities by policy-makers.

Nash, J. and Safa, H. (eds.) (1980) *Sex and class in Latin America. Women's perspectives on politics, economics and the family in the Third World*, New York: J. F. Bergin Publishers Inc.
Sixteen papers, including five on Brazil and three on Chile, dealing with the situation of women in relation to the family and ideological

subordination, labour force participation and productive roles, and
political mobilization.

Randall, M. (1982) *Sandino's daughters: testimonies of Nicaraguan
women in struggle*, London: Zed Press
Vivid description of the important role played by women in the
Nicaraguan revolution.

Young, K. (1978) 'Modes of appropriation and the sexual division of
labour: a case study from Oaxaca, Mexico', in Kuhn, A. and Wolpe,
A-M. (eds.) *Feminism and Materialism*, London: Routledge and Kegan
Paul.
The study examines the relationship between women's productive and
reproductive roles through change in two communities, 1870 to 1970,
under capitalist development. The socialization process under which
women accepted exclusion is also considered.

References and selected bibliography

Abdullah, M. (1983) *Dimensions of intra household food and nutrient allocation: a study of a Bangladesh village*, Ph.D. thesis (unpublished), London School of Hygiene and Tropical Medicine.

Abdullah, M. and Wheeler, E. F. (1985) 'Seasonal variations and the intra-household distribution of food in a Bangladesh village', *American Journal of Clinical Nutrition*, **41**, 1305–13

Acharya, M. (1979) 'Statistical profile of Nepalese women: a critical review', *The Status of Women in Nepal*, **1** (1), Kathmandu: CEDA

Adeyokunnu, T. C. (1976) 'Agricultural development, education and rural women in Nigeria', unpublished paper presented at the *Conference on Nigerian Women and Development in Relation to Changing Family Structure*, University of Ibadan

Agarwal, B. (1984) 'Rural women and the high yielding variety rice technology', *Economic and Political Weekly*, Review of Agriculture, **19** (13), 31 March

Agarwal, B. (1986) 'Women, poverty and agricultural growth in India', *The Journal of Peasant Studies*, **13** (4), July

Agency for Industrial Mission (1976) *Another blanket* (2nd edn), Netherlands

Ali, M. D. (1968) 'Malay customary law and the family', in Buxbaum, D. C. (ed.) *Family law and customary law in Asia: A contemporary legal perspective*, The Hague: Martinus Nijhoff, 181–201

Allen, N. (1976) 'Approaches to illness in the Nepalese hills', in Londen, J. B. (ed.) *Social anthropology of medicine*, London: Academic Press

Allison, C. (1985) 'Women, land, labour and survival: getting some basic facts straight', *Bulletin of the Institute of Development Studies*, 16 (3), 24–30

Andrews, A. C. (1982) 'Towards a status-of-women index', *Professional Geographer*, **34** (1), 24–31

Anker, R. (1980) *Research on women's roles and demographic change: survey questionnaires for households, women, men and communities*, working document for restricted circulation, Geneva: ILO

Anker, R. (1982) 'Introduction' in Anker *et al.* (eds.)

Anker, R., Buvinic, M. and Youssef, N. M. (eds.) (1982) *Women's roles and population trends in the Third World*, London: Croom Helm

Antonov, A. M. (1947) 'Children born during the siege of Leningrad in 1942', *Journal of Pediatrics*, **30**, 250

Antrobus, P. (1984) 'Human development: new approaches and applications', address to the *Annual Conference for Non-Governmental Organisations on 'New Approaches to Development: Building a Just World'*, United Nations Headquarters, New York.

Antrobus, P. (1985) 'Lessons from the decade: a retrospective of practice', in Gallin, R. S. and Spring, A. (eds.) *Women creating wealth: transforming economic development*, Washington DC: Association for Women in Development, 15–20

Appadurai, A. (1981) 'Gastropolitics in South Asia', *American Ethnologist*, **8** (3), 494–511

Appadurai, A. (1984) 'How moral is South Asia's economy? – a review article', *Journal of Asian Studies*, **43** (3), 431–97

Aries, P. (1962) *Centuries of childhood: A social history of family life*, New York: Vintage Books

Arizpe, L. (1977) 'Women in the informal labour sector: The case of Mexico City', in Wellesley Editorial Committee (ed.) *Women and national development: the complexities of change*, Chicago: University of Chicago Press, 25–37

Arizpe, L. (1982) 'Women and development in Latin America and the Caribbean. Lessons from the seventies and hopes for the future', *Development Dialogue*, **1–2**, 74–84

Bagchi, D. (1981) 'Women in agrarian transition in India: impact of development', *Geografiska Annaler*, **63B**, 109–17

Bagchi, D. (1982) 'Female roles in agricultural modernization: an Indian case study', *WID Working Papers*, no. 10, East Lansing: Michigan State University

Balfour, M. I. (1938) 'The effect of occupation on pregnancy and neonatal mortality', *Public Health*, **51**, 106–11

Bandaranage, A. (1984) 'Women in development: Liberalism, Marxism and Marxist–Feminism', *Development and Change*, **15**, 495–515

Bangladesh Bureau of Statistics (1983) *Khulna district statistics*, Dhaka: Government of the People's Republic of Bangladesh

Bardhan, P. K. (1974) 'On life and death questions', *Economic and Political Weekly*, **9**, August

Bardhan, K. (1984) 'Work patterns and social differentiation: rural women in West Bengal', in Binswanger and Rosensweig (eds.), 184–207

Bardhan, P. K. (1984) *Land, labor and rural poverty*, Delhi: Oxford University Press

Barnes, D. F. and Allen, J. (1981) 'Deforestation and social forestry in developing countries', *Resources*, **66**, Washington

Barrell, R. A. E. and Rowland, M. G. M. (1979) 'Infant foods as a potential source of diarrhoeal illness in rural West Africa', *Transactions of the Royal Society of Tropical Medicine and Hygiene*, **73** (1), 85–90

Barrett, M. and McIntosh, M. (1980) 'The family wage: some problems for socialists and feminists', *Capital and Class*, **11** (summer)

Basham, A. L. (1954) *The wonder that was India: a survey of the culture of the Indian sub-continent before the coming of the Muslims*. London: Sidgwick and Jackson

Bay, E. (ed.) (1982) *Women and work in Africa*, Boulder: Westview

Beavon, K. S. O. and Rogerson, C. M. (1986) 'The changing role of women in the urban informal sector of Johannesburg, South Africa', in Drakakis-Smith, D. (ed.) *Urbanization and the developing world*, London: Croom Helm.

Becker, G. G. (1965) 'A theory of the allocation of time', *The Economic Journal*, **80** (299), 493–517

Beneria, L. (1981) 'Conceptualizing the labour force: the underestimation of women's economic activity', in Nelson, N. (ed.), 10–28

Beneria, L. (1982) 'Accounting for women's work', in Beneria, L. (ed.)

Beneria, L. (ed.) (1982) *Women and development: the sexual division of labor in rural societies*, New York: Praeger

Bennett, L. (1976) 'Sex and motherhood among the Brahmins and Chetris of East-Central Nepal', *Contributions to Nepalese Studies*, **3**, special issue, 1–52

Bennett, L. (1979) 'Tradition and change in the legal status of Nepalese women', *The status of women in Nepal*, **1** (2), Kathmandu: CEDA

Bennholdt-Thomsen, V. (1981) 'Subsistence production and extended reproduction', in Young *et al.* (eds.)

Benton, J. M. (1984) 'The changing position of Aymara women in Bolivia's Lake Titicaca region', in Henshall Momsen and Townsend, 86–91

Berkner, L. K. (1977) 'Peasant household organization and demographic change in Lower Saxony (1689–1766)', in Lee, R. D. *et al.* (eds.), *Population patterns in the past*, New York: Academic Press, 19–51

Bernstein, H., (1977), 'Notes on capital and peasantry', *Review of African Political Economy*, **10**, 60–73

Bernstein, H. (1982) *Migrant cocoa-farmers in southern Ghana*, Cambridge: Cambridge University Press

Bernstein, H. (1984) 'Notes on capital and peasantry', in Harriss, J. (ed.) *Rural Development*, London: Hutchinson

Binswanger, H. P. (1977) *The economics of tractors in South Asia: an analytical review*, Hyderabad: ADC/ICRISAT Monograph

Binswanger, H. P., Evenson, R. E., Florencio, C. A. and White, B. N. F. (eds.) (1980) *Rural household studies in Asia*, Singapore: Singapore University Press

Binswanger, H. P. and Rosensweig, M. R. (eds.) (1984) *Contractual arrangements, employment and wages in rural labor markets in Asia*, New Haven: Yale University Press

Binswanger, H. P. and Rosensweig, M. R. (1984) 'Contractual arrangements, employment and wages in rural labor markets: a critical review', in Binswanger and Rosensweig (eds.), 1–40

Binswanger, H. P. and Shetty, S. V. R. (1977) 'Economic aspects of weed control in semi arid tropical areas in India', *Occasional Paper*, no. 13, Hyderabad: Economics Program, ICRISAT

Birdsall, N. and McGreevey, W. P. (1983) 'Women, poverty and development', in Buvinic *et al*. (eds.), 3–13

Black, R. E., Brown, K. H., Becker, S., Abdul Alim, A. R. M. and Merson, M. H. (1982) 'Contamination of weaning foods and transmission of enterotoxigenic Escherichia coli diarrhoea in children in Bangladesh', *Transactions of the Royal Society of Tropical Medicine and Hygiene*, **76** (2), 259–64

Black, R., Brown, K. H., Beck, S. (1984) 'Malnutrition is a determining factor in diarrhoeal duration, but not incidence among young children in a longitudinal study in rural Bangladesh', *American Journal of Clinical Nutrition*, **37**, 89–94

Blaikie, P., Cameron, J. and Seddon, B. (1979) *The struggle for basic needs in Nepal*, Paris: OECD

Blaikie, P. *et al*. (1980) *Nepal in crisis*, Delhi: Oxford University Press

Blanchet, T. (1984) *Women, pollution and marginality: meanings and rituals of birth in rural Bangladesh*, Dhaka, Bangladesh: University Press

Bleiberg, F. M., Brun, T. A., Goihman, S. and Gouba, E. (1980) 'Duration of activities and energy expenditure of female farmers in dry and rainy seasons in Upper Volta', *British Journal of Nutrition*, **43**, 71–82

Blumberg, R. L. (1976) 'Fairy tales and facts: economy, family, fertility and the female', in Tinker, I., Bo Bramsen, M. and Buvinic, M. (eds.), *Women and world development*, New York: Praeger, 12–21

Blumberg, R. L. (1984) 'A general theory of gender stratification', in Collins, R. (ed.), *Sociological Theory 1984*, San Francisco and London: Jossey-Bass, 23–101

Board, C. (1976) 'The spatial structure of labour migration', in Smith, D. M. (ed.), 'Separation in South Africa: People and policies', Queen Mary College, Department of Geography, *Occasional Papers*, no. 6, 63–76

Boesen, J. (1979) 'Tanzania from ujamaa to villagisation', in Mwansasu, B. and Pratt, C. (eds.), *Towards socialism in Tanzania*, Toronto and Dar es Salaam: University of Toronto and Tanzania Publishing House

Bollinger, W. *et al*. (ed.) (1979) *Women in Latin America: an anthology*, Riverside, California: Latin American Perspectives

Boserup, E. (1970) *Women's role in economic development*, London and Baltimore: Allen and Unwin

Boulding, E. (1977) *Women in the twentieth century world*, New York: John Wiley and Sons

Boulding, E. (1983) 'Measures of women's work in the Third World', in Buvinic *et al*. (eds.), 286–99

Boulding, E., Nus, S., Carson, D. and Greenstein, M. (1976) *Handbook of international data on women*, New York: Halsted Press

Bourque, S. and Warren, K. B. (1981) *Women of the Andes*, Ann Arbor: University of Michigan Press

Bourque, S. and Warren, K. B. (1981) 'Rural women and development planning in Peru', in Black, N. and Cottrell, A. B. (eds.), *Women –*

World change: equity issues in development, Beverly Hills: Sage Publications Inc.

Brain, J. L. (1976) 'Less than second-class: women in rural settlement schemes in Tanzania', in Hafkin, N. J. and Bay, E. G. (eds.), *Women in Africa*, Stanford: Stanford University Press

Bridges, J. C. (1980) 'The Mexican family', in Das, M. S. and Jesser, C. J. (eds.), *The family in Latin America*, New Delhi: Vikas, 295–334

Bromley, R. (1982) 'Working in the streets: survival strategy, necessity or unavoidable evil?', in Gilbert, A. in association with Hardoy, J. E. and Ramirez, R. (eds.), *Urbanisation in contemporary Latin America: critical approaches to the analysis of urban issues*, Chichester: John Wiley, 59–77

Bronstein, A. (1982) *The tripple struggle: Latin American peasant women*, London: War on Want Campaigns

Brown, J. K. (1970) 'A note on the division of labor by sex', *American Anthropolgist*, **72**, 1074–8

Brown, J. K. (1975) 'Iroquois women: an ethnohistoric note', in Reiter (ed.)

Brown, N. L. (ed.) (1978) *Renewable energy resources and applications in the developing world*, Colorado: Westview Press

Brown, N. L. (1980) 'Renewable energy resources for developing countries', *Annual Review of Energy*, **5**, Hawaii: East West Centre

Browning, H. L. and Roberts, B. (1980) 'Urbanisation, sectoral transformation and the utilisation of labour in Latin America', *Comparative Urban Research*, **8** (1), 86–104

Brun, T. A., Bleiberg, F. M. and Goihman, S. (1981) 'Energy expenditures of male farmers in dry and rainy seasons in Upper Volta', *British Journal of Nutrition*, **45**, 65–75

Bryceson, D. F. (1980), 'The proletarianization of women in Tanzania', *Review of African Political Economy*, **17**, 4–27

Bryceson, D. F. and Kirimbai, M. (eds.) (1980), 'Subsistence or beyond? Money-earning activities of women in rural Tanzania', Dar es Salaam: UDSM, Bureau of Resource Assessment and Land Use Planning and UWT, *BRALUP Research Report*, **45**

Bryceson, D. F. and Mbilinyi, M. (1978) 'The changing role of Tanzanian women in production: from peasants to proletarians', Dar es Salaam: UDSM, Bureau of Resource Assessment and Land Use Planning, *BRALUP Service Paper*, 78/5

Buechler, H. C. (1980) *The masked media: Aymara fiestas and social interaction in the Bolivian highlands*, The Hague: Mouton

Bujra, J. M. (1978) 'Introduction: female solidarity and the sexual division of labour', in Caplan, P. and Bujra, J. M. (eds.), *Women united, women divided*, London: Tavistock Publications

Bukh, J. (1979) *The village woman in Ghana*, Uppsala: Scandinavian Institute of African Studies

Burfisher, M. E. and Horenstein, N. R. (1985) *Sex roles in the Nigerian Giv farm household. Women's roles and gender differences in development. Cases for planners*. West Hartford: Kumarian Press

Burley, J. (1982) 'Wood scarcity forces poor to change basic life patterns', *UN University Newsletter, Tokyo*, **7** (1), 3–4

Burton, M. L., Brudner, L. and White, D. R. (1977) 'A model of the sexual division of labor', *American Ethnologist*, **4** (2), 227–51

Buvinic, M. and Youssef, N. H., with Van Elm, B. (1978) *Women-headed households: the ignored factor in development planning*, Washington DC: Office of Women in Development, Agency for International Development

Buvinic, M., Lycette, M. A. and McGreevey, W. P. (eds.) (1983) *Women and poverty in the Third World*, Baltimore and London: Johns Hopkins University Press

Buxbaum, D. C. (1968) 'Islam and customary law in the Malaysian legal context', in Buxbaum, D. C. (ed.), *Family law and customary law in Asia: a contemporary legal perspective*, The Hague: Martinus Nijhoff

Byrne, P. R. and Ontiveros, S. K. (eds.) (1985) *Women in the Third World: An historical bibliography*, Research Guides Series no. 15, ABC: Clio

Cain, M. T. (1977) 'The economic activities of children in a village in Bangladesh', *Population and Development Review*, **3**, 3

Cain, M. T., Syed, R. K. and Nahar, S. (1979) 'Class, patriarchy and women's work in Bangladesh', *Population and Development Review*, **5**, 3

Cain, M. T. (1980) 'The economic activities of children in a village in Bangladesh', in Binswanger et al. (eds.), 218–47

Calcutta Metropolitan Development Authority (1980) *Health and socio-economic survey of the Calcutta metropolitan development area*, Calcutta: Indian Statistical Institute/CMBA

Caldwell, J. C. (1976) 'Towards a restatement of demographic transition theory', *Population and Development Review*, **2**, 321–66

Caldwell, J. C. (1978) 'A theory of fertility: from high plateau to destabilisation', *Population and Development Review*, **4**, 553–77

Caplan, P. (1981) 'Development policies in Tanzania – some implications for women', *Journal of Development Studies*, **17** (3), 98–108

Carlstein, T. (1982) *Time resources, society and ecology*, vol. 1, *Preindustrial societies*, London: Allen & Unwin

Carr, M. (1983) 'The long walk home', *Appropriate Technology*, **10** (1), 17–19

Carroll, T. F. (1983) *Women, religion and development in the Third World*, New York: Praeger

Casinader, R. A. (1983) 'Women workers in Sri Lanka Free Trade Zones', *Voice of Women*, Colombo

Cebotarev, E. A. (1982) 'Research on rural women: an international perspective', *Resources for Feminist Research*, **II** (1), 28–31

Cecelski, E. (1984) *The rural energy crisis, women's work and family welfare: perspectives and approaches to action*, Geneva: ILO

Chambers, R. (1979) 'Health, agricultural and rural poverty: why seasons matter', Institute of Development Studies, *Discussion paper*, 148, Sussex

Chambers, R., Longhurst, R. and Pacey, A. (eds.) (1981) *Seasonal dimensions to rural poverty*, London: Frances Pinter

Chan Lean Heng, Young, M. L. and Salih, K. (1983) 'Women workers in Malaysia: TNC's and social contradictions', unpublished paper presented at the *Conference on Industrialization and the Labour Process in Southeast Asia*, Copenhagen, 26–28 August

Chaney, E. M. (1983) *Scenarios of hunger in the Caribbean: migration, decline of smallholder agriculture and the feminization of farming*, Working Paper, 18, East Lansing: Michigan State University

Chant, S. (1984a) *Las Olvidadas: a study of women, housing and family structure in Querétaro, Mexico*, unpublished Ph.D. dissertation, University College, London

Chant, S. (1984b) 'Household labour and self-help housing in Querétaro, Mexico', *Boletin de Estudios Latinoamericanos y del Caribe*, **37**

Chant, S., (1984c) 'Women and housing: a study of household labour in Querétaro, Mexico', in Momsen and Townsend (eds.), 1–39

Chant, S. (1985) 'Family formation and female roles in Querétaro, Mexico', *Bulletin of Latin American Research*, **4** (1), 17–32

Chattopadhyay, M. (1982) 'Role of female labour in Indian agriculture', *Social Scientist*, **110**, 43–54

Chaudhuri, P. (1982) *Nutrition and health problems and policies: women and children in India*, British Society for Population Studies, Oxford Conference, mimeo quoted in Lipton (1983a)

Chen, L. C. (1982) 'Where have the women gone?', *Economic and Political Weekly*, March

Chen, L. C., Chowdhury, A. K. M. A. and Huffman, S. L. (1980) 'Anthropometric assessment of energy protein malnutrition and subsequent risk of mortality among preschool aged children', *American Journal of Clinical Nutrition*, **33**, 1836–45

Chen, L. C., Huq, E. and D'Souza, S. (1981) 'Sex bias in the family allocation of food and health care in rural Bangladesh', *Population and Development Review*, **7** (1), 55–70

Chen, L. C., Huq, E. and Huffman, S. L. (1981) 'A prospective study of the risk of diarrhoeal diseases according to the nutritional status of children', *American Journal of Epidemiology*, **114** (2), 284–92

Chinnappa, B. N. and Silva, W. P. T. (1977) 'Impact of the cultivation of HYVs of paddy on employment and income', in Farmer (ed.), 204–44

Chodorow, N. (1974) 'Family structure and feminine personality', in Rosaldo, M. Z. and Lamphere, L. (eds.), 43–66

Chowdhury, A. K. M. N., Alam, M. N. and Ali, A. M. K. (1981) 'Demography morbidity and mortality in a rural community in Bangladesh', *Bangladesh Medical Journal*, **7** (1), 22–39

Christopherson, S. (1983) 'Female labour force participation and urban structure: the case of Cuidad Juarez, Mexico.' *Revista Geográfica*, **97**, 83–5

Chulasai, L. et al. (1983) *Family labour, hired labour and employment* linkages in rural Thailand: a case study of Northern Thailand, Chiang Mai: Chiangmai University

Clark, A. (1983) 'Limitations on female life chances in rural central Gujurat', Indian Economic and Social History Review, 20 (1), 1–26

Clarke, E. (1966) My mother who fathered me (2nd edn), London: George Allen & Unwin

Clarke, J. I. and Kosinski, L. A. (eds.) (1985) Population and Development Projects in Africa, Cambridge: Cambridge University Press

Cohen, R. B. (1981) 'The new international division of labor, multinational corporations and urban hierarchy', in Dear, M. and Scott, A. J. (eds.), Urbanization and urban planning in capitalist society, London: Methuen, 287–315

Colclough, C. (1980) 'Some aspects of labour use in Southern Africa: problems and policies', Institute of Development Studies Bulletin, 11 (4), 29–39

Collins, R. (1971) 'A conflict theory of sexual stratification', Social Problems, 19, 3–21

Collins, R. (1975) Conflict sociology: toward an explanatory science, New York: Academic Press

Comitas, L. (1973) 'Occupational multiplicity in rural Jamaica', in Comitas, L. and Lowenthal, D. (eds.), Work and family life: West Indian perspectives, New York: Doubleday Anchor; 156–78

Connolly, P. (1981) 'El desempleo, subempleo y la pauperización urbana', paper presented at the Third Reunion of the Grupo Latinomericano de Investigacion, Mexico City, July 27–31

Conor, J. (1977) The market power of multinationals: a quantitative analysis of US corporations in Brazil and Mexico, New York: Praeger

Cormack, M. (1961) The Hindu woman, Bombay: Asia Publishing House

Coulson, A. (ed.) (1979) African socialism in practice: the Tanzanian experience, Nottingham: Spokesman

Coulson, A. (1982) Tanzania: a political economy, Oxford: Clarendon

Cuales, S. M. (1982) 'Accumulation and gender relations in the flower industry in Colombia', Research in Political Economy, 5, 109–37

Cunningham, S. (1979) Brazilian industrial development since 1960: a study of planning, policy and spatial aspects with special reference to the southeast region, unpublished Ph.D. thesis, University of London

Cunningham, S. (1983) 'Labour turnover and women's work: evidence from Brazil', Bulletin of Latin American Research, 3 (1), 93–103

Cutler, P. and Shoham, J. (1985) Responses to drought of famine refugees in Sudan, mimeo, London School of Hygiene and Tropical Medicine (draft)

Dahlberg, F. (1981) 'Introduction', in Dahlberg (ed.), 1–33

Dahlberg, F. (ed.) (1981) Woman the gatherer, New Haven and London: Yale University Press

Dauber, R. and Cain, M. L. (1981) Women and technological change in developing countries, AAS Selected Symposium 53, Colorado: Westview Press

Das, M. S. and Jesser, C. J. (eds.) (1980) *The family in Latin America*, New Delhi: Vikas

Da Vanzo, J. and Lee, D. L. P. (1983) 'The compatibility of child care with market and non market activities: preliminary evidence from Malaysia', in Buvinic *et al*. (eds.)

de Barbieri, T. (1982) 'Familia y trabajo domestico', presented at *Domestic Groups, Family and Society*, Mexico City, 7–9 July

Deere, C. D. (1976) 'Rural women's subsistence production in the capitalist periphery', *The Review of Radical Political Economics*, **8** (1)

Deere, C. D. (1979) 'Rural women's subsistence production in the capitalist periphery', in Cohen, R., Gutkind P. C. W. and Brazier P. (eds.), *Peasants and Proletarians: the struggles of third world workers*, London: Hutchinson, 133–45

Deere, C. D. (1983) 'The allocation of familial labour and the formation of peasant household income in the Peruvian Sierra', in Buvinic *et al*. (eds.)

Deere, C. M., Humphries, J. and Leon de Leal, M. (1982) 'Class and historical analysis for the study of women and economic change', in Anker *et al*. (eds.), 87–116

Deere, C. D. and Leon de Leal, M. (1983) *Women in Andean agriculture*, Geneva: ILO

Dey, J. (1981) 'Gambian women: unequal partners in rice development projects?', in Nelson, N. (ed)

Dixon, R. (1978) *Rural women at work*, Baltimore; Johns Hopkins University Press

Dixon, R. (1983) 'Land, labour and the sex composition of the agricultural labour force: an international comparison', *Development and Change*, **14** (3), 347–72

Dixon-Mueller, R. (1985) *Women's work in Third World agriculture*, Geneva: ILO

Djamour, J. (1959) *Malay kinship and marriage in Singapore*, London: Athlone Press

Djukanovic, V. and Mach, E. P. (1975) *Alternative approaches to meeting basic health needs in developing countries*, Geneva: WHO

Dobbing, J. (1981) 'Maternal nutrition in pregnancy: eating for two?', *Early Human Development*, **5**, 113

Douglas, M. (1966) *Purity and danger*, London: Routledge & Kegan Paul

Doyal, L. (1981) *The political economy of health*, London: Pluto

D'Souza, V. S. (1975) 'Family status and female work participation', in de Souza, A, (ed.), *Women in contemporary India: traditional images and changing roles*, Delhi: Indian Social Institute/Manohar Publishing House, 29–141

DSS (1976) *Demographic sample survey*, Kathmandu: General Bureau of Statistics

Dumont, L. (1970) *Homo Hierarchicus*, London: Weidenfeld and Nicolson

Dumont, R. and Mottin, L. C. (1979) *Self-reliant rural development in*

Tanzania twelve years after Arusha Declaration on socialist lines, Dar es Salaam: draft report for president's office; typescript

Dumont, R. and Morrin, M. F. (1983) *Stranglehold on Africa*, London: André Deutsch

Durant, W. (1935) *The story of civilization*, New York: Simon and Schuster

Dyson, T. and Moore, M. P. (1983) 'Kinship structure, female autonomy and demographic behaviour', *Population and Development Review*, **9** (1), 35–60

Earthscan (1980) 'Water and sanitation for all?', *Earthscan Briefing Document*, **22**

Edholm, F., Harris, O. and Young, K. (1977) 'Conceptualising women', *Critique of Anthropology*, **9**

Elliot, C. M. (1977) 'Theories of development: an assessment', in Wellesley Editorial Committee, *Women and national development, the complexities of change*, Chicago: University of Chicago Press

Elmendorf, M. (1977) 'Mexico: the many worlds of women', in Giele, J. Z. and Smock, A. C. (eds.), *Women: roles and status in eight countries*, New York: John Wiley, 127–72

Elson, D. and Pearson, R. (1981) 'The subordination of women and the internationalisation of factory production', in Young *et al*. (eds.)

Elu de Lenero, M. del C. (1980) 'Women's work and fertility', in Nash and Safa (eds.), 45–68

Ember, C. R. (1983) 'The relative decline in women's contribution to agriculture with intensification', *American Anthropologist*, **85**, 285–304

Engels, F. (1884, 1942, 1972) *The origin of the family, private property and the state* (English translation of the 1884 German original), New York: International Publishers

Episcopada de Bolivia (1975) *Los problemas de la poblacion*, La Paz: Episcopado de Bolivia

Epstein, T. S. and Watts, R. A. (eds.) (1981) *The endless day: some case material on Asian rural women*, Oxford: Pergamon

Epstein, T. S. (1982) 'A social anthropological approach to women's roles and status in developing countries', in Anker *et al*. (eds.), 151–70

Erikson, E. H. (1970) *Gandhi's truth: on the origins of militant non violence*, London: Faber and Faber

Evenson, R. E. (1978) 'Time allocation in rural Philippine households', *American Journal of Agricultural Economics*, **60** (2), 322–30

Evers, H-D. (1981) 'The contribution of urban subsistence production to incomes in Jakarta', *Bulletin of Indonesian Economic Studies*, **17** (2), 89–96

Evers, H-D. *et al*. (1984) 'Subsistence reproduction: a framework for analysis', in Smith *et al*. (eds.), 23–36

Ewen, S. (1976) *Captains of consciousness: advertising and the social roots of the consumer culture*, New York: McGraw Hill Book Co.

Farmer, B. H. (ed.) (1977) *Green revolution?*, London: Macmillan

Fawcett, J. T., Khoo, S-E. and Smith, P. C. (1984) *Women in the cities of Asia: Migration and urban adaptation*, Boulder, Colorado: Westview

Figueroa, B. and Anderson, J. (1981) *Women in Peru*, London: Change

Firebrace, J. (1985) *Never kneel down: drought, development and liberation in Eritrea*, Nottingham: Spokesman

Firestone, S. (1970) *The dialectic of sex*, New York: William Morrow

Fisher, J. (1978) 'Homo Hierarchicus Nepalensis: a cultural subspecies', in Fisher, J. (ed.), *Himalayan anthropology*, The Hague: Mouton

Fleuret, P. and Fleuret, A. (1978) 'Fuelwood use in a peasant community: a Tanzanian case study', *Journal of Developing Areas*, **12**, 315–22

Fong, M. (1980) 'Victims of old-fashioned statistics', *Ceres* (May–June), 23–32

Food and Agriculture Organization (1984) *Tanzania. Fuelwood consumption and supply in semi-arid areas*, Rome: Food and Agricultural Organization of the United Nations

Foweraker, J. (1981) *A political economy of the pioneer frontier in Brazil from 1930 to the present day*, Cambridge: Cambridge University Press

Frank da Costa, J. (1982) 'The United Nations Conference on Science and Technology for Development. A personal view', *Mazingira*, **6** (1). 24–39

Franke, M. (1985) *Las mujeres en el Peru*, Lima: Flora Tristan, Centro de la Mujer Peruana

Fraser, H. (1981) *The coming of the mass market, 1850–1914*, Hamden, Conn.: Archon Books

Friedl, E. (1975) *Women and men: an anthropologist's view*, New York: Holt, Rinehart and Winston

Friedman, K. (1984) 'Households as income-pooling units', in Smith *et al.* (eds.), 37–55

Friedmann, J. and Wolff, G. (1982) 'Future of the World City', unpublished paper presented at *Conference on Urbanization and National Development*, East–West Center, Honolulu, Hawaii

Fröbel, F., Heinrichs, J. and Kreye, O. (1980) *The New International Division of Labour: structural unemployment in industrialized countries and industrialization in developing countries*, Cambridge: Cambridge University Press

Galletti, R., Baldwin, K. D. S. and Dina, I. O. (1956) *Nigerian cocoa farmers: an economic survey of Yoruba cocoa farming families*, London: Greenwood Press

García, B., Muñoz, H. and de Oliveira, O. (1982) *Hogares y trabajadores en la ciudad de Mexico*, Mexico: UNAM

Garrow, J. S. (1981) *Treat obesity seriously. A clinical manual*, London: Churchill Livingstone

Gay, J. S. (1980) 'Basotho women migrants: a case study', *Institute of Development Studies Bulletin*, **11** (4)

Gibbons, D. *et al.* (1981) *Land tenure in the Muda irrigation area (final report)*, Penang: Centre for Policy Research, Universiti Sains Malaysia

Gissi, J. (1980) 'Mythology about women with special reference to Chile', in Nash, J. and Safa, H. (eds.), 30–45

Gomez, F., Galvin, R. R., Frenk, S., Munoz, J. C., Chavez, R. and Vazquez, E. (1956) 'Mortality in second and third degree malnutrition', *The Journal of Tropical Pediatrics* (September), 77–83

Gonzalez de la Rocha, M. (1984) *Urban households and domestic cycles in Guadalajara, Mexico*, Paper presented at the annual conference of the Society of Latin American Studies

Goode, W. J. (1963) *World revolution and family patterns*, New York: Free Press

Goody, J. (1976) *Production and reproduction*, Cambridge: Cambridge University Press

Goody, J. (1976) *Production and Reproduction*, Cambridge: Cambridge University Press

Goody, J. (1983) *The development of the family and marriage in Europe*, Cambridge: Cambridge University Press

Gopalan, C. and Nadamini Naidu, A. (1972) 'Nutrition and fertility', *The Lancet* (2), 1077–9

Gordon, E. (1981) 'An analysis of the impact of labour migration on the lives of women in Lesotho', in Nelson, N. (ed.), 59–76

Gordon, L. and Klopov, E. (1975) *Man after work*, Moscow: Progress Publishers

Gough, K. (1981) *Rural society in southeast India*, London: Cambridge University Press

Grant and Anthonio, Q. B. O. (1973) 'Women co-operative in the Western State of Nigeria', *Bulletin of Rural Economics and Sociology*, **8** (1), 7–36

Grant, J. P. (1986) *The state of the world's children, 1986*, Paris: UNICEF

Graves, P. (1976) 'Nutrition, infant behaviour and maternal characteristics: a pilot study in West Bengal, India', *American Journal of Clinical Nutrition*, **29**, 305

Greenough, P. R. (1982) *Prosperity and misery in modern Bengal: the famine of 1943–1944*, New York: Oxford University Press

Grigg, D. B. (1977) 'E. G. Ravenstein and the laws of migration', *Journal of Historical Geography*, **3** (1), 41–54

Gugler, J. (1981) 'The rural–urban interface and migration', in Gilbert, A. and Gugler, J., *Cities, poverty and development: urbanization in the Third World*, Oxford: Oxford University Press

Gugler, J. and Flanagan, W. G. (1978) *Urbanization and social change in West Africa*, Cambridge: Cambridge University Press

Gulati, L. (1975a) 'Female work participation: a study of interstate differences', *Economic and Political Weekly*, **10** (1–2), 35–42

Gulati, L. (1975b), 'Occupational distribution of working women: an interstate comparison', *Economic and Political Weekly*, **10** (43), 1692–1704

Gulati, L. (1978) 'Profile of a female agricultural labourer', *Economic and Political Weekly*, **13** (12), A27–A35

Habict, J. P., Delgado, Y., Yarbrough, C. and Klein, R. E. (1975)

'Repercussions of lactation on nutritional status of mother and infant', *Proceedings of the Ninth International Congress of Nutrition*, Mexico, 1972 Basel: Karger 2, 106–14

Hackenberg, R., Murphy, A. D. and Selby, H. A. (1981) 'The household in the secondary cities of the Third World', Wenner-Gren Foundation Symposium *Households: changing form and function*, New York, October 8–15

Hagerstrand, T. (1970) 'What about people in regional science?', *Papers of the Regional Science Association*, **24**, 7–24

Hamilton, S. B., Popkin, B. M. and Spicer, D. (1984) *Women and nutrition in Third World countries*, New York: Praeger

Hanger, J. and Morris, J. (1973) 'Women and the household economy', in Chambers, R. and Morris, J. (eds.), *MWEA An irrigated rice settlement in Kenya*, Munich: Welforum Verlag, 209–44

Hanley, S. B. (1977) 'The influence of economic and social variables on marriage and fertility in eighteenth and nineteenth century Japanese villages', in Lee, R. D. *et al.* (eds.), *Population patterns in the past*, New York: Academic Press, 165–200

Hannan-Andersson, C. (1982) 'Women, water and development in a Pare settlement, Tanzania', Dar es Salaam: UDSM, Bureau of Resource Assessment and Land Use Planning, *Research Report*, **52**

Hareven, T. K. (1974) 'The family as process: the historical study of the family cycle', *Journal of Social History*, **7**, 322–9

Hareven, T. K. (1977) 'Family time and historical time', *Daedalus*, **106** (2), 59–70

Hareven, T. K. (ed.) (1978) *Transitions, the family and the life course in historical perspective*, New York: Academic Press

Hareven, T. K. (1982) *Family time and industrial time*, Cambridge: Cambridge University Press

Harris, M. (1976) 'History and significance of the emic/etic distinction', *Annual Review of Anthropology*, **5**, 329–50

Harris, O. (1976) 'Women's labour and the household', discussion paper for the *British Sociological Association Workshop on the Peasantry*, mimeo

Harris, O. (1981) 'Household as natural units', in Young *et al.* (eds.), 49–68

Harris, O. and Young, K. (1981) 'Engendered structures: some problems in the analysis of reproduction', in Kahn, J. S. and Llobera, J. R. (eds.), *The anthropology of precapitalist societies*, London: Macmillan

Harriss, B. (1976) 'Paddy processing in India and Sri Lanka: a review of the case for technological innovation', *Tropical Science*, **18** (3), 161–86

Harriss, B. (1977) 'Paddy milling: problems in policy and the choice of technology', in Farmer, B. H. (ed.), 276–300

Harriss, B. (1979) 'Post harvest rice processing systems in rural Bangladesh: technology, economics and employment', *Bangladesh Journal of Agricultural Economics*, **2** (1)

Harriss, B. (1983) 'Food systems and society: the system of circulation of rice in West Bengal', *Cressida Transactions*, **2** (1–2), 158–250

Harriss, B. (1985) *Tamil Nadu's noon meal scheme*, mimeo, London School of Hygiene and Tropical Medicine

Harriss, B. (with Chapman, G. P., McLean, W., Shears, E. and Watson, E.) (1984) *Exchange relations and poverty in dryland agriculture*, New Delhi: Concept Publishing Co.

Harriss, B. and Kelly, C. (1982) 'Food processing: policy for rice and oil technology in S. Asia', *Bulletin, Institute of Development Studies*, **13**, 32–44

Harriss, J. (1977) 'Implications of change in agriculture for social relations at the village level: the case of Randam', in Farmer (ed.), 225–45

Harriss, J. (1981) *Capitalism and peasant farming*, New Delhi: Oxford University Press

Harriss, J. (ed.) (1982) *Rural development: theories of peasant economy and agrarian change*, London: Hutchinson

Harry, I. S. (1981) *Women in agriculture in Trinidad*, M.Sc Thesis, unpublished, University of Calgary, Canada

Hartman, B. and Boyce, J. (1983) *Quiet violence: view from a Bangladesh village*, London: Zed Press

Hay, M. J. (1976) 'Luo women and economics during the colonial period', in Hafkin, N. J. and Bay, E. G. (eds.), *Women in Africa: studies in social and economic change*, Stanford: Stanford University Press

Hazlehurst, L. W. (1966) 'Entrepreneurship and the merchant castes in a Punjab city', *Duke University Monograph*, no. 1, Commonwealth Studies Centre

Hecht, S. (forthcoming) 'The Latin America livestock sector and its potential impact on women'

Henshall, J. D. (1964) *The spatial structure of Barbadian peasant agriculture*, M.Sc Thesis (unpublished), Montreal: McGill University

Henshall, J. D. (1981) 'Women and small scale farming in the Caribbean', in Horst, O. H. (ed.), 44–56

Henshall Momsen, J. (1980) 'Women in Canadian Geography', *Professional Geographer*, **32** (3), 365–9

Henshall Momsen, J. (1984) 'Gender and geography: a Latin American perspective', paper presented at the *Anglo-Mexican Symposium in Geography*, Mexico City (September)

Henshall Momsen, J. and Townsend, J. (eds.) (1984) *Women's role in changing the face of the developing world*, Women and Geography Study Group of the Institute of British Geographers: Durham University, Geography Department

Hepner, R. and Maiden, N. (1971) 'Growth rate, nutrient intake and "mothering" as determinants of malnutrition in disadvantaged children', *Nutrition Reviews*, **29** (10), 219–23

Heyzer, N. (1981) 'Towards a framework of analysis', in Young (ed.), **3–7**

Hilder, A. S., and Steinhoff, M. C. (1983) *RUMSA Nutritional and immunisation status survey: preliminary report*, Vellore: Christian Medical College Hospital

Hill, P. (1963) *Migrant cocoa-farmers in Southern Ghana*, Cambridge: Cambridge University Press

Hill, P., (1982) *Dry grain farming families*, London: Cambridge University Press

Hirata, H. (1981) 'Division sexuelle du travail et le rôle de l'état: l'exemple brésilien', *Critiques de l'Economie Politique*, **17**

HMG (1976) *Basic health services project formulation*, Kathmandu: Ministry of Health

HMG (1977) *Analysis of the population statistics of Nepal*, Kathmandu: The Planning Commission

HMG (1979) *Mid term health review*, Kathmandu: Ministry of Health

HMG (1982) *National Census 1981; brief analysis*, Katmandhu: National Population Commission, mimeo

Horst, O. (1981) (ed.) *Papers in Latin American geography in honor of Lucia C. Harrison*, special publication no. 1., Muncie, Indiana, Conference of Latin Americanist Geographers

Hosken, F. P. (1976) 'Female circumcision and fertility in Africa', *Women and Health*, **1** (6), 1–11

Hoskins, M. (1979) *Women in forestry for local community development: a programming guide*, USAID

Hrdy, S. B. (1981) *The woman that never evolved*, Cambridge: Harvard University Press

Humphrey, J. (1984) 'The growth of female employment in Brazilian manufacturing industry in the 1970s', *Journal of Development Studies*, **20** (4), 224–47

Humphries, J. (1976) 'Women: scapegoats and safety valves in the Great Depression', *The Review of Radical Political Economics*, **8** (1)

Humphries, J. (1977) 'Class struggle and the persistence of the working class family', *Cambridge Journal of Economics*; **1** (2), 241–58

Huston, P. (1979) *Third World women speak out*, New York: Praeger

Hyden, G. (1980) *Beyond Ujamaa in Tanzania: underdevelopment and an uncaptured peasantry*, Nairobi: Heinemann

IBGE (1974) (Instituto Brasileiro da Geografía e Estatística) *Anuário estatístico do Brasil 1973*, Rio de Janeiro

IBGE (1980) *Industrial census*, Rio de Janeiro

IBGE (1981) *Tabulacoes avancadas*, Rio de Janeiro

IBGE (1983) *Demographic census 1980*, Rio de Janeiro

Ibrahim, A. (1975) *Islamic law in Malaya*, Singapore: Malaysian Sociological Research Institute

ICRISAT (1983) *Annual Report, 1982*, Hyderabad: International Crops Research Institute for the Semi Arid Tropics

Igben, M. S., Famoirye, S. and Adeyokunno, T. (1977) *The role of women in marketing gari and palm oil in some parts of Nigeria: a case study in the rural communities of Fashola, Ife, Okene and Ehor*, Ibadan: University of Ibadan

ILCA (1984) *Workshop on women in agriculture in West Africa*, Ibadan,

unpublished papers sponsored by International Livestock Centre for
Africa and the Ford Foundation

ILO, see International Labour Office

ILO (1983) *Yearbook of labour statistics*, Geneva: ILO

India (1981) *Census of India, 1981, Series 1, Paper 1 of 1981 provisional
population totals*, Delhi: Government of India

Indian Council of Medical Research (1981) *Recommended dietary
intakes for Indians*, Delhi: Indian Council for Medical Research

Institute of Medicine (1977) *Rural health needs. A study of Tanahu
District*, Kathmandu: Tribhuvan University

Institute of Medicine (1979a) *Rural Health needs. Study No. 2. A study of
Khankuta District*, Kathmandu: Tribhuvan University

Institute of Medicine (1979b) *Rural health needs. Study No. 3. A study of
Nuwakot District*, Kathmandu: Tribhuvan University

Institute of Medicine (1979c) *Surkhet District community health survey*,
Kathmandu: Tribhuvan University

International Labour Office (1975) *Woman power*, Geneva: ILO

International Labour Office (1977) *Labour force estimates and
projections, 1950–2000*, vols. I, II, III, Geneva: ILO

Islam, N. and Haq, S. (1981) *Population and migration characteristics of
Khulna city*, Dhaka: Centre for Urban Studies, University of Dhaka

Janelid, I. (1975) *The role of women in Nigerian agriculture*, Rome: FAO

Jay, P. (1970) 'The female primate', in Fanben, S. and Wilson, R. (eds.),
The potential of woman, New York: McGraw Hill

Jelin, E. (1977) 'Migration and labour force participation of Latin
American women: the domestic servants in the cities', in Wellesley
Editorial Committee (ed.), *Women and national development: the
complexities of change*, Chicago: University of Chicago Press, 129–41

Jones, D. (1977) *Aid and development in Southern Africa*, London:
Croom Helm

Jones, G. (ed.) (1984) *Women in the urban and industrial workforce:
southeast and east Asia*, Development Studies Centre Monograph, no.
33, Canberra: Australian National University

Jones, G. W. (1981) 'Trends in marriage and divorce', in Sidhu, M. S. and
Jones, G. W. (eds.), *Population dynamics in a plural society:
peninsular Malaysia*, Kuala Lumpur: UMCB Publications, 185–208

Jones, G. W. (1982) 'Economic growth and changing female employment
structure in the cities of Southeast and East Asia', unpublished paper
presented at the *Conference on Women in the Urban and Industrial
workforce in Southeast and East Asia*, Manila, Philippines, 16–19
November

Kakar, S. (1981) *The inner world: a psychoanalytic study of childhood
and society in India*, Delhi: Oxford University Press

Kamuzora, C. L. (1984) 'High fertility and the demand for labour in
peasant economies: case of Bukoba District, Tanzania', *Development
and Change*, **15** (1), 105–24

Kemp, G. J. (1983) 'Tel El-Amarna', in Smith, H. S. and Hall, R. (eds.),

Ancient centres of Egyptian civilisation, London: The Egyptian Education Bureau

Kershaw, G. (1975/6) 'The changing roles of men and women in the Kikuyu family by socioeconomic strata', *Rural Africana*, **29**, 20–9

Khor Kok Peng (1984) *Recession and the Malaysian economy*, Penang: Institut Mashkarakat

Kidron, M. and Segal, R. (1984) *The new state of the world atlas*, London: Pan and Pluto Press

King, E. and Evenson, R. E. (1983) 'Time allocation and home production in Philippine rural households', in Buvinic, M. *et al*. (eds.)

Kitching, G. (1982) *Development and underdevelopment in historical perspective: populism, nationalism and industrialisation*, London and New York: Methuen

Kleemeier, L. (1983) 'Domestic policies versus poverty-oriented foreign assistance in Tanzania', *Journal of Development Studies*, **20** (2), 170–201

Kuhn, A. and Wolpe, A. M. (eds.) (1978) *Feminism and materialism*, London: Routledge and Kegan Paul

Kurian, G. and Ghosh, R. (eds.) (1981) *Women in the family and the economy*, Connecticut: Greenwood Press

Kynch, J., and Sen, A. K. (forthcoming) 'Indian women: wellbeing and survival', *Cambridge Journal of Economics*

Lagbao, F. Y. and Pa, R. E. (1981) 'Transnationals and consumerism: impact on Filipino tastes and values', *State and Society*, **2** (1), 91–9

Lailson, S. (1980) 'Expansion limitada y proliferacion horizontal. La industria de la ropa y el tejido de punto', *Relactiones del Colegio de Michoacán*, **1** (3), 48–102

Lannoy, R. (1971) *The speaking tree: a study of Indian culture and society*, London: Oxford University Press

Latin American and Caribbean Women's Collective (1980) *Slaves of slaves: the challenge of Latin American women*, London: Zed Press

Lavrin, A. (ed.) (1978) *Latin American women: historical perspectives*, Connecticut: Greenwood Press

Lavrin, A. (1981) 'Women in Latin American history', *History Teacher*, **15**, 387–99

Lavrin, A. (1984) 'Recent studies on women in Latin America', *Latin American Research Review*, **19** (1), 181–9

Lee, D. (forthcoming) 'Women and geography, 1985: A bibliography', *Transition*

Lee, R. B. (1968) 'What hunters do for a living, or how to make out on scarce resources', in Lee, R. B. and DeVore, I. (eds.), *Man the hunter*, Chicago: Aldine

Leghorn, L. and Parker, K. (1981) *Woman's worth: sexual economics in the world of women*, Mass.: Routledge and Kegan Paul

Lele, U. (1986) 'Women and structural transformation', *Economic Development and Cultural Change*, **34** (2), 195–222

Leon, M. (1984) 'Measuring women's work: methodological and

conceptual issues in Latin America', *Bulletin of the Institute of Development Studies*, **15** (1), 12–17

Leon de Leal, M. (ed.) (1977) *La mujer y el desarrollo en Colombia*, Bogota: ACEP

Leon de Leal, M. (ed.) (1980) *Mujer y capitalismo agrario*, Bogota: ACEP

Leon de Leal, M. (ed.) (1982) *La realidad Colombiana: debate sobre la mujer en America Latina y el Caribe*, vol. 1, Bogota: ACEP

Levinson, F. J. (1972) *An economic analysis of malnutrition among young children in rural India*, Cambridge, Mass.: MIT/Cornell University Press

Lewis, G. J. (1982) *Human migration: a geographical perspective*, London: Croom Helm

Lewis, O. (1958) *Village life in northern India*, New York: Vintage Books

Lim, L. (1980) 'Women in the redeployment of manufacturing industry to developing countries', *UNIDO Working Papers on Structural Changes*, **18**

Lim, S. G. (1982) 'Mr Tang's girls', *Asiaweek*, 1 October, 42–51

Lim Teck Ghee (1977) *Peasants and their agricultural economy in colonial Malaya, 1874–1941*, Kuala Lumpur: Oxford University Press

Lin, V. (1985) 'Health, women's work and industrialization, women workers in the semiconductor industry in Singapore and Malaysia', paper presented to *International Sociological Association Conference*. University of Hong Kong, August

Lindsay, B. (ed.) (1980) *Comparative perspectives on Third World women*, New York: Praeger

Lipton, M. (1983a) 'Poverty, undernutrition and hunger', *World Bank Staff Working Papers*, Washington: IBRD

Lipton, M. (1983b) 'Demography and Poverty', *World Bank Staff Working Papers*, 623, Washington: IBRD

Lipton, M. (1984) 'Family, fungibility and formality: rural advantages of informal non-farm enterprise versus the urban–formal state', in Amin, S. (ed.) *Developing countries*, vol. 5 in *Human resources, employment and development*, London: Macmillan, 189–242

Lisansky, J. (1979) 'Women in the Brazilian frontier', *Latinamericanist*, **15** (1), University of Florida

Little, K. (1973) *African women in towns*, Cambridge: Cambridge University Press

Lomnitz, L. A. de (1977) *Networks and marginality – life in a Mexican shanty town*, New York: Academic Press

Long, N. (ed.) (1984) *Family and work in rural societies: Perspective on non-wage labour*, London: Tavistock Publications

Lopez de Piza, E. (1979) 'La familia matrifocal como mecanismo de adaptación de la mujer a su marginalidad', *Vinculos, Revista de Antropologia del Museo Nacional de Costa Rica*, **5** (1–2)

McCall, M. (1983) 'Environmental and agricultural impact of Tanzania's villagisation programme', Enschede: Twente University, *Technology and Development Group Working Paper*, no. 6

Macfarlane, A. (1976) *Resources and population*, Cambridge: Cambridge University Press

Macfarlane, A. (1981) 'Death, disease and caring in a Himalayan village', in Furer-Haimendorf, C. von (ed.) *Asian highland societies in anthropological perspective*, New Delhi: Sterling

McGee, T. G. (1982) 'Women workers or working women? Some preliminary thoughts on the proletarianization process in the export processing zone of Southeast and East Asia', unpublished paper presented at the *Conference on Women in the Urban and Industrial Workforce in Southeast and East Asia*, Manila, Philippines, 16–19 November

McGee, T. G. (1983) 'Circuits and networks of capital. The internationalisation of the world economy and national urbanisation', unpublished paper presented at the *Conference on Urban Growth*, University of British Columbia, Vancouver, 1–5 August

McGee, T. G. (1984) 'Middle class households and the creation of the mass market in Malaysia – a proposal', unpublished paper presented at the *Research Seminar on Third World Urbanization and the Household Economy*, Universiti Sains Malaysia, Penang, 16–17 August

McGee, T. G. (1985) 'Mass markets: little markets, some preliminary thoughts on the growth of consumption and its relationship to urbanization: a case study of Malaysia', in Plattner, S. (ed.), *Markets and Marketing*, Lanham: University Press of America, 205–33

McGee, T. G. (forthcoming) 'From "Urban involution" to "Proletarian Transformation": Asian Perspectives', in McGee, T. G. (ed.), *Proletarianization in Asia and the Pacific*, Melbourne: Centre for Southeast Asian Studies, Monash University

McHenry, D. E. (1979) *Tanzania's Ujamaa villages: the implementation of a rural development strategy*, Berkeley: University of California, Institute of International Studies, Research Series, **39**

McInnis, R. M. (1977) 'Childbearing and land availability: some evidence from individual household data', in Lee, R. D. *et al.* (eds.), *Population patterns in the past*, New York: Academic Press, 201–27

Mackintosh, M. (1981) 'Gender and economics: the sexual division of labour and the subordination of women', in Young *et al.* (eds.)

Maclachlan, M. D. (1983) *Why they did not starve: biocultural adaptation in a south Indian village*. Philadelphia: Institute for the Study of Human Issues

McLoughlin, P. F. M. (ed.) (1970) *African food production systems*, London: Johns Hopkins Press

McNeill, G. (1984) *Energy undernutrition in adults in rural south India: progress report*, London School of Hygiene and Tropical Medicine, mimeo

McStay, J. R. and Dunlap, R. E. (1983) 'Male–female differences in concern for environmental quality', *International Journal of Women's Studies*, **6**, 291–301

Madeley, J. (1985) 'Giving poor credit for better living standard',
   Guardian, Manchester and London, 23 October
Maeda, N. (1978) 'The Malay family as a social circle', *Southeast Asian
   Studies*, **16**, 216–45
Magles, El-Shoura (House of Senates) Arab Republic of Egypt, (1984) *Final
   report of the services committee on the promotion of women as a part
   of comprehensive development*, Cairo: House of Senates (Arabic)
Mahler, H. (1974) 'An international "health conscience" ', *WHO
   Chronicle*, **28**, 207–11
Mair, L. (1984) *Anthropology and development*, London: Macmillan Press
Malaysia, Government of (1970) *Second Malaysia Plan 1971–75*, Kuala
   Lumpur: Government Press
Mamdani, M. (1972) *The myth of population control: family, caste and
   class in an Indian village*, New York: Monthly Review Press
Manderson, L. (ed.) (1983) *Women's work and women's roles: economics
   and everyday life in Indonesia, Malaysia and Singapore*, Canberra and
   New York: Australian National University, Development Studies
   Center, Monograph no. 32
Maro, S. and Mlay, W. F. (1976) *The spatial perspective of
   decentralisation*, Dar es Salaam: UDSM, Decentralisation Research
   Project, Working Paper
Maro, S. and Mlay, W. F. (1979) 'Decentralisation and the organisation of
   space in Tanzania', *Africa* **49** (3), 291–301
Mars, Z. (1982) 'Women and development', *Development Research
   Digest*, **7**
Martin, A. (1956) *The oil palm economy of the Ibibio farmer*, Ibadan:
   Ibadan University Press
Martin, M. K. and Voorhies, B. (1975) *Female of the species*, New York:
   Columbia University Press
Martin, V. M. and Rogerson, C. M. (1984) 'Women and industrial change.
   The South African experience', *The South African Geographical
   Journal*, **66** (1), 32–46
Martorell, R., Leslie, J. and Moock, P. R. (1984) 'Characteristics and
   determinants of child nutritional status in Nepal', *American Journal of
   Clinical Nutrition*, **39**, 74–86
Mascarenhas, O. and Mbilinyi, M. (1983) *Women in Tanzania: an
   analytical bibliography*, Uppsala and Stockholm: Scandinavian
   Institute of African Studies & SIDA
Massey, D. (1984) *Spatial divisions of labour: social structure and the
   geography of production*, London: Macmillan
Mazey, M. E. and Lee, D. R. (1983) 'Her space, her place: a geography of
   women', Association of American Geographers, *Resource Publications
   in Geography*, Washington
Mbilinyi, M. (ed.) (1984) *Cooperation or exploitation? Experiences of
   women's initiatives in Tanzania*, Geneva: ILO
Meaney, A. (1980) *The cashew industry of Ceara, Brazil*, MA Thesis,
   unpublished, University of Calgary, Canada

Meillassoux, C. (1981) *Maidens, meal and money: capitalism and the domestic community*, Cambridge: Cambridge University Press

Mencher, J. (1980) 'The lessons and non lessons of Kerala: agricultural labour and poverty', *Economic and Political Weekly*, **15**, 1781–802

Mencher, J. and Saradamoni, K. (1982) 'Muddy feet, dirty hands: rice production and female agricultural labour', *Economic and Political Weekly*, Review of Agriculture, December

Merrick, T. W. and Schmink, M. (1983) 'Households headed by women and urban poverty in Brazil', in Buvinic, M. *et al.* (eds.), 244–71

Meza Vargas, M. A. (1982) 'Desarrollo industrial en el estado', in PRI, *Consulta popular en las reuniones nacionales: Querétaro*, 22–24, Mexico City: PRI

Mickelwait, D., Riegelman, K. A. and Sweet, C. (1977) *Women in rural development: a survey of the role of women in Ghana, Lesotho, Kenya, Nigeria, Bolivia, Paraguay and Peru*, Boulder, Colorado: Westview

Mies, M. (1978) *Consequences of capitalist penetration for women's subsistence reproduction in rural India*, paper read at University of Bielefeld, 21–23 April, mimeo

Mies, M. (1982) *The lacemakers of Narsapur. Indian housewives produce for the world market*, London: Zed Press

Miller, B. (1981) *The endangered sex: neglect of female children in rural north India*, Ithaca, New York: Cornell University Press

Mitra, A. (1978a) *India's population: aspects of quality and control*, New Delhi: Abhinar Publications

Mitra, A. (1978b) 'Implications of the sex ratio in India', in Mies

Mohamad, M. (1984) 'Gender, class and the sexual division of labour in a rural community in Kedah', *Kajian Malaysia*, **II** (2), 101–22

Molyneux, M. (1981) 'Women's emancipation under socialism: a model for the Third World?', *World Development* **9** (9/10), 1019–37

Molyneux, M. (1982) 'Feminism in the realm of the possible', *Guardian*, Manchester and London, 15 October

Momsen, J. H. and Townsend, J. G. (eds.) (1984) *Women's role in changing the face of the developing world*, Durham: Women and Geography Study Group of the Institute of British Geographers

Monk, J. (1981) 'Social change and sexual differences in Puerto Rican rural migration', in Horst, O. (ed.), 28–43

Monk, J. (1984) 'Human diversity and perceptions of place', in Haubrich, H., *Perception of people and places through media*, vol. 1., Freiburg: Pedagogische Hochschule Freiburg, 45–67

Monk, J. and Hanson, S. (1982) 'On not excluding half of the human in human geography', *Professional Geographer*, **34**, 11–23

Monk, J. and Momsen, J. Henshall (1984) 'Gender and Geography in the Caribbean', paper presented to the *Conference of the National Council for Geographic Education*, Jamaica, October

Monyake, A. M. (1973) 'The size and age-sex characteristics of the populations for the six lowland townships, 1971/72', *Monographs on urban populations*, **1**, Maseru: Bureau of Statistics, mimeo

Moore, M. P. (1974) *Some economic aspects of women's work and status in the rural areas of Africa and Asia*, Institute of Development Studies, Sussex

Morris, M. (1979) *Measuring the condition of the world's poor: the PQLI index*, New York: Pergamon

Moser, C. (1978) 'Informal sector or petty commodity production: dualism or dependence in urban development?', *World Development*, **6** (9–10), 1041–64

Moser, C. (1981) 'Surviving in the surburbios', *Bulletin of the Institute of Development Studies*, **12** (3), 19–29

Moser, C. and Young, K. (1981) 'Women of the working poor', *Bulletin of the Institute of Development Studies*, **12** (3), 54–62

Moubray, G. A. (1931) *Matriarchy in the Malay peninsula and neighbouring countries*, London: Routledge and Kegan Paul

Mueller, E. (1979) *Time use in rural Botswana*, Ann Arbor: University of Michigan, Population Studies Center

Mueller, E. (1982) 'The allocation of women's time and its relation to fertility', in Anker *et al.* (eds.), 133–50

Mukherjee, M. (1983) 'Impact of modernisation on women's occupations: a case study of the rice husking industry of Bengal', *Indian Economic and Social History Review*, **20** (1)

Murdock, G. P. (1949) *Social structure*, New York: Macmillan

Murdock, G. P. and Provost, C. (1973) 'Factors in the division of labor by sex; a cross-cultural analysis', *Ethnology*, **12**, 203–35

Murphy, Y. and Murphy, R. F. (1974) *Women of the forest*, New York: Columbia University Press

Murray, C. (1981) *Families divided: the impact of migrant labour in Lesotho*, Cambridge: Cambridge University Press

Muzaffar, C. (1979) *Protector?*, Penang: Aliran

Muzaffar, C. (1979) 'Urban interlude: some aspects of internal Malay migration in West Malaysia', *International Migration Review*, **8** (2), 301–24

Nag, M., White, B. N. F. and Peet, R. C. (1980) 'An anthropological approach to the study of the economic value of children in Java and Nepal', in Binswanger *et al.* (eds.), 248–88

Nagata, J. (1974) 'Urban interlude: some aspects of internal Malay migration in West Malaysia', *International Migration Review*, **8** (2), 301–24

Nalven, J. (1978) *The politics of urban growth: a case study of community formation in Cali, Colombia*, Ph.D. dissertation, University of California at San Diego, reprinted by Ann Arbor: Michigan

Nardi, B. A. (1984) 'Infant feeding and women's work in western Samoa: a hypothesis, some evidence and suggestions for future research', *Ecology, Food and Nutrition*, **14**, 277–86

Narli, A. N. (1984) 'Development, Malay women and Islam, in Malaysia', *Kajian Malaysia*, **II** (2), 123–35

Nash, J. (1975) 'Certain aspects of the integration of women in the development process: a point of view', United Nations Document E/CONF. 66/BP/5

Nash, J. (1977) 'Women in development: dependency and exploitation', *Development and Change*, **8** (2), 161–82

Nash, J. and Safa, H. (eds.) (1980) *Sex and class in Latin America*, New York: Bergin

Navera, E. R. (1978) 'The allocation of household time associated with children in rural households in Laguna, Philippines', *Philippine Economic Journal*, **36**, 47–59

Nazir, N. (1965) *Women in Egypt's ancient history*, Cairo: Dar-el-Qallam (Arabic)

Nelson, N. (1979) 'How women and men get by: the sexual division of labour in the informal sector of a Nairobi squatter settlement', in Bromley, R. and Gerry, C. (eds.), *Casual work and poverty in Third World cities*, Chichester: John Wiley and Sons, 283–302

Nelson, N. (ed.) (1981) *African women in the development process*, London: Frank Cass; also published as special issue of the *Journal of Development Studies*, **17**

Nepal (1975) *Nepal national nutritional status survey*, Kathmandu: Government of Nepal/USAID

Nerlove, S. B. (1974) 'Women's workload and infant feeding practices: a relationship with demographic implications', *Ethnology*, **13** (2), 207–14

Newfarmer, R. and Mueller, W. (1975) *Multinational corporations in Brazil and Mexico*, Washington: Report to Subcommittee on Multinational Corporations, Committee on Foreign Relations, US Senate GPO

New Internationalist (1985) *Women: a world report*, London: Methuen

Newman, K. S. (1970) 'Women and law: land tenure in Africa', in Black, N. and Cottrell, A. B. (eds.), *Women and world change, equity issues in development*, Beverly Hills: Sage

NFE center project highlights (1981) *The NFE Exchange*, **22**, East Lansing: Nonformal Information Center, Michigan State University

NFS (1976) *Nepal fertility survey*, Kathmandu: Ministry of Health

Ngwenya, M. A. R. (1978) *The supply of labour and demand for migrants in Southern Africa: the case of Lesotho*, National University of Lesotho

Njelango, J. (1981) *Impact of villagisation in Dodoma Region*, Dar es Salaam: UDSM, Department of Geography, unpublished BA dissertation

Nkhoma, A. G. (1984) 'Beer-brewing as an income generating activity in Utengule village, Mbeya Region', in Mbilinyi, M. (ed.)

Nkonoki, S. R. (1983) *The poor man's energy crisis*, Dar es Salaam: UDSM, Institute of Development Studies, Tanzania Rural Energy Consumption Survey, Research Report

Nyerere, J. K. (1977) *The Arusha Declaration ten years after*, Dar es Salaam: Government Printer (reprinted in Coulson, A. (ed.) (1979))

Oakley, A. (1972) *Sex, gender and society*, London: Temple Smith

Obbo, C. (1981) *African women: their struggle for economic independence*, London: Zed Pres

O'Brien, L. N. (1981) 'Asian women and the new international division of labour', paper presented to *Workshop on women in Asia*, Asian Studies Association of Australia, University of New South Wales (June)

Okali, C. and Berry, S. (1985) 'Alley farming in West Africa in comparative perspective', *Discussion Paper*, 11, Boston University, African Studies Center

Okali, C. and Cassidy, K. (1985) 'Community response to a pilot farming project in Nigeria', *Discussion Paper*, 10, Boston University, African Studies Center

Oluwasanmi, H. A., Sema, I. S. *et al.* (1966) 'Uboma: a socio economic and nutritional survey of a rural community in Eastern Nigeria', World Land Use Survey, *Occasional Paper*, 6, Geographical Publications Ltd, Bude, Cornwall

Omvedt, G. (1978) 'Women and rural revolt in India', *Journal of Peasant Studies*, **5** (3), 370–403

Oppong, C. (1982) 'Family structure and women's reproductive and productive roles: some conceptual and methodological issues', in Anker *et al.* (eds.), 133–50

Ortner, S. B. (1974) 'Is female to male as nature is to culture?', in Rosaldo and Lamphere (eds.), 67–87

Osuntogun, A. (1976) 'Rural women in agricultural development: a Nigerian case study', unpublished paper, *Conference on Nigerian Women and Development in Relation to Changing Family Structure*, University of Ibadan

Pacey, A. and Payne, P. (eds.) (1985) *Agricultural development and nutrition*, London: Hutchinson

Padmanabha, P. (1982) 'Mortality in India: A note on trends and implications', *Economic and Political Weekly*, August

Padmarasha, P. (1981), see India (1981)

Pahl, R. (1984) *Divisions of labour*, London: Macmillan

Pala Okeyo, A. (1980a) 'Daughters of the lakes and rivers: colonisation and the land rights of Luo women', in Etienne, M. and Leacock, E. (eds.) *Women and colonisation, anthropological perspectives*, ch. 8, New York: Praeger, 186–213

Pala Okeyo, A. (1980b) 'The Joluo equation. Land reform = lower status for women', *Ceres* (May–June), 37–42

Palmer, I. (1979) *The Nemow case. Case studies of the impact of large scale development projects on women: a series for planners*, International programs, working paper no. 7, New York: The Population Council

Palmer, I. (1979) 'New official ideas on women and development', *Institute for Development Studies*, **10** (3), 42–53

Palmer, I. (1985) *The Nemow case. Women's notes and gender differences in development: cases for planners*, West Hartford: Kumarian Press

Panigrahi, L. (1973) *British social policy and female infanticide in India*, New Delhi: Munshiram Manoharlal Press

Papanek, H. (1976) 'Women in cities: problems and perspectives', in Tinker *et al.* (eds.) 54–69

Parry, J. P. (1979) *Caste and kinship in Kangra*, London: Routledge and Kegan Paul

Parthasarathy, G. and Rama Rao, G. D. (1973) 'Employment and unemployment among rural labour households: a study of west Godavari', *Economic and Political Weekly*, Review of Agriculture, **8** (52), A118–32 (December)

Patel, A. U. and Anthonio, Q. B. O. (1973) *Farmers' wives in agricultural development: the Nigeria case*, unpublished Seminar Paper, University of Ibadan

Paul, A. A., Muller, E. M. and Whitehead, R. G. (1979) 'The quantitative effects of maternal dietary energy intake on pregnancy and lactation in rural Gambian women', *Transactions of the Society for Tropical Medicine and Hygiene*, **73** (6), 686–92

Paulme, D. (ed.) (1963) *Women of tropical Africa*, London: Routledge and Kegan Paul

Payne, A. (1985) in Pacey and Payne (eds.)

Pearson, M. (1983) 'Western medicine and the underdevelopment of health in Nepal', *Proceedings of Primo Seminario Internationale di Geográfica Médica*, Perugia, 389–95

Pedrero, M. and Rendon, T. (1982) 'El trabajo de la mujer en Mexico en las setentas', in Secretaría de Programación y Presupuesto (ed.), *Estudios sobre la mujer, el empleo y la mujer. Bases teoricas y metodologicas y evidencia empírica*, Mexico DF: Secretaría de Programación y Presupuesto, 437–58

Perera, W. D. A. (1983) 'The nutritional status surveys of preschool children in Sri Lanka', in Government of Sri Lanka, *Nutritional status: its determinants and intervention programmes*, Colombo: Food and nutrition policy planning division, Ministry of Plan Implementation, 14–15

Perry, J. W. B. (1976) 'Lesotho: environment and tradition hamper development', *Focus*, **26** (3), 8–16

Pescatello, A. M. (ed.) (1973) *Female and male in Latin America*, Pittsburgh: University of Pittsburgh

Pescatello, A. M. (1976) *Power and pawn: The female in Iberian families, societies and cultures*, Westport, Conn., Greenwood Press

Phongpaichit, P. (1980) 'Rural women of Thailand: from peasant girls to Bangkok masseuses', *Women, Work and Development Series*, no. 2, Geneva: ILO (WEP 10/WP 14)

Pike, K. L. (1967) *Language in relation to a unified theory of the structure of human behaviour*, The Hague: Mouton

Popkin, B. M. (1981) 'Influence of maternal nutritional factors affecting birth weight', *American Journal of Clinical Nutrition*, **34** (4), supplement, 775–84

Popkin, B. M. (1981) 'Time allocation of the mother and child nutrition', *Ecology of Food and Nutrition*, **34** (4), supplement, 775–84

Popkin, B. M. (1983) 'Rural women, work and child welfare in the Philippines', in Buvinic, M. *et al.* (eds.)

Pred, A. (1984) 'Place as historically contingent process: structuration and the time-geography of becoming places', *Annals of the Association of American Geographers*, **74** (2), 279–97

Rajaraman, I. (1983) 'Economics of bride price and dowry', *Economic and Political Weekly*

Raman, L. (1970) 'Influence of maternal factors affecting birth weight', *American Journal of Clinical Nutrition*, **34** (4), supplement, 775–84

Randeria, S. and Visaria, L. (1984) 'Sociology of bride price and dowry', *Economic and Political Weekly* (April)

Rastogi, B. K. and Reddy, Y. V. R. (1982) *A study on farm structures in dry farming areas*, Hyderabad: All India Co-ordinated Research Project on Dryland Agriculture

Ravenstein, E. G. (1885) 'The laws of migration', *Journal of the Statistical Society*, **48** (II), 167–227

Rawson, I. G. and Valverde, V. (1976) 'The etiology of malnutrition among preschool children in rural Costa Rica', *Environmental Child Health* (February), 12–17

Redclift, M. (1984) *Development and the environmental crisis: red or green alternatives?* London and New York: Methuen

Reejal, P. R. (1979) 'Integration of women in development. The case of Nepal', *The status of women in Nepal*, **1** (5), Kathmandu: CEDA

Reiter, R. (ed.) (1975) *Toward an anthropology of women*, New York: Monthly Review Press

Rengert, A. (1981) 'Some sociocultural aspects of rural out-migration in Latin America', in Horst (ed.), 15–27

Rezende, F. *et al.* (1976) *Aspectos da participacâo do governo na economia, IPEA Serie Monografica*, **26**, Rio de Janeiro

Rivers, J. P. W. (1982) 'Women and children last: an essay on sex discrimination in disasters', *Disasters*, **6** (4), 256–67

Roberts, S. B., Paul, A. A., Cole, T. J. and Whitehead, R. G. (1982) 'Seasonal changes in activity, birth weight and lactational performance in rural Gambian women', *Transactions of the Royal Society of Tropical Medicine and Hygiene*, **76** (5), 668–78

Robinson, S. (1982) 'A change from Nasi Lemak', *Business Times*, Singapore (26 June)

Roff, W. R. (1980) *The origins of Malay nationalism*, Kuala Lumpur: Universiti Malaya Press

Rogers, B. (1980) *The domestication of women: Discrimination in developing societies*, London: Tavistock Publications

Rohrlich-Leavitt, R. (ed.) (1975) *Women cross-culturally: change and challenge*, The Hague: Mouton

Roider, W. (1971) *Farm settlements for socio-economic development. The western Nigeria case*, Munich: Weltforum Verlag

Rosaldo, M. Z. and Lamphere, L. (eds.) (1974) *Woman, culture and society*, Stanford: Stanford University Press

Rosensweig, M. R. (1984) 'Determinants of wage rates and labor supply behaviour in the rural sector of a developing country', in Binswanger, H. P. and Rosensweig, M. R. (eds.), 211–41

Rosensweig, M. R. and Schultz, T. P. (1980) 'Market opportunities, genetic endowments and the intra family distribution of resources: child survival in rural India', *American Economic Review*, **63**

Rosser, C. (1979) 'Social mobility in the Newar caste system', in Furer-Haimendorf, C. von (ed.), *Caste and kin in Nepal, India and Ceylon*, Delhi: East West Publications

Rossi, A. S. (ed.) (1970) *J. S. Mill and Harriet Taylor: essays on sex equality*, Chicago: University of Chicago Press

Rubbo, A. (1975) 'The spread of capitalism in rural Colombia: effects on poor women', in Reiter, R. (ed.)

Rubbo, A. and Taussig, M. (1983) 'Up off their knees: servanthood in southwest Colombia', *Latin American Perspectives*, **4**, 5–23

Rubens, B. (1978) 'The gold widows', *Observer* colour supplement (11 June), 32–42

Ryan, J. G. (1982) *Progress Report*, no. 38, Hyderabad: ICRISAT

Ryan, J. G. and Ghodake, R. D. (1984) 'Labor market behaviour in rural villages in south India: effects of season, sex and socio-economic status', in Binswanger, H. P. and Rosensweig, M. R. (eds.), 169–83

Sabot, R. H. (1979) *Economic development and urban migration: Tanzania 1900–1971*, Oxford: Clarendon Press

Sachs, C. (1983) *The invisible farmers: women in agricultural production*, New Jersey: Rowan and Allanheld

Sacks, K. (1975) 'Engels revisited: women, the organization of production and private property', in Reiter, R. (ed.)

Saffiotti, H. (1978) 'Female labour and capitalism in the United States and Brazil', in Rohrlich-Leavitt, R. (ed.)

Saffiotti, H. (1982) 'La modernización de la industria textil y la estructura de empleo femenino, un caso en Brasil', Leon, M. (ed.), *Sociedad, subordinación y feminismo: debate sobre la mujer en America Latina y el Caribe*, Bogotá: ACEP

Safilios-Rothschild, C. (1970) 'Toward a cross-cultural conceptualization of family modernization', *Journal of Comparative Family Studies*, **1** (1), 17–25

Safilios-Rothschild, C. (1982) 'Female power, autonomy and demographic change in the Third World', in Anker *et al.* (eds.), 117–32

Safilios-Rothschild, C. (1985) 'The persistence of women's invisibility in agriculture: theoretical and policy lessons from Lesotho and Sierra Leone', *Economic Development and Cultural Change*, **33** (2), 299–317

Sahlins, M. (1974) *Stone age economics*, London: Tavistock

Salaff, W. (1981) *Working daughters of Hong Kong*, New York: Cambridge University Press

Salih, K. (1981), *Malaysia and the world system: a perspective essay on* incorporation, social groups and the state (mimeo), Penang: Universiti Sains Malaysia

Salih, K. (1982) 'Urbanization in Malaysia: impact of the new economic policy', unpublished paper presented at the Parliamentarian Seminar, Kuala Lumpur, 5–6 October

Salih, K. and Young, M. L. (1982) 'Malaysia: urbanization in a multiethnic society – case of peninsular Malaysia', in Honjo, M. (ed.), Urbanization and regional development, UNCRD Regional Development Series, 6, Singapore: L Maruzen Asia, 117–47

Salih, K. and Young, M. L. (1982) 'Urbanization trends in Malaysia: some policy directions for the 80s', unpublished paper presented at the Joint Session of the IDRC Participatory Urban Services Meeting and East-West Center Population Institute Summer Seminar, Universiti Sains Malaysia, Penang, 1 July

Salih, K., McGee, T. G., Young, M. L. and Chan Lean Heng (1983) 'Industrialization, urbanization and labour force formation in Penang: a research proposal', paper presented at the Research Seminar on Third World Urbanization and Household Economy, Universiti Sains Malaysia, Penang, 27–29 June

Salih, K. et al. (1985) Young workers and urban services. A case study of Penang, Malaysia, Final report, Participatory Urban Services Project, Penang: Universiti Sains Malaysia, June

Samper, D. G. and Ladron de Guevara, L. (1981) Desarrollo y colonización: el caso colombiano, Bogota: Universidad Santo Tomás

Sanchez Macias, C. (1980) 'La estructura familiar y sus correlaciones históricas', in Corona Ibarra (ed.), Antropocultura, Guadalajara, Jalisco: Universidad de Guadalajara, 125–36

Sanday, P. R. (1974) 'Female status in the public domain', in Rosaldo and Lamphere (eds.), 189–206

Santos, M. (1979) The shared space: the two circuits of the urban economy in underdeveloped countries, London: Methuen

Sauer, C. O. (1961) 'Sedentary and mobile bents in earliest societies' in Washburn, S. L. (ed.), Social Life of Early Man, Chicago: Aldine, 256–66

Sauer, C. O. (1967) 'Seashore: primitive home of early man', in Leighly, J. (ed.), Land and Life, Berkeley: University of California Press

Schivji, Issa G. (1975) Class struggles in Tanzania, Dar es Salaam: Tanzania Publishing House

Schlegel, A. (1975) 'Toward a theory of sexual stratification', in Schlegel, A. (ed.), Sexual stratification: a cross-cultural view, New York: Columbia University Press, 1–40

Schmidt, C. F. (1975) 'A spatial model of authority–dependency relations in South Africa', Journal of Modern African Studies, 13 (3), 483–90

Schmink, M. (1977) 'Dependent development and the division of labour by sex', Latin American Perspectives, 4 (1–2), 153–79

Schmitz, H. (1982) Manufacturing in the backyard, London: Frances Pinter

Schroeder, R. and Schroeder, E. (1979) 'Women in Nepali agriculture: all work and no power', *Journal of Development and Administrative Studies*, Kathmandu: CEDA

Schultheis, M. J. (1982) 'Rural institutions and incentives: the dynamics of village development', Dar es Salaam: UDSM, *Economic Research Bureau Seminar Paper*

Schumacher, E. G. (1976) *Small is beautiful*, London: Harper and Row

Scott, J. W. and Tilly, L. A. (1981) 'Women's work and the family in nineteenth century Europe', in Anderson, M. (ed.) *Sociology of the Family*, Harmondsworth: Penguin, 126–63

Selat, N. (1970) 'Some facts and fallacies with regard to the position of men in Adat Perpatih', *Federal Museums Journal*, **XV**, 101–20

Selat, N. (1976) 'Sistem Sosial Adat Perpateh', *Utusan Melayu*, Kuala Lumpur

Selby, H., Murphy, A., Cabrera, I. and Castaneda, A. (1981) 'Battling urban poverty from below: a profile of the poor in two Mexican cities', paper prepared for the Wenner-Gren Foundation Symposium *Households: Changing Form and Function*, New York, 8–15 October

Selby, R. L. (1979) *Women: industrialization and change in Querétaro, Mexico*, Ph.D. dissertation, Department of Anthropology, University of Utah, reprinted by Ann Arbor: Michigan

Selwyn P. (ed.) (1980) 'Southern Africa: the political economy of inequality', *Institute of Development Studies Bulletin*, **11** (4)

Sen, A. K. (1981) *Poverty and famines: an essay in entitlements*, Oxford: Clarendon

Sen, A. K. (1984) *Resources, values and development*, London: Blackwell

Sen, A. K. and Sengupta, S. (1983) 'Malnutrition of rural Indian children and the sex bias', *Economic and Political Weekly*, **18** (19–21), 855–64

Sen, G. (1982) 'Women workers and the green revolution', in Beneria, L. (ed.)

Sharma, R. (1982) 'Greening the Indian countryside', *Mazingira*, **6**, (1), 80–2

Sharma, U. (1978) 'Women and their affines: the veil as a symbol of separation', *Man* (June), 218–33

Sharma, U. (1980) *Women, work and property in north west India*, London: Tavistock Publications

Sharp, H. S. (1981) 'The null case: the Chipewyan', in Dahlberg (ed.), 221–44

Shivji, I. G. (1975) *Class struggles in Tanzania*, Dar es Salaam: Tanzania Publishing House

Sicoli, F. (1980) 'Women in rural development: recommendations and realities', *Ceres*, **75**, 15–22

Simmons, A. B. (1976) 'Opportunity space, migration and economic development: a critical assessment of research on migrant characteristics and their impact on rural and urban communities', in Gilbert, A. (ed.), *Development planning and spatial structure*, London: Wiley

Simmons, G. B., Smucker, C., Misra, D. D. and Majumdar, P. (1978) 'Patterns and causes of infant mortality in rural Uttar Pradesh', *Tropical Pediatrics, Environment and Child Health*, **24**, 207–16

Simon, D. (1984) 'Responding to third world urban poverty: women and men in the "Informal Sector" in Windhoek, Namibia', in Henshall Momsen and Townsend (eds.), 95–130

Singhanetra-Renard, A. (1981) 'Mobility in North Thailand: A view from within', in Jones, G. and Richter, H. (eds.), *Population mobility and development: Southeast Asia and the Pacific*, Development Studies Centre Monograph no. 27, Canberra: Australian National University

Singhanetra-Renard, A. (1982) *Northern Thai mobility 1870–1977: A view from within*, unpublished Ph.D. dissertation, University of Hawaii

Singhanetra-Renard, A. (1984) 'Effect of female labour force participation on fertility: the case of construction workers in Chiang Mai City', in Jones, G. (ed.)

Sivard, R. L. (1985) *Women . . . a world survey*, Washington: World Priorities

Skar, S. L. (1982) *Fuel availability, nutrition, and women's work in highland Peru*, mimeographed World Employment Program Research Working Paper, restricted, Geneva: ILO

Skutsch, M. (1983) *Why people don't plant trees: the socio-economic impacts of existing woodfuel programs: village case studies, Tanzania*, Washington DC: Resources for the Future, Center for Energy Policy Research

Smith, D. S. (1977) 'A homeostatic demographic regime: patterns in West European family reconstitution studies', in Lee, R. D. *et al.* (eds.), *Population patterns in the past*, New York: Academic Press, 19–51

Smith, J., Wallerstein, I. and Evers, H. D. (eds.) (1984) *Households and the world-economy*, Beverly Hills, London, New Delhi: Sage

Smith, K. (1981) 'Determinants of female labour force participation and family size in Mexico City', *Economic Development and Cultural Change*, **30** (1), 129–207

Smith, R. T. (1960) 'The family in the Caribbean', in Rubin, V. (ed.), *Caribbean studies: a symposium*, Seattle: University of Washington Press, 67–75

Smith, T. C. *et al.* (1977) *Nakahara – the family farming and population in a Japanese village, 1717–1830*, Stanford: Stanford University Press

Solien, N. L. (1959) *The consanguineal household among the black Caribs of Central America*, Ph.D. Thesis, University of Michigan

Sopher, D. E. (1980) 'The geographic patterning of culture in India', in Sopher, D. E. (ed.), *An exploration of India*, Ithaca, New York: Cornell University Press

d'Souza, S. and Chen, L. C. (1980) 'Sex differentials in mortality in rural Bangladesh', *Population and Development Review*, **6**, 257–70

Spiro, H. (1979) *The role of women in farming and trading in Oyo State, Nigeria: a case study in the fifth world*, unpublished Ph.D. dissertation, Manchester University

Spiro, H. (1981) *The fifth world: women's rural activities and time budgets in Nigeria*, occasional paper, **19**, Queen Mary College, London University

Spiro, H. (1984) 'Agricultural development strategies: the experience at ILORA', see ILCA

Spiro, H. (1985) *The Ilora Farm Settlement in Nigeria. Women's roles and gender differences in development, cases for planners*, West Hartford, Connecticut: Kumarian Press/Population Council

Sri Lanka (1982) Government of Sri Lanka, Department of Statistics, Ministry of Plan Implementation, *Census of Population and Housing, Sri Lanka, 1981*, Tables based on a 10 per cent sample, preliminary release, Colombo

Srinavas, M. N. (1976) *The remembered village*, Delhi: Oxford University Press

Stamp, E. (1975/6) 'Perceptions of change and economic activity among Kikuyu women of Mitero, Kenya', *Rural Africana*, **29**, 173–94

Standing, G. and Sheehan, G. (eds.) (1978) *Labour force participation in low income countries*, Geneva: ILO

Standing, G. (1981) *Labour force participation and development* (2nd edn.), Geneva: ILO

Stanley, L. (1984) 'Should "sex" really be "gender" – or "gender" really be "sex"?', in Anderson, R. J. and Sharrock, W. W. (eds.), *Applied Sociological Perspectives*, London: Allen and Unwin

Staudt, K. A. (1978) 'Agricultural productivity gaps: a case study of male preference in government policy implementation', *Development and Change*, **9** (3), 439–57

Steckler, J. (1972) 'Effects of industrialization on food consumption patterns: a study in two Ewe villages, University of Ghana', *Technical Publication Services*, no. 20

Stewart, A. J. and Winter, D. G. (1979) 'The nature and causes of female suppression', *Signs*, **2** (3), 531–53

Stewart, F. (1985) *Planning to meet basic needs*, London: Macmillan

Stinner, W. F., de Albuquerque, K. and Bryce-Laporte, Roy S. (eds.) (1982) *Return migration and remittances: developing a Caribbean perspective*, Washington DC: Smithsonian Institute

Stolcke, V. (1981) 'Women's labours: the naturalisation of social inequality and women's subordination', in Young, K. *et al.* (eds.)

Stoler, A. (1977) *Class structure and female autonomy in rural Java, woman and national development: complexities of change*, Chicago: University of Chicago Press

Stone, L. (1976) 'Concepts of illness and curing in a central Nepal village', *Contributions to Nepalese Studies*, **3**, special issue, 83–105

Stone, L. (1979) *The family, sex and marriage in England 1500–1800* (abridged version), New York: Harper and Row

Suleiman El-Said Suleiman (1983) *Village markets in Sharkiya Province*, unpublished Ph.D. Thesis, presented to Ain Shams University, Cairo (Arabic)

Sundar, P. (1981) 'Characteristics of female employment: implications of research and policy', *Economic and Political Weekly* (May)

Sundaram, J. K. (forthcoming) *A question of class*, Kuala Lumpur: Oxford University Press

Super, S. (1980) 'Women, key to reforestation', *Agenda*, USAID, **3** (1), 18–19

Sutcliffe, B. (1984) 'Industry and underdevelopment re-examined', *The Journal of Development Studies*, **21** (1), 121–33

Suzigan, W. (1976) 'As empresas do governo e o papel do estado na economía Brasileira', in Rezende, F. *et al.*

Swantz, M. L. (1977) 'Strain and strength among peasant women in Tanzania', Dar es Salaam: UDSM, *BRALUP Research Paper*, **49**

Swift, M. G. (1954) 'Men and women in Malay society', in Ward, B. E. (ed.), *Women in the new Asia*, Paris: UNESCO, 268–86

Swift, M. G. (1965) *Malay peasant society in Jelebu*, New York: Athlone Press

Tadesse, Z. (1982) 'Women and technology in peripheral countries, an overview', in D'Onofio-Flores, P. M. and Pfathie, S. M. (eds.), *Scientific-technological change and the role of women in development*, Boulder, Colorado: Westview Press

Tavares, M. da and Souza, P. (1983) 'Employment and wages in industry: the case of Brazil', in Urquidi, V. and Reyes, S. (eds.), *Human Resources, Employment and Development*, vol. 4, *Latin America*, London: Macmillan

Taylor, A. (ed.) (1975) 'Africa's food producers: the impact of change on rural women', *Focus*, **25**, 1–7

Taylor, C. E. (1951) 'A medical survey of the Kali Gandaki and Pokhara Valley of Central Nepal', *Geographical Review*, **41**, 428–31

Taylor, D. (1985) 'Women: an analysis', New Internationalist, 1–98

Thadani, V. N. (1980) *Property and progeny: an exploration of intergenerational relations*, Working Paper 62, New York: Center for Policy Studies, The Population Council

Tham, S. C. (1977) *Malays and modernization*, Singapore: Singapore University Press

Thiele, G. (1983) *Development plans and the economics of household and village in Dodoma Region, Tanzania*, Cambridge University, Anthropology, unpublished Ph.D. dissertation

Thomas, I. (1985) 'Development projects and aspects of population redistribution in Tanzania', in Clarke, J. I. and Kosinski, L. A. (eds.), *Population and development projects in Africa*, Cambridge: Cambridge University Press

Thomson, A. M., Billewitz, W. Z., Thomson, B. and McGregor, I. A. (1966) 'Body weight changes during pregnancy and lactation in rural African (Gambia) women', *J. Obstet. Gynaec. Brit. Cwlth.*, **73**, 724–33

Thomson, B. and Rahman, A. K. (1967) 'Infant feeding and child care in a West African village', *Journal of Tropical Paediatrics*, **13** (3), 124–38

Tiger, L. (1970) *Men in groups*, New York: Vintage

Tiger, L. (1977) 'The possible biological origin of sexual discrimination', in Brothwell, D. (ed.), *Biosocial Man*, London: Eugenics Society

Tilly, L. A. and Scott, J. W. (1978) *Women, work and family*, New York: Holt, Rinehart and Winston

Tinker, I. (1976) 'Introduction', in Tinker I. *et al.* (eds.)

Tinker, I., Bo Bramsen, M. and Buvinic, M. (eds.) (1976) *Women and world development*, Washington DC: Overseas Development Council

Tinker, I. (1980) *Women and energy: program implications*, Washington DC: USAID

Tinker, I. (1982) 'Energy needs of poor households', *WID Working Paper*, **4**, East Lansing: Michigan State University

Todaro, M. P. (1981) *Economic development in the Third World*, New York: Longman

Tomkins, A. N. (1981) 'Nutritional status and severity of diarrhoea among preschool children in rural Nigeria', *The Lancet*, **1**, 560–2

Townsend, A. R. (1986) 'Spatial aspects of the growth of part-time employment in Britain', *Regional Studies*, **20** (4)

Townsend, J. G. (1976) 'Land and society in the middle Magdalena Valley, Colombia', unpublished D.Phil. thesis, Oxford

Townsend, J. G. (1977) 'Perceived worlds of the colonists of tropical rainforest, Colombia', *Transactions, Institute of British Geographers*, new series, **2** (4), 430–57

Townsend, J. G. (1984) 'Seasonality and capitalist penetration in the Amazon Basin', in Hemming, J. (ed.), *Change in the Amazon basin, The frontier after a decade of colonisation*, Manchester: Manchester University Press, 140–57

Townsend, J. G. (1985) 'Seasonal dimensions to rural poverty in the tropical Americas', *Rural Systems*, **3** (1), 63–74

Townsend, J., Barraclough, R. and Henshall Momsen, J. (1984) *Women in developing areas: a preliminary biography for geographers*, Durham: Women and Geography Study Group of the Institute of British Geographers

Trebat, T. (1983) *Brazil's state-owned enterprises: a case study of the state as entrepreneur*, Cambridge: Cambridge University Press

Tripp, R. B. (1981) 'Farmers and traders: some economic determinants of nutritional status in northern Ghana', *Journal of Tropical Paediatrics*, **27**, 5–22

UN *see* United Nations

UNECA (1974) *Data base on women in development and population factors in Africa*, Addis Ababa: UNECA

UNESCO (1980) *Participation of women in R & D – a statistical study*, current surveys and research in statistics, CSR-5-9, Paris: UNESCO

UNESCO (1983) *Development of education in the least developed countries since 1970: a statistical study*, current surveys and research in statistics, CSR-E-42, Paris: UNESCO

United Nations (1980) *Patterns of urban and rural population growth*, New York: United Nations

United Nations (1983, 1984) Demographic Yearbook 1982, 1983, New
  York: United Nations

US Council on Environmental Quality and Department of State (1981)
  The Global 2000 Report to the President, Harmondsworth: Penguin
  Books

Van Esterik, P. and Greiner, T. (1981) 'Breastfeeding and women's work:
  constraints and opportunities', Studies in Family Planning, 12 (4),
  184–97

Visaria, P. M. (1967) 'The sex ratio of the population of India and Pakistan
  and regional variations during 1901–1961', in Bose, A. (ed.), Patterns
  of population change in India, 1951–1961, Bombay: Allied Publishing
  Co.

Visaria, P. and Visaria, L. (1973) 'Employment planning for the weaker
  sections in rural India', Economic and Political Weekly 8 (4, 5, 6),
  267–276a

Visaria, P. (1977) 'Living standards employment and education in Western
  India', ESCAP-IBRD Project Working Paper, 1, Washington:
  IBRD

Vlassof, M. (1979) 'Labour demand and the economic utility of children:
  a case study in rural India', Population Studies, 33 (2), 415–28

Voigi, T. E., 'Leonardo da Vinci of smokeless chulas', Mazingira, 6 (4)

Wallman, S. (1969) Take out hunger: two case studies of rural
  development in Basutoland, London: Athlone Press

Wallman, S. (1972) 'Conditions of non-development: the case of Lesotho',
  Journal of Development Studies, 8, 251–61

Ward, K. B. (1984) Women in the world system: its impact on status and
  fertility, New York: Praeger

Ware, H. (1983) 'Female and male life cycles', in Oppong, C. (ed.), Female
  and male in West Africa, London: Allen & Unwin, 6–31

Waterlow, J. C. (1972) 'Classification and definition of protein calorie
  malnutrition', British Medical Journal, 3 (September), 566–9

Waterlow, J. C. and Thomson, A. M. (1979) 'Observations on the
  adequacy of breast feeding', The Lancet (2), 238–42

Watkinson, M. (1981) 'Delayed onset of weanling diarrhoea associated
  with high breast milk intake', Transactions of the Royal Society of
  Tropical Medicine and Hygiene, 75 (3), 432–5

Weil, P. M. (1973) 'Wet rice, women and adaptation in the Gambia', Rural
  Africana, 19, 20–9

Weisner, T. S. and Gallimore, R. (1977) ' "My brother's keeper": child
  and sibling caretaking', Current Anthropology, 18 (2), 169–90

Wells, J. (1977) 'The diffusion of durables in Brazil and its implications
  for recent controversies concerning Brazilian development',
  Cambridge Journal of Economics, I, 259–79

Wells, J. (1983) 'Industrial accumulation and living standards in the long
  run: the São Paulo industrial working class 1930–75', Journal of
  Development Studies, part I, 19 (2), 145–69, part II, 19 (3), 297–328

Whitaker, B., Guest, I. and Ennals, D. (1982) 'The Biharis in Bangladesh',

Minority Rights Group Report, **11**, London

White, B. (1976) 'Population, involution and employment in rural Java', *Development and Change*, **7**, 267–90

White, B. (1984) 'Measuring time allocation, decision-making and agrarian changes affecting rural women: examples from recent research in Indonesia', *Bulletin of the Institute of Development Studies*, **15** (3), 18–33

White, C. P. and Young, K. (eds.) (1984) 'Research on rural women: feminist methodological questions', *Bulletin of the Institute of Development Studies*, **15** (1)

Whitehead, A. (1979) 'Some preliminary notes on the subordination of women', *Bulletin of the Institute of Development Studies*, **10** (3), 10–13

Whitehead, A. (1981) 'A conceptual framework for the analysis of the effects of technological change on rural women', *World Employment Programme Working Paper*, 79

Whitehead, A. (1981) ' "I'm hungry mum": the politics of domestic budgeting', in Young, K. *et al.* (eds.), 88–111

Whitehead, A. (1984) 'Women's solidarity – and divisions among women', *Bulletin of the Institute of Development Studies*, **15** (1), 6–11

Whitehead, R. G. and Paul, A. A. (1981) 'Infant growth and human milk requirements: a fresh approach', *The Lancet* (25 July), 161–3

Whittaker, M. (1984) Preliminary results from fieldwork conducted during 1981–3, personal communication

WHO *see also* World Health Organization

WHO (1981) *Annual Statistics*, Geneva

WHO–UNICEF (1978) *Primary health care*, Geneva–New York: WHO–UNICEF

Whyte, M. K. (1978) *The status of women in preindustrial societies*, Princeton, NJ: Princeton University Press

Whyte, R. O. and Whyte, P. (1982) *The women of rural Asia*, Boulder, Colorado: Westview Press

Wilkinson, R. C. (1983) 'Migration in Lesotho: some comparative aspects, with particular reference to the role of women', *Geography*, **68** (3), 208–24

Wilkinson, R. C. (1985) *Migration in Lesotho: A study of population movement in a labour reserve economy*, unpublished Ph.D. thesis, University of Newcastle upon Tyne

Williams, J. C. (1971) 'Lesotho: economic implications of migrant labour', *South African Journal of Economics* (June), 149–78

Wilson, F. (1972) *Migrant labour in South Africa*, Johannesburg: South African Council of Churches and Spro-Cas

Wilson, P. J. (1967) *A Malay village and Malaysia – social values and rural development*, New Haven: HRAF

Women and Geography Study Group of the IBG (1984) *Geography and gender*, London: Hutchinson

Woolfe, J. A., Wheeler, E. F., Van Dyke, W. and Orraca-Tetteh, R., (1977) 'The value of the Ghanaian traditional diet in relation to the energy needs of young children', *Ecology, Food and Nutrition*, **6**, 175–81

World Bank (1978) *Agricultural land settlement*, Washington: IBRD

World Bank (1979) *Nepal*, New York: IBRD

World Bank (1983) *World Development Report, 1983*, London: Oxford University Press

World Bank (1983) *Perspectives on poverty and income inequality in Brazil*, World Bank Staff Working Papers, no. 601, Washington: IBRD

World Bank (1984) *Towards sustained development in Sub Saharan Africa: a joint program of action*, Washington: The World Bank

World Development Report (1984) New York: Oxford University Press for the IBRD

World Fertility Survey (1984) *World Fertility Survey's major findings and implications*, London: Voorburg

World Health Organization (1970) *The prevalence of nutritional anaemia in women in developing countries*, Geneva: WHO

World Health Organization (1980, 1983) *World Health Statistics*, Geneva: WHO

World Health Organization (1983) *Measuring change in nutritional status*, Geneva: WHO

World Health Organization (1984) *Annual Report 1983*, Geneva: WHO

World University Service (1984) *WUS women, education and development campaign*, London: WUS

Worth, K. M. and Shah, N. K. (1969) *Nepal health survey*, Honolulu: University of Hawaii Press

Young, K. (ed.) (1979) 'The continuing subordination of women in the development process', special issue, *Bulletin of the Institute of Development Studies*, **10** (3)

Young, K. (ed.) (1981) 'Women and the informal sector', special issue of *Bulletin of the Institute of Development Studies*, **12** (3)

Young, K. (1982) 'The creation of a relative surplus population: a case study from Mexico', In Beneria, L. (ed.), 149–77

Young, K. Wolkowitz, C. and McCullagh, R. (eds.) (1981) *Of marriage and the market*, London: Conference of Socialist Economists

Young, M. L. (1978) 'Migration and employment: a case study of a rural settlement within a development scheme in peninsular Malaysia', in Salih, K. (ed.), *Rural underdevelopment: the case of Malaysia*, UNCRD Country Monograph, Nagoya: UNCRD, 411–41

Young, M. L. (1978) 'Migrants and niches: economic structure in peninsular Malaysia, 1965–70', *Discussion Paper No. 7*, Penang: School of Social Sciences, Universiti Sains Malaysia, 1982.

Young, M. L. (1983) 'A survey of the bibliographic material on the Malay family in Malaysia', unpublished paper presented at the *Workshop on Family Research*, East–West Center Population Institute, Honolulu, Hawaii, 25–29 July

Yousseff, N. H. (1972) 'Differential labour force participation of women in Latin American and Middle Eastern countries: the influence of family characteristics', *Social Forces*, **51**, 135–53

Youssef, N. H. (1977) *Women and work in developing societies*, London: Greenwood Press

Youssef, N. H. (1982) 'The interrelationship between the division of labour in the household, women's role and their impact on fertility', in Anker, R. *et al.* (eds.), 173–201

Youssef, N. H. and Hetler, C. B. (1983) 'Establishing the economic condition of woman-headed households in the Third World', in Buvinic, M. *et al.* (eds.), 216–43

Youssef, N. H. and Hetler, C. B. (forthcoming) *Rural households headed by women: a priority issue for policy concern*, Geneva: ILO

Zachariah, K. C. and Conde, J. (1981) *Migration in West Africa: demographic aspects*, New York: Oxford University Press

Zaretsky, E. (1976) *Capitalism, the family, and personal life*, London: Pluto Press Ltd

Zeitlin, M. (1985) *Positive deviance in young children in developing countries*, report to UNICEF (draft)

Zelinsky, W., Monk, J. and Hanson, S. (1982) 'Women and geography: a review and prospectus', *Progress in Human Geography*, **6** (3), 317–66

Zuvekas, C. Jr (1978) *A profile of small farmers in the Caribbean Region*, Working document series, Caribbean Region, General working document no. 2, Washington DC: US Agency for International Development

Index

abortion 217
Abdullah, M. 91, 92
Acharya, M. 118, 120
Adeyokunna, T. C. 178
afforestation 331, 332
Afghanistan, 30, 32, 49, 51
Africa 43 (table), 51 (table), 73
(table), 327 (table), 328 (table);
anaemia 33; bridewealth 71;
economic activity 43, 69, 153,
178; education 235; food
production 167; gender
roles 185; labour reserve
regions 225; migration 52, 227,
239; sex ratio 86 (table); time
use 57–9, 329; see also names of
countries
Africa, East: colonial 156;
domestic service – male 56;
migration – female 233;
mutilation 38
Africa, North: 327 (table);
divorce 52; dowry 70;
economic activity 43; equality
rating 73 (table); literacy 49;
quality of life 35; sex ratio 33
Africa, Sub-Saharan: economic
activity 47, 73, 153–72; equality
rating 73 (table); life
expectancy 33, 75; literacy 75;
quality of life 35
Africa, West: colonialism 156;
female-headed households 52;
time use 25; traders 180
Agarwal, B. 101, 114, 215, 325–6,
334–6
age 179, 229 (table); 245–6 (table),
269, 285; and employment 285;
see also life cycle
Agency for Industrial
Mission 231, 232, 233

agriculture 44 (map), 250 (table),
262–3 (table), 267 (table), 280–1
(table), 284 (table), 296 (table),
344; and women 23, 118, 153,
174, 175, 231–2, 326, 329, 330,
334, 342, 343, 345;
processing 26, 309, 311, 315,
329, 342; production 25, 116,
334, 342; see also capitalist
penetration, economic activity,
farming system, modernization,
peasant, plantation, subsistence
alcohol 163, 220, 309, 316, 317;
see also beer brewing
Albania 30, 36
Algeria 49, 57, 73
Allison, C. 171
anaemia 18, 33
Andra Pradesh 89, 96, 98, 100,
101, 334–6
Andrews, A. C. 35–6, 77
Angola 32, 43
Anker, R. 61, 77
Anthropometry 91, 113, 134–5,
143, 253–5
Antrobus, P. 7, 16, 17, 22
Appardurai, A. 113
Argentina 18
Arizpe, L. 282
Asia 327 (table), 328 (table);
anaemia 33; consumption
needs 355, 357, 358; economic
activity 43, 79; education 76;
fertility 76; gender roles 153;
migration 227; sex ratio 33; see
also names of countries
Asia, South 73 (table);
discrimination 32–6; economic
activity 45; equality rating 73
(table); gender roles 69;
household size 133; life